ecpr PRESS

new nation-states and national minorities

Edited by
Julien Danero Iglesias, Nenad Stojanović,
and Sharon Weinblum

ecpr PRESS

First published by the ECPR Press in 2013

The ECPR Press is the publishing imprint of the European Consortium for Political Research (ECPR), a scholarly association, which supports and encourages the training, research and cross-national cooperation of political scientists in institutions throughout Europe and beyond.

ECPR Press
University of Essex
Wivenhoe Park
Colchester
CO4 3SQ
UK

Typeset by ECPR Press

Printed and bound by Lightning Source

British Library Cataloguing in Publication Data
A catalogue record for this book is available from the British Library

Hardback ISBN: 978-1-907301-36-0

www.ecpr.eu/ecprpress

ECPR – *Studies in European Political Science*

Series Editors:
Dario Castiglione (University of Exeter)
Peter Kennealy (European University Institute)
Alexandra Segerberg (Stockholm University)
Peter Triantafillou (Roskilde University)

ECPR – *Studies in European Political Science* is a series of high-quality edited volumes on topics at the cutting edge of current political science and political thought. All volumes are research-based offering new perspectives in the study of politics with contributions from leading scholars working in the relevant fields. Most of the volumes originate from ECPR events including the Joint Sessions of Workshops, the Research Sessions, and the General Conferences.

Books in this series
A Political Sociology of Transnational Europe
ISBN: 9781907301346
Edited by Niilo Kauppi

Europeanisation and Party Politics
ISBN: 9781907301223
Edited by Erol Külahci

Interactive Policy Making, Metagovernance and Democracy
ISBN: 9781907301131
Edited by Jacob Torfing and Peter Triantafillou

Perceptions of Europe
ISBN: 9781907301155
Edited by Daniel Gaxie, Jay Rowell and Nicolas Hubé

Personal Representation: The Neglected Dimension of Electoral Systems
ISBN: 9781907301162
Edited by Josep Colomer

Political Participation in France and Germany
ISBN: 9781907301315
Oscar Gabriel, Silke Keil, and Eric Kerrouche

Political Trust: Why Context Matters
ISBN: 9781907301230
Edited by Sonja Zmerli and Marc Hooghe

Please visit www.ecpr.eu/ecprpress for up-to-date information about new publications.

contents

List of Figures and Tables

List of Abbreviations

Contributors

Acknowledgements

Introduction: Recurrent Processes in Different Contexts
Julien Danero Iglesias, Nenad Stojanović, Sharon Weinblum   1

Chapter One: Nationalising States Revisited – Projects and Processes of Nationalisation in Post-Soviet States
Rogers Brubaker   11

Chapter Two: Against the Nation – Moldovan Political Discourse after the 2009 'Revolution'
Julien Danero Iglesias   39

Chapter Three: Inventing the Ukrainian Nation – Identity Building Between Dichotomies
Doris Wydra   59

Chapter Four: Group Empowerment and Cross-Ethnic Dialogue – Integration within the Polish National State
Magdalena Dembinska   79

Chapter Five: Majority as Minority – a Comparative Case of Autochthonous Slavs in Lithuania and Hungarians in Slovakia after the Second World War
Hanna Vasilevich   99

Chapter Six: Nationalising States and Nationalising Policies in Southeast Asia – Malaysia and Indonesia
Karolina Prasad   123

Chapter Seven: Nationalising Discourse Versus Minorities' Political Demands – the Case of the Palestinian Minority of Israel
Sharon Weinblum   149

Chapter Eight: The legacy of the Nation-State Building Process – Minority Politics in Greece and Turkey

Fulya Memisoglu   169

Chapter Nine: Whose Mobilisation? An Ontological Primer on the Mobilisation of National Minorities

Christina Isabel Zuber   191

Chapter Ten: Ethnicity and Strategic Voting in the 1998 Ukrainian Elections

Julian Bernauer   209

Chapter Eleven: On Fissions and Fusions of Ethnic Minority Parties

Edina Szöcsik and Daniel Bochsler   231

Conclusion: What's in a Comparison? Some Remarks About the Analysis of Recurrent Processes

Antoine Roger   255

Index   269

| list of figures and tables

Figures

Figure 6.1: Indonesia and Malaysia according to Freedom House report
on political freedoms, 1972–2010   134

Figure 10.1: Distribution of SF ratios by type of trailing party   219

Figure 10.2: U-shaped interaction effect of trailing minority party
moderated by share of Russians   221

Figure 10.3: Predicted variance of SF ratio based on Model 4.   222

Tables

Table 1.1: Titular and Russian share of population in last Soviet and
first post-Soviet census   16

Table 4.1: Integrating differences in a national state – group
empowerment and cross-ethnic dialogue   95

Table 9.1: Theoretical perspectives on ethnic identification   204

Table 10.1: Beta regression of strategic voting   227

| list of abbreviations

AIE	*Alianta pentru Integrare Europeana* (Republic of Moldova)
AMN	*Alianta Moldova Noastra* (Republic of Moldova)
BAPERKI	*Badan Permusjawaratan Kewarganegaraan Indonesia* (Consultative Body for Indonesian Citizenship)
BDZ	Bosniak Democratic Community (Serbia)
BJuT	Bloc Julia Timoshenko (Ukraine)
BN	*Barisan Nasional* (National Front, Malaysia)
BPN	*Białowieża National Park* (Poland)
CDA	Critical Discourse Analysis
CDR	*Convenţia Democrată Română* (Democratic Convention of Romania)
CEC	Central Elections Committee (Israel)
CEE	Central and Eastern Europe
CIS	Commonwealth of Independent States
CNMT	Hungarian National Council of Transylvania (Romania)
CNS	Szekler National Council (Romania)
CSES	Comparative Study of Electoral Systems
DANCEE	Danish Cooperation for Environment in Eastern Europe
DAP	*Parti Tindakan Demokratik* (Democratic Action Party, Malaysia)
DOS	*Demokratska opozicija Srbije* (Democratic Opposition of Serbia, Serbia)
DS	*Demokratska stranka* (Democratic Party, Serbia)
DSS	*Demokratska stranka Srbije* (Democratic Party of Serbia, Serbia)
DSVM	*Vajdasági Magyar Demokrata Párt* (Democratic Party of Vojvodina Hungarians, Serbia)
DZVM	*Vajdasági Magyarok Demokratikus Közössége* (Democratic Fellowship of Vojvodina Hungarians, Serbia)
EB	Ethnic behavior assumption
EI	Ethnic identification assumption
EPR	Ethnic Power Relation dataset
EU	European Union
Ex-USSR	Former Union of Soviet Socialist Republics
FSN	*Frontul Salvării Naţionale* (National Salvation Front, Romania)

GSM	Hungarian Civil Alliance (Serbia)
HZDS	*Ľudová strana – Hnutie za demokratické Slovensko* (People's Party - Movement for a Democratic Slovakia, Slovakia)
LDP	*Liberalno-demokratska partija* (Liberal Democratic Party, Serbia)
LPKB	*Lembaga Pembinaan Kesatuan Bangsa* (Institute for Promotion of National Unity, Indonesia)
OUN-UPA	Organisation of Ukrainian Nationalists in Western Ukraine
MCA	Malaysian Chinese Association (Malaysia)
MK	Member of the Knesset (Israel)
MN	Mniejszość Niemiecka (Party of the German minority in the Opolski Region, Poland)
MOS	Hungarian Civic Party (Slovakia)
MP	Member of Parliament
MSWiA	*Ministerstwo Spraw Wewnętrznych* (Ministry of Internal Affairs and Administration, Poland)
NATO	North Atlantic Treaty Organization
OKOOP	*Obywatelski Komitet Obrony Opolszczyzny* (Citizens' Committee for the Defence of Opolszczyzna, Poland)
PAS	*Parti Islam Se-Malaysia* (Pan-Malaysian Islamic Party, Malaysia)
PBB	*Pesaka Bumiputra Bersatu* (United Traditional Bumiputra Party, Malaysia)
PCM	Hungarian Civic Party (Romania)
PCRM	*Partidul Comunistilor din Republica Moldova* (Party of the Communists of the Republic of Moldova, Republic of Moldova)
PD	*Partidul Democrat* (Democratic Party, Romania)
PDM	*Partitul Democrat din Moldova* (Democratic Party, Republic of Moldova)
PKR	*Parti Keadilan Rakyat* (People's Justice Party, Malaysia)
PL	*Partidul liberal* (Republic of Moldova)
PLDM	*Partidul liberal-democrat din Moldova* (Liberal Democratic Party, Republic of Moldova)
PLP	Progressive List for Peace (Israel)
PMN	*Magyar Remény Mozgalom* (Hungarian Hope Movement, Serbia)
PNL	*Partidul National Liberal* (National Liberal Party, Romania)
PR	Proportional Representation
PRC	People's Republic of China

PSDR	*Partidul Social Democrat Român* (Social Democratic Party, Romania)
SBKRI	*Surat Bukti Kewarganegaraan Republik Indonesia* (Certificate of Indonesian Citizenship)
SDA	Party for Democratic Action (Serbia)
SDP	*Sandžačka Demokratska Partija* (Social Democratic Party of Serbia, Serbia)
SF	Second-to-first loser ratio
SLD	*Sojusz Lewicy Demokratycznej* (Democratic Left Alliance, Poland)
SMER	*sociálna demokracia* (Social Democracy, Slovakia)
SMK	*Strana maďarskej koalície – Magyar Koalíció Pártja* (Party of the Hungarian Coalition, Slovakia)
SNS	*Slovenská národná strana* (Slovak National Party, Slovakia)
SR	Slovak Republic
SSR	Soviet Socialist Republic
SUPP	*Parti Rakyat Bersatu Sarawak* (Sarawak United People's Party, Malaysia)
SVM	*Savez vojvođanskih Mađara* (Alliance of Vojvodina Hungarians, Serbia)
UCM	Hungaric Civic Union (Romania)
UDMR	*Uniunea Democrată Maghiară din România* (Organisation of the Hungarians in Romania)
UMNO	*Pertubuhan Kebangsaan Melayu Bersatu* (United Malays National Organisation, Malaysia)
UN	United Nations
UPE	Civic Association for Odorheiu Secuiesc (Romania)
WNI	*Waarga Negara Indonesia* (Indonesian citizen)
ZLS	*Zjednoczone Stronnictwo Ludowe* (United People's Party, Poland)

| contributors

JULIAN BERNAUER (PhD in Political Science, University of Konstanz, Germany) is a Postdoctoral Research Assistant at the Institute of Political Science, University of Berne, Switzerland. His research interests include political representation, empirical patterns of democracy, and quantitative methods. Recent publications have appeared in the *European Journal of Political Research* and *Electoral Studies* or are forthcoming with *Comparative Political Studies*.

DANIEL BOCHSLER (PhD in Political Science, University of Geneva) is Assistant Professor of Democratisation at NCCR Democracy at the University of Zurich, Switzerland. His main research interests include political representation, multi-ethnic societies, and democratisation of post-communist countries. His monograph "Territory and Electoral Rules in Post-Communist Democracies" has been published in Palgrave, and his articles have been published, among others, in *Acta Politica, Democratization, Electoral Studies, Ethnopolitics, Europe-Asia Studies, Politics and Policy, Public Choice, Regional and Federal Studies, the Swiss Political Science Review,* and the *European Yearbook for Minority Issues*.

ROGERS BRUBAKER is Professor of Sociology at the University of California, Los Angeles. He has written widely on social theory, immigration, citizenship, nationalism, and ethnicity. His books include *Citizenship and Nationhood in France and Germany* (1992), *Nationalism Reframed: Nationhood and the National Question in the New Europe* (1996), *Ethnicity without Groups* (2004), and *Nationalist Politics and Everyday Ethnicity in a Transylvanian Town* (2006).

JULIEN DANERO IGLESIAS (PhD in Political Science, Université libre de Bruxelles) is a postdoctoral fellow in Political Science at the Université libre de Bruxelles, Belgium. His PhD dissertation focused on the discursive construction of nationhood in the Republic of Moldova. He has interests in nationalism and minority studies, with a focus on Central and Eastern Europe. His current work focuses on nationalism and minorities in Moldova, Romania, and in Central and Eastern Europe in general.

MAGDALENA DEMBINSKA (PhD in Political Science, Université de Montréal) is an assistant professor at the Department of Political Science, Université of Montréal. Her research is situated in the subject of identity politics and conflict, nation-building, nationalism and diversity, in Eurasia and Central Europe. She is currently working on ethnopolitical mobilisation of Kashubs and Silesians in Poland, and on historical politics and identity transformations in de facto states (Transnistria, Abkhazia and Turkish Cyprus). Recent publications include *Vivre ensemble dans la diversité culturelle* (Presses universitaires de Rennes, 2012), and articles in *Ethnopolitics, Études internationales, Canadian Journal of Political Science, Comparative Political Studies,* and *Nations and Nationalism*.

FULYA MEMISOGLU (PhD in Politics and International Relations, University of Nottingham) is an Assistant Lecturer in International Relations at Cukurova University, Turkey. She has research interests in Europeanisation of minority politics, international and regional human rights institutions. Her current researches focus on minority nationalism, migration and asylum policies.

KAROLINA PRASAD (MA in Political Science, University of Warsaw) is a PhD candidate at the Universität Hamburg and at the German Institute of Global and Area Studies GIGA, Hamburg, Germany. She has research interest in ethnic politics, ethnic identity change and nationalism. Her work focuses on ethnic minorities in Malaysian and Indonesian Borneo.

ANTOINE ROGER (PhD in Political Science, University of Bordeaux, France) is Full Professor of Political Science at Sciences Po Bordeaux, member of Institut universitaire de France and Head of Centre Emile Durkheim (CNRS, University of Bordeaux). He has research interests in comparative politics and political sociology. His current work focuses on the political representation of peasants and the claims against European policies in France and Romania. Recent publications have appeared in *Revue française de science politique, Sociologie du travail, Politix* and *Cultures & Conflits*.

NENAD STOJANOVIĆ (PhD in Political Science, Zurich) is a Senior Research Fellow at the Centre for Democracy Studies in Aarau (ZDA), Switzerland, and an Assistant Lecturer at the universities of Zurich, Lausanne and Geneva. He has research interests in comparative politics, political theory and Swiss politics, with a focus on prospects for democracy in multicultural societies. His current work is on challenges of direct democracy in multilingual societies. Recent publications have appeared in *Representation, Politique et Sociétés, Transitions, Ratio Juris,* and *Nations and Nationalism*.

EDINA SZÖCSIK (MA in Political Science) is currently a guest researcher at the Political Science Department of the Vrije Universiteit Amsterdam. She was part of the PhD program "Civil Society and External Democratisation in Post-Socialist Europe" which was based on the cooperation between the ETH Zurich and the European University Viadrina Frankfurt (Oder) and funded by the Heinrich Boell Foundation. In her dissertation, she analysed the radicalisation process of ethnic minority parties in Central and Eastern Europe.

HANNA VASILEVICH (MA in International Relations and Diplomacy, Anglo-American University in Prague, MES in European Integration and Regionalism, the University of Graz and the Autonomous University of Barcelona) is a PhD candidate at the Metropolitan University in Prague, Czech Republic, and assisting editor of the quarterly *Belarusian Review*. Her research interests cover national identities, interethnic relations and national minorities in the CEE region in historical and contemporary perspectives. Her current work focuses on national identity and state policies in Belarus after the collapse of the Soviet Union.

SHARON WEINBLUM (PhD in Political Science, Université libre de Bruxelles, Belgium) is a postdoctoral research fellow at Harvard University and an associate member of the Université libre de Bruxelles. Her research interests include security studies, discourse theory, democracy and ethnic studies. Her previous work explored the security-democracy nexus in the Israeli parliamentary discourse. Her current research focuses on the political discourse on non-Jewish migrations in Israel. She recently published in *Revue Internationale de Politique Comparée, Interdisciplinary Political Studies* and *Politique et Sociétés*.

DORIS WYDRA (MA in Political Science, LLD University of Salzburg) is Senior Scientist at the Department of Political Science and Executive Director of the Salzburg Centre of European Union Studies. Her research focuses is on democracy and human rights promotion as aspects of external governance of the European Union, the European Neighbourhood Policy and the relations between the European Union and Russia. She has published on the question of the democratic development in Russia and Ukraine, minority legislation in Russia and a book on the Autonomous Republic of Crimea from the perspective of international law. Recent publications have appeared in *Osteuropa Recht, Österreichische Zeitschrift für Politikwissenschaft* and *International Journal of Social Ecology and Sustainable Development*.

CHRISTINA ISABEL ZUBER (Dr.rer.pol., University of Cologne) is a research associate at the Chair of Comparative Politics, University of Cologne, Germany. She has research interests in comparative political institutions, party politics and ethnic politics. Her current work focuses on the role of ethnicity in party competition in European democracies. Recent publications have appeared in *Comparative Political Studies* and *Party Politics*.

| acknowledgements

This edited volume is the result of a workshop held at the 2010 ECPR joint sessions of workshops in Münster. We are indebted to all the participants of the workshop for their stimulating contributions and for their supportive enthusiasm about the idea of this book.

We would like to thank all those who, by their suggestions and critiques, have helped refining the first versions of the various chapters, among whom particularly Ilana Kaufman, Régis Dandoy, and Josué Mathieu. We are grateful to Jean Blondel, Jean-Benoit Pilet, and Emilie van Haute for their opinion and comments on the very first project of the book. Dario Castiglione and Mark Kench of ECPR Press were extremely supportive in helping to guide this project to completion.

For proof reading, word processing and other assistance in the preparation of the manuscript, we also thank the team from ECPR Press, as well as Colin Shepherd, Simon Toubeau, Katya Long, and Anja Giudici. Finally, we acknowledge the financial support provided by the Université libre de Bruxelles.

Julien Danero Iglesias, Nenad Stojanović, and Sharon Weinblum
Aarau and Brussels, March 2013

introduction | recurrent processes in different contexts

Julien Danero Iglesias, Nenad Stojanović, Sharon Weinblum

The original puzzle

Despite the widespread expectation that modernity might lead to the decline of the nation-state, nationalism persists in its role as a 'quasi religion' (Smith J. E. 1994). Most states that emerged during the twentieth and twenty-first centuries were established on the basis of the classical nineteenth century nation-state – and most of these states derived crucial legitimisation by drawing on the force of this model. The First World War helped contribute to this development – especially in Eastern and Central Europe, where new countries gained independence on a national basis. One can also readily observe the nation-state's continued dominance in the wake of communist rule (in the states of the ex-USSR, ex-Yugoslavia, and ex-Czechoslovakia).

More recently, and in spite of the nationalist and ethnic wars that have so recently devastated the European continent, Africa, the Middle East, and South-east Asia (indeed, most parts of the inhabited world), new states have been established following the nation-state model, and nationalism remains a major driving force in world affairs (Smith A. D. 2001). Even a cursory consideration of the states recognised by the international community in the first decade of the twenty-first century reveals the narrative of the nation-state's enduring power and the degree of legitimacy it still confers upon political actors. In 2006, Montenegro gained independence from Serbia on the basis of an ethnic rationale. In much the same manner, Timor-Leste (known as East Timor), which recovered independence from Indonesia by force at the end of the 1990s, appeared on track to be a new nation-state until what has been presented as an ethnic conflict broke out in 2006. In addition, South Sudan declared independence in 2011, on the grounds of ethnic and religious dissimilarities between its population and that of North Sudan. Finally, other states emerged at the beginning of the twenty-first century on the same ethnic or nation-based argumentation, but without being granted formal recognition by the international community. The most striking case of this is no doubt Kosovo, which declared national independence in 2008, but has not been recognised by countries such as Spain or Romania, which are somewhat apprehensive when it comes to ethnic minorities' claims. This type of situation can also be observed in various post-Soviet de facto states, such as Transnistria, South Ossetia, Abhkazia and Nagorno-Karabakh, where ethnic/national issues appear to be at stake.

This reality – along with growing regionalist demands and particularism – has been at the root of our extended inquiry into the following contradiction: recently established states tend to continue implementing and giving legitimacy to the nation-state model despite the fact that it has time and again revealed problematic for the national minorities living in those countries (Lecours and Moreno 2010). Indeed, the affirmation of the nation-state model, whether merely at the rhetorical level (i.e. in the political discourses of the elites) or at a policy level (in matters of education, budget allocation, cultural rights, and so on), has important consequences in terms of the relationship between the state and the citizens of these minorities. In the most extreme cases, individuals belonging to national minorities have been denied full citizenship in their new states. In other cases, minorities have been excluded or discriminated against in the name of an alleged necessity to defend the emerging nation-state and its identity.

While this volume focuses on this tension – between the continued defence of a particular national identity and the incorporation of national minorities within the borders of the state territory – it does *not* delve into the roots of the nation-state's continued legitimacy nor into causes of the apparent paradox between nationalism and modernity (an issue that has already been explored at length elsewhere; see, among others, Badie 1995 and Dieckhoff 2000). Instead, we propose to explore the various dynamics generated by the implementation of the nation-state model – a model often considered outdated and unworthy of analysis – by states that gained independence during the last century. More specifically, this volume is concerned with the *consequent processes* engendered by the adoption of such a state model in terms of the minority-majority relationship, minority integration and, more generally, citizenship. It aims to explore the implications of this self-chosen model of national identification as it relates to state-building processes, identity construction, national minorities' rights and inclusion, minorities' mobilisation and expression, citizenship and inter-group relations.

The specific approach of the volume

While nationalism has received more and more attention from political scientists since the fall of communism, a huge part of this literature is devoted to explaining and classifying theories of nationalism (for example Dahbour and Ishay 1995; Hutchinson and Smith A. D. 1994; McCrone 1998; Ozkirimli 2000). Confronted by this proliferation of theories, authors such as Hall (1993) argue that the focus should instead be on the creation of typologies.

Besides, recent national minority studies have mostly approached nationalism either from a political theory point of view or from the perspectives of social mobilisations, secessionism (Gurr 2011; Hale 2008) and violence (Laitin 2007). In the latter studies, the concepts of ethnicity, ethnic mobilisation and violence have often been mobilised to refer to actors generally considered as primordial entities defined by their ethnic characteristics. Under this perspective, processes such as identity construction and the dynamics between state national practices and discourses have been left out of the analytical framework.

Hence, despite a large amount of research on nationalism on the one hand, and national minorities on the other, few volumes have tackled the specific relationship between new nation-states and national minorities and made the link between nationalism studies and national minorities. While several works have been published on case studies, such as Israel (Ghanem 2000; Kaufman 2010; Peled 1992; Smooha 1989), post-Soviet or post-Communist states (Beissinger 2002; Brubaker 1996; Bunce 2005; Commercio 2010; Hale 2008; Motyl 2001), this issue has rarely been discussed through the lenses that eschew single regional studies. This is precisely what our volume intends to offer, by reflecting on various cases worldwide, from Ukraine to Israel, Turkey or Malaysia.

More substantially, the various case studies and comparative analyses included in this volume have been developed in an original perspective that permits us to draw unique and insightful theoretical conclusions. In order to analyse the relationship between new nation-states and national minorities, the authors of this volume draw on various common concepts and categories derived from Brubaker's triadic nexus model and its critiques.

Instead of describing nations as substantial entities, collectivities or communities, Brubaker presents them as conceptual variables (Brubaker 1996: 16) – theorising a single relational nexus as a triad, linking national minorities, the newly-nationalising states in which they live, and the external national 'homelands' to which they belong (or can be construed as belonging) via an ethno-cultural affinity, though not by legal citizenship (1996: 4). In this manner, the three terms are linked, but they are not fixed or taken as given; each constitutes arenas of struggle that can be seen as a number of differentiated and competitive positions or stances, adopted by different organisations, parties, movements, or individual political entrepreneurs (1996: 61).

Consequently, and to follow Brubaker (1996: 60), a national minority may be seen as a family of related yet mutually-competing stances, which can be characterised by:

- a public claim to membership within an ethno-cultural nation different from the numerically- or politically-dominant ethno-cultural nation;
- the demand for state recognition of this distinct ethno-cultural nationality; and
- the assertion, on the basis of this ethno-cultural nationality, of certain collective or political rights.

A nationalising state may be seen as a family of related yet competing stances, characterised by the tendency to see the state as an 'unrealised' nation-state, and the concomitant disposition to remedy this perceived defect – something that leads to nationalising practices, policies or events on behalf of what is seen as 'the state' (1996: 63). External national homelands may be seen as a family of related yet competing stances surrounding an axiom of shared nationhood across the boundaries of state and citizenship, united by the idea that this shared nationhood makes the state responsible not only for its own citizens, but also for its ethnic co-nationals living in other states and who possess other citizenships (1996: 66–7). The triadic relation between these three terms is thus as *between relational fields*, characterised by the close interdependence of relations within and between fields, by the responsive and interactive character of the triadic relational interplay between the fields, and by the mediated character of this responsive interplay. Taking a responsive, interactive stance may be mediated by representations of stances in an external field – representations that may be shaped, in turn, by stances already provisionally held (1996: 67–9).

Drawing on the concept of the triadic nexus, Smith has argued that a fourth term should be taken into consideration, since international organisations have so strongly influenced the relationships between national minorities, nationalising states, and external national homelands – as has been seen in the case of Estonia (Smith D. 2002; see also Coppieter *et al.* 2004 and Johns 2003). By contrast, however, in a study on Russian national minorities in Latvia and Kyrgyzstan, Commercio argues that the role minorities' external homelands play may be over-stated and that other factors (e.g. local economic conditions) have a greater impact on minority perceptions than one external homeland's foreign policy practices (Commercio 2010: 19). The most vocal critique of Brubaker's triadic nexus comes from Kuzio (2001), who argues that one of Brubaker's three terms – the nationalising state – should be equated with nation building, and cannot be selectively applied only to former communist countries, mainly Ukraine and Kazakhstan (Arel 1995; Wilson 1997; Cummings 1998; Kubicek 1999; Lieven 1999) with Russia excepted (Smith G. *et al.* 1998; see Kuzio 2001: 139–42). Indeed, Kuzio (2001: 136) argues that if we agree that all civic states have ethno-cultural cores, then they are all de facto nationalising, since historical myths, state languages, anniversaries, symbols and flags are never neutral.

While taking these critiques into account and discussing them, the authors of the chapters of this volume, including Brubaker, take into consideration the extent to which the nationalising processes in the states that have emerged from the start of the twentieth century give the impression of *déjà vu* (Frandsen 2001: 302). Further, they explore ways in which nationalising states and policies can be analysed in cases across the globe.

Hence, this volume offers a series of studies that share a common conceptual framework and that pursue the same general objective: addressing the interaction between newly-established nationalising states and national minorities. The authors' focus on this interaction represents the linchpin of the volume and expresses its general motivation. In doing so, this volume aims to present new analytical tools and empirical examples to better understand the different processes brought about by the impact of nationalising patterns upon minorities, and the impact national minorities have had upon such patterns.

Outline of the volume

To address these issues in an in-depth manner, this volume integrates a series of chapters, focusing on specific dimensions of the general research question. More precisely, the volume is structured along three research axes and parts:

- The first part tackles how national identity is constructed in new nation-states. It considers the different ways in which these new states may constitute arenas of struggle between competing groups and discourses that try to impose their narrative on the state identity.

- The second part of this volume is dedicated to the analysis of the impact of the nationalising state on national minorities living in those states. The chapters assess the consequences of nationalising discourses and practices carried out by state elites.

- The last part of this volume explores the position of national minorities.

The investigation is conducted along two dimensions:

(1) how national minorities perceive themselves, and their identity, in a nationalising state; and

(2) what kinds of mobilisation this self-perception engenders.

In Chapter One, Rogers Brubaker begins by addressing different manifestations of the nationalising state. He looks back at the conclusions of his previous work discussing the nationalising state and suggests using this concept with significant caution. In particular, he holds that the notion of a 'nationalising state' should not be looked upon as a theory, or as a device for classifying states as nationalising or non-nationalising. Rather, he holds that it should be viewed as an analytical prism that allows us to better grasp nationalising discourses, policies and processes – one that should be used:

> in conjunction with other political, economic, social structural and cultural modes of analysis in specifying the material and symbolic interests at stake, the forms of social closure in operation and the patterns of state consolidation, economic transformation and cultural reorganisation that are under way.

In Chapter Two, Julien Danero Iglesias offers a study of the different discourses articulated by elites in the Republic of Moldova. Working within the framework of an electoral competition, he reveals how these political elites have repeatedly mobilised the concept of 'nation' in a way that seems devoid of specific content and in a manner that serves their particular interests. Drawing on Breuilly's definition of nationalism, this chapter shows how, in this case, the concept of nation serves above all as a tool for mobilising voters and *not* as something greater. In employing the term or idea of 'nation', the most important thing for these actors seems to be obtaining power.

Working from a different theoretical perspective, Doris Wydra examines, in Chapter Three, how nationalising narratives in Ukraine have been transformed into political narratives. She argues that Ukraine has been a battlefield of competing identity narratives. Indeed, she suggests how its main national minority (Russians), by virtue of its political and linguistic power, does not constitute a typical minority and therefore presents a constant challenge to the nation-building project of Ukraine's political elite.

The second part of the volume focuses on the impact nationalising practices have on minorities and minority rights. In Chapter Four, Magdalena Dembinska looks at political arrangements that favour the political integration of minorities in nationalising states, with a special focus on Belarusians and Germans in Poland after 1989. She suggests that the mere presence of ethnic parties in democratic institutions is not a sufficient indicator of integration, and that 'real' integration takes place when ethnic parties become regional parties that are open to members of other groups.

Hanna Vasilevich, in Chapter Five, gives further insights on the situation of national minorities, in two nationalising states: Poles and Belarusians in Lithuania, and Hungarians in Slovakia. Her main interest concerns the impact international organisations (especially the EU) and external national homelands (Poland, Belarus, Hungary) have had on the status of these minorities, on the articulation of their political claims, and on inter-ethnic relations. Drawing on Brubaker's 'triadic nexus', this chapter evaluates Brubaker's scheme and provides empirical discussion.

The relations between nationalising states and minorities in two Asian countries, specifically Malaysia and Indonesia, are at the centre of Karolina Prasad's contribution. In particular, in Chapter Six, Prasad examines the role that ethnic minorities (the Chinese in Indonesia, and the Chinese and Indians in Malaysia) have played in their nations' democratisation processes, against the background of their distinctive positions in the two countries (i.e. a long record of discrimination against the Chinese in Indonesia, and the more tolerated and politically-active Chinese and Indian presence in Malaysia).

Sharon Weinblum, in Chapter Seven, is also interested in the relationship between democracy and nationalising states. In her chapter on Israel, she presents an analysis of political discourses in the Israeli political arena in order to assess the concrete significance of the claim that Israel is both Jewish and democratic. Her empirical findings indicate that the demands of the Palestinian/Arab minority have been perceived by the dominant political elite, from centre-left to right, as a threat to the state and its core nation. The author labels this a 'differentialist nationalising discourse', and claims that, under such circumstances, the only possibility for the Palestinian minority to be integrated in the polity rests on the legitimisation of the so far marginal pluralist discourse accommodating the Jewish and democratic dimensions of the state.

Coming back to the borders of Europe, Chapter Eight explores the evolution of minority rights' protection in post-Ottoman Turkey and in the long-standing nation-state, Greece, with a special focus on the situation of the Turkish/Muslim minority in Greece and the Greek minority in Turkey after the 1923 Treaty of Lausanne. Using an approach informed by historical institutionalism, Fulya Memisoglu shows how path-dependent patterns have resulted in policies of 'negative reciprocity' that have threatened the very existence of these minorities in the two countries in question.

In the final part of this volume, the authors focus on minorities' responses to nationalising practices and discourses. In Chapter Nine, Christina Zuber argues that, before engaging in a discussion of the mobilisation of national minorities in nationalising states, we should first determine whose mobilisation we are talking about. In this manner, she proposes an exploration of the ontological assumptions inherent in the study of minority mobilisation. By doing so, she rightly criticises the essentialist approach that pervades most studies on ethnic mobilisation, as an approach that too quickly – indeed, 'without further argument', as she puts it – assumes that national minorities are collective entities. Zuber demonstrates greater sympathy for constructionist-leaning approaches, but still suggests that employing such ontologies may lead 'to an overestimation of the capacity of ethnic entrepreneurs to strategically manipulate flexible – qua constructed – identity categories'. In light of this, she suggests that a third approach, called 'naturalised constructivism', may be better. This approach treats ethnic groups as if they were a natural given, while acknowledging that they are social constructs. It is suggested that proceeding in this manner, which is also championed by authors such as Brubaker, Gil-White and Mallon, better enables researchers to understand minority mobilisation in nationalising states.

In Chapter Ten, Julian Bernauer explores the different ways in which members of the Russian minority have responded to nationalising processes in Ukraine, depending on their population share in a given district. His analysis of 'strategic voting' (i.e. voting for a party other than the most preferred one) in the 1998 parliamentary elections shows that the Russian voters used this strategy more often in electoral districts in which their population share was very low (below 15 per cent). This contradicts the author's initial expectation that strategic voting would be less readily observed among ethnic minority voters, who tend to stick with their ethnic parties even when it means 'wasting' their votes. The author further argues that, in places with salient ethnic cleavages, pure majoritarian systems do not lead to moderation and that, in the context of Ukraine, the move to full PR after the 2002 election 'likely reduces the probability of ethnic conflict'.

While Bernauer's focus centres on the electoral behaviour of ethnic minority voters, Chapter Eleven deals with the behaviour of ethnic *parties*. Edina Szöcsik and Daniel Bochsler examine the processes of fission and fusion that can be observed in minority ethnic parties, as a consequence of their participation in government. By considering developments visible in the political organisations of the Hungarian minorities in Romania, Serbia, and Slovakia, as well as those of Bosniaks in Serbia, Szöcsik and Bochsler suggest that government participation weakens the political unity of ethnic minorities, on the grounds that it often causes internal splits or sharpens competition between existing rival organisations.

The final chapter of the volume draws general conclusions from the different case studies. Antoine Roger first asks the question of the status of comparisons. How can we be sure that cases are comparable? Do the various cases enable us to formulate universal rules of causality? Advocating a re-examination of the epistemological bases of comparison, Roger proposes to substitute positivism with critical realism. Secondly, the author looks again at the causal mechanisms identified by Brubaker (instruments of public action, academic inputs, external inputs and everyday practices) and shows that multiple combinations between them help understand the prominence given to ethnicity and nationality in specific contexts. The author concludes with an invitation to pursue further comparative studies in this field.

References

Arel, D. (1995) 'Language politics in independent Ukraine: towards one or two state languages?', *Nationalities Papers*, 23(3): 597–622.

Badie, B. (1995) *La Fin des territoires*, Paris: Fayard.

Beissinger, M. R. (2002) *Nationalist Mobilization and the Collapse of the Soviet State*, New York: Cambridge University Press.

Brubaker, R. (1996) *Nationalism Reframed: Nationhood and the national question in the new Europe*, Cambridge: Cambridge University Press.

Bunce, V. (2005) 'The national idea: imperial legacies and post-communist pathways in eastern Europe', *East European Politics and Societies*, 19(3): 406–42.

Commercio (2010) *Russian Minority Politics in Post-Soviet Latvia and Kyrgyzstan: The transformative power of informal networks*, Philadelphia: University of Pennsylvania Press.

Coppieters, B., Emerson, M., Huysseune, M., Kovziridze, T., Noutcheva, G., Tocci, N. and Vahl, B. M. (2004) *Europeanization and Conflict Resolution: Case studies from the European periphery*, Ghent: Academia Press.

Cummings, S. (1998) 'The Kazakhs: demographics, diasporas, and "return"', in C. King and N. Melvin (eds) *Nations Abroad: Diaspora politics and international relations in the former Soviet Union*, Boulder: Westview, pp. 133–52.

Dahbour, O. and Ishay, M. (eds) (1995) *The Nationalism Reader*, Atlantic Highlands: Humanities Press.

Dieckhoff, A. (2000) *La nation dans tous ses Etats. Les identités nationales en mouvement*, Paris: Flammarion.

Frandsen, S. (2001) 'Beyond the multinational states: the revival of nations and nationalism', *Contemporary European History*, 10(2): 295–305.

Ghanem, A. (2000) 'The Palestinian minority in Israel: the "challenge" of the Jewish state and its implications', *Third World Quarterly*, 21(1): 87–104.

Gurr, T. (2011) *People and States: Minorities at risk in the new century*, Washington: United States Institute of Peace.

Hall, J. (1993) 'Nationalisms: classified and explained', *Daedalus*, 122(3): 1–28.

Hale, H. (2008) *The Foundations of Ethnic Politics: Separatism of states and nations in Eurasia and the world*, Cambridge: Cambridge University Press.

Hutchinson, J. and Smith, A. D. (eds) (1994) *Nationalism*, Oxford: Oxford University Press.

Johns, M. (2003) '"Do as I say, not as I do": the European Union, eastern Europe and minority rights', *East European Politics and Societies*, 17(4): 682–99.

Kaufman, I. (2010) 'Escalating minority claims: the Arab "visions documents" of 2006–2007 in Israel', in A. Lecours and L. Moreno (eds), *Nationalism and Democracy: Dichotomies, complementarities, oppositions*, London, New York: Routledge, pp. 184–208.

Kubicek, P. (1999) 'What happened to the nationalists in Ukraine?', *Nationalism and Ethnic Politics*, 5(1): 29–45.

Kuzio, T. (2001) '"Nationalising states" or nation-building? A critical review of the theoretical literature and empirical evidence', *Nations and Nationalism*, 7(2): 135–54.

Laitin, D. (2007) *Nations, States and Violence*, Oxford: Oxford University Press.

Lecours, A. and Moreno, L. (eds) (2010) *Nationalism and Democracy: Dichotomies, complementarities, oppositions*, New York: Routledge.

Lieven, A. (1999) *Ukraine and Russia: A fraternal rivalry*, Washington: United States Institute of Peace.

McCrone, D. (1998) *The Sociology of Nationalism: Tomorrow's ancestors*, London: Routledge.

Motyl, A. (2001) *Imperial Ends: The decay, collapse, and revival of empire*, New York: Columbia University Press.

Ozkirimli, U. (2000) *Theories of Nationalism*, New York: St Martin's Press.

Peled, Y. (1992) 'Ethnic democracy and the legal construction of citizenship: Palestinian-Arab citizens of the Jewish state', *American Political Science Review*, 86(2): 432–43.

Smith, A. D. (2001) *Nationalism: Theory, ideology, history*, Malden: Blackwell.

Smith, D. (2002) 'Framing the national question in central and eastern Europe: a quadratic nexus?', *The Global Review of Ethnopolitics*, 2(1): 3–16.

Smith, J. E. (1994) *Quasi-Religions, Humanism, Marxism, and Nationalism*, London: Macmillan.

Smith, G., Law, V., Wilson, A., Bohr, A. and Allworth, E. (1998) *Nation-Building in the Post-Soviet Borderlands: The politics of national identities*, New York: Cambridge University Press.

Smooha, S. (1989) *Arabs and Jews in Israel*, vol. 1., Boulder: Westview Press.

Wilson, A. (1997) *Ukrainian Nationalism in the 1990s: A minority faith*, Cambridge: Cambridge University Press.

chapter one | nationalising states revisited – projects and processes of nationalisation in post-soviet states

Rogers Brubaker

Introduction[1]

Twenty years ago, the political landscape of East Central Europe and Eurasia underwent a radical reconfiguration. Previously, multinational political space was reorganised along national lines in a vast region that spanned eleven time zones. Twenty-four national successor states emerged from the breakup of the multinational Soviet and Yugoslav and bi-national Czechoslovak states. At a moment when Western Europe seemed to be moving beyond the nation-state, Eastern Europe and Eurasia appeared to be moving back to the nation-state, entering not a post-national but a post-multinational era.

Writing in *Ethnic and Racial Studies* shortly after that great reconfiguration, I suggested that the successor states could usefully be analysed not simply as national, but as *nationalising* states (Brubaker 1996a). The dynamic implications of the term pointed to the unfinished and ongoing nature of nationalist projects and nationalising processes. The achievement of independent statehood, on this account, did not mark an end to nationalist politics, but a transition to a new kind of nationalist politics. The reorganisation of political space had produced (nominally) independent states; it had not produced 'genuine' nation-states. The new states were national in form, but not in substance. From a nationalist point of view, the states were organisational shells that had to be filled with national content, bringing population, territory, culture, and polity into the close congruence that defines a fully-realised nation-state.

Five motifs, I suggested, were characteristic of nationalist discourse in the successor states and used to justify nationalising policies in a variety of domains:

(1) the idea that the state contains a *core nation* or nationality, understood in ethno-cultural terms, and distinguished from the citizenry or permanent resident population of the state as a whole;

(2) a claim to *ownership* or *primacy* – the state is understood as the state *of* and *for* the core nation;

(3) the claim that the core nation is in a *weak* or unhealthy condition;

---

1. The present chapter is reproduced from an article previously published in November 2011 in *Ethnic and Racial Studies*, 34 (11): 1785–1814.

(4) the claim that *state action* is needed to strengthen the core nation, to promote its language, cultural growth, demographic robustness, economic welfare, or political hegemony; and

(5) the claim that such action is *remedial* or *compensatory*, needed to redress previous discrimination or oppression suffered by the core nation.

The notion of nationalising states emerged from the comparative study of interwar era and post-communist forms of nationalism, and from an analysis of the legacy of Soviet nationality policy. Like the post-World War I successor states to the Habsburg, Romanov, and Ottoman empires, the successor states to the Soviet Union, Yugoslavia, and Czechoslovakia were extraordinarily heterogeneous in ethno-linguistic and ethno-religious terms, yet they claimed legitimacy as the states of and for independently existing ethno-cultural 'nations,' and they too have been concerned to 'nationalise' their heterogeneous populations and territories. In both eras, the nationalising agenda was lent urgency by the existence of large, alienated, and presumed dangerous national minorities, connected to and supported by neighbouring ethno-national 'kin' or 'patron' states across the border.

The broader economic, political, and cultural contexts of nationalist politics, to be sure, differed substantially between interwar East Central Europe and post-communist Eastern Europe and Eurasia. The post-communist successor states have been more tightly enmeshed – though to very differing degrees – in a web of international organisations such as the European Union, the Organisation for Security and Cooperation in Europe, the Council of Europe, and the North Atlantic Treaty Organisation. These organisations have promoted models of civic nationhood, multiculturalism, integration, and minority rights towards which successor state elites have been obliged at least to gesture, and they have sought with some success to persuade post-communist states, most notably Estonia and Latvia, to moderate certain nationalising policies (Kelley 2004).[2] Post-communist successor states have also been enmeshed in denser webs of economic interdependence, and models of autarchic nationalism have lost their allure. Yet despite these contextual differences, the similarities arising from a nationalising stance, discourse and policies between interwar and incipient post-communist successor states seemed striking.

Two aspects of the Soviet legacy, I suggested, were contributing to the prevalence of nationalising discourse and policies in the incipient successor states.[3] One was the distinctive Soviet system of institutionalised multi-nationality; the other was the manner in which centralised rule and state-wide economic integration led to linguistic and demographic 'Russification'. The Soviet regime went to unprecedented lengths in institutionalising nationhood on a sub-state level (Suny 1993:

---

2. For a differing interpretation, stressing the primacy of domestic politics over international embeddedness and focusing on the issue of irredentism in post-communist Eastern Europe and Eurasia, see Saideman and Ayres 2008.

3. A similar argument applies, *mutatis mutandis*, in the Yugoslav and, to a considerably lesser extent, Czechoslovak cases.

Chapter Three; Slezkine 1994; Brubaker 1996b: Chapter Two; Martin 2001). More than fifty autonomous national 'homelands' were established and arrayed in a four-tiered ethno-federal hierarchy, each defined as the territory of and for a particular ethno-national group. Paralleling the national classification of territories was the national classification of persons. Every citizen was assigned an official ethno-cultural 'nationality'. This was ascribed at birth on the basis of descent, registered in personal documents, and recorded in bureaucratic encounters.

Constructing national territories as the polities of and for ethno-cultural nations, classifying and categorising people by 'nationality,' and giving preferential treatment to members of national groups in 'their own' territories fostered and legitimated the habit of distinguishing between the core, state-bearing nation, or 'titular nation', as it came to be called in Soviet and post-Soviet studies, and the total population of the republic. It also fostered and legitimated the sense of titular 'ownership' of or primacy within each republic.

Yet, while the Soviet regime constituted ethno-cultural nations and endowed them with 'their own' theoretically-autonomous, or even sovereign, territorial polities, it did not, of course, grant those polities substantive powers of self-rule. Quite apart from the massive repression directed against some ethno-national communities at certain junctures during Stalin's rule, large-scale migration and gradual linguistic Russification threatened to undermine the cultural and demographic bases of a number of the national polities. This had generated a discourse of titular weakness and ethnic redress already in the late Soviet period.

The first few years of independence, and even the final years of the Soviet era, furnished abundant examples of nationalising discourse and policies.[4] The key motifs of nationalising discourse – the distinction between core or titular nationality and others; the claim to titular primacy; the diagnosis of titular weakness; the call for remedial state action; and the justification in terms of compensation or redress – were so familiar as to constitute a kind of political common sense (Smith et al. 1998; Wilson 1997: Chapter Six; Schatz 2000: 83ff.). Laws promoting the national language were adopted in all of the incipient successor states even before independence. And Estonia and Latvia, where nationalising discourse was particularly strong and pervasive, adopted restrictive citizenship legislation that excluded about a third of the population from the citizenry.

The initial characterisation of successor states as nationalising states, however, was sketchy and speculative. Since then, a substantial literature has developed on various aspects of nation- and state-building in the new states. Building on this literature, I analyse in this chapter the dynamics of nationalisation in post-independence Estonia, Latvia, Ukraine, and Kazakhstan. These successor states had, proportionally, the largest Russian minorities at the end of the Soviet era; Ukraine

---

4.   Although I limit my attention in the text to the post-Soviet context, nationalising dynamics have been evident in the Yugoslav and Czechoslovak successor states as well, and figured centrally in the violent dissolution of Yugoslavia. For a discussion of the destabilising interplay between the incipient Croatian nationalising state, the incipient Serb national minority in Croatia, and the incipient 'kin' or 'homeland' state of Serbia, see Brubaker 1996b: 69–75.

and Kazakhstan also had, by far, the largest Russian minorities in absolute numbers. Nationalising discourses, policies, and practices have therefore been more central – and more sensitive – in these countries than elsewhere. These countries also capture a good deal of variation in patterns of incorporation into the Russian empire and Soviet Union (Laitin 1998) and in the strength of nationalist mobilisation in the last years of the Soviet era; this variation is related to the strength and form of nationalising discourses, policies, and practices.[5]

I focus on four domains: ethno-political demography, language repertoires and practices, the polity, and the economy. I consider the first two in detail, the latter two more briefly. This list of domains is neither exhaustive nor mutually exclusive.[6] However, concentrating on particular domains – rather than on nationalising discourses, policies, or processes in general – helps address both empirical and theoretical issues in a more differentiated and focused manner.

This chapter seeks to make both substantive and theoretical contributions. Substantively, it contributes to comparative work on nation- and state-building in Soviet successor states. Its main finding, to anticipate, is that differing modes of nationalisation have corresponded to different sorts of ethno-national boundaries between the 'core' or 'titular' nation and Russophone minority populations. Where boundaries have been strong, quasi-racial, and inter-generationally persistent, as in Kazakhstan, nationalisation (notwithstanding inclusive official rhetoric) has served primarily to strengthen and empower the titular nation at the expense of clearly distinct minority populations. Where ethno-national and linguistic boundaries have been blurred and permeable, as in Ukraine, nationalisation has worked primarily to reshape cultural practices, loyalties, and identities, thereby in effect redefining and enlarging the 'core nation'. Where boundaries have been strong, yet show signs of being inter-generationally permeable, as in Estonia and Latvia, nationalisation was initially oriented towards protecting, strengthening, and empowering the core nation as a sharply-bounded collectivity, but has subsequently become more 'assimilationist' and 'culturalist'.

This chapter contributes to the theoretical work on nationalism by reconsidering and reformulating the notion of 'nationalising states'. While my earlier discussion focused primarily on conspicuously nationalising *discourse* and *policies*, i.e. on expressly nationalising *projects*, I give equal attention to gradual, inconspicuous and anonymous nationalising *processes*. Projects and processes have distinct dynamics: nationalising projects do not necessarily produce their intended results, while nationalising processes may occur even in the absence of expressly nationalising discourse or policies. By highlighting the duality of projects and processes, I seek to provide a more nuanced understanding of the dynamics – and the limits – of nationalisation.

---

5.   Laitin's important 1998 study addresses the same four countries, but his focus is on the Russian-speaking minority population, not on the nationalising states per se.

6.   It does not include, for example, the domain of symbols and narratives (see illustratively Wanner 1998, Schatz 2004, Graney 2007, Wilson 1995, and Marples 2007).

Ethno-political demography

The first domain of nationalisation is what I will call ethno-political demography. By this I mean discourse, policies and processes bearing on the absolute or relative size of the core nation and significant minority ethno-national groups. Absolute and relative group size are the constant focal points of ethno-political concern in many settings; but, the large-scale Soviet-era migration of Russians and others into peripheral republics made this issue especially salient in the post-Soviet context, particularly in Estonia, Latvia, and Kazakhstan. How could these states be the states of and for their eponymous nations when titulars comprised, according to the last Soviet census in 1989, just 40 per cent of the population in Kazakhstan, a bare majority in Latvia, and just over 60 per cent in Estonia? In nationalist discourse, the very survival of the nation was at stake.

Migration per se has not been as salient an issue in Ukraine, but the absolute and relative size of the Russian minority has been a major focus of concern there too. The 11.4 million Russians comprised 22 per cent of the population in 1989, and a substantially higher share in borderland regions. In the Crimean peninsula (which had been part of Russia until it was transferred to Ukraine in 1954), Russians formed 66 per cent of the population; in the strategically important industrial region of the Donbass, their share was 44 per cent, while 66 per cent declared Russian as their native language (Wilson 1995: 267). Given Russian nationalist reluctance to recognise the permanent loss of Ukraine, the loyalties and identities of the population of the eastern borderlands have been a matter of vital concern.

On the eve of independence, then, the basic ethnic demography of the state was seen as deeply problematic in all four cases. By the time of the first post-Soviet censuses, a decade later, the ethno-demographic landscape had changed dramatically. In each country, the census documented a nationalising trend, with the titular share of the population increasing sharply and the Russian (and Russophone) share declining even more sharply (see Table 1.1). Gains by titulars were particularly dramatic in Kazakhstan, where the Kazakh share jumped from 40 per cent in 1989 to 53 per cent ten years later. Preliminary results from the 2009 census show rapid nationalisation continuing in Kazakhstan, with the Kazakh share now 63 per cent.[7]

This nationalising shift in the relative shares of the titular and Russian populations has been driven by three processes. In the Baltics and Kazakhstan, the most important has been the emigration of the Russian-speaking population. The first post-Soviet censuses recorded declines in the Russian population of 22 per cent in Latvia, 26 per cent in Estonia, and 28 per cent in Kazakhstan (39 per cent between 1989 and 2009); other predominantly Russophone minority populations suffered similar or even sharper declines. Most of this decline is attributable to emigration, but also a *consequence* of nationalisation. Migrations of 'ethnic unmixing'[8] have

---

7. Preliminary census results are reported on the website of the Statistical Agency of Kazakhstan: www.stat.kz/p_perepis/Pages/n_04_02_10.aspx (accessed 28 July 2010).

8. Migrations of 'ethnic unmixing' are caused by the fact that some ethnic groups did not mix with other populations and left the country for a country in which they have 'ethnic affinity'. Ethnic

Table 1.1: Titular and Russian share of population in last Soviet and first post-Soviet census

	Estonia		Latvia		Ukraine		Kazakhstan		
	1989	2000	1989	2000	1989	2001	1989	1999	2009
Titular nationality (%)	61.5	67.9	52.0	57.7	72.7	77.8	39.7	53.4	63.1
Russian (%)	30.3	25.6	34.0	29.6	22.1	17.3	37.8	29.9	23.7
Titular nationality (000)	963	930	1,388	1,370	37,419	37,542	6,535	7,985	10,099
Russian (000)	475	351	906	703	11,356	8,334	6,228	4,480	3,797

Sources:

Soviet figures 1989: Gosudarstvennyi Komitet po Statistike, Natsional'nyi Sostav Naselenia SSSR. Moscow: Finansy i Statistika (1991).

Estonia 2000: http://pub.stat.ee/px-web.2001/I_Databas/Population_Census/databasetree.asp (accessed 18 July 2010).

Latvia 2000: /www.csb.gov.lv/images/modules/items/item_file_2064_baltcen3.pdf (accessed 22 August 2010);

Ukraine 2001: /www.ukrcensus.gov.ua/eng/results/nationality_population/nationality_1/ (accessed 18 July 2010);

Kazakhstan 1999: Dave 2004a:442; Kazakhstan 2009: /www.stat.kz/p_perepis/Pages/n_04_02_10.aspx (accessed 28 July 2010).

regularly followed the reconfiguration of political space along national lines, when previously dominant ethno-national groups (such as Germans in the eastern provinces of Prussia, or Hungarians in Transylvania) found themselves transformed into national minorities in nationalising successor states (such as interwar Poland and Romania) (Brubaker 1996b: Chapter Six). The post-Soviet pattern has been similar.

Strong nationalising discourse and policies encouraged many Russians to leave Estonia and Latvia soon after independence. Russian-speaking immigrants were routinely characterised as unwanted and even illegal 'occupiers' or 'colonists', while mainstream politicians, reflecting titular public opinion, made no secret of their desire to see them emigrate (Laitin 1998:166). One relatively moderate statement from a leading politician who was Minister of Foreign Affairs from 1992–4 expressed the hope that 'a third or so [of non-Estonians] will become Estonian citizens, a third may remain here with Russian citizenship, and a third *at least* will leave' (Lieven 1993: 377; emphasis added). Among nationalists, it was commonly argued that all or most of the Soviet-era immigrants – and even their Estonian or Latvian-born children – should leave.

unmixing is a push factor at the point of origin, while ethnic affinity is a pull factor at the point of destination.

Restrictive legislation left large majorities of the Russian and Russophone population (and a third of the total population) without citizenship initially, and made naturalisation conditional on knowledge of the titular language. In these circumstances, it is scarcely surprising that about a quarter of the Russophone population emigrated. But the emigration wave peaked in the early 1990s, tapering off rapidly thereafter. Russophones have not felt welcome in Estonia and Latvia, but they have felt secure; and they could see a more promising future there – or perhaps in 'Europe' more broadly – than in Russia (Laitin 1998:161ff).[9]

Public discourse in Kazakhstan – at least discourse directed at Russophone and international audiences – has not been as important with regard to nationalising as in Estonia or Latvia. All residents were accorded citizenship, and President Nazarbaev, concerned about the economic disruption a massive exodus would entail, sought to reassure Russophones about their place in an independent multi-ethnic Kazakhstan. Informal signals and practices, however, have been important for nationalising. Kazakhstan is understood, by both Kazakhs and Russophone minorities, as the state of and for Kazakhs; and most Russophones believe they have no long-term future in the country (Laitin 1998: 98–9; 161, 171–6; Kuscu 2008: 86–9, 93; Dave 2007: 103, 127–8). This was already the case in the late Soviet era and Russophones had already started to leave Kazakhstan in the 1980s. The outflow picked up substantially in the 1990s, though without an immediate post-independence spike. While Russophone emigration from Estonia and Latvia had largely ceased by the mid-1990s, it has continued from Kazakhstan, and has acquired a self-sustaining dynamic (Laitin 1998: 171ff.; Dave 2007: 127–8).

Migration has contributed to the nationalisation of Kazakhstan not only through the emigration of Russophones, but also through the immigration of ethnic Kazakhs from neighbouring countries (the majority from Uzbekistan), who have been encouraged by the government to return to their 'historic homeland' (Kuscu 2008; Diener 2005). Nearly 740,000 *Oralmandar* (returnees) have resettled in Kazakhstan since independence, contributing substantially to the growth of the ethnic Kazakh population (International Federation for Human Rights 2009: 39). Internal migration, too, has had a nationalising effect, bringing Kakakhs from the south to the Russian-dominated north, especially to the new capital city of Astana; the capital was moved from Alma Ata in the south in part in an effort to strengthen the Kazakh presence in the north (Dave 2007: 122–3).

9. One factor that might lead to continued differential Russophone outmigration – among young people who have acquired Estonian or Latvian citizenship and know English – is the opportunity to work and eventually resettle in other EU countries. (Estonia and Latvia became EU members in 2004 and the last transitional restrictions on free mobility expired in 2011.) Children of Russophone families, especially those whose Estonian is less than fluent, might be more inclined than others to pursue such opportunities (Hughes 2005; Siiner 2006: 171–2). This is consistent with Laitin's data showing a stronger orientation to Europe on the part of Russian than Estonian youth in Estonia: 'It seems that Estonian independence opened up Europe for Russians, while it opened up Estonia for Estonians' (Laitin 2003: 213, 219–220).

The second process driving ethno-demographic nationalisation in Kazakhstan, though not in the other countries, has been differential fertility rates of titular and minority populations. While the size of the titular population in the other countries has been stable or declined slightly, it has grown by more than 50 per cent over twenty years in Kazakhstan. Some of this – perhaps a fifth to a quarter of the total growth in the Kazakh population – reflects the immigration of ethnic Kazakhs, but most reflects the high fertility rates and young age structure of the Kazakh population (Agadjanian 1999: 429; Centers for Disease Control and Prevention 2003: 25).

Ethno-demographic nationalisation in Ukraine reflects a third underlying process. The population identifying as Russian declined by some three million people between 1989 and 2001, amounting to more than a quarter of those who identified themselves as such in 1989. Yet, net emigration of Russians accounts for only about 5 to 10 per cent of this decline (Stebelsky 2009: 86; Heleniak 2004: 109). Russians have not been leaving the country; they have been re-identifying as Ukrainian (Rapawy 1998; Arel 2002b: 237–8; Stebelsky 2009). In other words, large numbers of people who previously identified their nationality as Russian (many of them presumably from the very large number of ethnically-mixed Ukrainian-Russian families)[10] appear to have identified as Ukrainian in the most recent census; and children from mixed nationality families who were being enumerated for the first time in the 2001 census were more likely to be identified as Ukrainian than were such children in previous censuses. The most thorough study of the matter suggests that re-identification accounts for more than two-thirds of the decline in the Russian population (Stebelsky 2009).

In Ukrainian nationalising discourse, such ethno-national re-identification represents a form of statistical redress, through which 'real' Ukrainians, having been denationalised and Russified during Soviet times, rediscover their 'true' identity (Arel 2002b: 237). But, essentially, this is a naive misunderstanding of ethnic demography. Mixed and fluctuating identities are characteristic of borderland populations, and constructivist research has demonstrated the malleability of ethnic identification in a wide range of settings. On a constructivist understanding, ethnic demography is not something prior and external to politics, affected only by demographic variables such as fertility, mortality, and migration; it reflects subjective practices of self-identification that are context-dependent and endogenous to political processes (Chandra and Boulet 2003).

But the seemingly objective facts of ethnic demography not only reflect the subjective self-identifications of individuals; they also reflect the counting and categorising practices of states. These too are symptomatic of political processes. As a number of scholars have argued, the procedures used by states to identify, count and categorise their populations do not provide a neutral and transparent

---

10. According to data on mixed marriages from the 1989 census (the most recent available), 22 per cent of all married couples in Ukraine were mixed Ukrainian-Russian couples, twice the share of Russian-Russian couples (Stebelsky 2009: 97).

record of social reality, but help constitute that reality (Hacking 1982; Anderson 1991: Chapter Ten; Arel and Kertzer 2002). The issue here is not the fabrication or falsification of data. It is that choices about counting and categorising – choices about *what* to count and *how* to count it – are always political, not simply technical choices. The data generated as a result of these choices can powerfully shape prevailing representations of state and society, and these representations, in turn, help shape political debate, frame policy options and legitimise particular stances and decisions.

In Kazakhstan, for example, the nationalising demographic trend was never in doubt, but it was uncertain whether the 1999 census would reveal a Kazakh majority – a symbolically resonant political and/or psychological threshold. This may have led officials to 'anticipate demographic superiority' (Kolstø 1998) by ensuring that the census would ratify an official demographic majority, in part by taking advantage of the flexibility and ambiguity involved in the counting of Russian and Kazakh migrants (Dave 2004: 453–4; Arel 2002a: 813–4).

Categorisation always involves decisions about lumping versus splitting, and disputes about combining or distinguishing categories have shadowed modern censuses from the beginning (Rothschild 1974: 88, 202). In the post-Soviet context, counting by ethnic nationality tends to represent minorities as smaller and as more fragmented than would other ways of counting (Arel 2002a: 815–6). In Kazakhstan, for example, distinctions of nationality among Russians, Ukrainians, Belarusians and Poles have little meaning or relevance for most people. These populations are overwhelmingly Russophone, and they are not divided by any significant social boundaries, such as barriers to intermarriage. In this context, counting by ethnic nationality – presenting statistics on Kazakhs and individual European nationalities, rather than on Kazakhs and Europeans or Slavs – serves to reduce the perceived size of the minority population. Similar techniques of statistical nationalisation have been used in Estonia and Latvia to minimise the size and exaggerate the fragmentation of the overwhelmingly Russophone minority population (*ibid.*).

Statistics on language have also been computed and presented in ways that understate heterogeneity. In Ukraine and Kazakhstan, for example, substantial fractions of the titular population still prefer to speak Russian. This linguistic divide among these groups is masked by using statistics on 'native language'. 'Native language' continues to be interpreted, as in Soviet times, as the language of one's ethnic nationality, regardless of whether, or how well, one speaks the language (Arel 2002a: 820). Thus while 98.5 per cent of Kazakhs named Kazakh as their native language in the 1989 census, observers suggested that about 40 per cent of Kazakhs – and a higher fraction of urban Kazkahs – spoke the language poorly or not at all (Fierman 2005: 405; Dave 2004a: 450). Kazakhs' knowledge of the Khazakh language has increased since independence – and will be discussed in the next section – but statistics on 'native language' continue to yield a very different picture than data on actual language use.

A similar point can be made about Ukraine: 85 per cent of ethnic Ukrainians – and two-thirds of the population – named Ukrainian as their native language in the 2001 census. But if statistics had been gathered and published on language of preference rather than 'native language', Ukraine would appear as more or less evenly divided between those preferring to speak Russian and those preferring Ukrainian (Arel 2002b: 238–243). These different representations of the population – either as predominantly Ukrainian-speaking or as evenly split between Ukrainian-speaking and Russian-speaking – can be used to justify very different policies. The latter, for example, could be used to argue for policies that would treat the Russian language on an equal footing with Ukrainian.

The analytical point is that statistics on nationality and language do not simply *measure* the progress of nationalising states; they help *produce* that progress. By publicly ratifying the nationalising trend, the post-Soviet censuses have strengthened the understanding and representation of the successor states as the states of and for particular nations. Statistics are in this sense a medium through which nationalisation is *effected*, not simply one through which it is *described*.

Language policies and practices

Language constitutes a second key domain for analysing nationalising discourses, policies, and processes. I have already touched on language statistics in connection with practices of counting and categorising; here I consider the aims, instruments, and results of policies that seek to alter language repertoires and practices.

Just as the large-scale Soviet-era migration of Russians and others into peripheral republics made ethnic demography a sensitive and salient issue in the successor states, so too the large-scale Soviet-era shift in language repertoires and practices made language an equally salient and sensitive issue. Migration and language shift were of course closely intertwined. But linguistic Russification was not simply a matter of Russophone in-migration; it was also a matter of a shift in the language repertoires and practices of the titular populations. And this involved not only the acquisition of Russian, but also, in some cases, the loss of competence in the titular language.

This shift led to large-scale discrepancies between language practices and official nationality, since official nationality – as inscribed in identity documents and recorded in the census – was much 'stickier' than language repertoires and practices. Members of various national groups increasingly spoke Russian in a wide range of contexts and domains, and in some cases they were unable to speak what was supposedly 'their own' language at all. Since language was and is generally understood to be constitutive of nationality, this language shift was widely interpreted as entailing or threatening de-nationalisation. This set the stage for one important strand of nationalising politics – to restore the congruence between nationality and language that nationalists saw as having been destroyed by decades of Russification. That this was an imagined and idealised congruence made it no less powerful as an inspiration for nationalising agendas (Siiner 2006: 173).

Restoring the congruence between nationality and language was relatively straightforward in Estonia and Latvia, where there had been little erosion in the titular population's command over the titular language. There was no need to change titulars' language repertoires or preferences; policies sought simply to make it possible for them to use their native language in the full range of domains and contexts, and throughout the territory of the state. This was done by mandating the use of the titular language in various domains, and by using language tests to exclude Russian monolinguals from positions involving contact with the public (Hogan-Brun *et al.* 2008).

The issue was more complicated in Ukraine and Kazakhstan, where substantial segments of the titular population could *not* speak or write the titular language, or simply preferred to speak Russian. It was easy enough for Russophone Ukrainians to learn Ukrainian; and it was easy enough to expand by decree the domains in which Ukrainian was used. And the prestige of Ukrainian has increased. Yet, a substantial and apparently stable fraction of ethnic Ukrainians continue to use Russian or a mix of Russian and Ukrainian in private (Bernsand 2001; Wilson 2002; Besters–Dilger 2007).

Restoring the congruence between language and nationality has been equally difficult in Kazakhstan. The prestige of Kazakh, like that of Ukrainian, has increased, and most Kazakhs have acquired at least a minimal competence in the language. Yet for many urban Kazakhs, this competence remains rudimentary, and the use of Kazakh is largely symbolic (Dave 2007: Chapter Five; Fierman 2006).

What about policies aimed at getting the non-titular population to learn or speak the titular language? Such policies have been largely symbolic in Kazakhstan, and secondary in Ukraine, given the primary focus on altering the language practices of titulars. But they have been taken quite seriously in the Baltic States. Such policies are often characterised, and criticised, as assimilationist. Yet there is surprisingly little talk of assimilation. Assimilationist discourse runs counter to prevailing international norms supporting multiculturalism and the preservation of minority languages and cultural identities. It also runs counter to the legacy of Soviet nationality policy, with its quasi-primordial understanding of ethnic nationality. Moreover, there is considerable ambivalence about assimilation, especially in the Baltics, where language is widely understood as a key ethnic boundary marker, and as the distinctive 'property' of an ethno-national group (Siiner 2006). And in Kazakhstan, where the difference between Europeans and Central Asians is widely understood in primordial or ethno-racial terms, assimilation is widely seen as inconceivable (Laitin 1998: 155).

In Estonia and Latvia, policies that seek to alter non-titulars' language repertoires and practices aim in the first instance to redistribute the burden of bilingualism. In the late Soviet era, Russophones could live and work as monolinguals throughout the territory of the state, while others were expected to be bilingual, even in their own republics. Nationalising language policies in Estonia and Latvia have sought to reverse this arrangement. Requiring Russophones to become bilingual in the titular language and Russian has made it easier for *titulars* to speak the titular language in a wider range of domains and contexts, instead of being obliged to speak Russian when interacting with Russian monolinguals. In practice, however, as Siiner (2006:179) notes with respect to Estonia, purist, protective and proprietary attitudes towards the titular language often leads titulars to speak Russian rather than 'hear Russian-speakers make mistakes while using Estonian'. Shifting the burden of bilingualism has also freed titulars to learn foreign languages other than Russian, notably English. It should be noted, however, that there remains considerable interest in learning Russian as a second foreign language: 35 per cent of children in Latvian language schools were studying Russian in 1999–2000 (Bloom 2008), while a 2002 survey reported that nearly half of Estonians wanted their children to study Russian[11] (see also Laitin 2003: 212).

Having considered the *aims* of nationalising language policies, I turn now to the primary *instruments* of these policies: prescriptive rules or mandates; language tests; and policies governing the language of instruction in the school system. Prescriptive rules mandate the use of the titular language in certain contexts in all four countries. The primary contexts include government and administration, the courts, the media, public signage, some workplaces, and parts of the educational system. Such rules have been justified by the fact that the titular language is formally the sole 'state language' in each country. They have also been justified by the assumption that it is the *majority* languages that require protection and promotion by the state, not, as in most other contexts, the *minority* languages. This is in keeping with the remedial character of nationalising policies and with the emphasis on redress, and it is a key part of what makes the post-Soviet context distinctive.

The second instrument is the use of language tests to regulate access to certain positions and status. In Estonia and Latvia, language tests have been used to control access to citizenship itself (see the next section). Language tests were also introduced for a wide range of private-sector as well as public-sector jobs that required 'contact with public' (Ozolins 2003: 223). This was in keeping with the aim of making it possible for titulars to conduct their everyday business exclusively in the titular language. In Kazakhstan, nationalist intellectuals have called repeatedly for language tests. But such tests would be highly divisive among Kazakhs themselves, and no formal tests have been implemented, though there are implicit requirements to learn Kazakh for those seeking work or advancement in government positions (Dave 2007: 107 and Dave, personal communication). Similarly, language tests have not been instituted in Ukraine, though the 1989 language law specified that officials must learn Ukrainian.

The third instrument of linguistic nationalisation – and in the long run, the most important – is the school system. Since the late nineteenth century, when states first began to provide universal and compulsory primary education, schools have served as the primary instrument of nationalisation in a wide range of cases. Yet schools can also work in a very different direction. Where primary, secondary, and even university education is provided in a minority language, schools can serve to reproduce minority 'communities' and languages (Brubaker *et al.* 2006: 269ff.). This was the situation in the Soviet Union, not only during the period of

---

11. The study of Russian remains obligatory in Ukraine (Besters–Dilger 2007) and Kazakhstan (William Fierman, personal communication).

korenizatsiia or 'nativisation' in the 1920s, when the regime made vast and un-precedented efforts to promote non-Russian languages and cultures (Martin 2001), but even (albeit unevenly) in the final decades of its existence. Comprehensive titular-medium school systems continued to exist in all Soviet republics, though Russian-medium schooling was also available throughout the Soviet Union (a fact that facilitated the migration of Russian and Russophone populations into the peripheral republics). In the late Soviet era, almost all titulars attended titular-medium schools in Estonia and Latvia. In Ukraine and especially in Kazakhstan, however, substantial fractions of the titular population attended Russian-medium schools.

Russian-medium education has contracted substantially in the successor states, though debates, policies and trends have varied. In Estonia and Latvia, where Russian-medium schools are used almost entirely by minorities, the proportion of all students being educated in Russian has declined steadily, even after the initial out-migration of Russophones: from 28 per cent in 1999–2000 to 20 per cent in 2006–7 in Estonia, and from 39 per cent in 1995–6 to 26 per cent in 2008–9 in Latvia (Estonian Ministry of Education and Research 2008, Latvian Ministry of Foreign Affairs 2010). In the 2009–10 school year, 17 per cent of Russians, and 20 per cent of all non-Latvians, were being educated in Latvian-medium schools.[12] Russian-medium schools have closed in areas without large concentrations of Russophones, and some Russophone parents have chosen to send their children to titular-medium schools.

In both countries, moreover, exclusively Russian-medium education is being phased out at the high-school level. Current policy in both countries calls for at least 60 per cent of the curriculum in grades 10–12 to be taught in the titular lan-guage (Galbreath and Galvin 2005; Verschick 2005; Latvian Ministry of Foreign Affairs 2010; Estonian Ministry of Education and Research 2008). The rationale is that this should improve the labour market integration of the graduates of Russian-medium schools. This represents a retreat from earlier plans in response to interna-tional pressure and domestic protest in both countries to abolish Russian-medium instruction altogether in secondary schools. Yet it still represents a substantial na-tionalisation of minority-language education.

In Kazakhstan, the nationalisation of education is aimed in the first instance not at minorities, but at Russified urban Kazakhs. While only about half of ur-ban Kazakhs were in Kazakh-medium classes in 1990, the share had increased to nearly three-quarters by 1995. However, there has been little change since then; a substantial share of urban Kazakhs continue to be educated in Russian-medium classes. Moreover, as Fierman (2006: 107; 2005) has shown, these figures overstate the degree of nationalisation, since 40 per cent of the urban students in Kazakh-medium classes are attending mixed schools, where the linguistic envi-ronment outside the classroom remains largely Russophone. And part of the in-crease reflects the heavy internal migration of non-Russified Kazkahs from the

---

12. Ministry of Education statistics, reported in personal communication from Stephen Bloom.

countryside, rather than a shift in language strategies on the part of the largely Russified elite. The urban Kazakh elite remains heavily invested in Russian as a language of mobility and opportunity, while also increasingly investing in English as well. As Dave (2007: 111) notes, it is virtually unheard of for children of the Kazakh elite to attend Kazakh-medium schools.

In Ukraine, too, the shift to titular-medium education was aimed in the first instance at titulars, and specifically at the 25 per cent of ethnic Ukrainian children who were being educated in Russian-medium schools in 1989 (Arel 1995: 604). Here too, nationalists sought to reverse decades of Russification and to restore what they understood to be the 'proper' congruence between nationality and language. In the early 1990s, the government strongly encouraged the shift to Ukrainian-medium education. And official statistics report a substantial increase in the proportion of students in Ukrainian-medium schools, from 58 per cent in 1995–6 to 78 per cent ten years later (Bilaniuk and Melnyk 2008: 353). But the increase has been uneven: while education is now almost exclusively in Ukrainian in the west and centre, Russian-medium education remains predominant in much of the east and south.

In addition to these formal policy instruments, linguistic nationalisation can be promoted or enforced through informal social pressures and informal linguistic 'policing'. Such policing is found in both intra-ethnic and inter-ethnic contexts. Laitin highlights the role of language 'vigilantes' in Ukraine, who seek to shame Russophone titulars into using Ukrainian (1998: 141–2, 341ff.); Dave (2007: 103, 109) notes a similar (though less effective) phenomenon in Kazakhstan, while Laitin (2003: 207) describes informal titular policing of Russophones' language practices in Estonia.

So much for the aims and instruments of linguistic nationalisation – what about the results of nationalising policies and practices? In Estonia and Latvia, where language policies have been 'thick' (Siiner 2006) and implementation serious, and where titulars have made what Laitin calls a 'credible commitment' to drop Russian from their linguistic repertoires, there have been strong incentives for Russophones, particularly the younger generation, to learn the titular language (Laitin 1998). The teaching *of* Estonian and Latvian in Russian-medium schools – and now the teaching of most subjects *in* Estonian and Latvian at the high school level – has made it possible, and increasingly necessary, for them to do so. Survey data, moreover, suggest that Russophones acknowledge not only the usefulness of learning the titular language, but the legitimacy of being required to learn it (Rose 2000; Laitin 1998: 205). Policies, incentives, and attitudes have been aligned in encouraging the learning of titular languages. Progress, however, has been slow, hampered – especially in Estonia – by continued social separation of Estonian and Russophone populations, even among the younger generation (Siiner 2006: 177ff.; Rannut 2008).

In Kazakhstan and Ukraine, the situation is more ambiguous. The 1999 Kazakh census, for example, reported that 99.4 per cent of Kazakhs were 'proficient' in the state language. The actual census question, however, did not ask about proficiency. It asked the respondent whether he or she 'knows,' 'knows weakly,' 'is learning,' or 'does not know' the state language; and instructions to census enumerators specified that knowing the language did not require the ability to read or write in Kazakh (Dave 2007: 112–3). Self-reported data on language competence are always of questionable value; here, given the normative expectations regarding knowledge of the state language, they are particularly dubious. Dave concludes that the state was 'less interested in capturing the actual patterns of linguistic behaviour' than in 'demonstrat[ing] the "steady success" of its ethno-linguistic policies' (*ibid.* 114).

In Ukraine, too, the official portrait of a steady and successful 'Ukrainisation' or 'de-Russification' of education has been challenged by data focused on actual practices. As indicated above, many of those who report their native language as Ukrainian prefer to speak Russian in everyday life. Some schools are classified as Ukrainian even if only a few subjects are taught in Ukrainian (Besters-Dilger 2007). A survey in Kiev – where, formally, a massive shift to Ukrainian-medium education has taken place – showed that only a fifth of schoolchildren spoke Ukrainian at school outside the classroom (*ibid.*; for ethnographic evidence, see Bilaniuk 2005: 47–8, 63–4). Print media remain Russian-dominated, while radio and television broadcast in both languages, often on the same channel. The over-all picture suggested by sociolinguistic research is that outside western Ukraine, Ukrainian often functions as a kind of government-supported 'artificial language' of education and administration, unable to compete on its own with Russian (Besters-Dilger 2007; for a more nuanced picture, see Bilaniuk and Melnyk 2008: 357–66 and Kulyk 2006; 2010).

The analytical point to underscore is that there are important limits to nation-alising policies in the sphere of language, even where policies are 'thick' and seri-ously enforced, as in the Baltics, and *a fortiori* in Kazakhstan and Ukraine. The state can mandate that the titular language be used in certain settings; but such mandates may or may not be enforced. In Ukraine, for example, legislation and licensing agreements require a certain fraction of broadcasting to be in Ukrainian, but these have been openly flouted (Besters-Dilger 2007; Bilaniuk and Melnyk 2008: 363). Language tests – or informal hiring policies – can create incentives for titulars and minorities to develop a certain competence in the titular language, but they cannot guarantee that the language will be used in practice. The state cannot legislate for change in linguistic preferences, nor can a liberal state do much to leg-islate for change in language practices, especially in the private sphere. Language shift is a very complex process; it is not something that can simply be decreed.

Yet despite the limits to nationalising *policies*, nationalising *processes* have their own dynamics. The gap between policies and processes is most striking in Kazakhstan. Nationalising language policies have been weak and largely symbolic (Dave 2007: 106ff.; Fierman 2005: 414). The 1997 Law on Languages stipulated a duty of every citizen to master Kazakh, but this was a purely symbolic gesture. There has been no serious expectation that Russians would learn the language; indeed, the language is widely understood as the exclusive possession of Kazakhs. And while Russified Kakakhs have been pressured to incorporate some Kazakh into their linguistic repertoire, they have encountered no 'major economic, professional or social pressure' to master the language or use it more actively (Dave 2007: 112). However, in the long run, the mass emigration of Russophones, substantial rural-urban and south-north migration of Kazakh monolinguals, and the rise of English as a contending language of opportunity, mobility and prestige are likely to erode the place of Russian and foster linguistic nationalisation (Fierman 2005: 419ff.; Laitin 1998: 359).

Polity and economy

Two other domains in which nationalising discourse, policies and processes are at work can be considered more briefly. In the political domain, the basic question is whether – and if so, how – discourse, policies and unofficial practices have promoted the political hegemony of the core nation or weakened the political power of national minorities. Three forms of nationalisation have been salient in the successor states: the nationalisation of the demos through restrictive citizenship policies; the nationalisation of government and administrative personnel through recruitment and promotion practices; and the limitation of the political voice of minorities through various means, including notably the rejection of demands for autonomy for minority-dominated regions.

The nationalisation of the demos through restrictive citizenship legislation has been key in Estonia and Latvia. Alone among the successor states, Estonia and Latvia rejected the inclusive model that based citizenship on residence in favour of a 'restored state' model that recognised as citizens at the moment of independence only those who had been citizens of interwar Estonia and Latvia and their descendants (Brubaker 1992). All others – including the great majority of the Russophone population – had to apply for naturalisation after a certain waiting period. Annual quotas on naturalisations were imposed in Latvia (though they were abolished in 1998); and fairly strict language tests have been a prerequisite for naturalisation in both countries. The pace of naturalisations has been slow, despite a certain easing of requirements, largely in response to international pressures.[13] Even today, nearly half of the Russophone population in both counties remains without Estonian or Latvian citizenship (Järve 2009; Krūma 2009).

The mass disenfranchisement of non-titulars ensured that the Russophone minority was largely excluded from the initial shaping of the basic structure of the new state (Järve 2009: 47). Russians, for example, did not hold a single seat in the first Estonian parliament elected after independence, and they held only 7 per cent of the seats in the first Latvian parliament, despite forming 34 per cent of the population in 1989 (Smith et al. 1998: 99).

Nationalisation of the personnel of the government and the state apparatus has followed from restrictive citizenship legislation in the Baltics. In Kazakhstan,

---

13. Regarding the influence of international organisations on Estonian and Latvian citizenship and language policies, see for example Kelley 2004, Jurado 2003. The influence of international organisations is evident at the margins; but the changes introduced in response to such pressures – especially in the context of applications for EU membership – have been modest.

citizenship has not been an issue, but informally nationalising recruitment and promotion practices led very quickly after independence to a substantial over-representation of Kazakhs among government and administrative personnel, especially in the Russian-dominated north (Smith *et al.* 1998: Chapter Seven; Dave 2007: 151ff.; Kolstø 1998: 61–2; Holm-Hansen 1999: 197).

Questions of regional autonomy were important and unsettled in the early post-independence years in Ukraine, Kazakhstan, and (to a lesser extent) Estonia, where minorities are territorially concentrated and form majorities in certain regions. Leaders of Ukraine and Kazakhstan skilfully resisted minority claims for territorial autonomy or federalism, framing such calls as threats to the integrity of the state (though concessions were made for the special case of Crimea) (Wolczuk 2002: 72–5; Dave 2007: 120).[14] The political voice of Russophones in Kazakhstan was further weakened by ethnic gerrymandering: district boundaries were redrawn so as to deprive northern districts, bordering Russia, of their prior Russian majorities (Dave 2007: 122–3; Arel 2002a: 814–15)). And organisations claiming to represent the Russian or Russian-speaking population in Kazakhstan have been hemmed in and effectively depoliticised through on-going emigration, fragmentation, intimidation, and surveillance (Dave 2007: 129–30, 136).

In the economic domain, the basic question is similar: whether – and if so, in what ways – discourses, policies, and practices have promoted the economic position and interests of the core nation over those of national minorities. In sharp contrast with interwar Eastern Europe – where successor state elites expressly sought to nationalise the ethno-nationally 'alien' urban economy, dominated by Jews, Germans, and other minorities – overtly nationalising economic discourse has not figured centrally in the successor states. Soviet-era preferential treatment policies already favoured members of titular nationalities in the economic domain, especially in white-collar jobs; as a result, the sense of titular weakness was less pronounced in the economic sphere than in demographic, cultural, and political domains.

Yet, if expressly nationalising discourse has been muted in the economic sphere, nationalising policies and practices have significantly shaped economic outcomes in the Baltics and Kazakhstan. Informal economic nationalisation has been particularly pronounced in Kazakhstan. The neo-patrimonial Kazakh regime has exercised close control and supervision of all key industries; major business and financial groups are dominated by Kazakhs with close ties to the president. Nationalisation is evident in the labour market as well. Already in the late Soviet era, Kazakhs had been displacing Russians in key positions. This process accelerated after independence, as informal hiring and promotion practices worked in a strongly nationalising direction (Dave 2007: Chapter Seven). This is what Smith *et al.* call 'nationalisation by stealth' (1998: 142), in that it did not involve explicit nationalising discourses or policies. Mass emigration has, of course, contributed

---

14. On the 1993 referendum supporting territorial autonomy for the small Russian-majority region in northeast Estonia, see Smith 2002.

to economic nationalisation, but emigration is itself in part a response to the pervasiveness of informal nationalising practices.[15]

Citizenship requirements have excluded non-citizens from some public-sector jobs in Estonia and Latvia, and language tests, as noted above, have limited access to private- and public-sector jobs involving 'contact with the public'. The exclusion of non-citizens has enabled citizens – belonging in their large majority to the titular nationality – to monopolise access to leading positions in a number of sectors (Smith *et al.* 1998: 99; Steen 2000). Minorities were also largely excluded from the mass restitution of state-expropriated or collectivised property to previous owners or their descendants in Estonia, and from the compensation vouchers that were issued in cases when the physical property was not returned, a process from which nearly half of ethnic Estonians benefited (Andersen 1997; on restitution see also Feldman 1999). Non-citizens were substantially disadvantaged in the privatisation process in both countries, and were barred from purchasing land for several years in both countries (Andersen 1997; Jubulis 2001:179). On the other hand, Russophones do have a significant presence among entrepreneurs in both countries. And a large-scale Norwegian-sponsored 1999 survey found the net effect of lack of citizenship on economic integration to be small in Estonia and Latvia, compared to education and region of residence (Aasland 2002). Thus, despite various disadvantages, one cannot speak of an economic marginalisation in any way comparable to the systematic political marginalisation of the Russophone population (Kolstø 2000: 120; Commercio 2008).

Discussion

Having considered nationalising discourse, policies, practices, and processes in four domains, I want to draw together the threads of the discussion and characterise the main patterns that emerge. In Kazakhstan, the boundary between the core nation and Slavic minorities is sharp, socially significant, and understood in primordial and ethno-racial terms as fixed and given. Nationalising discourse, policies, and practices *vis-à-vis* Russian-speaking minorities have been 'differentialist', not 'assimilationist'. They have not sought to turn Russians into Kazakhs, nor have they made serious efforts to get Russians to learn the Kazakh language. They have sought rather to promote the demographic robustness, economic strength, and political hegemony of Kazakhs *vis-à-vis* others; and in this collective mobility project they have succeeded. The state has been prevailingly understood, by Kazakhs and Russophones alike, as the state of and for Kazakhs. Official discourse has stressed the multi-ethnic character of Kazakhstan, but informal understandings and practices have been strongly nationalising. Nationalisation has been aided by large-scale Russophone emigration; but it has also contributed to that emigration. Nationalisation and emigration have been mutually reinforcing.

---

15. Commercio (2010: Chapter Seven) suggests that pressures for economic nationalisation in Kazakhstan have eased in recent years, allowing Russian-speakers a niche in the private sector, even though management positions tend to be monopolised by Kazakhs.

Linguistic nationalisation has produced more modest and ambiguous results. Nationalising discourse and policies – focused on Russified urban Kazakhs, not Slavic minorities – have been largely symbolic; despite the urgings of cultural nationalists, the state has not taken a stronger nationalising stand. Competence in and use of the Kazakh language has increased, but Russian remains strongly entrenched among urban Kazakhs as a language of opportunity, mobility, and prestige. Yet despite the only weakly nationalising language regime, the long-term prospects for linguistic nationalisation are bright.

In Ukraine, the linguistic and social boundaries between the core nation and the large Russian minority are blurred and permeable, as indicated not only by linguistic proximity, but by the very large number of mixed marriages. Ethno-demographic nationalisation has resulted from individuals reclassifying themselves across this blurred boundary, not from sharp ethnic differences in migration and fertility patterns, as in Kazakhstan. The state is understood as the state of and for a particular ethno-cultural nation, but that nation is not understood as sharply bounded. Primacy in the state is accorded not to a distinct and sharply-bounded ethno-national collectivity, as in Kazakhstan, but to a distinct language and culture. The state is understood as having the task of protecting and promoting that culture, rather than that of protecting and promoting the interests of a bounded collectivity.

Linguistic nationalisation, as in Kazakhstan, has been slowed by the continued strength of the Russian language among titulars (as well as Russians) in the east. But in the west, the Ukrainian language is solidly entrenched and the linguistic proximity between Russian and Ukrainian has made it relatively easy for Russian-speakers in that region to assimilate linguistically. The result is a core nation that is weakly bounded and easily joinable, but territorially and linguistically divided. Political struggles over nationalising policies have been articulated along regional and linguistic rather than ethno-national group lines; they have been intertwined with geopolitical and geo-economic questions concerning the relations of Ukraine with Russia on the one hand and with the European Union on the other.

In Estonia and Latvia, the linguistic and social boundaries between the core nation and the large Russian-speaking minorities have been sharp.[16] Nationalising discourse and policies were initially expressly oriented towards protecting, strengthening, and empowering the core nation as a bounded ethno-national collectivity, by excluding Soviet-era immigrants and their descendants from the demos and encouraging them to 'repatriate'. As in Kazakhstan, nationalisation was both cause and effect of Russophone emigration.

Over time, however, the boundary between the core nation and Russophones is likely to become more like that of Ukraine than that of Kazakhstan. The evidence today is admittedly equivocal. Young Russophones, educated and socialised largely in separate Russian-medium schools, remain for the most part strongly marked

---

16. Boundaries appear to be sharper in Estonia than in Latvia: the Russophone population is less integrated in Estonia on a variety of dimensions, including intermarriage (Steen 2000: 81–3).

as non-native speakers of titular languages; they are certainly not recognised as Estonians or Latvians, nor do they identify themselves as such. But the language skills of the younger generation are improving; titular and minority attitudes on a variety of dimensions have converged; and titulars have become more tolerant of Russophones. Most significantly, a substantial and increasing fraction of the Russophone population is being educated in titular-medium schools (20 per cent in Latvia in 2009–10), and a larger fraction has expressed an interest in doing so. If this trend continues, it will break down the social separation that follows from separate school systems, and rates of intermarriage can also be expected to increase. It is not implausible that a substantial fraction of the children or grandchildren of today's Russophones, schooled in the titular languages and no longer moving primarily in separate Russophone social circles, may come to identify – and be accepted – as Estonians and Latvians (Laitin 1998).

Ethno-national boundaries between core nation and Russophone minorities, in sum, have been strong, quasi-racial, and inter-generationally persistent in Kazakhstan, blurred and permeable in Ukraine, and strong but probably inter-generationally permeable in Estonia and Latvia. Patterns of nationalisation have corresponded to these kinds of boundaries. Nationalisation has been primarily differentialist or based on ethnicity in Kazakhstan, premised on a strong and clear boundary between core nation and Russophone minorities, and working to strengthen and empower the former at the expense of the latter. Nationalisation has been primarily assimilationist or culturalist in Ukraine, taking boundaries as permeable and linguistic repertoires and ethno-cultural identifications as plastic, and working to reshape cultural practices, loyalties, and identities. Nationalisation was initially differentialist and ethnicity-based in Estonia and Latvia, oriented towards protecting, strengthening, and empowering the core nation as a bounded collectivity, but has subsequently become more assimilationist and culturalist.[17]

Conclusion

The notion of nationalising states directs our attention to a rich nexus of discursive claims, symbolic representations, formal policies, informal practices and social processes. It offers a useful conceptual lens through which to bring into focus certain characteristic and distinctive aspects of nationalism and state-building in Soviet successor states, deriving from the dual Soviet legacy of elaborately institutionalised nation-building on the one hand and centralised rule, economic integration and demographic and linguistic Russification on the other. These include a deeply institutionalised ethno-cultural understanding of nationhood; an understanding of the state as the state of and for the ethno-culturally defined

---

17. The *rhetoric* of assimilation – globally out of fashion and locally inconsistent with the quasi-primordial understanding of nationality that is part of the Soviet legacy – has not been used in any of the successor states. But policies and processes can nonetheless be characterised as assimilationist in the sense specified in the text. For the most sustained treatment of assimilation in the post-Soviet context, see Laitin (1998).

'core' or 'titular' nation; the claim that the core nation is in a weak or unhealthy condition, and that its very survival is at stake; the argument that state action is needed to strengthen the demographic, cultural, economic or political position of the core nation; and the justification of such action as remedial or compensatory. Taken individually, these elements are found in many other settings; taken together, they comprise a configuration that is distinctive to post-Soviet and other 'post-multinational' settings such as East Central Europe after the collapse of the Habsburg, Ottoman, and Romanov empires.[18]

Several limitations to this analytical prism should be noted. First, the concept of nationalising states is not a theory. It does not enable one to predict *how nationalising* states will be, or – more interestingly – *how* they will be *nationalising*. Secondly, the concept of nationalising states is not (*pace* Kuzio 2001) a device for classifying states as nationalising or non-nationalising, or for ranking states as more or less nationalising, or still less for assessing the legitimacy of their policies and practices. It is not a device for posing yes-or-no questions like 'is Ukraine a nationalising state?' or 'is Latvia more or less nationalising than Estonia?'

Thirdly, the term 'nationalising state' is ambiguous. It suggests on the one hand that the state (narrowly understood as distinct from society) is *doing* the nationalising, and on the other hand that the state (broadly understood as the 'country' as a whole) is *undergoing* nationalisation. The state is understood in the former case as the *agent* of a nationalising *project*, and in the latter as the *subject* of a nationalising *process*. But there is something to be said for this ambiguity, for it highlights the important duality of project and process. Nationalising projects – articulated in discourse or embodied in policies – do not necessarily produce their intended results; conversely, nationalising processes – through which language repertoires, ethno-demographic patterns, or structures of economic and political dominance actually change – are driven by their own dynamics, and may occur even in the absence of expressly nationalising discourse or policies. The analysis of nationalising states must attend to both projects and processes. Strictly speaking, though, it makes more sense to speak of nationalising discourses, policies, practices or processes in particular domains than to speak of a 'nationalising state' *tout court*. The term 'nationalising state' is at best a shorthand device, pointing to an assemblage – and not necessary a coherent one – of discourses, policies, practices and processes, not to a single 'thing'.

Fourthly, and most importantly, using the notion of 'nationalising states' as

---

18. Kuzio (2001) suggests that the concept of nationalising states divides Europe into a civic west and an ethnic east and ignores cross-regional commonalities in forms of nation-building. Having myself criticised at length the civic-ethnic distinction (Brubaker 1999), I do not believe the first charge is warranted. As for the second, Kuzio is, of course, right that many other states have sought actively to homogenise their populations and that many other states have ethnic cores. My argument is not that homogenising policies or processes are distinctive to the post-Soviet or East European context. It is that the specific political and institutional legacy of multinational predecessor polities helps explain the prevalence in the successor states of a distinctive kind of nationalising discourse. As I have shown, nationalising discourse, policies, and processes take quite varied forms in Soviet successor states. Yet there is nonetheless a family resemblance deriving from the Soviet legacy that warrants taking the successor states as a legitimate domain – though not, of course, the only legitimate domain – of comparative analysis.

an analytical prism risks occluding other analytical perspectives. In particular, it risks contributing to what I have characterised elsewhere as an 'over-ethnicised' understanding of the social world (Brubaker 2004: 12; Brubaker *et al.* 2006:15).[19] Processes of state consolidation, for example, are at best imperfectly described and may be misleadingly described, if one focuses on nationalising discourses, policies, or practices. The same holds for processes of cultural transformation, and even more so for the process of economic transformation. Nationalising discourse – like the discourse of civic nationhood or multiculturalism – can conceal as much as it reveals, masking, for example, the pursuit of clan, clique, or class interests. Or what appear as nationalising processes on the aggregate level may mask underlying processes driven by different dynamics. The displacement of Russophone minorities by Kazakhs in key economic and political positions in Kazakhstan, for example, can be described as a process of nationalisation; yet, the networks that govern access to desirable positions and resources in Kazakhstan are structured along lineage, clan, or patron-client lines rather than ethno-national lines per se (Schatz 2000; 2004; Dave 2007). Thus what appears on the surface as nationalisation or 'Kazakhisation' is in fact a more complex process that involves considerable intra-Kazakh competition.

The notion of nationalising states is a useful sensitising concept, but it is not a self-sufficient analytical prism. It needs to be used in conjunction with other political, economic, social structural and cultural modes of analysis in specifying the material and symbolic interests at stake, the forms of social closure in operation, and the patterns of state consolidation, economic transformation and cultural reorganisation that are underway.

Focusing on nationalising discourses, policies, and processes is one way of capturing certain social, cultural, and political dynamics in Soviet successor states. The dual Soviet legacy of institutionalised multi-nationality and linguistic and demographic Russification helps explain the pervasiveness of nationalising discourse, and the attractiveness of nationalising policies, in the successor states. But this pervasiveness and attractiveness are by no means uniform between or within states or over time. Nationalising discourse is intertwined with other discourses, nationalising policies with other policies, nationalising processes with other process. The notion of the nationalising state is certainly not a 'master concept' that can capture the 'essence' of post-Soviet political, cultural and social life. It is simply one conceptual tool among others that may help pose some analytically-interesting comparative questions.

---

19. Hale's (2008) study of separatism in the late Soviet context argues similarly against attributing primary importance to pre-existing ethnic divisions or deeply-held ethnic identities.

References

Aasland, A. (2002) 'Citizenship status and social exclusion in Estonia and Latvia', *Journal of Baltic Studies*, 33(1): 57–77.

Agadjanian, V. (1999) 'Post-Soviet demographic paradoxes: ethnic differences in marriage and fertility in Kazakhstan', *Sociological Forum*, 14(3): 425–46.

Andersen, E. A. (1997) 'The legal status of Russians in Estonian privatisation legislation 1989–1995', *Europe-Asia Studies*, 49(2): 303–16.

Anderson, B. (1991) *Imagined Communities: Reflections on the origin and spread of nationalism*, London: Verso.

Arel, D. (1995) 'Language politics in independent Ukraine: towards one or two state languages?', *Nationalities Papers*, 23(3): 597–622.

— (2002a) 'Demography and politics in the first post-Soviet census: mistrusted state, contested identities', *Population-E*, 57(6): 801–28.

— (2002b) 'Interpreting "nationality" and "language" in 2001 Ukrainian census', *Post-Soviet Affairs*, 18(3): 213–49.

Arel, D. and Kertzer, D. I. (2002) 'Censuses, identity formation, and the struggle for political power', in D. I. Kertzer and D. Arel (eds), *Census and Identity: The politics of race, ethnicity, and language in national census*, Cambridge: Cambridge University Press, pp. 1–42.

Bernsand, N. (2001) 'Surzhyk and national identity in Ukrainian nationalist language ideology', *Berliner Osteuropa Info*, 17: 38–47.

Besters-Dilger, J. (2007) 'The Ukrainian language in education and mass media', *Harvard Ukrainian Studies*, 29 [publication delayed; volume forthcoming].

Bilaniuk, L. (2005) *Contested Tongues: Language politics and cultural correction in Ukraine*, Ithaca: Cornell University Press.

Bilaniuk, L. and Melnyk, S. (2008) 'A tense and shifting balance: bilingualism and education in Ukraine', *International Journal of Bilingual Education and Bilingualism*, 11(3): 340–72.

Bloom, S. (2008) 'Competitive assimilation or strategic nonassimilation? The political economy of school choice in Latvia', *Comparative Political Studies*, 41(7): 947–70.

Brubaker, R. (1992) 'Citizenship struggles in Soviet successor states', *International Migration Review*, 26(2): 269–91.

— (1996a) 'Nationalising states in the old "new Europe" – and the new"', *Ethnic and Racial Studies*, 19(2): 411–37.

— (1996b) *Nationalism Reframed: Nationhood and the national question in the new Europe*, Cambridge: Cambridge University Press.

— (1999) 'The manichean myth: rethinking the distinction between "civic" and "ethnic" nationalism', in Kriesi H., Armingeon, K., Siegrist, H., Wimmer, A. (eds), *Nation and National Identity: The European experience in perspective*, Zurich: Ruegger, pp. 55–71.

— (2004). *Ethnicity without Groups,* Cambridge: Harvard University Press.

— Brubaker, R., Feischmidt, M., Fox, J. and Grancea, L. (2006) *Nationalist Politics and Everyday Ethnicity in a Transylvanian Town*, Princeton: Princeton University Press.

Centers for Disease Control and Prevention (2003) 'Reproductive, maternal and child health in eastern Europe and Eurasia: a comparative report', Atlanta, U.S. Department of Health and Human Services. Online. Available / www.measuredhs.com/pubs/pdf/OD28/00FrontMatter.pdf (accessed 29 July 2010).

Chandra, K. and Boulet, C. (2003) 'A model of change in an ethnic demography', unpublished paper. Online. Available /www.math.cornell.edu/~cilanne/ Publications/ChangeEthnicDemography.pdf (accessed 27 January 2012).

Commercio, M. E. (2008) 'Systems of partial control: ethnic dynamics in post-Soviet Estonia and Latvia', *Studies in Comparative International Development*, 43(1): 81–100.

— (2010) *Russian Minority Politics in Post-Soviet Latvia and Kyrgyzstan: The transformative power of informal networks*, Philadelphia: University of Pennsylvania Press.

Dave, B. (2004) 'Entitlement through numbers: nationality and language categories in the first post-Soviet census of Kazakhstan', *Nations and Nationalism*, 10(4): 439–59.

— (2007) *Kazakhstan: Ethnicity, language, and power*, New York: Routledge.

Diener, A. (2005) 'Kazakhstan's kin state diaspora: settlement planning and the *Oralman* dilemma', *Europe-Asia Studies*, 57(2): 327–48.

Estonian Ministry of Education and Research (2008) 'Transition to Estonian-medium education'. Online. Available /www.hm.ee/index.php?148680 (accessed 4 August 2010).

Feldman, M. (1999) 'Justice in space? The restitution of property rights in Tallinn, Estonia', *Cultural Geographies*, 6(2): 165–82.

Fierman, W. (2005) 'Kazakh language and prospects for its role in Kazakh "groupness"', *Ab Imperio*, 2: 393–423.

— (2006) 'Language and education in post-Soviet Kazakhstan: Kasakh-medium instruction in urban schools', *Russian Review*, 65(1): 98–116.

Galbreath, D. J. and Galvin, M.E. (2005) 'The titularization of Latvian secondary schools: the historical legacy of Soviet Policy implementation', *Journal of Baltic Studies*, 36(4): 449–66.

Graney, K. (2007) 'Making Russia multicultural: Kazan at its millennium and beyond', *Problems of Post-Communism*, 54(6): 17–27.

Hacking, I. (1982) 'Biopower and the avalanche of printed numbers', *Humanities in Society*, 5: 279–95.

Hale, H. (2008) *The Foundations of Ethnic Politics: Separatism of states and nations in Eurasia and the world*, Cambridge and New York: Cambridge University Press.

Heleniak, T. (2004) 'Migration of the Russian diaspora after the breakup of the Soviet Union', *Journal of International Affairs*, 57(2): 99–117.

Hogan-Brun, G., Ozolins, U., Ramonienė, M. and Rannut, M. (2008) 'Language politics and practices in the Baltic states', *Current Issues in Language Planning*, 8(4): 469–631.

Holm-Hansen, J. (1999) 'Political integration in Kazakhstan', in P. Kolstø (ed.), *Nation-Building and Ethnic Integration in Post-Soviet Societies: An investigation of Latvia and Kazakhstan*, Boulder: Westview Press, pp. 153–226.

Hughes, J. (2005) '"Exit" in deeply divided societies: regimes of discrimination in Estonia and Latvia and the potential for Russophone migration', *Journal of Common Market Studies*, 43(4): 739–62.

International Federation for Human Rights (2009) 'Kazakhstan/Kyrgyzstan: exploitation of migrant workers, protection denied to asylum seekers and refugees'. Online. Available /www2.ohchr.org/english/bodies/cerd/docs/ngos/FIDH_Kazakhstan_76.pdf (accessed 27 January 2012).

Järve, P. (2009) 'Estonian citizenship: between ethnic preferences and democratic obligations', in R. Bauböck, B. Perchinig, and W. Sievers (eds), *Citizenship Policies in the New Europe*, rev. edn, Amsterdam: Amsterdam University Press, pp. 45–66.

Jubulis, M. A. (2001) *Nationalism and Democratic Transition: The politics of citizenship and language in post-Soviet Latvia*, Lanham: University Press of America.

Jurado, E. (2003) 'Complying with European standards of minority education: Estonia's relations with the European Union, OSCE, and Council of Europe', *Journal of Baltic Studies*, 34(4): 399–431.

Kelley, J. (2004) *Ethnic Politics in Europe: The power of norms and incentives*, Princeton and Oxford: Princeton University Press.

Kolstø, P. (1998) 'Anticipating demographic superiority: Kazakh thinking on integration and nation building', *Europe-Asia Studies*, 50(1): 51–69.

— (2000). *Political Construction Sites: Nation-building in Russia and the post-Soviet States*, Boulder: Westview Press.

Krūma, K. (2009) 'Checks and balances in Latvian nationality policies: national agendas and international frameworks', in R. Bauböck, B. Perchinig, and W. Sievers (eds), *Citizenship Policies in the New Europe*, rev. edn, Amsterdam: Amsterdam University Press, pp. 67–96.

Kulyk, V. (2006) 'Constructing common sense: language and ethnicity in Ukrainian public discourse', *Ethnic and Racial Studies*, 29(2): 281–314.

— (2010) 'Ideologies of language use in post-Soviet Ukrainian media', *International Journal of the Sociology of Language,* 2010(201): 79–104.

Kuscu, I. (2008) *Kazakhstan's oralman project: a remedy for ambiguous identity?*, unpublished thesis, Indiana University, United States.

Kuzio, T. (2001) '"Nationalising states" or nation-building? A critical review of the theoretical literature and empirical evidence', *Nations and Nationalism*, 7(2):135–54.

Laitin, D. (1998) *Identity in Formation: The Russian-speaking populations in the near abroad*, Ithaca, NY: Cornell University Press.

—   (2003) 'Three models of integration and the Estonian/Russian reality', *Journal of Baltic Studies*, 34(2): 197–222.

Latvian Ministry of Foreign Affairs (2010) 'Minority education in Latvia'. Online. Available /www.hm.ee/index.php?148680 (accessed 4 August 2010).

Lieven, A. (1993) *The Baltic Revolution: Estonia, Latvia, Lithuania, and the path to independence*, New Haven: Yale University Press.

Marples, D. R. (2007) *Heroes and Villains: Creating national history in contemporary Ukraine*, Budapest: Central European University Press.

Martin, T. (2001) *The Affirmative Action Empire: Nations and nationalism in the Soviet Union, 1923–1939,* Ithaca: Cornell University Press.

Ozolins, U. (2003) 'The impact of European accession upon language policy in the Baltic states', *Language Policy*, 2(3): 217–38.

Rannut, M. (2008) 'Estonianization efforts post-independence', *International Journal of Bilingual Education and Bilingualism*, 11(3): 423–39.

Rapawy, S. (1998) 'Ethnic reidentification in Ukraine', *Eurasia Bulletin*, Spring: 2–10. Online. Available /www.census.gov/ipc/www/ebspr98a.html (accessed 27 January 2012).

Rose, R. (2000) *New Baltic Barometer IV: A survey study,* Glasgow: Centre for the Study of Public Policy, University of Strathclyde. Online. Available /www.balticvoices.org/documents/spp-338.pdf (accessed 27 January 2012).

Rothschild, J. (1974) *East Central Europe Between the Two World Wars*, Seattle: University of Washington Press.

Saideman, S. and Ayres, R. W. (2008) *For Kin or Country: Xenophobia, nationalism, and war*, New York: Columbia University Press.

Schatz, E. (2000) 'Framing strategies and non-conflict in multi-ethnic Kazakhstan', *Nationalism and Ethnic Politics*, 6(2): 71–94.

—   (2004) 'What capital cities say about state and nation-building', *Nationalism and Ethnic Politics,* 9(4): 111–40.

Siiner, M. (2006) 'Planning language practice: a sociolinguistic analysis of language policy in post-Communist Estonia', *Language Policy,* 5(2): 161–86.

Slezkine, Y. (1994) 'The USSR as a communal apartment, or how a socialist state promoted ethnic particularism', *Slavic Review*, 53(2): 414–52

Smith, D. J. (2002) 'Narva Region within the Estonian Republic: from autonomism to accommodation?', *Regional and Federal Studies*, 12(2): 89–110.

Smith, G., Law, V., Wilson, A., Bohr, A. and Allworth, E. (1998) *Nation-building in the Post-Soviet Borderlands: The politics of national identities.* Cambridge: Cambridge University Press.

Stebelsky, I. (2009) 'Ethnic self-identification in Ukraine, 1989–2001: why more Ukrainians and fewer Russians?', *Canadian Slavonic Papers*, 51(1): 77–100.

Steen, A. (2000) 'Ethnic relations, elites and democracy in the Baltic States', *Journal of Communist Studies and Transition Politics*, 16(4): 68–87.

Suny, R. G. (1993) *The Revenge of the Past: Nationalism, revolution, and the collapse of the Soviet Union*, Stanford: Stanford University Press.

Verschik, A. (2005) 'The language situation in Estonia', *Journal of Baltic Studies*, 36(3): 283–316.

Wanner, C. (1998) *Burden of Dreams: History and identity in post-Soviet Ukraine*, University Park: Pennsylvania State University Press.

Wilson, A. (1995) 'The Donbas between Ukraine and Russia: the use of history in political disputes', *Journal of Contemporary History*, 30(2): 265–89.

— (1997) *Ukrainian Nationalism in the 1990s: A minority faith*, Cambridge: Cambridge University Press.

— (2002) 'Elements of a theory of Ukrainian ethno-national identities', *Nations and Nationalism*, 8(1): 31–54.

Wolczuk, K. (2002) 'Catching up with "Europe"? Constitutional debates on the territorial-administrative model in independent Ukraine', *Regional and Federal Studies,* 12(2): 65–88.

chapter two | against the nation – moldovan political discourse after the 2009 'revolution'

Julien Danero Iglesias

Introduction

Twenty years after its independence was proclaimed, the Republic of Moldova still appears to be an 'unrealised' nation-state (Brubaker 1996: 63), where 'different organisations, parties, movements, or individual figures within and around the state' are 'competing to inflect state policy in a particular direction, and seeking, in various and often mutually antagonistic ways, to make the state a "real" nation-state, the state of and for a particular nation' (Brubaker 1996: 66). The Party of the Communists of the Republic of Moldova (*Partidul Comunistilor din Republica Moldova* (PCRM)), which held power between 2001 and 2009, and their opponents from the Alliance for European Integration (*Alianţa pentru Integrare Europeana* (AIE)), which has held power since 2009, constantly seem to be struggling over what the Moldovan nation is, and who constitutes the core nation of the Republic ethnically.

Between 2001 and 2009, the communist vision of the nation, called 'Moldovanism', prevailed. Boasting the existence of a Moldovan people different from neighbouring Romanians, it was put into practice via several laws (rewriting of history textbooks, language and cultural policies, etc.). This Moldovan nationalism, originating in a Soviet justification for the inclusion of Moldova in the Soviet Union, has been fervently contested by Romanianist AIE parties, which consider Moldovans to be Romanians who were separated artificially by the Tsarist Empire and the Soviet Union.

In light of these two oppositional visions of the Moldovan nation, the Republic can be seen as a 'nationalising state' (Brubaker 1996: 63), in which the parties in power intend to implement policies aiming at strengthening a 'Moldovanist' or 'Romanianist' Moldovan nation. This struggle is the main focus of this chapter, which takes Moldova's status as a nationalising state as a precondition of the investigation, and therefore does not discuss Brubaker's theory and triadic nexus, as introduced in *Nationalism Reframed*. The purpose of this chapter is, instead, to analyse the internal 'arena of struggle' (Brubaker, 1996: 60) at a given time, in order to explore the internal dynamics of each of Brubaker's three terms – nationalising states, national minorities, and external national homeland (1996: 60–75).

In 2009, Moldova was host to two legislative elections: the first on the 5th April and the second on the 29th July. After eight years of communist rule, the 5th April elections marked a new victory for the PCRM. Nevertheless, after violent demonstrations in Chisinau (the capital city of the country) on the 7th April, political tensions between the communists and the opposition parties grew to a point of institutional impasse. While the elected communists held a parliamentary majority of sixty seats out of a total 101, they lacked the one seat needed to proceed with the election of the president. The oppositions' deputies under the then-established AIE coalition categorically refused to cede this one vote to the communist candidate, and boycotted the voting session. Thus, early elections were called on the 29th July.

A new electoral campaign began in the aftermath of the April demonstrations, with every electoral candidate positioning himself around what has generally been referred to as the 'events' (or the 'revolution'). This particularly polarising campaign is our starting point. It serves as a fruitful locus for analysis, since all of the electoral candidates invoked the protection of the country, the preservation of its sovereignty and its statehood against internal or external enemies in their campaign speeches. Indeed, the candidates' positions only differed in so far as which of these enemies they said the country needed to be protected from.

Following Roger's classification of nationalism (2001: 5), the present chapter considers nationalism as a tool for legitimising a politically-dominant position (Roger 2001: 139–61). Starting from this electoral campaign, I aim to determine how the dominant Party of the Communists used the 'events' in question to its advantage, and how they appealed to the Moldovan nation to maintain what had been their position. I also investigate how the opposition parties used the *same* discursive elements to reach the dominant position. The main question of the chapter concerns how the 'events' and the Moldovan nation, respectively, were constructed in the candidates' discourses, and how these discourses achieved the legitimisation of the parties' respective stances. As it investigates these issues, the chapter also argues, following Breuilly's definition that 'nationalism is, above and beyond all else, about politics and that politics is about power' (1993: 1). The content of the 'nation' invoked in the electoral discourse can thus be seen as floating – dependent on the need for parties to maintain or to gain power.

The first part of this chapter will introduce a brief theoretical presentation of nationalism (as it is conceived in this chapter) and will present methodological elements to study it, inspired by the methods of critical discourse analysis. The second part will concentrate on the context of the two 2009 legislative elections, in order to establish the bases of the arena in which the struggle occurred. The final part of the chapter will focus on the discursive construction of the Moldovan nation in the campaign speeches of the electoral candidates.

Nationalism as politics and discourse

Defining nationalism as a 'tool for a civic-territorial persuasion', Hermet suggests that 'by using an appropriate symbolic identity, the state may give an appearance of reality to the principle of popular sovereignty and conceal [...] that representative democracy actually works to the benefit of a few' (1996: 85–113). This particular definition of nationalism, taken from Gellner and Anderson, can be supplemented by part of Breuilly's conception of the same term. In his view, nationalism (as mentioned in the introduction to this chapter) is primarily 'a form of politics', because '[its] central task is to relate nationalism to the objectives of obtaining and using state power' (1994: 1). Nationalism is thus a political doctrine built upon three basic assertions:

(1) that there exists a nation with an explicit and peculiar character;
(2) that the interests and values of this nation take priority over all other interests and values; and
(3) that the nation must be as independent as possible (Breuilly 1994: 2).

In this way, nationalism can be seen as an ideology that is not an expression of national identity, nor an arbitrary invention of nationalists, but as a force that arises out of a need to make sense of complex social and political arrangements. The need is itself shaped by the kinds of intellectual traditions and patterns that any intellectual scheme evokes when it is activated. Nationalists have the same characteristics: they operate from a fund of intellectual assumptions about society and its organisation, which they relate to their own political projects. They then argue that these claims speak for the nation even though their projects and their implementation are products of a certain situation, rather than an expression of national needs (Breuilly 1994: 63). Nationalism thus depends on a structural change, but the way it is *used* by players influences it in crucial ways.

Following this logic, one can say that actors maintain and legitimise their power via an ad hoc design of their nation. Beyond ideology, however, nationalism can also be understood as 'the pre-eminent rhetoric for attempts to demarcate political communities, claim rights of self-determination and legitimate rule by reference to "the people" of a country' (Calhoun 1993: 211). Calhoun describes the importance of discourse in his definition of nationalism: the actors use the 'nation' and it takes the form of a speech.

According to this particular definition of nationalism, a discourse on the nation is seen merely as a tool used by elites to gain power. To investigate this discourse and, more specifically, the discursive construction of Moldovan nationhood, this chapter starts from the methodology of the Vienna school of critical discourse analysis (CDA). Our approach is 'discourse-historical', meaning that the 'context' is an inherent part of the analysis (Wodak 2001: 67) and that the analysis looks at three 'interwoven dimensions of analysis' in the discourse: contents, strategies, and 'means and forms' of realisation (Wodak *et al.* 2009: 30). Before beginning in earnest, we shall introduce a few contextual elements, related to the outburst of violent demonstrations after the 2009 Moldovan legislative elections. With these established, we will commence our analysis of the relevant parties' electoral campaign discourses, which came right after the 'events'.

Information on the parties' discourses was taken from the two main Moldovan daily newspapers in the 'state language',[1] *Moldova Suverana (Sovereign Moldova)*

---

1. According to the Constitution of the Republic of Moldova (article 13), 'the state language [...] is the Moldovan language written in the Latin script' while 'the state recognises and protects the right of the Russian language as well as other languages spoken on the territory to preservation,

and *Timpul* (*The Time*), which may be considered as the Communist Party's newspaper and as the opposition parties' newspaper[2] respectively. Articles about the parties in both newspapers were systematically analysed for a period of one month before the 29th July 2009 elections. This included twenty-seven articles in *Moldova Suverana* for the Communists, and forty-four articles in *Timpul* for AIE opposition parties. Following methodology of the CDA, we analysed the content of each article by looking at the main arguments, determining the discursive strategies used, and searching for the means of realisation, such as metaphors or the way the pronoun 'we' was used. By taking the results of this discourse analysis in the third part of this chapter, together with the context described in the second part of the chapter, we then draw conclusions concerning how discourse and legitimation were linked in the Moldovan electoral context, which are presented in the final part.

The 'events' of April 2009

After eight years of neo-communist rule in Moldova,[3] legislative elections were called for the 5th April 2009. Before the elections, party campaigns were marked by multiple violations of the country's electoral legislation: there were problems with the use of public resources, pressure and influence on the election runners and voters, partisan news programs, etc. (Info-Prim Neo 7th April 2009a). After a quiet election day, preliminary official results were made public by the Central Electoral Commission on the 5th April. Of the 2.5 million Moldovans with the right to vote, 59.52 per cent took part in the elections, and gave 49.91 per cent of their votes to the PCRM, making the party victorious for the third consecutive time. Together, the opposition parties obtained about 35 per cent (Info-Prim Neo 6th April 2009).

Following these preliminary results, a demonstration was held in Chisinau's main square, challenging the election outcome. The 6th April 2009 was declared 'a day of national mourning' and another protest was held on the 7th April (Info-

---

development, and functioning'.

2. According to figures of 2004, the press is the main source of information for 8 per cent of Moldovans, the radio is the main source for 11 per cent, and television for 50 to 70 per cent (Cazacu and Trifon 2010: 111). In a context where 63 per cent of Moldovans expressed their confidence in the media, while not trusting political parties, (*Monitor Media* 31st May 2011) The Independent Journalism Centre characterises the Moldovan press as widespread 'propaganda' (ICJ 2008: 2). In this way, Moldova presents a somewhat paradoxical context, where the media, which citizens *do* generally trust, serves the interests of political parties that the citizens largely do not trust. A political party's interest in availing itself of the services of the media is therefore obvious.

3. The Party of the Communists of the Republic of Moldova came into power in 2001 and was able to win re-election in 2005. Heir of the Moldovan section of the former Communist Party of the USSR, the party is considered by Luke March to be 'socialist populist' and not 'communist' – attempting to represent the 'vox populi' rather than the proletariat, and appealing to local identity while diminishing internationalism and class issues. However, the preservation of the label of communism is an important symbol, and an important motivation for the party and its members (March 2005: 2–3).

Prim Neo 7th April 2009b). On the morning of the 7th April, approximately 15,000 young people gathered in downtown Chisinau in order to protest against what they called 'rigged elections'. At about 12.00 pm, the first minor incidents were reported (Info-Prim Neo 7th April 2009c), starting what the *New York Times* called the first 'Twitter Revolution' (Barry 7th April 2009) in which the protesters, mobilised by mobile phones and text messages, assaulted the parliament and the presidential offices. Computers were hurled into the streets, tables and chairs were heaped onto a bonfire outside the buildings, and fires were lit inside (Euractiv 8th April 2009).

The police took hold of the parliament and presidential offices during the night. Arrested were 193 protestors – including eight minors – while ninety-six policemen were treated for injuries, according to officials (Info-Prim Neo 8th April 2009). Reports of fatalities and detainee mistreatment in connection with the demonstration and the detentions that followed were made public. Media NGOs expressed concern about the degradation of press freedom in the country, the violation of the public's right to access to information of public interest, and cases of journalist harassment (IJC 9th April 2009).

Ratifying the official reports confirming the Communists' victory (Info-Prim Neo 9th April 2009a), monitors from the OSCE declared the elections democratic and fair (Euractiv 8th April 2009). Because of the limited nature of the evidence presented by the opposition parties, the Moldovan constitutional court chose not to investigate allegations of electoral fraud. The election was declared legal and mandates were validated. Nevertheless, the newly-elected parliament failed to elect the new president in two attempts, on the 20th May and the 3rd June. The parliament was dissolved and new elections were called for July 2009 (OSCE, 16th June 2009: 3).

The Moldovan communist authorities alleged that these developments were a cover for an attempted *coup d'état* involving foreign special services (OSCE 16th June 2009: 2), and during a TV interview on the 29th April Vladimir Voronin called it a 'chromatic revolution' attempt (Botan 30th June 2009). On their part, opposition parties condemned 'the actions of the communist authorities' and invited 'president Voronin not to seek the guilty in other places, but to look in the mirror and realise that he is responsible for the "events" of the 7th April' (Info-Prim Neo 9th April 2009b). These allegations set forth the incentives that guided the campaigns leading up to the July elections, which we shall now analyse.

Analysis of the electoral campaign

Compared to the campaign preceding the April elections, the July election campaign proved 'tougher' and was considered by Moldovan experts to be a 'historical moment'. According to Igor Munteanu, a Moldovan political analyst, 'for the first time after the dissolution of the soviet state, preconditions for a real political guerrilla war were created in Moldova, [with] the authorities acting as instigators of this war' (Info-Prim Neo 20th July 2009). All of the candidates addressed the protests in their speeches, 'exploiting the polarisation of society to minimise the chances of their opponents gaining seats in Parliament' (IJC 26th January 2010: 2).

The campaign focused on the notion of protecting the motherland against its enemies—the Motherland being threatened by a *coup*. And because of this, the parties' discourses (as seen in the press at the time) are of utmost interest in that they present contrasting visions of nationhood in Moldova. Analysing these visions of nationhood will be the object of the third part, and the main purpose of this chapter.

Communists: fighting against the Romanian betrayal

The PCRM's campaign discourse focused on two main arguments: first, the elections were presented as 'historical', since the nation was perceived to be in danger; and secondly, the PCRM asserted that if the nation was in danger, it was because of the opposition parties (future members of the AIE coalition). Aside from these two arguments, one can also observe different versions of the 'other' and of the 'we' in the PCRM's discourse, but the national arguments that constitute the focus of this chapter appear more at the margins of the general discourse.

First and foremost, the PCRM asserted that Moldova – on the eve of the early elections of July 2009 – was at a moment that was 'critical to the future existence of the Republic of Moldova as a State' (MS12):

> The parliamentary elections of the 29th July will be the most important in the history of the Republic of Moldova. The question is very simple: to be or not be our country? Thus, voters will give their votes not for parties but for the independence and the future of our country (MS2).

In this way, the party constructed the atmosphere in which the elections took place as a moment of utmost importance, suggesting that the very fate of Moldova would depend on the voters and their choices. Concurrently, the party introduced itself as the *sole* representative on the side of democracy and as the sole supporter of Moldova and its statehood. Of its opponents, the PCRM declared 'the opposition parties [are] weak and liars' (MS1), and pejoratively characterised them as being 'demagogue and populist' (MS8), assigning to them an intent to 'destabilise the situation in the country' (MS3). The PCRM even went so far as to argue that the opposition 'prepared' for the 'events' that occurred on the 7th April, aiming to achieve 'the liquidation of our country as a state' (MS1).

The discursive strategy in play here aims to unify voters against the perceived threat of a great danger, and seeks to portray the situation in black and white— implying, naturally, a positive self-presentation. The two main arguments of the communist discourse – upon which the rest of their argumentation relies – are as follows: that the opposition seeks to pursue what the communists deem to be 'petty goals' (MS12), and that opposition parties are supported by the 'special services of certain states in order to cause mass unrest in our Moldova' (MS1). This is presented as a betrayal of the nation that can be explained by the opposition's desire to come to power. Opposition parties are therefore seen as 'aggressive' (MS9) and as upholding a mentality along the lines of 'the more things go wrong in the country, the better for us!'(MS6). The Communists consider the opposition parties to be interested in only 'one thing – power for power ['s sake]' (MS6), while 'the citizens are in the last place' of their interests (MS9):

> If on the 7th April president Voronin had not thought about the people, we would have woken up to the threshold of a civil war. Clearly, they [the opposition parties], they wanted to take power by a coup, an alleged colour revolution, by putting before them, for $20, the children of the people (MS4).

In this excerpt, one can identify a two-stranded conception of what the Communists call a 'betrayal' of Moldova: first, the opposition is portrayed as guilty of an attempted coup, and secondly, it is portrayed as guilty of corrupting Moldovan youth. Speaking in a similar vein, a pensioner quoted in an article supporting the PCRM helps cast light on why the 'unification' between Moldova and Romania is presented as such a betrayal:

> I'm going to vote for the Party of the Communists, the only party which is able to organise things, to preserve our country. The opponents have shown their true face and purpose – unification with Romania. We do not want this thing. We do not want the appearance of a new frontier – with Gagauzia. We do not want war (MS11).

Following this argument – in which the 'we' refers to 'Moldovans' – one can observe a Moldovan objection to unification on the grounds that Moldovans are different from Romanians and especially from the representatives of the opposition. It is implied that unification would disrupt harmonious relations with ethnic Gagauz and would trigger war. Moldovans are presented as tolerant and peaceful, and as protective of their right to live together. A similar conception can be seen in the words of a Moldovan citizen, included in the minutes of a PCRM meeting. In the following excerpt, there is a decidedly unitary and cultural inflection to the Moldovan 'we':

> What should one believe about the idea of union with Romania? I am categorically against. Why? Because we are a unitary nation – the Moldovans. And if you're a dog-wolf, you cannot change race and become a poodle or a pug. We, must be Moldovan and eat our Moldovan bread. We should not eat Romanian polenta[4] (MS13).

In this excerpt, the Moldovan 'we' is presented as culturally different from its Romanian counterpart and a clear strategy of differentiation emerges – a strategy that is similar to the aforementioned, i.e. portraying campaign conflicts in black and white. At the same meeting, another attending citizen expressed the view that the differentiation argument could be taken even further – emphasising the distance between Moldovans and their neighbours:

> I will vote for the communists! Only they are capable of granting the stability and prosperity of Moldova. They are fighting for it. But Romania ...! (Censored) (MS13).

---

4.   One of Romania's national dishes (called *mamaliga*) made from boiled cornmeal.

In this construction, Moldovans and Romanians are presented as two different peoples and opposition parties are accused of being willing to subjugate themselves – as well as the whole Moldovan population – to what is constructed as a clearly distinct 'other'.

Once the 'other' has been constructed as such, a positive construction of Moldovans ('we') serves to reinforce the speaker's line of argumentation. While Romanians are the 'other', the Moldovans, are presented as good people; to vote for the communists – presented in the articles of the party as an incarnation of the 'righteous' Moldova – is to vote for the well-meaning 'we'. Such a construction also appears in the next excerpt, which describes why the entire population of a village called Doroțcaia will support the PCRM:

> This town, located on the left bank of the Dniester, where military action took place seventeen years ago,[5] recovered difficultly from the endured shock. The concrete expression of good, in Doroțcaia, can be read on the [people's] faces. People do not make war. They have understood that they cannot divide poverty. And they also have realised that to escape poverty, we must choose people who think of them to lead the country. During the elections, the village of Doroțcaia votes, normally, for statehood (MS4).

Moldova is presented as a poor but worthy country, where the wisdom of the people leads them to vote normally or naturally for the communists. Such an idea is echoed by the inhabitants of Tomai, another village in the country where communists hold a meeting:

> All of these words [of support for the party] came from heart, they relied on the experience of life and on the natural intelligence of the country. The people of Tomai cannot be deceived, they are real patriots (MS5).

In this context, being a 'patriot' means sharing this natural intelligence. It also means being willing to interrupt a busy day of labour to attend a communist electoral event (MS7), or not hesitating to remain under the heat of a burning sun in order to discuss the national interests and the political struggle of the party (MS11). Moldovans are depicted as particularly concerned about the future of their country, but, more importantly, as a group exhibiting a 'natural' wisdom and intelligence – a trait that protects them from being cheated and or taken in by the 'lies' of the opposition parties (MS13).

Besides this emphasis on who 'we, Moldovans', are, the party also puts forward the notion of a civic Moldovan nation, once more pursuing a strategy of unification. The party emphasises how respect is shown towards minorities in the country and presents itself as 'the only party of "our" country to represent most extensively the poly-ethnic people of Moldova' (MS10). The above-mentioned

---

5. Reference to the civil war that occurred between 1991 and 1992 in the aftermath of the fall of the Soviet Union when Transnistria separated from Moldova. For more information about the conflict, see for example King 2001.

'unitary nation' thus becomes one that is open to minorities. This is almost certainly why, at a meeting in the south of the country where the Gagauz minority[6] is sizable, the party's candidates spoke in Gagauz in front of a grateful audience and an admiring journalist:

> At the meeting, a candidate attended, Oleg Garizan, mayor of the village of Copceac, a person well known in Gagauzia. It is difficult to say what he discussed with the residents of Tomai, because he spoke in Gagauz, but the emotions in the room confirmed the interest in the speeches and the applause showed the importance for the people of what has been said (MS5).

While the emphasis here is on what the communists call a 'poly-ethnic' nation, these terms may not be quite accurate, in light of statements about the country's atmosphere of tolerance and respect towards minorities such as the Gagauz. For example, Irina Vlah, first secretary of the Gagauz section of the PCRM, expresses her gratitude to the 'Moldovan people' and the PCRM 'for the favourable conditions of development created for ethnic Gagauz' (MS12). From this point of view, it seems that the Moldovan nation is more unitary than poly-ethnic and that it is only thanks to tolerance that national minorities can live peacefully in the country. Similarly, the speeches of the representatives of national minorities invited to a meeting with Vladimir Voronin follow the same line of reasoning: they emphasise the multi-ethnic character of the Moldovan people, while insisting on their own cultural characteristics (MS10).The notion of a poly-ethnic or civic people of Moldova is thus a fiction; indeed, the overriding narrative is one of a Moldova *constituted by ethnic Moldovans* who have magnanimously *accepted the presence* of other national minorities.[7]

Overall, in this first part of our analysis of the discourse that took place during the July 2009 electoral campaign, we have deliberately focused on the communist construction of an 'other' and of a 'we'. To summarise – the 'other' has been presented as being comprised of the opposition parties who, according to the communists, are 'traitors', willing to sell the country to neighbouring Romania (an entity seen as completely different from 'we' Moldovans). Moldovans are viewed as the core of a unitary nation of the Republic of Moldova, and the language of discourse references national minorities as entities that are 'tolerated' – even if the notion of Moldova as a poly-ethnic nation is sometimes promoted. Nevertheless, such matters seem almost marginal compared to the party's core arguments concerning the danger facing the nation and the constant blaming of the opposition parties. With these observations established, we shall now look at the opposition parties' discourse to see whether the same kind of arguments and constructions can be observed.

---

6. One of Moldova's national minorities (147,500 according to the 2004 Moldovan census, 4.4 per cent of the total population of the country), a Turkish ethnic group converted to Christian orthodoxy.

7. Along Moldovans (accounting for 75.8 per cent of the total population of the country according to the 2004 Moldovan census), national minorities are Ukrainians (8.4 per cent), Russians (5.9 per cent), Gagauz (4.4 per cent), Bulgarians (1.9 per cent).

Opposition parties: fighting against the communist dictatorship

The discourse of the parties described as 'opposition parties' by the communists is structurally similar to that of the communists, in that it also presents two main ideas:

(1) it suggests the historic character of the current elections; and
(2) it emphasises a dichotomy between the sides of democracy and of tyranny, from which one can determine a definition of 'other' and 'we'.

We shall look at each of the AIE parties separately, though it quickly becomes apparent that their discourses follow and complement each other.

These parties are grouped together here because they were the four 'opposition' parties to achieve victory in the July elections. These four parties were able to successfully found a coalition called the Alliance for the European Integration (*Alianta pentru Integrarea in Europa* (AIE)), comprising the Liberal Party (*Partidul liberal* (PL)), the Liberal-Democrat Party of Moldova (*Partidul liberal-democrat din Moldova* (PLDM)), the 'Our Moldova' Alliance (*Alianta 'Moldova Noastra'* (AMN)), and the Democratic Party of Moldova (*Partidul Democrat din Moldova* (PDM)). The latter garnered 12.54 per cent of the votes in July after Marian Lupu, the former communist speaker of the parliament and the second candidate on the PCRM list in the April elections, left the party with his team. Thanks to an impressive and expensive campaign, the PDM, led by Lupu, was able to win parts of the former communist vote – this, even after the party failed to pass the 5 per cent threshold in April. The PCRM obtained 44.69 per cent of the votes, while opposition parties and the PDM accounted for approximately 51 per cent[8].

The AMN and the dictatorship of Voronin

For the AMN – the first party of the future ruling AIE coalition – the Republic of Moldova is in danger of remaining under a de facto dictatorship, run by the president Vladimir Voronin. In their discourse, Voronin is presented as the head of a mafia-like clan (T2) controlling the country. The AMN also compares Moldova to a totalitarian regime, marked by propaganda, misinformation, collusion between the regime and all the country's institutions (media, justice, and police), and general hatred. According to the party, this injustice will end only with the defeat of the communists. The tone of the discourse is hard and the images used are strong, with the AMN constructing a *locus terribilis* that will improve dramatically if people vote against the communists:

> The philosophy of the PCRM is subject to the vagaries and complexities of a single man, the dictator Voronin, who has always started from division, conflict,

---

8. The results of all Moldovan elections since independence can be found on the website of the Moldovan Association for Participatory Democracy "ADEPT": www.e-democracy.md (accessed 27 September 2012).

and the creation as well as the accusation of some virtual enemies. Everything must be divided into two, three, seven – one separates and rules as he wants. He is the one who started the division of society in the first year of government. […] Now he resorts to the most dangerous division, the interethnic one. […] Is that strengthening society? Is that defending the homeland? Or is it protecting his own Power over a divided people to manipulate and dispossess? (T3).

According to the party discourse, Moldovans live within an ongoing tragedy, and are aware that the communist regime has come to a dead end – singling out how the regime has mistreated and neglected the country's youth (and, thus, the nation's future). The strategies used are thus very much the same as those employed by the communists, only with the guilty party changed. The communists are also accused of 'betraying' the country by selling it to Russia, while the AMN advocates a pragmatic approach to the country's relations with Russia and insists on the Moldovan European stance (T8). Furthermore, the AMN asserts that the communists 'divide' the population along ethnic criteria:

> First, we need a civic peace in the Republic of Moldova, a coalition government composed of parties showing a democratic vocation, and also eliminate the communists of the political spectrum (T9).

Aside from this strategy of unification and advocating civic peace, it appears that the articles of the AMN never mention national minorities. The discourse remains vague about who does or does not belong to the nation – to this 'home' in which we must remain the 'masters', according to the slogan of the party. The slogan of the party – 'be the master in your home' (T1) – thus has a symbolic force that is oriented primarily against the communists. The construction of a Moldovan 'we' relies fairly exclusively on the party's opposition to communism and on the promotion of Moldovan democracy.

The PLDM and the return to normality

The PLDM – the second coalition party – mainly expressed a desire to bring Moldova back to 'normal' (T11) – presenting a 'we' unwilling to accept the current situation of the ('our') country:

> The massive recruitment of managers of pre-university education in the ranks of the Party of the Communists, the return to the Bolshevik practices of ideological corruption of children and young people, the reactivation of the pioneer organisations and youth, the excessive interference of the central and local government structures in the management of education institutions – all this undermines the school system. After more than fifteen years of scientific and historical truth, children learn the Stalinist clichés and concepts specific to the ideology of the party-state. It's very sad that these things happen here at the centre of Europe in the early twenty-first century (T5).

Appointing itself the party of democracy and normality, the PLDM thus depicts the communists as direct heirs of the worst aspects of the country's recent Soviet past. And, by a strategy of continuation, it presents Vladimir Voronin as an heir to Stalin. Following a strategy of unification, the PLDM thus works to address all of the country's citizens with this rhetoric, and especially the young people. Just as in the communists' argument, the party insists on a need to protect the 'fatherland', which is currently in danger:

> For me, the true home is where you are proud anytime and anywhere you hear its name pronounced. That is why I will defend my country, and not the one of Voronin the mutant who has deported a million of patriots (T4).

Once again, the 'we' is conceptualised as an entity that stands in opposition to communism and the Party of the Communists; here, 'being patriotic' means to desire the good of the country, and thus to not vote for the communists. The communists comprise the single-pointed 'other' in this discourse, and their regime is portrayed as being held at bay. It is suggested that the communist leaders will be called to account for their abuses of the 7th April in front of a court. But, like the AMN, the party also accuses the president of 'dividing' the population along ethnic lines, while saying nothing more about the national minorities. The PLDM intends to address all citizens of the country, even though minorities are never mentioned.

The limited campaign of the PL

The campaign discourse of the PL, the third future coalition party, is somewhat limited compared to the AMN and PLDM. However, it can be stated that the arguments and discursive strategies of the PL follow in the same vein as those put forth by the two larger parties, i.e. emphasising unity in a 'fight' against the re-election of the communists. Here, the essence of the PL's argument lies in ending the communist 'dictatorship' (T7/T10) and restoring 'good' in the country. Again, the party says nothing about a Moldovan 'we', except that it is 'democratic', 'European' and 'anti-communist' (T7/T10). Ethnic minorities are not of particular concern; at most, they are embedded in a discourse aimed at 'citizens', regardless of their ethnicity, such as in the following excerpt:

> The Communist Party means dictatorship, terror, torture, murder, poverty and corruption! The communists are the crisis and the problem! The Liberal Party is the solution and the future! The Liberal Party means freedom, democracy, rule of law, economic prosperity, integration into the European Union, a secure future for all citizens, regardless of their ethnicity (T7/T10).

Thus, the main strategy of the party is one of portraying the situation in black and white. The PL promotes a view in which 'we' refers to a Moldova that is democratic and 'good', and in which 'they' – comprised of the communists –is bad, and synonymous with a malevolent dictatorship.

The correct solution of the PDM

Like the three above-mentioned opposition parties, the PDM – before joining the AIE coalition after the elections, it competed alone – strikes out against the ruling party. Nevertheless, its critique is broader, questioning the entire political land-scape (not just the communists). Consequently, it has been seen by the communists as traitorous and by the three above-mentioned parties (AMN, PLDM and PL) as suspicious, because of Lupu's communist past. Only *after* the elections did the PDM join the three opposition parties. Even though their arguments were con-structed along the same lines – that of depicting a communist dictatorship – they were sufficiently different to remain apart.

Lupu, the new leader of the party, hoped to be a unifier, heroically leading the country out of 'war' and restoring 'peace':

> We want to transform Moldova into a country which we can be proud of, where we can live happily and which we leave as a legacy to our children and our grandchildren with peace of mind (T6).

This conception of 'we' is synonymous with peace and ethnic 'tolerance' – something that makes sense in a country that wants to keep its sovereignty, while also integrating into the European Union. The discourse of the party is mainly concerned with ending the dominant political discord; the ethnic issue is hardly discussed. Nevertheless, an expression used by the party gives an indication of the position in relation to its home: 'A correct solution for our common homeland' (T6). This expression is identical to one put forth by the communists, and assumes the same contradictions; Moldova is seen as a 'common house', an expression derived directly from Soviet discourse.

The discourses of the four opposition parties can thus be characterised by the emphasis they put on restoring democracy and on getting rid of the communists. The four parties call for unification against the PCRM as their main strategy. Compared to the ruling party's discourse on the 'poly-ethnicity' of the Moldovan nation, the opposition parties – with the exception of the 'common house' of the PDM – are not particularly concerned with minorities. Even if they make refer-ences to the 'nation', and even if they speak of the need to preserve it, one can eas-ily observe that this 'we' merely means 'democratic' (as opposed to a 'communist other') and that the word 'nation' lacks any content.

Conclusion

Following Hermet and Breuilly, this chapter started from the assumption that na-tionalism is a discourse that helps legitimise a politically-dominant position. Our analysis took as its focus the electoral campaign that occurred during the institu-tional impasse following the April 2009 legislative elections in Moldova and the 'events' that occurred in its aftermath, and sought to determine how the concept of 'nation' was used during this campaign.

In the context of a highly-polarised election – where the political spectrum was divided between the communists and their opponents – our analysis focused on the discourse found in two general national newspapers, *Moldova Suverana* and *Timpul*.

In the Moldovan political arena, the parties seem to be engaged to a great extent in a kind of 'mirror' discourse: communist and opposition parties struggled for what they both considered a 'historic' moment, with the Moldovan statehood seen as being in danger after the chaos of the April elections. On both sides, the arguments proved very similar, and so were the issues addressed and the strategies used, namely the portrayal of the situation in black and white and attempts to unify voters under the banner of 'real' democracy. All of the parties used the same register of language: dramatic and with references to history, and sometimes derogatory. Strong language was used – 'hostages', 'Nazis', 'fascist', 'clan', 'clique', 'diabolic', etc. – to present the July early elections as the very moment when Moldova, as a state, would fail or survive for the better. Arguments – such as that of betrayal – were sometimes exactly the same on both sides, with the only difference being who was seen as responsible or at fault.

Even if the preservation of statehood was at the very centre of everyone's argument, the most important discourse element rested in identifying who was *responsible* for this threat and who had the moral duty to protect the nation from it. In the same way, the April elections were highly polarised, as were the 'events' that immediately followed, and also the electoral campaign for early elections in July.

From this analysis, one can argue that attributing guilt, or responsibility, is much more important to the political parties' discourse than the notion of the preservation of the state of Moldova itself. Starting from a 'presumption of guiltiness' (Botan 30th June 2009), the parties blame each other – insulting each other in what Lupu identifies as a 'political war', while scarcely referring to what Moldova represents.

This leads us to the first conclusion: compared with the toughness of the accusations concerning who was responsible for the April events, the arguments for the preservation of the Moldovan state – which lacked meaningful content concerning the state's actual character, and about who constituted its membership – seem much less important in the context of the campaign, even if these arguments were the mobilising reference of every political address. The April events were referenced, implicitly or explicitly, in every single discourse, as the moment in which the very existence of the Republic was at stake. So, while a party's electoral opponent was inevitably presented as acting against the interests of the Moldovan state, such references to the nation served merely as a means for mobilising voters. Indeed, the 'nation' seems less important here than dragging the opponent's party's name through the mud.

Nevertheless, the few comments about the 'nation' that *were* available in the party discourses allow us to draw a second conclusion (one that is in line with findings of the Vienna school of critical discourse analysis): no purely civic nation can exist, it will always shows elements of an ethnic nation. Indeed, the communists may have implied the existence of a multi-ethnic state in which minorities had their due say. And they may have insisted on the support of minorities, saying that 'their' Moldova was a 'common house' for a 'unitary, multi-ethnic and poly-cultural people'. But this represents the most advanced development one can find in their discourse. The PDM, boasting a conciliatory position – orienting itself against the campaign's 'ethnic war' – presented a very similar vision, describing Moldova as a 'common homeland'. But the explanation does not go further. The opposition parties advocated the need to preserve ethnic and civic peace for all – for every 'citizen' – but they never explicitly mentioned the content of the nation that they were advocating, and they never explicitly referenced what problems minorities might possibly encounter in the country.

The use of 'nation' here is thus a tool, employed to legitimise a party's position in the context of an important and turbulent electoral contest. The PCRM, which was in power in 2009, strongly emphasised huge differences between Moldovans and Romanians, thereby legitimising the Republic of Moldova as an independent state. Furthermore, even if the idea of a 'poly-ethnic' nation contradicts the unitary Moldova it sometimes put forward, the PCRM nevertheless emphasised this 'poly-ethnic' status, in the hope of garnering the electoral support of minorities. For their part, the opposition parties did not actually talk about the nation in meaningful terms, but rather used it to put forward a 'democratic' opposition   a force serving as the sole champion of peace in the country. In this manner, they strove to attain power as defenders of an independent republic, without advocating unification with a neighbour. Indeed, doing so would be politically unwise: advocating strong Romanianist elements, such as promoting a Romanian identity for Moldovans, would implicitly call for unification and would therefore render the existence of Moldova as a state meaningless.

Subsequent developments in the Moldovan political environment are in line with this analysis. A new AIE government was appointed, but no president could be elected since the new majority did not hold the mandatory number of seats (61 out of 101). The AIE candidate, Marian Lupu, was called a 'traitor' by Vladimir Turcan, a leader of the Party of the Communists, and denounced for promoting a 'radical nationalist policy' (Euractiv 18th August 2009). Since the constitution does not allow for more than two elections in a year, new elections were not held until the 28th November 2010. The AIE coalition was formed again, and a president was finally elected in March 2012. And even though Romanianist nationalising reforms have been on the agenda – including measures aimed at revising the communist history textbooks, commemorating the victims of the Soviet occupation, and reconsidering the status of the state language, among other things – AIE parties have not promoted the end of the Moldovan state and unity with Romania, even though diplomatic relations between the two states have warmed since the AIE came to power.

Thus, one can conclude that, in Brubaker's 'arena' in the nationalising state of Moldova, electoral candidates are struggling violently. Nevertheless, on the occasion of the early July elections, it is not clear whether they intend to make the state a 'real' nation-state, i.e. a state of and for a particular 'nation'. Looking at the aftermath of the April events, statehood and nationhood appear to be essential in the discourse, but only because such words have a powerful attraction. Drawing on Breuilly's definition of nationalism, one may comfortably assume that the preservation of the nation served largely as a tool for mobilising the voters during this campaign and *not* as something greater. Ultimately, these circumstances seem to attest to the notion that, in a fraught political context, the most important thing is to reach power, by whatever means available. Furthermore, the most interesting idea apparent from our analysis is that the parties blame *each other* for this emphasis on reaching power by any means, while saying that *they, themselves,* are the ones truly fighting for the citizens and for the preservation of the country.

References

Barry E. (2009) 'Protests in Moldova explode, with help of Twitter', *The New York Times*, 7 April. Online. Available /www.nytimes.com/2009/04/08/world/europe/08moldova.html (accessed 15 June 2009).

Botan, I. (2009) 'Presumption of guiltiness', 30 June. Online. Available http://www.e-democracy.md/en/monitoring/politics/comments/200906301/ (accessed 15 September 2012).

Breuilly, J. (1994) *Nationalism and the State*, 2nd edn, Chicago: The University of Chicago Press.

Brubaker, R. (1996) *Nationalism Reframed: Nationhood and the national question in the New Europe*, Cambridge: Cambridge University Press.

Calhoun, C. (1993) 'Nationalism and ethnicity', *Annual Review of Sociology*, 19: 211–39.

Cazacu, M. and Trifon, N. (2010) *Un Etat en quête de nation. La République de Moldavie*, Paris: Non-Lieu.

Euractiv (2009) 'Moldova calls for help after election riot outbreak', 8 April. Online. Available /www.euractiv.com/en/east-mediterranean/moldova-calls-help-election-riot-outbreak/article-181134 (accessed 15 June 2009).

— (2009) 'Moldova political crisis in deadlock', 18 August. Online. Available /www.euractiv.com/en/east-mediterranean/moldova-political-crisis-deadlock/article-184600 (accessed 1 September 2009).

Hermet, G. (1996) *Histoire des Nations et du Nationalisme en Europe*, Paris: Le Seuil.

Independent Journalism Centre (2008) 'Relatiile dintre mass-media si autoritatile de stat – spre transparenta si responsabilitate (noiembrie 2007 – septembrie 2008). Raport final', Independent Journalism Centre: Chisinau.

— (2009) 'Declaration of media NGOs from Moldova on the situation of the press, violations of the right to access to information and attacks on journalists', 9 April. Online. Available /www.azi.md/en/print-story/2198 (accessed 15 June 2009).

Info-Prim Neo (2009) 'PCRM wins elections according to preliminary official results', 6 April. Online. Available /www.azi.md/en/print-story/2089 (accessed 15 June 2009).

— (2009a) 'Coalition 2009: Unfair and partially free elections. Electoral process tainted before elections', 7 April. Online. Available /www.azi.md/en/print-story/2132 (accessed 15 June 2009).

— (2009b) 'About 10,000 young people challenge election outcome in Chisinau', 7 April. Online. Available /www.azi.md/en/print-story/2113 (accessed 15 June 2009).

— (2009c) 'Protest in downtown Chisinau takes proportions', 7 April. Online. Available /www.azi.md/en/print-story/2118 (accessed 15 June 2009).

— (2009a) 'About 200 protesters were arrested last night?', Online, 8 April. Available /www.azi.md/en/print-story/2140 (accessed 15 June 2009).

—   (2009a) 'PCRM won 49.48 per cent of the poll, official results', 9 April. Online. Available /www.azi.md/en/print-story/2171 (accessed 15 June 2009).

—   (2009b) 'And the Liberal Party accuses Communist Authorities of vandalism acts', 9 April. Online. Available /www.azi.md/en/print-story/2194 (accessed 15 June 2009).

—   (2009) 'Voters – prisoners of political war', 20 July. Online. Available / www.azi.md/en/print-story/4552.

—   (2009) 'International observers say identified irregularities did not affect elections', 30 July. Online. Available /www.azi.md/en/story/4850 (accessed 1 September 2009).

King, C. (2001) *The Moldovans: Romania, Russia, and the Politics of Culture*, Stanford: Hoover Institution Press.

March, L. (2005) ,'The Moldovan Communists: from Leninism to democracy?', *Eurojournal.org*, September: 1–25.

Monitor Media (2011) 'Sondaj: Moldovenii au încredere în mass-media', 31 May. Online. Available /www.azi.md/ro/print-story/18690 (accessed 5 June 2011).

Roger, A. (2001) *Les grandes théories du nationalisme*, Paris: Armand Colin.

Wodak, R. (2001), 'The discourse-historical approach', in R. Wodak and M. Meyer (eds), *Methods of Critical Discourse Analysis*, London: Sage.

Wodak, R., de Cillia R., Reisigl M. and Liebhart K. (2009) *The Discursive Construction of National Identity*, 2nd edn, Edinburgh: Edinburgh University Press.

Primary sources: PCRM articles

MS1: Grozavu, V. (2009), 'Fraudarea alegerilor serveste drept tertip pentru opozitia slaba si mincinoasa', *Moldova Suverana*, 1 July, p. 3.

MS2: PCRM Press Services (2009), 'Alegerile din 29 iulie vor fi cele mai importante in istoria Republicii Moldova, *Moldova Suverana,* 3 July, pp. 1–2.

MS3: Grozavu, V. (2009), 'Si peste hotare s-a votat corect in pofida afirmatiilor mincinoase ale opozitiei', *Moldova Suverana,* 3 July, p. 3.

MS4: Grozavu, V. (2009), 'Dorotcaia : O suta la zero in folosul lui Vladimir Voronin', *Moldova Suverana,* 7 July, p. 3.

MS5: Anon. (2009), 'Fata in fata cu propria soveste', *Moldova Suverana,* 10 July, p. 2

MS6: Anon. (2009), 'Locuitorii satului Dubasari Vechi sint cu PCRM', *Moldova Suverana,* 14 July, pp. 1–2.

MS7: Anon. (2009), 'Invinge PCRM, invinge Moldova!', *Moldova Suverana,* 15 July, pp. 1–2.

MS8: Grozavu, V. (2009), 'Tineretul comunist vrea sa-i spuna lui Filat adevarul despre evenimentele din 7 aprilie ', *Moldova Suverana,* 15 July, pp. 1–3.

MS9: Anon. (2009), 'Scoreni: Vom vota PCRM, unicul partid care va continua dezvoltarea tarii', *Moldova Suverana,* 22 July, p. 2.

MS10: Anon. (2009), 'PCRM este partidul cu cea mai mare reprezentare a minoritatilor etnice din Republica Moldova', *Moldova Suverana,* 22 July, pp. 1–3.

MS11: Anon. (2009), 'Raionul Cantemir : Noi votam comunistii pentru ca ei merita', *Moldova Suverana,* 22 July, p. 2.

MS12: Anon. (2009), 'Alegatorii din UTA Gagauzia sint convinsi ca PCRM nu are alternativa la guvernare in Republica Moldova', *Moldova Suverana,* 24 July, p. 2.

MS13: Anon. (2009) 'Locuitorii satului Racovat sint buni gospodari. De aceea vor vota comunistii', *Moldova Suverana,* 24 July, p. 2.

AIE articles

T1: Alianta 'Moldova noastra' (2009), 'O saptamana de intoxicare la TRM', *Timpul*, 6 July, p. 3.

T2: Alianta 'Moldova noastra' (2009), 'TRM – fabrica comunista de spalare a creierilor', *Timpul,* 9 July, p. 4.

T3: Alianta 'Moldova noastra' (2009), 'Atacand opozitia, comunistii ataca majoritatea poporului', *Timpul,* 10 July, p. 8.

T4: Cojocaru, S. (2009), 'Patria mutanţilor', *Timpul*, 10 July, p. 5.

T5: Damian, A. (2009), 'Comunistii distrug intenţionat invatamantul', *Timpul*, 10 July, p. 5.

T6: Partidul Democrat din Moldova (2009), 'APEL al Congresului VI extraordinar al Partidului Democrat din Moldova catre cetatenii Republicii Moldova', *Timpul*, 21 July, p. 7.

T7: Partidul liberal (2009), no title, *Timpul*, 21 July, p.8

T8: Alianta 'Moldova noastra' (2009), 'Moldova este in pericol, iar pericolul se cheama Voronin', *Timpul*, 22 July, p. 6.

T9: Alianta 'Moldova noastra' (2009), 'Serafim Urechean : 'Comunistii vor raspunde in fata Tribunalului de la Haga', *Timpul*, 23 July, p.4.

T10: Partidul liberal (2009) no title, *Timpul*, 24 July, p. 6

T11: Filat, V. (2009), 'Impreuna pentru viitorul copiilor nostri! Impreuna pentru Moldova!', *Timpul*, 27 July, p. 5.

chapter three | inventing the ukrainian nation – identity building between dichotomies

Doris Wydra

Introduction – a difficult heritage

Ukraine – one of the countries that emerged on Soviet territory after the demise of the USSR – has existed within its current borders only since 1939. Before the Soviets united the territory, Ukraine's regions had developed within the frameworks of neighbouring states: Western Ukraine (Galicia) had been part of Poland and the Habsburg monarchy, and Eastern Ukraine – the historic centre of ancient Rus – had long been dominated by the Russian empire. The call for Ukrainian independence in 1991 was thus not so much a call for national rebirth after coercive repression (as was the case in the Baltic States), but a product of widespread hopes for greater prosperity. Even in Crimea and the Donbas, a majority voted for an independent Ukraine, regardless of ethnic affiliations (Morrison 1993: 685).

Like other successor states of the Soviet Union, Ukraine has a specific ethnic heritage. The USSR was always characterised as a multi-ethnic federation, first defined by the concept of '*korenisacija*' ('rootage'), and then later by policies aimed to create a 'homo sovieticus', dominated by Russian culture and language. Hobsbawn (1990: 168) argued that 'fear and coercion kept the USSR together', and helped prevent ethnic and communal tensions from degenerating into mutual violence. These tensions were transferred to the successor states of the Soviet Union, when it dissolved along the lines of its quasi-federal territorial structures.

In 1996, the Ukrainian Constitution was adopted 'on behalf of the Ukrainian people – citizens of Ukraine of all nationalities' (*vid imeni Ukraïns'kogo narodu – gromadjan Ukraïny vsich nacional'nostej*). While ethnic Ukrainians continue to hold the majority, 17.3 per cent of the Ukrainian population are ethnic Russians, 0.61 per cent are Belorussians, 0.55 per cent are Moldovans, and 0.52 per cent are Crimean Tatars; in addition, a number of smaller groups (such as Bulgarians, Hungarians, Romanians, Poles, and Jews) often live in compact settlements in the Ukrainian regions.[1] Like other post-communist states, Ukraine has had to confront the challenges of building a state and consolidating national authority, while at the same time struggling with ethnic and regional mobilisation (Hughes and

---

1. Main minority groups 2009, Source: State Committee on Nationalities and Migration in Ukraine. Online. Available /www.scnm.gov.ua/control/uk/publish/category?cat_id=131554 (accessed 31 March 2010).

Sasse 2002: 21). And while ethnic Russians are a relatively small group in Ukraine numerically speaking, viewing them merely as a national minority would not account for their full influence.

In a general sense, this chapter deals with a very specific minority – the Russian minority in post-Soviet Ukraine – and a first aim is to show that it does not fit well with the prevalent sociological definition of a 'minority', since it cannot really be characterised as 'non-dominant group'.[2] Contemporary Ukraine is notably bi-ethnic in nature, as evidenced by a bilingual set-up (with Ukrainian and Russian enjoying near-equal popularity) and pronounced regional differences (Shulman 2006: 250). Furthermore, Ukrainian identities do not simply draw upon Ukrainian or Russian ethnic roots. Indeed, Ukrainian national identities are constructed through complex narrative framing processes, and may be conceptualised based on discourses on history, ties with a specific territory, national and ethnic characteristics, and *also* by the notion of 'what one is not'. In his analysis of nationalism, Brubaker (1996: 60ff.) uses the term 'nationalising state' to characterise an arena of political struggle, especially with regard to the position of national minorities and these minorities' relationships with their homelands. Consequently, as its second aim, this chapter sets out to analyse the different 'nationalising narratives' within Ukraine – looking specifically at their use of history, territory and citizenship, the pure nation, and an imagined 'other', by drawing on the vast literature published during the past years that deals with the fact that Ukraine seems to be split between Russian and Ukrainian ethnic narratives not only as a society, but also as a political entity.

Finally, as our third aim, we focus more specifically on the political dimension of identity discourse, exploring the fact that these identities are not just relevant on an individual level, but in the political arena as well. In this context, they are taken up by political parties, and flow into political programmes and finally become law, since ruling elites structure state policies. So, taking as our starting point the narratives that form the imagined political community of Ukraine, our main line of inquiry is concerned with how these nationalising narratives are transferred into political narratives – and whether one identity narrative is becoming more influential in the country's political discourse than the other.

Constructing identities – building a nation

A nation can be seen as a named human population, sharing a historic territory, culture and common legal rights (Smith 2001: 19). Politicising an ethnic subset as a nation – imposing power structures, and structuring and differentiating territory – means building a state (Anderson 2005: 172ff.). Anderson (2005: 18) defines nations as imagined communities, characterised by their limits and their sovereignty.

---

2. According to Francesco Capotorti, a minority is a group 'numerically inferior to the rest of the population of a state, in a non-dominant position' (Special Rapporteur of the United Nations Sub-Commission on the Prevention of Discrimination and Protection of Minorities, E/CN.4/Sub.2/384/Rev.1, para. 568).

Ernest Gellner (1983) argues that the large-scale socio-economic transformations that led to the formation of nation-states in the nineteenth century aimed at homogenising diverse populations, especially via education and mass public culture, and were thus also aimed at reducing perceptions of heterogeneity between groups. This notion leads us to expect that a common language, religion, ethnicity and values promote a stronger national identity and unity (Shulman 2006: 249). And, ultimately, it leads us to the question: is nationalism, defined as the construction of common ethnic and cultural roots, necessary for building a stable state?

National identities are produced and reproduced, transformed and dismantled. The members of a nation are acculturated in many heterogeneous and often conflicting regional, sub-regional, cultural, linguistic and ethnic identities. Each of those identities involves inclusion and exclusion (Wodak *et al.* 2009: 4ff.). Studies by Shulman (2005) and Pirie (1996) have demonstrated that identity concepts in Ukraine are multi-layered, volatile and hard to grasp. While Shulman (2005: 68) distinguished between an ethnic Ukrainian and an Eastern Slavic national identity, Pirie (1996: 1982ff.) emphasised that ethnic self-identification in Ukraine also includes cases of identification with two or more ethnic groups, and of ethnic nihilism. Still, building a nation means constructing uniqueness and difference. Even conflicting identity constructions must be connected with each other in order to form an epistemically plausible whole – creating not just imagined communities, but their imagined boundaries as well (Benhabib 2006: 384). State-building means exercising power and authority, and having external and internal sovereignty (Habermas 1998: 107). And in this sense, nation-building and national identity formation are political products (Cinpoes 2008: 6). Stressing civic elements allows for the building of a 'demos' across ethnic cleavages, emphasising common legal principles and the uniting aspect of citizenship (Vlachová and Reháková 2009: 255). Stable political systems require at least a permissive consensus. And as we will see in the following section, these solidarity-building narratives are still fragile in Ukraine, something that makes the country prone to strident political antagonisms.

Nationalising narratives endeavour to give meaning to a specific territory, as well as to the relationships between ethnic groups, while also making claims for state-structuring power (Hall 1996: 615; Wodak *et al.* 2009: 24). At the same time, they strive to conceptualise notions of anticipation and future orientation (Kolakowski 1995). Thus, these narratives do not merely define the present state of a national community, they also give meaning to its past and future. Competing narratives operate in persistent interaction and change and adapt within the context of this interaction. In light of this ever-shifting environment, we ask the question: despite strong regional identification within Ukraine, are there prospects for a development towards greater coherence?

In our analysis of the competing narratives on Ukrainian history, territory and citizenship, on the pure nation, and on images of the 'other', it is helpful to keep in mind that these narratives are of strong political salience; later, we will see how these narratives are transformed into policies in greater detail.

Ukrainian identity – overlapping narratives

Article 11 of the Ukrainian Constitution yields a helpful starting point for understanding constitutive narratives, stating:

> The State promotes the consolidation and development of the Ukrainian nation (*ukraïns'koï naciï*), of its historical consciousness, traditions and culture, and also the development of the ethnic, cultural, linguistic and religious identity of all indigenous peoples and national minorities of Ukraine.

These narratives build the basis of the imagined political community of the Ukrainian nation and aim at legitimising its existence as an independent state within its given territory. Authors like Hall, Kolakowski and Wodak have applied the tools of critical analysis to reveal how national communities are constructed through discourses and narratives. Inspired by these authors, we aim to frame Ukrainian identity narratives and emphasise the different layers of identity building. The narratives highlighted in the following sections should give readers a close-up view of the struggle to define the Ukrainian nation, as a national and political construct. In many cases, this struggle is one that centres on a constant contestation between Ukrainian, Russian and pan-ethnic narratives. After all, this competition holds the promise of state-building, despite all the disruptive forces we have witnessed in the contemporary Ukrainian political arena. Only through contestation can a development towards coherence occur (that is, *if* this contestation is structured by rules all parties have to obey). Without contestation, identities would remain fixed and distant, without the potential to develop into a basis for a stable community.

Contesting history

The Ukrainian Constitution, which emphasises the 'centuries-old history of Ukrainian state-building', highlights the importance of historic narratives for the legitimacy of state-building. Historical myths establish links between ethnic groups and specific territories, thereby constructing and legitimising claims for political power. Contemporary claims to rule are rooted in historic entitlements, and historic deprivations of ruling power are defined as coercive and illegitimate intrusion. The Kievan Rus is regarded as the glorious starting point of the Ukrainian nation (Kolakowski (1995) calls this a 'nameable beginning for national consciousness') and is used to show that Ukrainians were able to build an independent territorial entity that only later had to submit to foreign oppression. Furthermore, Ukraine's connection to the European civic tradition can be connected to historic narratives about the Kievan Rus, which may be used to promote the liberal characteristics of its administrative structure (Rjabtschuk 2009: 145). Kolossov (1999: 78) uncovers four historical myths about the Ukrainian nation: the myth of the Kievan Rus being homeland only to the Ukrainian people (and not a motherland for all East-Slavic peoples); the myth of the independent, democratic nature of the Zapporozhian polity in the seventeenth and eighteenth centuries and its destruction by Catherine the Great (which serves as a symbol for Russian oppressive power); that of the colonial character of the Russian empire (depicted as causing irreversible demographic changes to the Ukrainian people); and the myth of the imposition of Soviet dominance by force through the destruction of the Ukrainian state by Bolshevik chauvinist intervention.

The contestation of identities begins with historic memory, however. And the accusation of Ukrainisation is closely linked to what appears to be a reinterpretation of historic facts. Pirozhenko (2010) criticises a vulgar variant of a Ukrainian history that interprets the Ukrainian state as a continuation of the Kievan Rus, and views events such as the 'holodomor'[3] as being symbolic of Russian oppression (while defining the OUN-UPA as a liberation army[4]), only to neglect any mention of brotherly relations between the Russian and Ukrainian peoples. This stands in stark contrast to the traditional Russian historiography, under which the Kievan state is regarded as the birthplace of Eastern Slavic history (Morrison 1993: 681), and the Treaty of Perejaslav (via which the Cossacks swore allegiance to the Tsar in Moscow in 1654) is interpreted by Ukrainian Russians as an important founding document for uniting brotherly nations, while ethnic Ukrainians regard it as the beginning of colonial oppression (Morrison 1993: 681).[5] The period under the Soviet Union has also become a reference point for identity narratives. Nikolayenko's analysis (2008: 252) of Soviet nostalgia among adolescents in post-Communist Russia and Ukraine revealed remarkable differences between different Ukrainian regions. While in L'viv, 91.8 per cent rated the demise of the Soviet Union as positive, in Donetsk this was only the case for 31.4 per cent of the respondents (a number very close to the results found for Russian cities). A sociological survey conducted in 1995 showed that the Donbas and Crimea (the regions with the highest proportion of ethnically-mixed families) were by far the most 'Soviet' (Pirie 1996: 1090).

Contesting territory and citizenship

According to Wodak et al. (2009: 26), narratives on the national body link territories, landscapes, and also people (e.g. ethnic groups) to narratives on national identity, thereby defining the size and limitations of a state. Narratives on territory and citizenship are both narratives of 'belonging. The question of territory is especially crucial for Ukraine, since Ukrainian regions '[moved] in and out of Ukrainian history at different times' (Sasse 2002: 73). Ukraine – consisting of

---

3. The famine killed about four million people in the Ukrainian Socialist Soviet Republic in 1932/33.

4. The Organisation of Ukrainian Nationalists in Western Ukraine fought against Polish oppression and later against the Red Army. Its aim was an independent Ukraine; its most prominent representative Stepan Bandera.

5. In 1992, the treaty was renounced, but its legacy still lingers on. When Ukrainian president Kravchuk signed the tripartite agreement to establish CIS in 1992, this was interpreted by some as following in Khmelnytsky's footsteps, arguing that any security guarantees offered by Russia are as worthless as the Tsar's promises (Morrison 1993: 680).

twenty-four regions and the Autonomous Republic of Crimea – is thus a good locus for exploring strong regional differences in the context of narratives related to
identity and belonging (Kolossov 1999: 73). Wilson (2002) describes a variety of
local identities, often described with the term *'tuteshni'* ('coming from here'). The
Donchanin (Donbas) identity, for instance, is based on the myth of an urban melt-
ing pot, dissolving particularities of ethnicity into a common labour culture. Such
a conception highlights the influence that economic narratives can have on regional identities (and indeed, the regions are very diverse when it comes to economic
structure, with a heavily industrialised east and south) (Hutchinson 2005: 35). The
Chornomortsi (Black Sea) identity presents a myth of multi-ethnic immigration to
a virgin coastal territory and the adoption of Russian as the voluntary lingua franca. The identity of the *krymskii narod* (Crimean people) is defined by a myth of
historical exceptionalism and geographical semi-isolation. The Carpathian *rusyny*,
for their part, have usually been divided between advocates of Russian, Ukrainian,
Hungarian and Slovak identities. And Galician nationalism, by contrast, defines
itself as 'oppositional' to the rest of Ukraine, with a strong self-imposed identity as
the 'true Ukrainian people (Wilson 2002: 43). It should be noted that while these
regional identities are important, one must not forget that there has also been a
strong history of federalism in Ukraine – although the Crimeans have made claims
for more autonomy since independence, along with the Hungarians in Zakarpattya
and the Russians of the Donbas area (Sasse 2002: 83ff.).

However, a state is not defined merely by its territory; it is also defined by its
citizens. In his analysis, Barrington (2001: 150) concluded that 'citizenship is a
powerful inclusionary device in the post-Soviet region'. In a survey conducted by
Zimmermann in 1994, Ukrainians adopted a rather tolerant attitude towards citizenship, not taking an exclusivist view (Zimmermann 1998: 49). Such consensus
on citizenship implies some recognition of a shared fate, and may even evidence
the development of a Ukrainian political community and some kind of differentiation between Ukraine and Russia (Zimmermann 1998: 54). Here, it is helpful to
keep in mind Lehning's distinction between objective and subjective citizenship:
while objective citizenship concerns the extent to which rights are extended to
individuals, subjective citizenship is the extent to which individuals 'actually con-
ceive themselves as citizens' (i.e. as belonging to the entity) (Lehning 2001: 273).
Drawing once again from the analysis of Nikolayenko (2008: 255), it seems that
Ukrainian citizenship is viewed more positively among western Ukrainian adolescents than by those in the east (Donetsk). The overall results, however, show that
majorities in both regions have positive attitudes towards Ukrainian citizenship.
For example, in L'viv and Donetsk respectively 97.2 per cent and 80.1 per cent of
the respondents to the study chose the category of 'having a great deal of national
pride'. The re-orientation from a Soviet identity towards a Ukrainian one proved
to be especially difficult for ethnic Russians. In economic, political, and territorial
terms, they identify themselves as part of the Ukrainian demos, but in ethnic terms
(culture, language and history), they see themselves as Russians. Gorodjanenko
(2009: 92) illustrates this re-orientation with concrete numbers: while only 34
per cent of the Russian minorities surveyed regarded themselves as citizens of

Ukraine in 2004, the number rose to 42.9 per cent in 2006. At the same time, the number of those who still felt some connection to the Soviet Union fell from 21.8 per cent in 2004, to 14.5 per cent in 2006. In explaining this phenomenon, Gorodjanenko points towards the development of a notion of mixed citizenship, wherein Russians either find it difficult to claim a Russian or Ukrainian identity, or feel a 'complex incompleteness typical of Russians in Western Ukraine, who are often characterised as "unwanted citizens"'.

Contesting the purity of the nation

In this volume, Rogers Brubaker (see Chapter One) stresses the importance of the belief that the state contains a core nation and that the bad state of this core nation can only be cured through state actions. Strengthening this core is at the heart of the nationalising movements of the Soviet successor states. Today, 78 per cent of the Ukrainian population are ethnic Ukrainians – so we might conclude that the pure (core) nation is the Ukrainian one and that the political community has developed along its characteristics – leaving only a minority position for the Russians, with limited regional significance. When it comes to the language of this community, however, this narrative on the pure Ukrainian nation is heavily contested. On the surface, we can consider the conclusions of Herder, who asserts that each nation has its own national education and language (Anderson 2005: 72). For the Ukrainian language, the Ukrainian poet Taras Shevchenko is certainly seen as the most important poet and early advocate of a Ukrainian national state.[6] The Ukrainian Constitution holds that Ukrainian is the only state language.

But language in Ukraine is much more complicated; it is often presented as a main factor dividing society. While the western part is inhabited mostly by Ukrainian-speaking Ukrainians, the east is mainly home to Russian-speaking Ukrainians and ethnic Russians. In the Russian ethno-political tradition, language plays a central role for the formation of an ethnicity (Guboglo 2003: 29; Chimiris 2007: 40). In the 1989 Soviet census, 72.7 per cent of the Ukrainian population classified themselves as Ukrainian, and nearly 65 per cent cited Ukrainian as their mother tongue – something that gives the impression that Ukraine was rather homogenous. But interviews conducted after independence revealed that the percentage of Russian-speaking Ukrainians was much higher (Chmelko and Oksamitnaja: 2008: 1), especially when taking into account the language of preference rather than mother tongue. Surveys show that only a minority of the overall population (that is to say, 20 million out of 50 million) preferred Ukrainian over Russian and about 30 per cent of the population freely used either language, depending on circumstances (Wilson 2002: 36; see also Brubaker in this volume on the Ukrainian language).

---

6. Anderson cites Seton Watson, saying that the Ukrainian language owes everything to Taras Shevchenko as his use of the Ukrainian language in his works was decisive for the development of an Ukrainian national consciousness (Anderson 2005: 79).

There is an increasing number of multi-ethnic families, which may also give an explanation for the rising number of bilingual persons (in 2001, approximately 22.8 per cent were bi-ethnic). Bi-ethnics are more likely to choose Russian as mother tongue (Chmelko and Oksamitnaja: 2008: 3ff.), but they are also more likely to define themselves as Ukrainian nationals, which is also a kind of re-identification (Rapawy 1997). Taking these different language narratives into account, proposals for language policy were developed, but they met with resistance. In his seminal essay, Gorodjanenko (2009: 93) accuses the Ukrainian state of massive linguistic discrimination, especially in the educational system and in mass media, and suggests this discrimination has led to the spread of negative attitudes towards the Russian language (and, subsequently, to everything connected with Russia). He also stresses the fact that a growing percentage of the population speaks *surzhik*, which is a mixture of Russian and Ukrainian. Chimiris (2007: 53), by contrast, posits three possible solutions for the language situation. First, he imagines advocating a continued preference for the Ukrainian language, putting Russian ever more squarely into the status of a minority language, and thereby also moving Russians to the position of an ethnic minority and an ethnic group that does not have nation-building character for Ukraine. Secondly, he suggests that Russian could be given an official status as a state or regional language, something that may, by contrast, complicate Ukrainian identity-building. Thirdly, he suggests the possibility of strengthening the bilingual aspect of Ukrainian society.

Despite their differences, all of these approaches to language suggest that the narrative on the pure nation, with its 'ethnic language', is heavily contested and seems unlikely to be easily resolved. While examples like Finland or Switzerland demonstrate that bilingual or multi-lingual settings do not necessarily present disruptive elements for the national whole, Ukraine will probably need more time to progress towards the acceptance of Russian as a mere instrument of communication. The Ukrainian language is characterised as an essential element for national uniqueness and national rebirth, while Russian has been the language of the Soviet Union. In Ukrainian discourse (and here, 'Ukrainian' is understood in a political context), Ukrainian is the language of the Ukrainian state: a state of the Ukrainian people, which has given them back the political power to decide about their own faith – a power that was withheld from them by the Soviet (i.e. Russian) oppressors. Russians hold no constitutive power in this state; Russian, therefore, cannot be a state language. In this conceptualisation, Russians are most definitely the 'others'.

Contesting images of the 'other'

According to Sheila Benhabib (2002), constructing the 'other' not only determines the differences between peoples, but also defines the borders of the self's identity and reshapes it. In Ukraine, the question of ethnic national identity is particularly contentious. The two identity complexes noted by Shulman (2004: 40) – the ethnic Ukrainian and Eastern Slavic complex – differ in their assessment of the unifying and distinguishing features of Ukrainian national identity and the compatibility of

Ukrainian and Russian identities. Ethnic Ukrainian identity discourse describes Ukraine as a natural homeland that has been oppressed by Soviet 'russification'. Its main competitor is perceived to be the Eastern Slavic identity, which sees the Ukrainian nation as founded on Ukrainian and Russian ethnicity, language and culture. In this fashion, Ukraine is conceptualised as being a bi-ethnic, bilingual, bi-cultural nation. These ethnic Ukrainian identity concepts disagree mainly on who is the primary 'other' – Russia or Europe.

Russia and Ukraine have been at odds over a wide range of issues (e.g. the Black Sea Fleet, the division of former Soviet property, Crimea, gas deliveries, etc.) ever since the dissolution of the Soviet Union. Particularly in the early 1990s, there was a consensus that building an independent Ukraine was incompatible with any form of political or economic integration with Russia, though in the long run, especially with regard to energy supplies, this strategy led Ukraine into severe economic crisis (Morrison 1993: 685). It was economic development that proved to be of crucial importance for the country's domestic stability, especially with regard to Ukraine's eastern territories. In 1993, the Ukrainian economy started to perform worse than the Russian economy (Morrison 1993: 681) and it became apparent that the construction of the Russian 'other' was not as strong a narrative in the eastern regions as it was in the western ones, and did not override the economic concerns in the east as readily as it did in the west. It was clear that being different from Russia was not more important than achieving economic stability. However, the ethnic Ukrainian narrative about the dominance of a 'pan-Russian national identity' also made it difficult to construct a unique Ukrainian identity.

Furthermore, depending on the context, Ukrainians' image of Europe is either one of the 'other' or the 'similar'. During the presidency of Kuchma, approximation towards the European Union had already become a top-level priority, although Wolczuk (2003) tagged this development with the term of 'declarative Europeanisation', since no active political steps followed. Opinion polls show a stable approval rating for European integration, with support of around 55 per cent. But in all these discourses, Europe is framed in different ways, often following ethnic, social, linguistic and even generational cleavages.

Above, we have presented the various antagonisms found in each layer of the discourse on a developing Ukrainian identity. We saw a (slightly exaggerated) nationalising Ukrainian narrative: going back to the Kievan Rus in order to build a founding myth of a Ukrainian people, whose drive for independence was manifested in the Zapporozhian Sich. This myth presented a people who kept their language, traditions and culture despite Russian oppression; a people whose future is thought to lie in moving towards European civilisation, and away from Eurasian dictatorship.

The opposing narrative, by contrast, stresses the brotherhood of East Slavic nations (comprised of different linguistic, cultural and ethnic groups, but united by Russian language). This version presents a nation that had its basis in the Kievan Empire, was consolidated by the treaty of Perejaslav and, ultimately, found its perfection in the Soviet Union. This narrative views the current conflict as artificial, i.e. as something to be overcome (at the very least) by pursuing closer political and economic cooperation with Russia.

There are signs of a developing coherence and amalgamation, but the process is still nascent. Speculation that the newly-formed state might break apart along ethnic divisions have not been realised – and such possibilities are becoming ever more unlikely, despite the secessionist movements in Crimea during the 1990s.

As noted in the introductory paragraphs, after providing an outline of the different nationalising narratives and the interpretative structures upon which they are built, our aim is to connect these identity narratives with political narratives.

Turning identities into policies

Identity narratives as political narratives

These different constructs of identity are mobilised within the political narratives of Ukrainian political parties. Centre-periphery, regional and ethno-linguistic dividing lines are the main factors for party identification. Their main role is to structure political competition and to legitimise the leadership of individual politicians (Wilson and Birch 2007). This analysis concentrates on parties that are presently represented within the Ukrainian parliament. This includes the Party of Regions (the party of president Yanukovych), Our Ukraine – National Self-Defence (the party of former president Yushchenko), BJuT (Bloc Julia Timoshenko), and the Bloc Lytvyn – People's Party (the party of the chairmen of the Supreme Rada), as well as the Communist Party of Ukraine. Most of these groups are actually alliances, made up of multiple political parties. The current governing coalition, which was made possible by a change in the rules of procedure of the Ukrainian parliament that occurred immediately after the presidential elections, allows individual members of elected fractions to break away from their party and to form a coalition together with other parliamentary groups. The coalition is made up of the Party of Regions (192 seats), the Communist Party (25 seats) and the Lytvyn Bloc (20 seats). Parties in opposition consist of the BJuT (105 seats) and Our Ukraine (67 seats).[7]

Ukrainian history is a strongly contested field and in political discourse this history becomes a reference point for present-day challenges. Lytvyn's People's Party demonstrates the importance of history in the development of a new state ('A state that does not understand its history, has no future'[8]). Practical examples that highlight the deep cleavages in Ukrainian history can be seen in the cases of Stepan Bandera; in the historic roles of the hetmans Bohdan Chmelniyckyj and Ivan Mazepa; and also in the 'Great Fatherland War'. In January 2010, then-president Yushchenko honoured Stepan Bandera by declaring him a national hero of Ukraine. This decree was finally overturned by the Constitutional Court of Ukraine in 2011. As a result of this decision, the BJuT accused president Yanukovych of

7. Verchovna Rada Ukraina. Online. Available /w1.c1.rada.gov.ua/pls/site/p_fractions (number of deputies per faction; accessed 31 July 2011).

8. 'Oficijnyj sajt Narodnoi partii – Tochka zoru, Pamjat' o proshlom kak fundament budushego', 6 May 2010. Online. Available /narodna.org.ua/news (accessed 31 May 2011).

pressurising the courts to neglect Bandera's important role in Ukrainian history.[9] And while certain subsets of Ukrainians, such as the communists, believe that there is a clear connection between fascism and persons like Stepan Bandera – indeed, they are quick to emphasise that the fight against fascism is still a pressing issue[10] (especially in the western parts of Ukraine, which are characterised as being under nationalist and fascist pressure[11]) – the People's Party sees no conflict in according national historical significance to Bohdan Chmelniyckyi and the victory over fascist Germany ('no page of the national history should be torn out, just because somebody does not like it').[12]

Likewise, other historic events are mobilised within political discussions. The treaty on the extension of the lease of the Ukrainian seaports to the Russian part of the Black Sea fleet was signed – according to the BJuT – on the eve of the destruction of the Zapporozhian Sich, which also rejected the development of the Ukrainian state for a long time. By employing this reference, the BJuT once again portrays Russia as denying Ukraine free development, emphasising the deployment of Russian armed forces on Ukrainian territory.[13] While the period under the Soviet Union is remembered by most Ukrainian parties (and especially by Our Ukraine) as a time of oppression, the Communist Party stresses the consolidation of Ukrainian territory under Soviet rule.[14]

In the matter of the narrative of the pure nation in particular, we can observe pronounced antagonism between the Party of Regions and Our Ukraine. The party programme of Our Ukraine stresses the importance of grounding the development of the nation in an ethno-cultural development of its people, i.e. in basing a national identity on the traditions of the titular Ukrainian nation, since it will only be able to survive within its own state.[15] Our Ukraine stands firmly behind the status of Ukrainian as the single state language, while also supporting the right for free development for minority languages, such as Russian. So while there is a strong belief within Our Ukraine that the Ukrainian state must be built on an ethnic

9. 'Rishennja Janukovicha ne vplivne na rol' ta misce Stepana Banderi v ukrains'kij istorii'. Online. Available /byut.com.ua/news, 12 January 2011; 'Julija Timoshenko: Janukovych vdaet'sja do repressij spravzhnich geroiv' Ukrainy, http://byut.com.ua/news, 13 January 2011 (both articles accessed 30 June 2011).

10. 'Sergej Gmyrja: Bandera i Shukhevich imejut prjamoe otnoshenie k fashismu', 1 July 2011. Online. Available /www.kpu.ua (accessed 31 July 2011).

11. 'Aleksandr Zuchevskij: Nacionalisti mogut sprovocirovat' „l'vovskij' konflikt v ljubom zapadnoukrainskom gorode', 30 June 2011. Online. Available /www.kpu.ua (accessed 31 July 2011).

12. 'Oficijnyj sajt Narodnoi partii – Tochka zoru, Pamjat' o proshlom kak fundament budushego, 6 May 2010. Online. Available /narodna.org.ua/news (accessed 31 May 2011).

13. Opozicija zhe dopustyt ratyfikacii ugody pro prodovzhennja perebuvannja rocijs'kogo flout', 22 April 2010. Online. Available /http://byut.com.ua/news, (accessed 31 May 2011).

14. 'Programma Kommunisticheskoj partii Ukrainy'. Online. Available /www.kpu.ua/programakpu/ (accessed 31 May 2011).

15. 'Programma Narodnogo Sojuzu "Nasha Ukraina"'. Online. Available /www.razom.org.ua/documents/ (accessed 30 June 2011).

Ukrainian core,[16] the state is bi-ethnic and bilingual for the Party of Regions. According to the Party of Regions, the importance of the Russian language as means of everyday communication must be recognised, especially in light of the fact that during the 'orange years', the development of minority languages suffered severely within the nationalising environment.[17] The BJuT, by contrast, heavily criticises the weakening status of Ukrainian as the sole state language under the presidency of Yanukovych – the president has practically formed a Russian state-administration, and Russian has once again taken on the position of first state language in practice.[18]

'Europe' and 'Russia' are highly-contested designations in the political arena. For Our Ukraine and BJuT, 'the other' is clearly the Russian Federation and its perceived aspirations to undermine Ukrainian sovereignty.[19] According to the party programme of Our Ukraine, Ukraine is a European state, built on the principles of market economy, democracy, and the rule of law.[20] For former president Yushchenko and his supporters (hailing mainly from western Ukraine) the prospect of membership in the European Union would have meant the final affirmation of Ukrainian independent statehood, with Ukraine becoming an equal partner in a union of democratic, pluralist, and culturally-European states. This was regarded as final confirmation of Ukrainian sovereignty within recognised borders.[21] This sovereignty frame mobilises discourses on the long-standing European tradition of Ukraine, which was perceived as lost through subordination under Russian domination.[22]

At the other end of the spectrum is the Communist Party of Ukraine, which is still strongly rooted in the idea of a common Soviet past, and rather critical towards the pressures of Western capitalism (in the form of the European Union, the World Trade Organisation and NATO membership), which they see as poised to overturn Ukrainian society structures. A possible renewal of a voluntary union between the post-Soviet countries is still on the party agenda. Closer cooperation with former members of the USSR in the Commonwealth of Independent States (CIS) and the Customs Union, together with Russia, Belarus and Kazakhstan, is regarded by the communists as serving Ukrainian interests' best.[23] However,

16. 'Programma Narodnogo Sojuzu 'Nasha Ukraina'. Online. Available /www.razom.org.ua/documents/ (accessed 30 June 2011).

17. 'Nacionalnye men'shinstva Ukrainy osudili „dvojnye standarty' komissara OBSE Knuta Vollebeka', 18 March 2011. Online. Available /www.partyofregions.org.ua/ru/news/faces/show/273 (accessed 31 May 2011).

18. Rosijs'ka vzhe stala pershoju derzhavnoju. Online. Available /http://byut.com.ua/news, 5 March 2010 (accessed 31 May 2011).

19. E.g. 'Julia Tymosheko: Janukovch namagaet'sja peretvoryty Ukrainy na votchynu Rossij'. Online. Available /http://byut.com.ua/news, 9 June 2010 (accessed May 2011).

20. 'Programma Narodnogo Sojuzu 'Nasha Ukraina'. Online. Available /www.razom.org.ua/documents/ (accessed 30 June 2011).

21. 'Evropejskij vibir'. Online. Available /www.razom.org.ua/documents/ (accessed 31 May 2011).

22. 'Party programme of "Our Ukraine"'. Online. Available /www.razom.org.ua/documents/443/ (accessed 31 May 2011).

23. 'Programma Kommunisticheskoj partii Ukrainy', /www.kpu.ua/programakpu/; Evgenij Car'kov:

equally strong importance is accorded to the idea of cultivating closer relations with the communist countries of Asia and, most of all, China, which the party perceives to be crucial to the country's strategic future.[24] Europe is viewed as a foreign power that places obligations on Ukraine, without providing it with the chance to play an equal part in norm creation. Equality is only seen as possible in Ukraine's relationships with Russia and Belarus.[25] By contrast, the idea of an equal relationship with Russia is merely a phantasm for Our Ukraine, at least in any situation where Ukraine is not part of a bigger bloc like NATO or the European Union ('if Russia recognises any weakness, it will exploit it').[26] Lytvyn's People's Party and the Party of Regions take the middle ground on this issue; while the party of Regions takes a slightly more sympathetic stance towards Russia, the Lytvyn Bloc skews more towards the European Union.[27] President Yanukovych and his Party of Regions strive for further integration into the European economy, but also for closer cooperation with the Russian Federation, Kazakhstan and Belarus, within the Common Economic Space.[28] Their platform stresses that Russia approaches Ukraine with words of friendship, while the European Union speaks only about democracy.[29] To the People's Party, the European Union is an optimal model of social economy and public institutions.[30] The nationalist ideas of Our Ukraine are criticised by Lytvyn for having brought about serious ideological conflicts with Moscow; the victory of Yanukovych at the presidential elections has been the predictable result. He opts for a third way, moving the country in the direction of Europe, but without incurring exhausting confrontations with Russia.[31] Such a multi-vectored foreign policy is a necessity, as long as one vector supports the economic development and the other guarantees security.[32]

Tol'ko polnocennoe uchastie Ukrainy v Tamozhennom sojuze mozhet snjat' vse zaprety I kvoty. Online. Available /www.kpu.ua (accessed 31 May 2011).

24. 'Ukraina vybrala strategichesckij kurs na kommunizm', 23.06.2011. Online. Available /www.kpu.ua (accessed 30 June 2011).

25. 'Interview Simonenko'. Online. Available /www.kpu.ua/petr-simonenko-ukraina-%E2%80%93-nesvobodnoe-gosudarstvo/ (accessed 31 October 2010).

26. 'Volodymyr Ohryzko: Vidnosyny z Rosieju mozhut buty rivnopravnymy lyshe v tomu razi, koly b Ukraina stala chlenom Evropejs'kogo Sojuzu i NATO'. Online. Available /www.razom.org.ua/opinions (accessed 31 July 2011).

27. 'Infomacijniyj bjuleten' Narodnoi Partii No. 103 (7.3.2011–11.3.2011), Shodo vnutrishn'oi polityky Ukrainy'. Online. Available /narodna.org.ua/news (accessed 30 June 2011).

28. 'Predvybornaja programma partii regionov'. Online. Available /www.partyofregions.org.ua/opposition-a-z/46c593c3e2c58/ (accessed 31 May 2011).

29. 'Inna Bogoslovskaja: Rossija prikryvaet svoj interesy druzhboj, a ES – demokratiej, no Ukraine nuzhno dumat' o sebe i svoem proizvodstve', Online. Available /www.partyofregions.org.ua/deputy_faction/activities/show/2763 (accessed 30 July 2011).

30. 'Infomacijniyj bjuleten' Narodnoi Partii No. 111 (10.05.2011–13.05.2011), Shodo Evropejs'koi integracii Ukrainy'. Online. Available /narodna.org.ua/news (accessed 30 June 2011).

31. 'Ukrainska perspektiva: do Evropi – zaruku z Rosieju', 12 May 2010. Online. Available /www.narodna.org.ua/news.php?AYear=2010&AMonth=5&ADay=12&ArticleI (accessed 31 October 2010).

32. Vladimir Lytvyn: 'My ne mozhem otkazatsja ot mnogovektornosti', *Gazeta ,, Izvestija v Ukraine'*, 1 April 2010. Online. Available /izvestia.com.ua/?/articles/2010/04/01/211316-5 (accessed 31

Transferring identities into law

The governing coalition under president Yanukovych (Party of Regions, People's Party and Communists) has settled on a pragmatic course towards Europe, on openness towards Russia – stressing a common bi-ethnic, bilingual Slavic identity (by rhetorically emphasising the importance of the Russian language) – and on opposing the 'nationalist claims promoted by Western Ukraine'. Two legislative decisions can be held up as examples of how these identity narratives – presented by the parties in power – have been transformed into law. In April 2010, the Ukrainian parliament had already issued a law allowing for the Russian part of the Black Sea Fleet to stay in the port of Sebastopol (Crimea) until 2042, following an agreement between the Russian president, Medvedev, and the Ukrainian president, Yanukovych.[33] This new law was characterised by the opposition (the BJuT and Our Ukraine) as 'against the constitution, against the national interests of Ukraine and its territorial integrity'. Both sides accused the other of betraying Ukrainian sovereignty: Our Ukraine and the BJuT were characterised as forcing a division of the country by completely breaking with Russia; and the governing coalition was depicted as turning Ukraine into a vassal of Russia.[34]

The second law that resulted in profound arguments among the different factions in the Ukrainian parliament was the 'Law on the basic principles of domestic and foreign policies of Ukraine'.[35] The law, based on a legal initiative promoted by president Yanukovych, was issued by the Ukrainian parliament on 1st July 2010. It was ambitious in scope: aiming to regulate all fundamental principles for developing statehood and local self-government, to stimulate the development of the regions, and to form institutions of civil society, national security and defence in economic, social, and humanitarian areas. The new law has been the subject of heated criticism, and not without reason. It is a political programme rather than a legal basis for domestic and foreign policy. Its swift adoption was attributed to the newly elected president's desire to ensconce his understanding of national policies (including the relations between linguistic groups, the socio-economic development and relations towards the Russian Federation and the West) within some kind of legal framework. The result is a new law that reflects different – and rather contradictory – ideas of foreign policy, without any clear mechanisms for their implementation. Indeed, if taken as written, the law could result in a number of changes to existing legislation, in areas as far-ranging as national security strategy, the military doctrine, election laws, and laws on local self-government. Even the

---

October 2010).

33. 'Verchovna Rada Ukrainy, Zakon vid 27.04.2010, Pro ratifikaciju Ugodu mizh Ukrainoju ta Rosijs'koju Federacijeiju z pitan' perebuvannja Chornomors'kogo flout Rosijs'koi Federacii na terytorii Ukrainy'. Online. Available /www.rada.kiev.ua (accessed 31 July 2011).

34. 'Stenographic Protocol Supreme Rada', 27 April 2010. Online. Available /www.rada.kiev.ua, (accessed 31 October 2010).

35. 'Verchovna Rada Ukrainy, Zakon vid 01.07.2010, Pro zasady vnutrish'noi I zovnish'noi polityky', *VVR 2010*, N40, st. 527.

constitution itself would be subject to major changes under the new law.

Central principles of the law's stance on domestic policy include the strengthening of regional self-government, the expansion of competencies of local organs by way of decentralisation, and the harmonisation of national, regional and local interests (article 4 paragraph 1). Article 10 aims at realising a national language policy. What is interesting in this regard is that the law does not mention a 'state language', although one goal is to guarantee the development and functioning of the Ukrainian language in all areas of social life throughout Ukraine, while also guaranteeing the free development, use and protection of the Russian language, as well as other languages of Ukrainian citizens. At the same time, the paragraph also refers to the principles of international law, an aspect that has often been stressed by the Party of Regions, who accuse the 'orange government' of discrimination against the Russian language, especially in the area of education, suggesting that it violates the Convention on the Rights of the Child.[36]

Perhaps most important, and also most controversial, has been the regulation on the principles of the foreign policy of Ukraine. The provision against entering into NATO membership represents a sharp break from former Ukrainian policy, which had favoured close cooperation with NATO within the Special Partnership Framework, and had placed the country on a course towards full membership since 2002. During the discussions in parliament, the opposition parties, and especially the representatives of Our Ukraine, protested strongly against this new law. They stressed that the independence of the Ukrainian nation had been a 'return to the European home'. In their eyes, the reversal of this trend and the suddenly renewed emphasis on the Eurasian sphere of influence also meant doing away with Ukrainian sovereignty and independence. 'When the president signed the agreement on the Black Sea fleet, he lost the chance to be president of the whole of Ukraine' was one characteristic argument that was expressed.[37] Furthermore, Leonid Kravchuk, the first president of Ukraine after independence, described the new agreement on the Black Sea Fleet as a first step in delimiting Ukrainian sovereignty. Under the new law, all further steps towards European integration would have to be agreed with Russia.[38] The BJuT stressed that in their opinion the law was a clear sign that the Ukrainian government was fulfilling Russian orders and limiting the possibilities of the Ukrainian state – going so far as to describe the law as being 'an instrument of the Kremlin to destroy the Ukrainian state'.[39]

The law was finally passed with 171 votes from the Party of Regions, twenty-seven from the Communists, and nineteen from the Lytvyn Bloc – but also with twenty-five from BJuT and thirteen from Our Ukraine. The Party of Regions, supported by the Communists and the Lytvyn Bloc, argued during the session

---

36. Again e.g. in 'Obrazovanie na rodnom jazyke: prichot' cheloveka ili objazannost' gosudarstva?', Online. Available /www.partyofregions.org.ua/ru/news/faces/show/152 (accessed 31 July 2001).

37. 'Antidepressant dlja opposicii', *Den'*, No. 72, 23 April 2010.

38. 'Antidepressant dlja opposicii', *Den'*, No. 72, 23 April 2010, Commented by Leonid Kravchuk.

39. 'Opasnosti «vneblokovosti'», Pavel Koval', *Den'*, 1 April 2010.

of the Supreme Rada that this pragmatic policy style was a necessity to trigger reform in Ukraine. As self-described realists, they believe that to overcome the state's financial and economic problems – which also block Ukraine's way into the European Union – Ukraine needs to maximise the potential of its good relations with all of its strategic partners (especially its relations with Russia, its most important ally in this area). The attempt to distance the country from the Russian Federation has, after all, resulted in considerable economic loss. So by moving back towards Russia, a swifter integration into Europe may well become possible. In their view, Ukraine's multi-vectored policy is likely to bring economic and social benefits – and most importantly, it follows the will of the people of Ukraine.

Conclusion

In 1905, Ivan Franko demanded the building of a Ukrainian people out of the ethnic masses, thus constructing a common cultural organism. As Zhulinskij (2009) stresses, Ukraine succeeded in achieving independence, but still lacks a common language, mythology, consciousness and symbols. Ukraine is a state with various layers of identities, which are constantly in flux. Gorodjanenko (2009: 91) argues that, instead of Ukraine being an imagined community in and of itself, the Russian-speaking minority in Ukraine is such an imagined community, and this hinders the construction of a common all-Ukrainian identity. National identities in Ukraine are produced and reproduced, transformed and dismantled. The notion that the nationalising Ukrainian state is an arena for such contestation becomes manifest in its narratives on history, territory and citizenship, the pure nation and images of the 'other'.

On the one hand, these narratives imagine a Ukrainian state that has a clear right to existence, built on the uniqueness of the Ukrainian people and its differences from a Russian identity. On the other hand, a Russian minority – one that is not a traditional minority in terms of its political influence – together with Russian-speaking citizens, promote a bilingual, pan-ethnic, Slavic discourse. Looking beyond these factors, however, we can see the different layers of identity construction in play, and how they are transferred into the realm of politics. Surveying this broader picture, we wondered: can an 'imagined community' be built, overcoming all the cleavages we have analysed so far? Is Ukraine on its way to a stable democratic state? Our investigation of how these identity narratives are turned into political narratives has revealed how antagonism has hindered stabilisation in Ukraine. Indeed, political disputes centre not only on diverging economic and social programmes, but also on the very identity of the state, and its direction, factors that always seem to be perilously at stake. With this in mind, a compelling question is: must we accustom ourselves to seeing 'lively' discussions in the Ukrainian parliament, with deputies resorting to their fists when they feel their arguments are no longer heard (as was the case during the session that dealt with the prolongation of the deployment of the Russian Black Sea Fleet)? Or is there the chance that the permissive consensus necessary for a stable political community may emerge? As stated before, competition is vital to the transformation of identities; after all, without competition, identities remain immobile. But, for this to work, the contesting parties must play by the rules. When they do, processes, institutions, and constitutional rules can become reference points for identity building and the narratives we have analysed so far can be accommodated within these processes and lose their disruptive character. And therefore these rules – the democratic game and the constitutional framework – must be stable, transparent, valid for all participants in the game and recognised as a legitimate basis for power. Based on this line of reasoning, it would seem that the state's procedural and institutional deficiencies – its sometimes instable and arbitrary processes – have a stronger tendency towards mere disruption than towards fruitfully-diverging identity constructions.

References

Anderson, B. (2005) [1983] *Die Erfindung der Nation. Zur Karriere eines folgenreichen Konzepts*, Frankfurt and New York: Campus Verlag.

Barrington, L. (2001) 'Russian-speakers in Ukraine and Kazakhstan', *Post-Soviet Affairs*, 17(2): 129–58.

Benhabib, S. (2002) *The Claims of Culture: Equality and diversity in the global era*, Princeton: Princeton University Press.

— (2006) 'The "claims" of culture properly interpreted: response to Nikolas Kompridis', *Political Theory*, 34(3): 383–88.

Brubaker, R. (1996) *Nationalism Reframed: Nationhood and the national question in the new Europe*, Cambridge: Cambridge University Press.

Chimiris, E. (2007) 'Faktor jazykovoj identichnosti v ukrainskoj politike', *Kosmopolis*, 18(2): 39–52.

Chmelko, W. E. Oksamitnaja, S. N. (2008) *Russko-ukrainskaja bietnicheskaja identichnost b lingvo-etnicheskaja geterogennost v Ukraine*. Online. Available /www.isras.ru/publications_bank/1225745240.pdf (accessed 1 October 2010).

Cinpoes, R. (2008) 'From national identity to European identity', *Journal of Identity and Migration Studies*, 2(1): 3–14.

Gellner, E. (1983) *Nations and Nationalism*, Ithaca: Cornell University Press.

Gorodjanenko, V. G. (2009) 'Polozhenije Russkich v Ukraine i problemy ich identichnosti', *Etnosociologija*, 1: 89–95.

Guboglo, M. N. (2003) *Identifikacija identichnosti: Etnosociologicheskie ocherki*, Moskva: Nauka.

Habermas, J. (1998) *The Inclusion of the Other: Studies in political theory*, Cambridge: Polity Press.

Hall, S. (1996) 'The question of cultural identity', in S. Hall, D. Held, D. Hubert and K. Thompson (eds) *Modernity: An introduction to modern societies*, Massachusetts: Blackwell Publishers, pp. 595–634.

Hobsbawn, E. (1990) *Nations and Nationalism since 1780: Programme, myth and reality*, Cambridge: Cambridge University Press.

Hughes, J. and Sasse, G. (2002) 'Comparing regional and ethnic conflicts in post-Soviet transition states', in J. Hughes and G. Sasse (eds) *Ethnicity and Territory in the Former Soviet Union: Regions in conflict*, London and Portland: Frank Cass, pp. 1–35.

Hutchinson, J. (2005) *Nations as Zones of Conflict*, London: Sage Publications.

Kolakowski, L. (1995) 'Über kollektive Identität', in K. Michalski (ed.) *Identität im Wandel: Castelgandolfo-Gespräche 1995*, Stuttgart: Institut für die Wissenschaften vom Menschen, pp. 47–60.

Kolossov, V. (1999) 'Ethnic and political identities and territorialities in the post-Soviet space', *GeoJournal*, 48(2): 71–81.

Lehning, P. P. (2001) 'European citizenship: towards a European identity?', *Law and Philosophy*, 20(3): 239–82.

Morrison, J. (1993) 'Perejaslav and after: the Russian-Ukrainian relationship', *International Affairs*, 69(4): 677–703.

Nikolayenko, O. (2008) 'Contextual effects on historical memory: Soviet nostalgia among post-Soviet adolescents', *Communist and Post-Communist Studies*, 41(2): 243–59.

Pirie, P. S. (1996) 'National identity and politics in southern and eastern Ukraine', *Europe-Asia Studies*, 48(7): 1079–104.

Pirozhenko, V. A. (2010) 'Istorija "nozhnic" i "kleja" kak sredstvo formirovanija ukrainskoj etnicheskoj nacii'. Online. Available \www.hist.msu.ru/Labs/ UkrBel/pirozenko.doc (accessed 1 September 2010).

Rapawy, S. (1997) 'Ethnic reidentification in Ukraine', *IPC Staff Paper 90*, Washington: Unites States Bureau of the Census. Online. Available / www.census.gov/ipc/www/ebspr98a.html (accessed 1 September 2010).

Rjabtschuk, M. (2009) 'Ambivalentes Grenzland: die ukrainische Identität zwischen Ost und West', in T. Meyer and J. Eisenberg (eds) *Europäische Identität als Projekt*, Wiesbaden: VS Verlag für Sozialwissenschaften, pp. 143–60.

Sasse, G. (2002) 'The "new" Ukraine: a state of regions', in J. Hughes and G. Sasse (eds) *Ethnicity and Territory in the Former Soviet Union: Regions in conflict*, London and Portland: Frank Cass, pp. 69–100.

Shulman, S. (2004) 'The contours of civic and ethnic national identification in Ukraine', *Europe-Asia Studies*, 56(1): 35–56.

— (2005) 'National identity and public support for political and economic reform in Ukraine', *Slavic Review*, 64(1): 59–87.

— (2006) 'Cultural comparisons and the consequences for nationhood in Ukraine', *Communist and Post-Communist Studies*, 39(2): 247–63.

Smith, A. D. (2001) 'Nations in History', in M. Guibernau and J. Hutchinson (eds) *Understanding Nationalism*, Cambridge: Polity, pp. 9–31.

Vlachová, K. and Reháková, B. (2009) 'Identity of non-self-evident nation: Czech national identity after the break-up of Czechokslovakia and before accession to the European Union', *Nations and Nationalism*, 15(2): 254–79.

Wilson, A. (2002) 'Elements of a theory of Ukrainian ethno-national identities', *Nations and Nationalism*, 8(2): 31–54.

Wilson, A. and Birch, S. (2007) 'Political parties in Ukraine: virtual and representational', in P. Webb and S. White (eds) *Political Parties in New Democracies: Trajectories of development and implications for democracy*, Oxford: Oxford University Press, pp. 53–84.

Wodak, R., de Cilia, R., Reisigl, M. and Liebhart, K. (2009) *The Discursive Construction of National Identity*, 2nd edn., Edinburgh: Edinburgh University Press.

Wolczuk, K. (2003) 'Ukraine's policy towards the European Union: a case of "declarative Europeanization"', working paper. Online. Available /www. batory.org.pl/ftp/program/forum/eu_ukraine/ukraine_eu_policy.pdf (accessed 20 September 2010).

Zimmermann, W. (1998) 'Is Ukraine a political community?', *Communist and Post-Communist Studies*, 31(1): 43–55.

Zhulinskij, N. (2009) 'O nacionalnoj identichnosti', *Den*, 9 December.

chapter four	group empowerment and cross-ethnic dialogue – integration within the polish national state

Magdalena Dembinska

'*Voice, rather than votes, is the vehicle of empowerment*'

Simone Chambers

Introduction

This chapter explores political arrangements favourable to the integration of minorities in nationalising states. Political scientists have developed various institutional and electoral rules of power-sharing for divided societies, aimed at countering the risk of marginalisation faced by minorities. According to some analysts, however, too much importance is given to the political representation of minorities, i.e. to the presence of ethnic parties in the legislature (Alonso and Ruiz-Rufino 2007; Bieber 2004: 240). After all, the mere presence of these parties is not necessarily indicative of the ethnic group's successful integration. In the past few years, more and more analysts have expressed the notion that further thought should be given to the concept of 'living together' in the long run. As O'Flynn and Russell (2005: 6) describe it, 'even where it is not possible to opt for integration in the first instance, it should nevertheless remain a fundamental objective, actively pursued by policy makers in a determined fashion.' The objective of this chapter is to contribute to this debate by exploring political practices that enable the integration of diversity in nationally-defined states. Specifically, we investigate the question: if ethnic representation alone is not enough, what alternative/complementary means are there for promoting the issues important to minority groups on the political agenda, that at the same time indicate integration?

Using writings from the field of political philosophy as my guide, I define integration in opposition to unity, acculturation or assimilation. 'Integration' means taking into account different perspectives while elaborating public policies. Following Alain-G. Gagnon (2002: 128), I hold that integration has a twofold goal: *to empower group identities while ensuring common grounds for dialogue.* The now-classic controversy between Lijphart (1977) and Horowitz (1985) presents the two key dimensions of integration nicely. The former puts emphasis on group empowerment, and the latter on cross-ethnic dialogue. What political practices exist that can effectively reconcile these goals? To answer this question, this chapter proposes an intermediate way of understanding and practicing integrative politics. As in Lijphart, I consider the institutional representation of group perspectives to be important – but I also note that such representation may take a plurality of shapes, that are tailor-made. And as in Horowitz, I believe that cross-ethnic interests should be promoted, but with care taken not to eradicate ethnic-based institutions *a priori*. After all, only when all perspectives are represented can a debate on common interests be undertaken (Young 2000). And only through such a debate can group-based institutions adjust and attenuate ethnic-based (hostile) claims within nationalising policies. The argument here is quite normative in nature; I do not present a hypothesis or undertake subsequent systematic demonstration. Instead, this chapter explores the question of integration of difference by looking into political practices dealing with the political representation and participation of minorities in a national state, in order to uncover mechanisms that may help promote this normative aim. In this fashion, I hope to discover indicators that analysts may use to more effectively explore integration – viewed as group empowerment *and* cooperation – in divided societies.

In pursuit of these goals, I take as my analytical locus the case of minorities in Poland, specifically Germans and Belarusians, in the years between the fall of communism in 1989 and the EU accession in 2004. Though often considered a mono-ethnic state, Poland has numerous small minorities, whose relations with the Polish majority are quite sensitive due to the hostilities that have marked their histories as well as the forced homogenisation during the communist period. The resulting tensions, while devoid of the potential to escalate into armed conflict, represent a serious challenge for the state, which defines itself as Polish-national, but still aspires to fulfill European norms. Some degree of integration is required – something that is no small task, given that the Polish nation is proud and determined to assert its recovered sovereignty, a sovereignty that has been violated so many times in history by the neighboring nations that are now partly within the Polish state (the German minority, for instance).

Interwar Poland served as Brubaker's (1996) paradigmatic nationalising state. And while the Second World War and the changing of borders in 1945 shifted the demographic structure of the state, communist Poland espoused homogenising policies. In the period after 1989, the post-communist elites revised policies towards minorities, but still defined the state in national terms. Thus, for our purposes, Poland can be considered a nationalising state, if we work from a rather loose definition of the now-contested term. One of the concept's critics, Kuzio (2001), convincingly argues that *all* civic states have a national core, and that all modern states have been developed via nation-building policies similar to those observed in the post-communist world. In light of this, placing states into either civic or ethnic categories can be somewhat misleading; indeed, it may be more productive to think of the degree to which they demonstrate nationalising policies, and in the context of the period which corresponds simultaneously to state-building. 'The majority of the former European communist states can no longer be defined as "nationalisers". The majority of them are territorial, civic and inclusive democracies (although, clearly, they are not all consolidated), as defined by their willingness to allow integration for all into the societal culture' (Kuzio 2001:

149). Indeed, like the majority of liberal democratic states, they have a 'dominant culture and value system' (Kymlicka 1995) that sometimes makes minorities feel marginalised. Nation-builders must decide which language to make official, what historiography and national values to promote through the media and education system, what national symbols and anthem to endorse, and whether to single out any religious denomination as the state's official one (Kuzio 2001: 148). Polish elites chose to define the state by the core nation's dominant language and culture, and to promote the Polish nation – its culture, traditions, and the Catholic Church – in the public sphere. Thus, it is a national state, and a 'nationalising state'. In light of this, our questions are: to what degree, and how, can ethnic minorities be integrated into such a political sphere? Can a national state be (or become) accommodating?

The chapter is organised as follows. The first section presents a theoretical framework discussing ethnic political representation and its alternatives, as means for promoting the integration of minorities' interests and perspectives. The second section presents different electoral situations, in order to illustrate ethnic parties' presence in the Polish legislature. It demonstrates the limits of electoral engineering as a means of promoting equal representation and the integration of difference. In subsequent sections, two questions are considered: When does convergence occur between the minorities represented via ethnic political parties and the majority group? And, how can non-represented minorities still be empowered to participate in public matters that affect them?

Representation and cooperation – integrating minority interests and perspectives

A common argument in the literature holds that an appropriate way to deal with ethnic tensions is to make institutions more accessible to ethnic groups. This argument follows from Arendt Lijphart's work on consociational democracy – specifically, on the need for proportional ethnic political representation. According to Burg (1996: 129), consociationalism remains the preferred strategy of most analysts of ethnic conflict. Roeder (2004: 214) argues, however, that in less divided societies, 'the power-sharing institutions usually recommended by political scientists to manage the problems of national diversity in democratising states actually made matters worse'. Indeed, consociational democracy requires highly-cohesive subcultures to keep the proportional ethnic vote for the grand coalition to be representative. For this reason, it can have the unintended effect of strengthening differences between groups, and cultivating divisions at the expense of integration between the segments of the society. This observation leads us to realise once more: identities are fluid and require flexible and dynamic institutions (Simonsen 2005).

A less demanding alternative for multicultural societies consists of making political institutions more accessible to minorities by facilitating ethnic political parties' presence in parliaments. The proponents of this view argue that parliamentary representation allows the participation of minorities in the political arena and, as a consequence, offers ethnic organisations incentives to abandon extra-institutional action strategies (Alonso and Ruiz-Rufino 2007). According to other authors, however, excessive significance is attached to the political representation of minorities, while ignoring the issues of education and social and economic equity – matters that are often more important for ethnic groups such as the Roma, for example (Bieber 2004: 240). Unlike Lijphart, Horowitz (1985) argues for the need to reduce the divisions between subcultures through electoral law that would break the ethnic vote. Working from this point of view, the electoral system would provide incentives for cooperation between parties and between subcultures. To be elected, one would have to win electoral support from different segments of society.

Preventing *a priori* ethnic political representation seems rather extreme and conflict-prone, however. After all, it would be unthinkable, for example, to rewrite the electoral rules in Canada to dissolve the separatist party (the Bloc Québécois). Even in civic states that typically promote their core national culture to some degree, as noted above, minorities are challenged by policies and rules that are not culturally neutral – and aspire to recognition and political representation that will give them greater power and visibility. The very act of curbing such activity can be a great source of conflict. In sum, between the extremes of ethnic political representation at any price and the impossibility of having such representation, alternatives for group empowerment should be explored, paying particular attention to whether this empowerment provides grounds for dialogue.

My investigation builds upon the work of two political theorists, Ann Phillips and Marion Iris Young. Phillips (1995) argues that there are two types of representation: 'political ideas' are represented by ideological parties advocating certain values and principles that set policy direction, without necessarily identifying the means; and descriptive representation of a marginalised group, which she labels the 'politics of presence' (also Williams 1998). Responding to the question of 'when does a person feel represented,' Young (2000: 134–7) distinguishes three elements, each an integral part of her reply:

(1) a person feels represented when her *interests* are represented – mainly via interest groups seeking to gain political influence;

(2) a person feels represented when her *opinions* are represented (similar to Phillips's 'ideas'), a role mainly performed by political parties; and

(3) a person feels represented when her *perspectives* are represented.

Young (2000: 136) maintains that it is different perspectives that justify the need for the representation of marginalised groups, such as cultural minorities, 'because differently positioned people have different experience, history, and social knowledge derived from that positioning'.

Ethnic political parties include the three types of representation. They represent minorities' perspectives (views and perceptions formed according to their respective position within the society and throughout the history), their interests (collective rights), and their opinions (in the case of a religious group, for example).

Lijphart's consociational democracy takes into account different perspectives but fixes them in time. In contrast, Horowitz sees the representation of perspectives as undesirable, and instead promotes the convergence of interests of all communities. On the one hand, emphasising the need for political representation along ethnic lines maintains ethnic divides, which might otherwise be fluid (Jesse and Williams 2005; Kaufman 2001; Simonsen 2005; Smith 1999). On the other hand, breaking the ethnic vote from the start can be counter-productive: the ethnic perspective, rather than confining itself to a circumscribed set of conditions, consists of a set of questions, experiences and assumptions from which reasoning can begin (Young 2000: 137). After all, consensus-building connotes a discussion – where perspectives, opinions and interests must be confronted. Only when diverging interpretations, questions and ideas are fully taken into account can parties claim to have reached a consensus. And consensus – being the result of the exposure of and to different perspectives – is a sign of integration (i.e. of group empowerment and cross-ethnic dialogue). Only through the participation of diverse cultural perspectives can the convergence of ethnic interests – and of these same perspectives – be achieved, effecting a political process that transforms the electorate and the ethnic parties. Groups' representatives who remain intensely at odds, and who champion extreme claims, hinder integration (which might itself be a strategy and aim). Robotin and Salat's (2003) comparative study on minority-majority relations in Macedonia, Romania and Slovakia, confirms this line of thought. They find that inter-ethnic peace in Romania and Slovakia was possible thanks to the participation of ethnic parties in non-ethnic politics, while the 2001 conflict in Macedonia broke out because of a lack of dialogue on topics of common interest, despite the Albanian minority's political party representation.

The limits of electoral rules – similar German and Belarusian minorities, different results

Allegedly, the most direct way to make parliaments more accessible to ethnic minorities is to establish proportional electoral regimes. Changing Polish electoral rules from the 1990s show that proportionality does not necessarily lead to the representation of minority ethnic parties. Despite the granting of privileges, most ethnic groups have failed to enter the parliament (Budyta-Budzyńska 2003: 113–34; Łodziński 2003: 91–5). Moreover, as shown by Alonso and Ruiz-Rufino (2007: 238), higher levels of representation in parliament do not automatically lead to a moderation of ethnic conflict – and being in parliament is no guarantee that the minority ethnic parties will really have a say in decision making.

In 1989, ethnic groups were allowed to participate in elections for the first time since the interwar period. Under the majority electoral system – and with no electoral privileges at the time – they received no parliamentary seat. However, a Ukrainian and a Belarusian were elected on the lists of the Citizens' Committee of Solidarity and ZSL (a party loyal to the former Communist Party), respectively. In the 1990 by-elections, following the death of a Senator representing the region of Opole, the German minority proved very successful, however, even though their candidate, Henryk Kroll, did not win the seat (Barska and Michalczyk 1997: 167). The casting of over 84,000 votes (39 per cent) for Kroll resulted in a second round, pitting him against Dorota Simonides of Solidarity – who ultimately was elected, benefitting from the votes of Poles who had mobilised following the 'German surprise' in the first round (Kurcz 1995: 225; Rabagliati 2001: 111–13).

The 1991 elections were proportional, with no thresholds imposed, and minorities obtained a special provision facilitating the registration of their lists on the regional and national levels. Five ethnic electoral committees participated in the campaign: two Germans, two Belarusians and the Bloc of National Minorities representing the Lithuanians, Ukrainians, Slovaks and Czechs. Only two committees succeeded in electing their representatives: seven German deputies, one German senator and a Belarusian from the Orthodox Committee. Despite a relatively high ethnic vote, no other minority won a seat, even among candidates affiliated with Polish majority parties.

In 1993, the electoral law was amended to prevent partisan fragmentation. A threshold of 5 per cent was introduced for parties, and a threshold of 8 per cent was introduced for coalitions. Minorities were exempted from the obligation to reach one of these thresholds, at their discretion. The change of rules elicited modified strategies from ethnic organisations. Territorially-concentrated Germans and Belarusians chose to present candidates only on regional lists. The dispersed minority of Ukrainians chose to present its candidates on non-ethnic lists. The Germans elected four deputies and one senator – and one Ukrainian and one Belarusian were elected from lists of non-ethnic political parties. Under the same electoral rules in 1997, only two German MPs entered parliament, and none entered the senate. Two representatives of the Belarusian minority obtained seats on the SLD list, however (Democratic Left Alliance, successor of the Communist Party). In 2001, the privileges governing the registration of regional lists were set aside. Except for the German minority, the new rules forced minority organisa- tions to participate through lists of non-ethnic political parties. Two German deputies, a Belarusian deputy and a senator on the SLD list, and a Kashubian – Edmund Wittbrodt, who became Minister of Education – were elected. The same electoral system remained in place for the following elections, in which only the German minority gained entry to the legislature with two deputies in 2005 and one in 2007.

Three things become clear from these results. First, the ethnic vote declined steadily in the period after 1991. Minority committees received 180,000 votes in 1991, compared to 120,000 in 1993, 93,500 in 1997 and 55,000 in 2001. This fall-off can be explained in part by changes in the rules governing the electoral strategies of minorities – changes that resulted in a shift from minorities organising themselves in ethnic electoral committees (predominantly the case in 1991) toward participating in nation-wide political parties – leaving only the two German Committees on the electoral arena (in 2001). This situation could also be explained by an evolving situation, wherein over time ethnic issues were dealt with by the state and thus lost salience for voters.

Secondly, it is clear that when looking into ethnic political representation, one should pay attention not only to the ethnic parties, but also to the MPs of the majority parties who identify themselves as members of ethnic minorities. These MPs can present the perspectives and interests of minorities in various forums. For example, the Belarusian, Eugeniusz Czykwin (elected first on the ZSL list, then on the Orthodox Committee list, and then on the SLD list), member of the Parliamentary Commission on Minorities, was an active participant in the development and promotion of the Act on National and Ethnic Minorities and the Regional Language, adopted in 2005 after years of debate. Certain relevant ministerial positions – such as the position of Education Minister occupied by Wittbrodt from the Kashub group – are also highly significant in matters pertaining to the advancement of minority interests and political visibility (note that since 2007 the Polish Prime Minister, Donald Tusk, is also from the Kashub group).

Thirdly, one can observe that geographically-concentrated minorities began to turn to political representation at the local level. Belarusians and Lithuanians failed to garner enough votes across the country, and the representation of Germans in parliament had little strategic importance. All of these groups had significant representation at the municipal level, however, despite the lack of electoral privileges. Since the 1990 local elections, the German community has been represented almost proportionally to their population share in the region. In the Opole region, some 30 per cent of councilors were from the German Committee, and the German minority held the majority in twenty-six municipalities out of sixty-four (Brink 1999: 364). It was much the same for the Lithuanians, a relatively small national minority, but locally concentrated in Puńsk and Sejny. Ukrainians were dispersed and did not enjoy such an alternative representation; as for concentrated Belarusians, their performance was much less impressive.

Like the Germans, Belarusians have typically been concentrated in one area, and are sufficiently numerous to access the legislative seats (Budyta-Budzyńska 2003: 165). After enjoying relative success in 1991, when Czykwin was elected on the list of the Orthodox Committee by an electorate comprised mostly of Belarusians (but also Orthodox Ukrainians and Poles), Belarusians disappeared from the ethnic electoral scene. How can one explain this difference, as compared to the Germans? The same rules do not yield similar results for the two minorities – and in this way demonstrate the de facto limits of electoral engineering for ethnic representation.

Under communism, German cultural expression was severely repressed. In contrast, Belarusians could engage in cultural activities and form a sociocultural organisation, albeit one under state control. Belarusians, mostly poorly-educated peasants whose organisational networks were controlled by the party, have long been under pressure to assimilate (Rabagliati 2001: 358–9). Moreover, the industrialisation led by the communist government in the region incited the migration of Belarusians to the cities, contributing to the weakening of their predominantly rural community culture. Industrialisation had the additional effect of changing the political outlook of the majority of Belarusians, who came to believe that communism contributed to civilising the area (Fleming 2002: 536). The Belarusian identity within Polish society was weakened – and was invariably and gradually replaced by Orthodox religious identification. Thus, unlike the injured and oppressed German minority, Belarusians were more liable to assimilate into the majority Polish nation (Budyta-Budzyńska 2003: 168).

Cumulatively, these observations also suggest another important factor in understanding the Belarusians' electoral defeat. While the Germans are united in the quest for their group survival, the Belarusians are divided. And this is a recipe for defeat in the Polish context; as Rabagliati (2001: 364) remarks, 'the relatively small size of the national minorities in Poland has meant that only if the activists and the population can unite on a common political platform will they be in a strong enough position to achieve their aims'. Three ideologically different Belarusian groups have competed for the same ethnic electorate (Budyta-Budzyńska 2003: 165; Rabagliati 2001: 352): one from the sociocultural organisation closely associated with the communist regime, a second created by young people who oppose this nomenclature, and a third representing Orthodox people, mostly Belarusians but with an inter-ethnic background.

The respective availability of resources and diverging external support constitute additional factors that explain the poor electoral performance of the Belarusian minority relative to that of the German minority. First, in terms of economic development, Poland can be seen as divided between the rich western 'Poland A' and the poor eastern 'Poland B' (Fleming 2002: 536). The German minority lives in the former, and the Belarusian minority in the latter. Secondly, the fall of communism and the opening of the borders allow Polish citizens of German nationality to go to work in Germany. Emerging minority organisations also enjoy a measure of financial support from the German government. Furthermore, the new geopolitical situation and the Polish states' aspirations for joining the European structures both give an unprecedented strength to the German minority. The Belarusian minority, by contrast, does not enjoy such benefits since neighbouring Belarus, being poor and authoritarian, is much less attractive, and less able to sustain its external minorities. Also, since the region inhabited by Belarusians is in more pronounced need of economic improvements than cultural ones, the interests of this community are formulated in economic rather than in ethnic terms (Fleming 2002: 539).

As we have seen in the above, applying the same electoral rules to similar ethnic demographics and geography may not produce similar results, because of differences in these groups' abilities to mobilise – something that is related to the resources available to these groups, as well as to specific past group experiences and affiliations. In light of this, it seems reasonable to assert that electoral engineering does not necessarily ensure the inclusive representation of ethnic parties, and that ethnic political representation is not a measure of integration. Therefore, I turn my attention to the question: what are the indicators of converging ethnic interests and perspectives within ethnic institutional representation, and without?

Integration with ethnic political representation – German minority case

During the 1989 elections in Poland, the political divide was very simple: the communists against 'Solidarity', the latter being a movement comprised of members with different interests and ideas but a common perspective – one that viewed the Soviet system as an oppressor and enemy. The landslide victory of Solidarity led its members to power, but once the common enemy disappeared, the movement quickly split into a variety of parties with diverging ideologies and interests. Synthesising the logic of this situation more generally, I propose that when a majority nation is no longer considered hostile, the political mobilisation of the ethnic minority is likely to lose momentum: either ethnic claims have been taken into account and dealt with satisfactorily, or they can be channelled differently. It is the development of increasingly-converging inter-ethnic perspectives, and of interests and opinions that go beyond ethnic boundaries, that indicate the integration of diversity. After all, as noted by May, Mohood and Squires (2004: 9–10):

> The varying confluence of ethnicity, language, class, religion and gender will result in a full repertoire of social identifications and trajectories among individual members of a particular ethnic group. [...] [These] groups are themselves not solidary groups but have their own broad-based internal divisions.

Thus, despite the mobilisation capacity and relative integrity of the German minority (the only group represented in the legislature), the movement split into two distinct clusters. One group was centered on the Socio-Cultural Association of Germans in Opole (TS-KMN), and the other was based in the adjacent regions of Katowice and Gliwice, under the banner of the Community of German Workers 'Reconciliation and Future' (Budyta-Budzyńska 2003: 181; Fleming 2003: 395). There was also a generational divide in play. As Fleming (2003: 395) notes:

> For the older generation (55+), the political issue was clear – 'We are Germans' – and the demand was to be able to live as Germans in Poland [...]. This allowed the broad spectrum of social positioning to be subsumed within a rather narrow political programme.

Initially, the possibility of going west to well-paid jobs encouraged young people to identify with a German nationality and to support the demands by the minority entrepreneurs. However, these young Polish citizens not only earned much less than their German colleagues, they also felt condescension from their German counterparts. As a result, claiming a German identity lost its appeal and German organisations in Poland became dominated by the elderly. These older Germans, mostly pensioners, had markedly different social and economic interests than the young Germans, whose main priority was job creation (Fleming 2003: 396). Consequently, indifferent to the political projects of ethnic organisations, these young people were more likely to vote for the majority Polish political parties (Berlińska 1999: 232; Rabagliati 2001: 352). The cleavages within the German minority along economic and social lines mark the convergence and development of inter-ethnic perspectives. Petra Meier (2000: 115) rightly emphasises that:

> what should be kept in mind [...] is to what extent guarantees of representation that arise out of a specific need for presence are conceived in absolute terms or whether they are conceived as temporary mechanisms that can be adapted to evolving needs.

The German Minority (MN) electoral programme was initially centered on the issue of the free expression of German identity, but the aforementioned generational factors and the favorable evolution of Polish policies weakened the minority ethnic discourse. Claims for German language classes and for the free cultural expression were fairly well satisfied by the mid-1990s. Thus, the organisation looked for opportunities to redefine itself, by transforming its ethnic objectives into regional ones. The identity link with neighbouring Germany weakened, and was reoriented to the *Heimat*, a geographical space inhabited by a community sharing a common history – in this case, a region located in Poland (Rabagliati 2001: 359 and 366).

At this point the emphasis shifted to cooperation and coexistence with the Poles. Locally, election campaigns began taking up the issue of the reconstruction of infrastructures, the development of private enterprises, aid to farmers, and also environmental concerns (Leciak n.d.; Rabagliati 2001: 115 and 249–50). Their slogans were inclusive: 'We will build Europe here', and 'For our common home'. The easing of ethnic claims and the inclusion of non-ethnic themes in the German minority program ensured the survival of the organisation, and also stood as indicators of the convergence of inter-ethnic regional interests. These were signs of the integration of difference: a dialogue on joint projects and work towards the good of the whole regional community, without erasing ethnic identities.

One of the earliest manifestations of inter-ethnic cooperation and the importance of the German minority leadership in the region came in the form of collective opposition to the 1998 governmental reform on administrative territories. At this time, the government had planned to reduce the number of administrative areas from forty-nine voivodships (first level sub-state administrative units) to twelve – merging, among others, the region of Opole into the region of Katowice. The project was opposed not only by the German minority, but also by the Polish inhabitants of Opole. Indeed, it was argued that the reform would disadvantage Opole by weakening its relative power as a region. It was estimated that in the projected regional Katowickie Parliament, only eight out of fifty seats would remain filled by representatives from Opole, including two theretofore held by the German minority (Rabagliati 2001: 222). A campaign to maintain Opolskie's status as a separate administrative entity was then initiated. The Citizens' Committee for the Defense of Opolszczyzna (OKOOP) was formed, uniting members from different parties, different ethnic groups, youth groups, and veterans' organisations. According to a survey conducted by *Gazeta Wyborcza*, 91.8 per cent of residents of Opolszczyzna opposed the elimination of the region (in Rabagliati 2001: 224). Importantly, the main argument in this struggle focused on the region's particular cultural richness, and the unique co-habitation between ethnic groups.

The Territorial Reform Act was finally adopted in July 1998. It reduced the number of voivodships to sixteen, but left the Opolskie untouched. This victory indicated considerable changes in the inter-ethnic relations in the region. First, unlike the Senate by-elections of 1990 (during which the Polish population of Opole mobilised against the German candidate Henryk Kroll), the events of 1998 signalled inter-ethnic cooperation. Secondly, the Poles in the region came to appreciate the minority presence and even made it the main argument of their 'special case' in the fight against the authorities in Warsaw. Finally, the role of the German minority's leader, Henryk Kroll, as a spokesman for the entire movement, demonstrated the minority organisation's ability to represent not only ethnicity, but *all* of the regional population, the *Heimat* (Rabagliati 2001: 227–8).

In this way, the German minority established itself as a regional organisation. Locally, there are now Poles who support it and who are included within the organisation's ranks. Furthermore, the joint territorial reform victory and the positive results brought about by representatives from the MN on living conditions in the region have made this integration possible. The stable constant vote for the MN in the region was not secured by the maintenance of ethnic questions on the agenda, but rather by its ability to secure financing for regional development (Fleming 2002: 538) and its efforts to build sewers, a water supply, telephone lines, road improvements and job creation (which resulted in a low unemployment rate) (Kurcz 1997: 105). Rabagliati (2001: 362 and 371) concludes that:

> it was crucial for the consolidation of the movement that these were shown to be competent people, carrying out their jobs well and acting for the good of the entire community, and not just for the minority [...]. German minority leaders managed to create a programme that enabled the organisation to break out from purely minority to create a full-scale regional movement.

This transformation from a purely ethnic organisation into an organisation with regional concerns, demonstrates a convergence of interests and the development of inter-ethnic integration.

Integration without ethnic political representation – alternative channels

Because of small numbers, or because of insufficient resources for mobilisation, some minorities may fail to achieve effective ethnic political representation. However, there are other mechanisms they may pursue in the hope of having their issues put on the agenda. Non-represented group interests can be forced on to the political agenda with the aid of third parties, or by pursuing some alternative channels institutionalised from above. While group interests are included within government politics in the first-case scenario, they are not synonymous with integration. Interests may be forced, yet be still perceived as hostile by the majority, i.e. received with no understanding, and no rapprochement of ethnic perspectives, as the 'Białowieża saga' shows. The second form of political practice for non-represented groups (i.e. consultation from above when minorities are called upon to participate in the elaboration of policies affecting them) is, however, an indicator of (a process of) integration since it shows a willingness to learn and understand ethnic perspectives and interests.

The expansion of Białowieża National Park (BPN) in north-eastern Poland represents an example of the de facto empowered Belarusian minority lacking cross-ethnic dialogue. The change of the administration and the extension of the Park affected the local economy and the ethnic demography structure of the region.

First, in 1991, the Nature Conservation Act transferred the responsibility of the BPN from the *powiat* (the administrative territorial entity whose representatives are elected by its inhabitants) to its superintendent, who has no real obligation to listen to the locals. Then, in the mid-1990s, the Polish authorities were faced with a campaign conducted by the World Wildlife Fund to expand the territory of the park (which was the only primary forest in Europe) and to stop any human activity that might endanger it. Consequently, the BPN almost doubled in size in 1996, and the World Conservation Union accorded it Class II status. Simultaneously, since the conservation of the Park was said to be threatened by the surrounding infrastructure (UNESCO/IUCN 2004), railway lines were closed, cutting communication between the municipalities inhabited most by Belarusians, and urban centers (Fleming 2002: 542). The extension of the Park led to a large-scale migration to the cities. The scope of the reforms is qualitatively different for the Poles than it is for the Belarusian minority, which is concentrated in this region. Indeed, migration to cities has threatened the survival of Belarusian's mainly rural culture, increased assimilation pressures, and altered the demographic structure of the entire region. Complaints from the locals seem to go unheard by the Polish government.

The Danish government agency, DANCEE, has taken up these local interests. And thanks to pressures from outside – primarily motivated by an interest in the survival of the BPN, of course – the concerns of Belarusians finally came under consideration. Foreign-aid intervention helped to develop agro-tourism, for instance, which reoriented the regional economy (van der Linden *et al.* 2004). These external pressures also focused on the cultural richness of the region, promoting it as a tourist attraction. This shift allowed local people to organise themselves differently, and reduced the threat of a wholesale change in the ethnic structure of the region, at least insofar as it is perceived by the Belarusian minority. The 'Bialowieża saga', as it is called by Fleming, seemed to take a positive turn when the aforementioned environmental needs were reconciled with the economic development of the local population and with the survival of the Belarusian minority and its culture. In the context of our argument, it should be noted, however, that these are *external* institutions that have come to the rescue of Belarusians. They have empowered the ethnic group without dialogue, and thus without integration within the national state.

Integration means including groups despite their disadvantaged economic or international position. And while there have been a number of cases in which minority perspectives have been ignored, one should also pay attention to positive developments. Various consultation forums have been established in Poland since 1989 (Łodziński 1998): the Parliamentary Commission on National and Ethnic Minorities, Ombudsman, specific departments in the Ministries of Culture and Education, plenipotentiaries at the voivodship level, the Joint Commission of the Government and the National and Ethnic Minorities. While elaborating the Minorities Act (adopted in 2005) and implementing the Education Act of 1991, not only were minority representatives invited to participate in the process, taking place in Warsaw, but also members of the Commission also conducted numerous field trips. These initiatives from above, put forth by Members of Parliament, sought to bring the perspectives of all those concerned into the debate.

Furthermore, media policies – newspaper, radio and television – play an important role in the development of culture and language, and also in the formulation and dissemination of group interests. Put concisely, media are used to influence public opinion (Klimkiewicz 1998; Tereskinas 2002). Officials from the Ministry of Culture have suggested that 'minority periodicals should be specially protected, since they are surrogate cultural institutions, they are centres of community life and they forge the minority's elite' (Berdychowska quoted in Klimkiewicz 1998: 11).

The accessibility of the media to minorities was debated widely between 2002 and 2004 as part of the Parliamentary Commission on Minorities. Three special meetings were held, in addition to meetings focused on other issues, but still dealt with the topic. One meeting focused on minority television and radio (12 February 2002), another on minority press (17 February 2004) and another was devoted to issues dealing with the inclusion of ethnic and national minorities' issues in the public media for Polish listeners (30 October 2003). Representatives of minorities (Tatar, Belorussian, Slovak, Roma, Ukrainian, German, Kashubian, Kazakh, Russian), of the national public media, regional media, government and of the Media Training Center were present. The meetings served as a consultation forum for exchanging ideas and information about the solutions implemented in different regions. There was also discussion concerning funding procedures and problems – all taking place in a sometimes-turbulent atmosphere (marked by insults and accusations). Following these exchanges, the Minorities Act of 2005 introduced, in article 35, an addendum to the 1992 Law on Radio and Television, which ensured the presence of minority representatives on programming boards. The issues raised by minority representatives in this forum also inspired article 18, paragraph 3, which provided minorities an exemption from the obligation to participate in competitions for funding in cases where activities that contribute to the development of their communities are concerned, including the media. This process, along with the subsequent public funding of minority media and the promotion of the official claim for the importance of media in producing and promoting the interests and the formation of public opinion, are signs of inclusive political practices conducive to integration.

In studying the integration of difference, another case worth exploring is the elaboration and implementation of educational policies. Ideally, such policies evolve in a process of trial and error, adjusting over time to meet the on-the-ground needs of the populace and to take stock of particularities on a case-by-case basis. As Sanguin and Puk (1994: 337) have noted, 'an ethnic minority can maintain its existence only if it has an education system and school. [...] For a language to survive and resist in an age of mass communication, it needs a press, radio and TV'. In Poland, issues relating to minority education are dealt with in the 1991 Education Act and its subsequent amendments. In article 13, the Act explicitly states that it is schools' prerogative – if desired – to teach minority languages and their respective histories in public schools in order to ensure the development of their national, ethnic, linguistic and religious identity.

A written statement from parents, addressed to a school's principal, typically serves as the impetus for creating classes/schools for minorities. The principle of stated parental willingness is important, since it does not limit the teaching of a group's mother tongue – or teaching *in* it – to the regions inhabited by that particular minority. The 1992 Decree of the Minister of Education has also provided for:

(1) schools where teaching is conducted in the language of the minority, and where history and geography curricula reflect the history and culture of the minority;

(2) bilingual schools;

(3) Polish schools with additional courses in the language of the minority that are mandatory for students who file the required declaration; and

(4) inter-school classes that include students from different schools, in order to teach the minority language (an important provision in the case of dispersed minorities, or for minorities living in rural areas).

Examinations are conducted in the teaching language and diplomas are issued in both Polish and in the minority language. Textbooks must be approved by the Ministry of Education, which fully funds and distributes them free of charge to students. In sum, different possibilities have been made available that suit the specific needs of each minority.

The process has not been perfect by any means. Indeed, over the past several years, the whole Polish education system has experienced funding problems, and the demands made by minority organisations in this area echo the requests made by Polish schools. Abuse and misuse of funds for education in minority languages has been present to an extent. The most recurrent problem has been the over-reporting of the number of students belonging to minorities, resulting in excessive subsidies. For our purposes, however, it is most important to note that corrective changes and adjustments have been made to the education system in response to specific minority problems – speaking to an atmosphere in which there has been minority incorporation and cross-cultural dialogue.

For example, in 2003, the number of parental statements required to form a minority class at the college level was reduced from fourteen to seven, due to the difficulty of forming such classes, and the fact that students often had to travel long distances to attend them – factors that minorities' representatives successfully brought to the attention of education officials. When school principals received parents' statements at the beginning of each school year, the difference between the schools' budget year (1st September) and the government budget year (1st January) posed difficulties in the calculation and transfer of subsidies (determined by the number of students enrolled). After interventions by minority organisations, the government introduced a system of 'equalising subsidies', thus solving the financial problems faced by these schools. In addition, the government introduced special funding policies for schools with only small numbers of students, which had been in danger of closure since teachers' salaries are typically proportional to the number of students enrolled in a school. In the same vein, in order to address the shortage of teachers in minority languages – as was the case for the Kashubs, for instance – temporary appointments of teachers without university qualifications (who first received the special approval of the Kashubian-Pomeranian Association) were allowed. The same dispensation was given for retired Lemko teachers. School buses for inter-school classes in areas where minority students are spread over a wide area have presented an answer to such challenges – although some practical issues are still being ironed out.

A case-by-case approach has also been adopted in the creation of projects and educational programmes tailored to the particularities of each minority and each region. Such programmes have been developed for the Lithuanian and German minorities. So far, the most controversial programme has been one designed specifically for the Roma, aimed at their inclusion into society and enabling Roma children's literacy. The project has faced difficulties stemming from the reluctance of the Roma, from the fact that there are several Romani dialects, and from the absence of a clear reference area with regard to the teaching of history and geography. The countries of Central Europe present similar challenges. Adjustments have been made to fit the particular context, however: childcare for Roma children has been put in place and Roma group members have been hired as 'education assistants' in order to better allay the misgivings.

The new Joint Commission, which was established by the 2005 Law on Minorities and is involved with the executive and state administrations, is an additional forum, and one that has been claimed by all minorities for some years now. The Commission serves as a body for consultation, with a mandate to assess laws and projects, to locate funding for minorities, to share information about the problems encountered in the implementation of minority provisions, and to propose solutions. The Joint Commission may also intervene in cases of discrimination against members of minorities. Apart from representatives of public administration (Ministries of Public Administration, Culture, Education, Finance, Labour and Social Security, Justice, Home Affairs, Foreign Affairs, the Council of Ministers, the Statistics Bureau and the Council of Remembrance), each *recognised* minority listed in the 2005 Law is able to delegate representatives to the Commission: two each for Belarusians, Lithuanians, Germans, Ukrainians, Lemkos, Roma, Kashubians; and one each for Czechs, Armenians, Russians, Slovaks, Jews, Tatars and Karaims. The Commission is also part of the Ministry of Internal Affairs and Administration (MSWiA). While officials may be replaced after elections when there is a change of government, representatives of minorities typically remain in place, unless their position is revoked by their respective ethnic organisations. In this manner, minorities are co-opted into the executive organs of the state.

The beginnings of this Commission's workings were rather difficult. The minutes from the meeting of the Parliamentary Commission on Minorities and the Joint Commission held on the 24th October 2006 – whose purpose was to discuss problems encountered in the work of the Joint Commission – made these quite clear. Many bitter comments were made during the course of the meeting, and minorities within the Joint Commission have attested to the lack of dialogue with their government colleagues, describing the meetings as monologues (Grzegorz

Kuprianowicz, Ukrainian organisation). They felt as though they were not being treated so much as partners, but as intruders and claimants (Helena Duc-Fajfer, Lemko organisation). Problems with the definition of tangible tasks were also discussed: some minority representatives denounced what they saw as a failure to resolve specific local problems they had brought before the Commission. Others stressed that the Commission should serve as a body handling matters of *principle* rather than cases. Positions, interests and perspectives differed, but the Commission has nevertheless proved integral to politics and policy elaboration. This makes sense, since convergence is by nature a process involving diverging perspectives and interests. The Commission serves as a forum for articulating such difference; the debate on various interpretations, as tumultuous as it may sometimes be, is the only way to possible consensus.

The examples above outline a way to look into group empowerment beyond ethnic political representation. The constant adjustments made with the participation of the minorities in question and the ongoing dialogue are signs of a diversity integration process. It is a dialogue without an endpoint, according to Bernard Crick (2002), as conflicts of interests and values are ever present; its importance rests in how it allows for learning about and understanding the other, and bringing about possible consensus. It is important to note, however, that co-option and consultative spaces are provided only to recognised minorities: Silesians are not invited, although their status and available public arenas are evolving and adjusting in a process of trial and error (Dembinska 2008).

Conclusion

One of the fears of minorities is that their interests and perspectives will not be taken into account in governmental decision-making processes. If the long-term integration of difference within states is desirable to reduce the risk of domination and marginalisation of minority groups, one must consider different mechanisms for including minorities in state policy elaboration. The mere presence of ethnic minorities in the political arena should not be the objective; integration of 'difference', understood as both group empowerment and cross-ethnic dialogue, is called for. While admitting the importance of ethnic parties noted by Lijphart, this chapter upholds that the maintenance of ethnic cleavages prevents the integration of diversity – à la Horowitz. Beside electoral rules facilitating the representation of ethnic parties, which are necessary but not sufficient, it is as well to look for other indicators of integration. It is the convergence, over time, of the majority electorate and members of minority parties that indicates integration. It is the participation of ethnic parties in non-ethnic policies that sustains integration. Integration occurs when intra-ethnic social and economic cleavages emerge and take precedence over ethnic issues; when ethnic party membership and electorate transforms to include majority nation members; and when the ethnic party transforms into a regional party. In the case of non-represented minorities, consultation bodies may well take over the role that would be performed by a formal presence in the legislature. The co-option of minorities in the executive arena, the invitation to participate in the legislative process, and field trips by decision-makers all stand out as signs of a desire to learn, to know, and to understand the perspectives and interests of minorities – and this makes possible tailor-made policies and their subsequent adjustment. Instances of permanent or ad hoc consultations are forums in which differences are expressed. The affirmation of and exposure to differences is a first step toward eventual convergence. Thus, different practices and political mechanisms – other than, and also complementary to, electoral designs – should be explored to ensure the integration of diverging ethnic perspectives and interests. Table 4.1 presents a schematic view of the observations expressed above.

As for the category of nationalising states, it behoves us to reiterate that this is a question of degree and of time. Policies are continuously evolving, and if they indicate greater group empowerment and cross-ethnic dialogue, integration of difference is in the making – something that allows for the prospect of establishing a civic-state, one that is never perfectly neutral, but organised along a core national culture. Integration is a never-ending process aimed at consensus in the context of ever-present conflicts of interests and values. A nationalising state moves on the civic-ethnic spectrum as it accommodates minority interests and integrates their perspectives. The Polish case shows that a national state may be accommodating and that nationalising policies, as proposed by Kuzio, should be considered as transitory, rather than fixed in time and space.

Table 4.1: Integrating differences in a national state – group empowerment and cross-ethnic dialogue

Source of tensions	Risks of nationalising policies	Integrative management	Indicators	Results
Distribution of power: political participation and representation	Majority nation domination	Facilitated ethnic political parties representation through electoral designs ⟶	– intra-ethnic cleavages – non-ethnic issues taken up by ethnic parties – transformation of ethnic parties – multi-ethnic membership	– convergence of group interests and/or perspectives – beyond ethnic presence – participation in decision-making – tailor-made minority policies, subsequently adjustable
	Exclusion and marginalisation of minority groups Lack of resources for ethnic mobilisation and representation	*and* Consultation from above with non-represented minorities ⟶	– institutionalised consultative bodies – exchange with minorities within institutions and on the ground (field trips by decision-makers)	

References

Alonso, S. and Ruiz-Rufino, R. (2007) 'Political representation and ethnic conflict in new democracies', *European Journal of Political Research*, 46: 237–67.

Barska, A. and Michalczyk, T. (1997) 'German minority in Opole Silesia', in M. S. Szczepański (ed.) *Ethnic Minorities and Ethnic Majority: Sociological studies of ethnic relations in Poland*, Katowice: Wydawnictwo Uniwersytetu Śląskiego, pp. 162–80.

Berlińska, D. (1999) *Mniejszość na Śląsku Opolskim w poszukiwaniu tożsomości*, Opole: Państwowy Instytut Naukowy.

Bieber, F. (2004) 'Power sharing as ethnic representation in post-conflict societies', in A. Mungiu-Pippidi and I. Krastev (eds) *Nationalism After Communism*, Budapest and New York: Central European University Press, pp. 231–48.

Brink, J. H. (1999) 'Les Allemands en Pologne', *Politique étrangère*, 64(2): 357–72.

Brubaker, R. (1996) *Nationalism Reframed*, New York: Cambridge University Press.

Budyta-Budzyńska, M. (2003) *Mniejszości narodowe–bogactwo czy problem?* Warsaw: Instytut Studiów Politycznych PAN.

Burg, S. L. (1996) *War or Peace?*, New York: New York University Press.

Crick, B. (2002) *Democracy: A very short introduction*, Oxford: Oxford University Press.

Dembinska, M. (2008) 'Adapting to the changing contexts of choice: nation-building strategies of unrecognised Silesians and Rusyns', *Canadian Journal of Political Science*, 41(3): 915–35.

Fleming, M. (2002) 'The new minority rights regime in Poland', *Nations and Nationalism*, 8(4): 531–48.

— (2003) 'The limits of the German minority project in post-communist Poland', *Nationalities Papers*, 31(4): 391–415.

Gagnon, A.-G. (2002) 'Problems and limits of multiculturalism', in B. Helmbrecht, J. Gebhardt and K. Lösch (eds) *Multiculturalism in Contemporary Societies,* Erlangen: Universitätsbund Erlangen, pp. 125–46.

Horowitz, D. L. (1985) *Ethnic Groups in Conflict*, Berkley: University of California Press.

Jesse, N. G. and Williams, K. P. (2005) *Identity and Institutions*, Albany: State University of New York Press.

Kaufman S. (2001) *Modern Hatreds,* Ithaca: Cornell University Press.

Klimkiewicz, B. (1998) 'Ethnic minorities and media in Poland: democracy without advocacy?', *International Development Studies Network*. Online. Available /www.idsnet.org/Papers/Communications/beata_klimkiewicz. htm (accessed 16 April 2009).

Kurcz, Z. (1995) *Mniejszość niemiecka w Polsce*, Wrocław: Wydawnictwo Uniwersytetu Wrocławskiego.

—   (1997) 'Mniejszość niemiecka w Polsce: geneza, struktury, oczekiwania', in Z. Kurcz (ed.) *Mniejszości narodowe w Polsce*, Wrocław: Wydawnictwo Uniwersytetu Wrocławskiego.

Kuzio, T. (2001) '"Nationalising states" or nation-building? A critical review of the theoretical literature and empirical evidence', *Nations and Nationalism*, 7(2): 135–54.

Kymlicka, W. (1995) 'Misunderstanding nationalism', *Dissent* 42: 130–5.

Leciak, B. (no date) 'German minority NGOs' public influence in Poland', *Institute of Development Studies, Civil Society and Governance (UK)*. Online. Available /www.ids.ac.uk/ids/civsoc/final/poland/pol1.html (accessed 6 December 2006).

Lijphart, A. (1977) *Democracy in Plural Societies*, New Haven: Yale University Press.

Linden, B. van der, Smeenge, H. and Verhart, F. (2004) 'Sustainable forest degeneration in Bialowieza'. Online. Available /www.franknature.nl/reports/SFD_bialowieza_text2.pdf (accessed 25 September 2006).

Łodziński, S. (1998) *Protection of National Minorities in Poland*, Warsaw: Instytut Europy Środkowo-Wschdniej, Uniwersytet Warszawski.

—   (2003) 'Dyskryminacja czy nierówność', in K. Iglicka (ed.) *Integracja czy dyskryminacja?*, Warsaw: Instytut Spraw Publicznych, pp. 21–43.

May, S. *et al.* (eds) (2004) *Ethnicity, Nationalism and Minority Rights*. Cambridge: Cambridge University Press.

Meier, P. (2000) 'From theory to practice and back again', in M. Saward (ed.) *Democratic Innovation*, London and New York: Routledge, pp. 106–16.

O'Flynn, I. and Russell, D. (eds) (2005) *Power Sharing*, London: Pluto Press.

Phillips, A. (1995) *The Politics of Presence*, Oxford: Clarendon Press.

Rabagliati, A. (2001) A Minority Vote: Participation of the German and Belarusian *minorities within the Polish political system 1989–1999*, Cracow: Zakład Wydawniczy 'Nomos'.

Robotin, M. and Salat, L. (eds) (2003) *A New Balance: Democracy and minorities in post-communist Europe*, Budapest: Open Society Institute, LGI Books.

Roeder, P. (2004) 'National self-determination and postcommunist popular sovereignity', in A. Mungiu-Pippidi and I. Krastev (eds) *Nationalism After Communism*, Budapest and New York: Central European University Press, pp. 199–230.

Sanguin, A.-L. and Puk, A. (1994) 'Entre disparition et renaissance', *Espace, populations, sociétés*, 3: 331–39.

Simonsen, S. G. (2005) 'Addressing ethnic divisions in post-conflict institution-building', *Security Dialogue*, 36(3): 297–318.

Smith, A. D. (1999) *Myths and Memories of the Nation*, Oxford: Oxford University Press.

Tereskinas, A. (2002) 'Minority politics, mass media and civil society in Lithuania, Latvia and Poland'. Online. Available /www.policy.hu/tereskinas/Research2002.html (accessed 21 August 2006).

UNESCO/IUCN (2004). *Report on the Joint UNESCO-IUCN Mission to Bialowieza Forest / Belovezhskaya Pushcha Forest, Poland and Republic of Belarus*. UNESCO/IUCN: Paris/Gland.

Williams, M. S. (1998) *Voice, Trust, and Memory: Marginalized groups and the failings of liberal representation*, Princeton, New Jersey: Princeton University Press.

Young, I. M. (2000) *Inclusion and Democracy*, Oxford: Oxford University Press.

chapter five | majority as minority – a comparative case of autochthonous slavs in lithuania and hungarians in slovakia after the second world war

Hanna Vasilevich

Introduction

Twenty years after the collapse of communism, there is still intensive debate over the roles that nationalism and nationalising policies played in the states that bear communist legacies. As a result of communism's demise, a number of new nationalising states emerged in the territories of former multinational states. This transition has done more than simply alter the political regimes of these newly-minted states – shifting then from communism to democracy. It has also strongly impacted on the national minorities of these states, which have found themselves within the new borders, under new nationalising policies and subject to new prevailing attitudes. Although the territorial and political changes in the region of Central and Eastern Europe (CEE) are significant and may even appear conclusive in some regards, Rogers Brubaker (1995: 107) argues that the national question has not been solved by any means in the countries in this region. Rather, he holds the question has been 'reframed', 'recast [...] in a new form'. In support of this notion, he offers an analysis of the national question that describes a triangle of relations between 'national minorities, nationalising states, and external national homelands' (1995: 107). In his view, the relationship between a nationalising state and an external national homeland will always be an oppositional one, due to the nature of the national politics (often assimilative) that govern the situation of the national minority.

Despite its generally acknowledged usefulness, Brubaker's scheme has been criticised and further developed by David J. Smith (2002: 3), who considers the influence of external factors – such as the presence of international organisations (e.g. the European Union, for the CEE region) – to be too important to be omitted. Smith points out how the EU's democratic values have served as a positive influence on the treatment of the minority in Estonia, in order to suggest the existence of a 'quadratic nexus'. Indeed, the example employed by Smith convincingly suggests the positive influence that the EU has in the aforementioned country, through its ability to improve the position of the Russian-speaking minority. In light of this, there is some reason to believe that the EU may be equally effective in guiding matters in its other member states.

Another critique of Brubaker's theory comes from Michele E. Commercio (2010: 19), who argues that Brubaker overestimates the role external homelands play in situations involving co-ethnic national minorities. Commercio's argumentation is based on his analysis of the situation of Russian-speaking minorities in Kyrgyzstan and Latvia, and focuses largely on the relationship between the minority and a nationalising state (minimising the influence of the external national homeland on this dyad) whose national politics may be described as 'ethnic differentiation, rather than ethnic integration' (Commercio 2010: 18). Working in this context, he depicts the development of inter-ethnic relations within a state as a majority-minority relationship, upon which the external homeland has only a limited impact.

Brubaker and his critics have set out with the aim of improving and developing a critical apparatus for systematising the processes that took place in the CEE region after the collapse of communism. However, the question remains: how deeply and universally does this scheme describe the essence of the majority-minority relations in the CEE? The critics' main points deal with the role played by external factors (Commercio's with the overestimation of the external national homeland; Smith's with the introduction of international organisations). Hence, Brubaker's theory and its critics consider the domestic majority-minority relationship while subsequent interpretations of this scheme – and the possible amendments and corrections one may make to it – deal with the roles external forces play in minorities' politics in the CEE region. Consequently, our analysis aims to consider the impact international organisations may have on these states, and to consider the scope of influence that may be exercised by external national homelands.

The role these two external factors play within Brubaker's scheme and the corrections suggested by Smith and Commercio, will be analysed on the basis of two case studies: the autochthonous Slavs (for the purposes of this research, we apply this collective term toward Belarusians and Poles in Lithuania, explaining our reasoning for doing so in the body of the text) of Lithuania, and the ethnic Hungarians of Slovakia. Our reasons for choosing these states and minorities for our analysis are as follows: both of these states have similar communist pasts; both have eagerly developed closer relations with the EU; and both—as a result—ultimately joined the EU, in 2004. Additionally, both of the minorities in question are relatively comparable *vis-à-vis* their size, their territorial compactness, and their historical roots (i.e. they are both autochthonous populations in the territories they currently occupy). In recent years, after their accession to the European Union, the development of the political situation in both countries has proved to be most problematic in cases where the minority issue is closely linked with national narratives. The minority issue has also significantly influenced Slovak-Hungarian and Lithuanian-Polish relations, and led to certain tensions and scandals. The EU's position on these matters allows us to assume that the minority issue largely remains a domestic one, and that the EU's scope of interest is limited. However, the very facts of these problems enable us to conclude that the existing EU and Council of Europe mechanisms do not work properly for Lithuania and Slovakia

– and that the issue depends predominantly on domestic legislation. In the case of Lithuania and its minorities, the issue goes beyond the scope of the EU and the matter of the Europeanisation of Belarus. Indeed, its perspectives on the interstate and inter-ethnic relations in the region come into question. In some sense, the idea of such open and transparent relations could significantly contribute to the implementation of the EU's standards for the protection of minorities: helping the government to overcome possible insecurity and instability and securing support of the Belarusian minority in Lithuania, as well as for the European integration of Belarus.

This chapter analyses the relevance of Brubaker's scheme and the aforementioned critiques in the context of majority-minority relations in Lithuania and Slovakia. And in doing so, it endeavours to provide answers about the role of the EU, and of these external national homelands, in the interethnic politics in Lithuania and Slovakia.

Constructing Lithuania and Slovakia – the older status quo reframed?

Lithuania and Slovakia are relatively small European countries, both in terms of territory and population. Having been parts of larger states (the USSR and Czechoslovakia, respectively) for more than forty-five years after the end of the Second World War, both of these countries enjoyed at least formal autonomy within these states, (one may question, of course, whether republics within the Communist USSR or Czechoslovakia enjoyed real autonomy. However, in both cases, these republics had all of the formal institutions in place required to exercise at least some degree of independence.) After the collapse of the USSR in early 1991 in Lithuania's case, and after the dissolution of Czechoslovakia in 1993 in Slovakia's case, these countries became independent states. Both opted for European and Euro-Atlantic integration, and both joined the European Union and NATO in 2004. Both Lithuania and Slovakia contain similar percentages of their original titular nations, relative to their present overall populations (roughly 84–85 per cent). In both countries, the minorities, the principal subject of this research, are of autochthonous and irredental character. In both cases, the minorities are concentrated in one particular area (Vilnius County, or eastern and east-southern Lithuania, and southern Slovakia respectively). In both cases, these minorities constitute the majority in these specific areas.

Hungarians in Slovakia – minority or dispossessed former masters?

It may be assumed that the Treaty of Trianon was, on the one hand, a national trauma for Hungarians and, on the other hand, a turning point in Hungarian-Slovak inter-ethnic relations. And even though it was ratified in 1920, it has affected Hungarian-Slovak relations to the present day. Prior to the signing of the treaty, 'for more than 1,000 years the Slovaks were under the rule of Magyars (Hungarians) – a rule that became notoriously heavy-handed in the nineteenth century – and was marked by a systematic 'Magyarisation' (Stein 1997: 26).

Without going into too much evaluative detail about the processes and policies of Magyarisation prior to 1918, we can agree with Stein (1997: 26) in his conclusion that, at the moment when the Czechoslovakia was established, 'the Slovak society lacked practically any upper or middle class, intelligentsia, or culture of its own'. Such an idea can also be found in the thesis of Hanák (1994: 39), who argues convincingly that Magyarisation policies had only the slightest effect on the popular strata of the minorities.

While securing its strategic and economic aims, interwar Czechoslovakia obtained large territories populated by ethnic Hungarians, and the Czechoslovak-Hungarian state frontier found itself 'much further south than the Slovak-Hungarian language border' (Lanstyák and Szabómihály 2005: 48). Despite the fact that these territories were attributed to Slovakia, the Slovak lands were governed directly by Prague. Therefore, if one leaves out the fascist Slovak state lead by Jozef Tiso, it can be concluded that, prior to 1945, Slovaks did not have any experience of statehood, relative to Czechs or Hungarians. After the Second World War, when the communist regime in Czechoslovakia was established, Slovakia found itself in a somewhat intermediate position, as it set about trying to obtain equal status with the Czech lands and to accommodate its minorities. Hence, Slovakia may be categorised as a nationalising state.

First, it is important to note that, although Slovakia had its own 'education system, an entrepreneurial class, a press, and a layer of intelligentsia and artists' under the communist regime, the Communist Party 'pursued the ethnic policy of a unitary socialist Czechoslovak nation' (Stein 1997: 27–9). Thus, for Slovaks the main issue during the Prague Spring was to ensure a truly federal Czechoslovak state, where Slovaks would receive rights equal to those enjoyed by Czechs. This was embodied into a slogan: 'Federation first, then democratisation!' (Kusý 1997: 170).

Secondly, one must also note that the minorities in question were predominantly concentrated in Slovakia, and Hungarians constituted the largest one. Minority rights were implemented 'on a federal level by constitutional legislation' (Kusý 1997: 172). Thus, Prague was seen as playing the role of a sort of impartial referee and guarantor in the relations between the Slovak majority and Hungarian and other minorities in Slovakia.

An additional factor worth noting is the relative importance of religion in Slovakia (not only among Slovaks, but also among Hungarians and other minorities). Surveys have shown that religion has played a much more important role in Slovakia, with less than 10 per cent of people identifying as non-religious – something that stands in stark contrast to Bohemia and Moravia, where the percentage of non-identifiers was near 40 per cent (Stein 1997: 29). Thus, despite the fact that there are no significant differences in religious affiliation between the Slovak majority and Hungarian minority in Slovakia (Lanstyák and Szabómihály 2005: 55), religion plays an important factor in the peoples' identities – serving as an additional mobilising factor of both communities.

After the Second World War, when the current (Czecho) Slovak-Hungarian border was settled, the country' relations with their ethnic Hungarian minorities changed significantly. Czechoslovakia, as the name suggests, was a bi-national state (i.e. both Czechs and Slovaks were regarded as titular nations). In the post-war history of Hungarians in Slovakia, from 1945 to 1948, a number of legal acts, known as the Beneš decrees, were implemented to enable deportations and other acts of repression. Particularly important was the Constitutional decree of the President of the Republic on August 2, 1945 (33/1945) concerning the modifi-cation of Czechoslovak citizenship for persons of German and Hungarian ethnic-ity. In Slovakia, its implementation deprived members of the Hungarian minor-ity of their citizenship, as well as most of their basic rights, including the right to a Hungarian education system (Spiesz 2006: 242). By granting Czechoslovak citizenship to those ethnic Hungarians who 'underwent' a 're-Slovakisation', i.e. declared themselves as Slovaks, the Czechoslovak government tried to solve the minority issue in the southern Slovakia (Kirchbaum 1995: 225–6). The intensity of these policies can be seen in the fact that speaking Hungarian in public was almost forbidden (Lanstyák and Szabómihály 2005: 55). This decree was revoked in April 1948 by the Communist Government, allowing the 400,000 or so ethnic Hungarians who remained in the country to rehabilitate their rights. However, the consequences of nearly three years of such discriminatory national policies led to various complications in the foreign relations of Czechoslovakia and its two successor states. Moreover, to the present day 'the application of the principle of collective guilt to the Hungarians (Magyars) remains a stain on the Slovak conscience' (Spiesz 2006: 242). Paradoxically, this remains in line with the view-point promoted by Slovak nationalists, who view Hungarians in Slovakia 'not merely as a minority, but as the dispossessed former masters' (Data Assessment for Hungarians in Slovakia 2006).

As a result of the revocation of this law, the Hungarians who remained in Czechoslovakia had their citizenship, educational, and electoral rights restored. However, the post-war period was still characterised by growing Slovakisation, as seen in how the Slovak language took over more space in the nation's public life and (more importantly) how Slovaks took over leading roles in the governing bodies. Another interesting feature of the situation in Slovakia comes in the form of the symbolic dissemination of elements of Slovak culture and nationalism into the nation's predominantly ethnically-Hungarian areas. This phenomenon can be seen in the renaming of many settlements with Hungarian majorities after pro-found figures of the Slovak national movement. In this manner, Párkány became Štúrovo, Gúta became Kolárovo, Ógyalla became Hurbanovo, and so on. These visible name changes were solely of ideological import – speaking to the domina-tion of the Slavic element over its Hungarian counterpart – and thus validating the (at least partial) achievement of Slovak dominance in the state. Nevertheless, the Data Assessment for Hungarians in Slovakia (2006) demonstrates that, despite such revelations, 'Slovak nationalism was largely kept in check by the strongly centralist Prague regime'.

After the Prague Spring, the changes for the Hungarian minority may be de-scribed as occurring in three contexts: the ethnically-neutral Prague-based cen-tre; the growing assimilation processes in Slovakia; and the Hungarian minority's weak willingness for inclusion.

The positions described above had one common facet worth noting, however. If Prague, as a federal centre, and Bratislava, as a Slovak republican centre, were able to operate as subjects in politics, then the Hungarian minority served as little more than an object. In other words, if Prague held influence over both Bratislava *and* the Hungarian minority, and Bratislava held its own influence over both Prague and the Hungarian minority, then the Hungarian minority itself demonstrated little capacity to make any reciprocal impact – either on the republican or the federal centre. Serving as a sort of judge, Prague had legally secured the status of minorities and influenced the politics of Bratislava, particularly in its adjustment of Slovak nationalism. Bratislava, in contrast, demanded federalism, which 'gave greater scope to Slovak nationalism' after 1968 (Data Assessment for Hungarians in Slovakia 2006). This same source claims that such achievements at the federal level led to the 'progressive Slovakisation of education, elimination of Hungarian place-names from signs, bans on using Hungarian in administrative dealings and in institutions and workplaces, and pressure to Slovakise Hungarian names'. Thus, influenced both by Prague and Bratislava, the Hungarian minority opted not to integrate into the Czechoslovak state system, something that, combined with a lack of sufficient knowledge of Slovak, placed considerable limits on Slovak Hungarians' economic and political participation in the state. This unwillingness can likely be attributed to their historic experience of a significant national trauma, to their severe repression just after the Second World War, and to their general mistrust of the communist system, since it had led to under-representation of the Hungarian minority in the political and social life of Czechoslovakia. This allows us to classify this minority as an *object* of politics, i.e. as an entity influenced by other entities.

Hence, we may conclude that Slovakia's society is rather traditional and conservative in nature. And we may infer, additionally, that the dissolution of Czechoslovakia likely left the Hungarian minority (*vis-à-vis* Slovak majority) without an impartial or neutral guarantor of the status quo. In Slovakia's accession to the European Union, it sought to demonstrate its capacity to serve as an independent arbitrator. The effectiveness of these actions will be examined in the following parts of this chapter.

Autochthonous Slavs in Lithuania – one Lithuania, different meanings

Despite having various competing identities, Poles and Belarusians in Lithuania are often perceived as a unified group, constituting a single cultural mass. As Burant points out, Belarusians have argued that 'the Slavs of the region surrounding Vilnius – identifying themselves as Poles for most of this [the twentieth] century – are really Belarusians who ought to be reunited with the motherland' (Burant 1997: 650). Furthermore, the 'Polonisation of the Vilnius region appears to have been accomplished by the choice of the people themselves and by repression of competing foci of allegiance.' Similarly, Józef Mackiewicz (2002) states that some months of Lithuanian rule in 1939 accomplished what the Polish national policy did not manage to achieve in twenty years. The author further emphasises the fact that 'Polish patriotism swelled into flame and embraced indifferent peasants, mostly Belarusians. People who were officially reported by the Polish authorities as "those without clear ethnic affiliation" and who called themselves locals converted to conscious Poles.' Therefore, Belarusians and Poles of Vilnius County may be regarded as carriers of the same cultural values and customs that, in their turn, are different from those of the Lithuanian majority.

Despite the fact that Lithuania gained independence in 1918, the final design of the country's current territory took shape only in 1939–1945, with the direct participation of the Soviet Union. Simultaneously, during this period, Lithuania itself became a part of the USSR, where it existed as one of fifteen (for a total of sixteen) union republics. Without venturing into any interpretation of Lithuania's presence in the USSR, it can be noted that both the interwar and current Republic of Lithuania were referred to as the Grand Duchy of Lithuania, since it represented itself as a sole continuer of this medieval state (Kaścian 2008 290–7).

Here, one important point should be clarified, since it may help explain some of the tensions and conflicts over the Vilnius area (where Polish and Belarusian minorities are currently concentrated in Lithuania). The importance of the legacy of the Grand Duchy, which both Belarusian and Lithuanian nationalisms claim as their own historical state, can be seen in the significant role it played in the development of the national narratives of both nations.[1] Belarusians and Lithuanians coexisted peacefully in this multinational state along with Jews, Tatars, Ukrainians and other ethnic groups. Another consideration involves the historical connection of the Grand Duchy of Lithuania to Poland, something that dates back to the Union of Kreva, when the Grand Duke Jahajła succeeded to the Polish throne, thereby uniting the Grand Duchy of Lithuania with the Kingdom of Poland. An important legal act is the Union of Lublin Act of 1569, which formed the Commonwealth of Both Nations – the Kingdom of Poland and the Grand Duchy of Lithuania. Hence, from 1569 until 1795, the Kingdom of Poland and the Grand Duchy of Lithuania existed as a Commonweal with one King/Grand Duke, but with different government and legal systems.

Moreover, the words 'Lithuania' and 'Lithuanian' have had different meanings at different moments in time. In the Lithuanian national movement, language has been a major issue, and a 'Lithuanian' is defined as one who speaks the Lithuanian language (Lietuvių kalba) (Eriksonas 2004: 277). In contrast, the very name of Belarus, in its present incarnation, is of relatively recent origin (Zaprudnik 1975: 50). Indeed, as Zaprudnik points out, 'during the second half of the twentieth century, western parts of Belarus and even the region of Minsk were referred as "Litva" [Lithuania]'. Consequently, those Belarusians who inhabited these areas were referred to as 'Litviny' [Lithuanians]. Hence, it is important to point out the

---

1.   In their historical narratives, both Slavic Belarusians and Baltic Lithuanians refer to the medieval Grand Duchy of Lithuania as the cradle of their statehood. These narratives present strictly antipodal views on the formation of this medieval state and the roles of the ancestors of Belarusians and Lithuanians in its creation and development.

contextual divergence between the Grand Duchy of Lithuania and the modern Republic of Lithuania (Snyder 2003: 13–102).

Having described the origins of Poles and Belarusians in Lithuania, as well as the divergence between them, we can also assume that for these people the Lithuanian authorities were considered foreign. Thus, presuming that the identity of each person was a matter of personal choice, we can conclude that their embracement of 'Polishness' may have been a sort of protest – against both Lithuanianisation, and Sovietisation. Such a 'neophyte', when moving between Belarusian and Polish identities, would probably have considered their Belarusian identity to be weaker and more associated with the Soviet regime. Moreover, Belarusians in Soviet Lithuania were banned from their schools and 'the post-war Vilnius University excluded them' (Snyder 2003: 94), while the Lithuanian SSR authorities tolerated secondary education in Polish.

It is worth noting the particular status Lithuania enjoyed compared to other Soviet republics of the European part of the former USSR. Indeed, the post-communist societies in these countries espouse different perceptions of their communist pasts – ones that are exploited differently by different spectra of ruling political elites in these countries. With a small number of exceptions, international scholarship has given only limited attention to comparative analysis of the democratic preconditions of the countries of this region. However, when one considers these nations' experiences under communism in the context of their nationalism or historical narratives, it is clear that they underwent markedly different experiences. Within the federation (USSR, Yugoslavia) different nations had different opportunities to exercise nationalism within the communist society. This possibility later became a crucial element for national mobilisation. An example of such an occurrence was described by Timothy Snyder in his book *The Reconstruction of Nations: Poland, Ukraine, Lithuania, Belarus, 1569–1999* (2003). In it, he demonstrates how Lithuania represents a unique example, noting how the Soviets focused on the personality of a particular Lithuanian SSR leader, Antanas Sniečkus, who, as a veteran of interwar politics, perfectly understood the centrality of Lithuanian nationalism in its society and succeeded in earning support for the national policies of the Lithuanian SSR from the authorities in Moscow. Contrary to the cities of Minsk, Riga and Tallinn, which faced massive pan-Soviet migrant influxes as a result of the subsequent Russification of the capitals, Moscow permitted the Lithuanianisation of Vilnius, and consequently 'under Soviet rule, Lithuanian identity in Vilnius had assimilatory force'. Snyder calls it 'National Communism' and points out its uniqueness in the Soviet Union. Thus, Lithuanian nationalism was never completely eliminated from Lithuanian society under Soviet rule, even though it had been limited to serve the communist needs. Even though the loss of independence in 1940 has long been considered a national trauma in Lithuania (analogous to events in Estonia and Latvia) the linguistic issue and the treatment of minorities never became serious problems for Lithuania. Compared to the cases of Latvia and Estonia, Belarus was affected by Soviet policies to a greater degree – circumstances that influenced its identity and nationalism, and reflected in the policies of the country. As Snyder argues, contrary to the cases of Estonia and Latvia, Belarus was not allowed to have a local-language university. This aspect, combined with other methods of Russification, largely contributed to the subsequent decline in the prestige and use of the Belarusian language in society (indeed, the language's usage is now limited largely to the country's peasants and humanitarian intelligentsia). In this manner, relative prosperity during the Soviet time became a key factor for the Belarusian authorities, who used it to implement policies aimed at the restoration of a scaled-down, Soviet-like system.

This example reveals how important it is to describe the preconditions of the societies in the countries of Central and Eastern Europe before democracy, in order to understand their development and the role of nationalism. Nationalism is *particularly* important, since some of these countries, such as Lithuania, have occupied much more advantageous positions, as a result of the presence of nationalistic forces during communist times. As a result, Lithuania proved better able to overcome the setbacks of communism, relative to other post-Soviet countries (such as Ukraine and, particularly, Belarus) that first had to reconsider the positive image of communism in their societies.

Thus, we may conclude that the Slavic majority in Vilnius County considered the Lithuanian element as foreign, or at least not local. By contrast, one can see how the role of Moscow in the case of the autochthonous Slavs in Lithuania notably differed from the similar position held by Prague in the case of Hungarians in Slovakia. By allowing Lithuanian communists to Lithuanianise the Vilnius County and the city of Vilnius, Moscow limited itself to the role of supervisor of this process (and notably, it did not function as a guarantor or referee for the autochthonous Slavs). Any influence on the part of Minsk or Warsaw on Moscow – and consequently, on communist Vilnius – seemed impossible. The consequences of these policies will be examined below.

Are Slovakia and Lithuania nationalising states?

The nationalising state represents one of the key elements of Brubaker's 'triadic nexus', which is not seriously questioned by Commercio or Smith. This term applies to: 'new or newly reconfigured nationalising states, ethnically heterogeneous yet conceived as nation-states, whose dominant elites promote [...] the language, culture, demographic position, economic flourishing, and political hegemony of the nominally state-bearing nation [...]' (Brubaker 1995: 109).

Within this model, the political elites of a certain country act in such a way as to serve exclusively the interests of the titular nation – notably, to dominate and thus promote its interests in domestic politics, economy and culture. These measures are generally embodied in the country's domestic legislation and in its subsequent interpretation. Within Brubaker's scheme, these endeavours imply the considerable and deliberate alienation of national minorities, leading the latter to resist actual assimilatory policies and processes.

This chapter provides an overview of the nationalising policies in Slovakia and Lithuania in regard to the treatment of the national minorities in these countries. The overview presented above provides the basis for assessing the impact external factors have had on inter-ethnic relations in those countries – an assessment that reveals the limited influence that those external factors (namely external national 'homelands' and international organisations, such as the European Union) seem likely to play in these processes.

Nationalising Slovakia – minorities as subjects of politics or as groups with additional obligations?

As at 2001, the Hungarian minority represented about 9.7 per cent of Slovakia's population, and lived mainly in the southern part of Slovakia, adjacent to Hungary.

The entire post-communist and pre-accession period can be characterised as two-sided. First, Hungarians took the advantage of the chance to establish themselves politically and institutionally in the new democratic system (Topidi 2003: 12). For the first time since the end of the Second World War, Hungarians in Slovakia became a *subject* in political and economic life, as opposed to the object, i.e. they became active in defending their rights and representing themselves as a single entity.

Secondly, the status of ethnic Hungarians in Slovakia did not improve. In describing this matter, several scholars have independently emphasised the mediating role the federal government in Prague had played, noting how its elimination led to the growth of Slovak nationalist rhetoric. Initially, such rhetoric had been connected with the establishment of federalism of Czechoslovakia and, later, with the call for Slovak independence. With the Czechs and the federal government eliminated from the political agenda, Slovak nationalists sought a new target for their patriotic campaigns: 'resident and foreign Hungarians whose political representation is supposed to threaten the new state by requesting minority rights' (Kusý 1997: 172). Such targeting became particularly apparent under Vladimír Mečiar's rule. Severely criticised for his entire political programme – which caused complications in Slovakia's accession to the European Union – Mečiar expressed the opinion in August 1997 that the 'dissatisfaction of Hungarians from Slovakia may be solved by their transfer to Hungary' (Rupnik 2003: 40). While representatives of the Party of the Hungarian Coalition were later included in the ruling coalition led by Mikuláš Dzurinda, in our opinion this did not so much change the status quo as enable Slovakia to achieve its short-term goals regarding accession to the EU. As Rupnik notes, the improvement of the situation was reflected not only in Hungarian-friendly amendments to the language law, *but also* in the Slovak government's attempts to maintain effective regional cooperation with Prague and Budapest, in order to coordinate EU accession activities and strategies (Rupnik 2003: 40).

At this stage it is important to review current Slovak minority protection laws, since this is one of the essential elements of a democratic state. In the Slovak case, the protection of national minorities is regulated by both domestic and international legal acts. The constitution of the Slovak Republic, under article 12, prescribes the inviolability and inalienability of the legally-secured basic rights and liberties of all persons, regardless of language, religion, national or social origin, descent or affiliation to a nation or ethnic group. The same article also provides for citizens' freedom of choice in regard to their right to claim any nationality, and guarantees that no pressure or other assimilatory or discriminatory measures will be exerted on them in this matter. Other articles of the constitution guarantee freedoms of speech, assembly and religion, as well as the right to information and the right to elect and be elected on an equal basis. Special attention should also be paid to article 34, which specifically refers to national minorities and requires individuals' loyalty to the state. This article guarantees citizens who are members of national minorities or minority ethnic groups a number of rights: the right to develop their own culture; the right to disseminate and receive information in their mother tongue; the right to associate in national minority associations; and the right to set up and maintain educational and cultural institutions.

Additionally, the constitution guarantees that minorities have rights to education in their own language, to use their language in dealings with the authorities, and to participate in public policy concerning national minorities and ethnic groups. However, these rights are *dependent* on additional laws, and *on* citizens' ability to master the state language. Such a formulation not only puts the Slovak language in a favoured position relative to the other languages spoken in Slovakia, but also creates room for possible restrictions of the rights cited above. In this matter, the most important passage is one prescribed in part 3 of this article of the constitution. It is formulated as follows:

> The enactment of the rights of citizens belonging to national minorities and ethnic groups that are guaranteed in this Constitution must not be conducive to jeopardising the sovereignty and territorial integrity of the Slovak Republic or to discrimination against its other inhabitants.

Such a formulation reveals a kind of mistrust on the part of the Slovak state towards its ethnic minorities. On the one hand, it *does* allow minorities to create any kind of territorial autonomy they may desire while, on the other hand, it reserves the state's power to impose strict control over their activities.

According to the SR constitution, members of a national minority or ethnic group in the Slovak Republic enjoy certain guarantees – in particular:

- the right (together with other members of their minority or group) to expand their culture;
- the right to broadcast and receive information in their native language; and
- the right to unite in national associations; and the right to establish and maintain educational and cultural institutions.

Further Slovakian national legislation on national minorities is consistent with the provisions of the constitution, and we will focus on the Law of the State Language later in this chapter.

In terms of international law, the most important legal acts binding Slovakia to a duty to protect its national minorities include the Framework Convention for the Protection of National Minorities and the European Charter for Regional or

Minority Languages. Slovakia was one of the first nations to sign the Convention on the 1st February 1995, and after the document's ratification, it entered into force on the 1st February 1998. The Charter was signed on the 20th February 2001 and it entered into force for Slovakia on the 1st January 2002.

As described above, the Slovak constitution has all the necessary attributes to be considered as being in compliance with pre-eminent democratic standards. However, the provision of article 34.3 hints at a certain mistrust of the country's minorities, and practically requires any representative of any minority to express an additional level of loyalty towards the Slovak state, its sovereignty and territorial integrity. In this manner, Slovakia's national legislation secures the nationalising policies that take effect in the country.

Nationalising Lithuania – does international law have any relevance?

Although it is a relatively homogeneous country – with Lithuanians constituting more than 83.4 per cent of the population – Lithuania accommodates about 115 different national minorities, most notably the Poles (6.7 per cent), Russians (6.3 per cent), Belarusians (1.2 per cent), Ukrainians (0.65 per cent) and Jews (0.1 per cent) (The Euromosaic Study). The autochthonous minorities are concentrated in Vilnius County, particularly in the Vilnius/Wilno/Vilnia and Šalčininkai/ Soleczniki/Salečniki communes. An analysis of demographic tendencies *vis-à-vis* the ethnic distribution in Lithuania's population reveals the following tendencies, which came into being after the country attained independence:

- the total population of Lithuania decreased;
- the population in each of the four biggest ethnic groups of Lithuania decreased;
- the percentage of ethnic Lithuanians increased; and
- the percentage of each of the three biggest national minorities decreased.

These tendencies call for an analysis of both the Soviet and present treatment of minorities in Lithuania. While we have already described the political dimension of the Lithuanian SSR's national policies, it is necessary to point out some of the cultural effects that are a result of these measures. The Lithuanian nationality enjoyed an increase in prestige, particularly in Vilnius. The cultural system of the Soviet Lithuania was relatively favourable towards Poles, even though there was a negative trend in the number of pupils enrolled in Polish schools, and even though Russian culture was dominant in the USSR. In contrast, Belarusians were banned from developing schools of their own under the Lithuanian SSR. In light of these facts, one can sense how different national policies were used in Soviet Lithuania towards different minorities. Such experiences created different starting points for the various ethnic groups in an already-independent Lithuania and contributed to the current circumstances of Belarusian and Polish minorities.

However, it is important to address a key legislative issue. The constitution of Lithuania is the principle legal act of the country, and 'any law or other act, which is contrary to the constitution, shall be invalid' (article 7). However, the Lithuanian constitution lacks provisions that specifically apply to the country's national minorities. Those articles concerning national minorities 'are of mostly general, [but] imperative character' (Lopata 1998: 20).

Such 'general' provisions apply to all the citizens of Lithuania, regardless of their ethnicity. And, describing it as 'an integral and directly applicable act', the constitution guarantees equality of persons before the law (article 6). Human rights and freedoms are proclaimed 'innate' (article 18), and it is stated that 'freedom of thought, conscience and religion shall not be restricted' (article 26). Article 29, for its part, provides for the equality of every person before the law, the court, and other state institutions and officials. This article also ensures equality regardless of gender, race, nationality, language, origin, social status, belief, convictions, or views; distinctions based on these criteria should neither give privileges nor cause restrictions, it says.

Article 10 specifies that the territory of Lithuania 'shall be integral and shall not be divided into any State-like formation'. This provision emphasises Lithuania's nature as a unitary state, all of whose parts enjoy same rights and have same obligations. And in addition, it legally excludes any possibility for the establishment of national or territorial autonomous units within the territory of the country. Thus, under the constitution, areas where minorities constitute majorities are specifically precluded from making claims of political autonomy.

There are only two articles in Lithuania's constitution that refer directly to the country's 'ethnic communities'. Article 37 decrees that minorities shall 'foster their language, culture and customs' as well as 'independently manage the affairs of their ethnic culture, education, charity, and mutual assistance' (article 45), which shall also be supported by the state.

Thus, despite the absence of a definition for the term 'ethnic community' in the constitution, we may infer three general criteria for these groups: the presence of specific language, culture and customs. In order to enjoy the rights described in the constitution, however, Lithuanian citizenship is required. Thus, only a Lithuanian citizen may be considered a part of any national minority. And accordingly, national minorities in Lithuania can consist only of Lithuanian citizens.

The international dimension of minority protection in Lithuania can be seen in the country's participation in most of the international conventions related to human rights protection in general and to national minorities' rights in particular. Here we will draw attention to the three conventions set down by the Council of Europe: the *Framework Convention for the Protection of National Minorities*, the *Charter for Minority and Regional Languages*, and the *Charter for Local Governments*.

On the 1st February 1995, Lithuania became one of the first countries to sign the Framework Convention for the Protection of National Minorities. However, it was not ratified until the 23rd March 2000, and subsequently entered into force on 1st July of the same year. Lithuania did not present any reservation, declaration or other communication, which means that the provisions of this document extend to all of the different ethnic groups residing within the territory of the country. In other words, any provision of this Framework Convention shall be applicable in

Lithuania and Lithuanian legislation shall be brought into conformity with the provisions of this document.

The Charter for Minority and Regional Languages presents a completely different situation. Lithuania, 'for some reason' (National minorities in Lithuania and Estonia 2009), neither signed nor ratified this document.[2] Lopata (1998: 18) refers to the Recommendation of the Parliamentary Assembly of the Council of Europe, which stated that, in Lithuania 'the right to use national minority languages is legally secured, in accordance with the principles of the European Charter for Regional or Minority Languages'. However, since this document was never signed, we may assume that the Lithuanian Government has decided that the national legislator will be given the right to determine if the country's domestic legislation should indeed comply with the provisions of the Charter. Therefore, this charter provides no protection for minority languages in Lithuania and domestic law still regulates these issues.

Thus, the constitution establishes Lithuanian as the state language (article 14) and holds, according to the law on state language, all personal names, names of companies and organisations, and names of goods and services provided in Lithuania, must be in the state language. The law on state language also states that 'the Law shall not regulate unofficial communication of the population and the language of events of religious communities as well as persons, belonging to ethnic communities'. This means that minority languages may be used in public life, but their official use is strictly limited. These 'official' limits extend to the way personal names are written on official documents and to a prohibition on street signs in minority languages.

In its Resolution 'On Writing of Names and Family Names in Passports of Citizens of the Republic of Lithuania', the Supreme Council of the Republic of Lithuania declared that 'in passports the names and family names of citizens of the Republic of Lithuania who are of Lithuanian and non-Lithuanian nationality shall be written in Lithuanian letters'. This means that representatives of national minorities are not allowed to officially write their names as the grammar rules of their mother tongues may require.[3] In its ruling, 'On the compliance of the 31st January 1991 Supreme Council of the Republic of Lithuania', the Constitutional Court of Lithuania established the Resolution 'On Writing of Names and Family Names in Passports of Citizens of the Republic of Lithuania' in the 'Constitution of the Republic of Lithuania', and declared that the Resolution was 'in compliance with the Constitution of the Republic of Lithuania'. Under these measures, representatives of ethnic minorities in Lithuania are deprived of the right to write their personal names according to the dictates of their mother tongues (i.e. using letters that do not exist in the Lithuanian alphabet).

---

2. This issue may be interpreted differently by different political groups. It seems that the Lithuanian state would not willingly welcome the existence of the officially multilingual capital region.

3. Compare: Lithuanian Valdemar(as) Tomaševski(s) vs. Polish Waldemar Tomaszewski.

The rules involving street signs in areas that have significant minority popula-tions are rather similar. In February 2009, the Supreme Administrative Court of Lithuania made a decision that street signs in the Vilnius districts where Poles constitute majorities must be written *only* in Lithuanian. Much as in the case of the Constitutional Court's ruling on the writing of personal names, this decision is final and absolute. Thus, despite the fact that the Law on National Minorities declares that languages other than Lithuanian (i.e. minority languages) can be used in the administration, as well as in other offices in regions that are densely populated by the minorities, minority languages have practically been barred from public use. Indeed, they are basically only allowed in private communication between people.

Officially, Lithuania is considered a 'success story' insofar as its handling of minority issues is concerned; it is seen as a Baltic state that avoided scandalous violations of minority rights and other serious conflicts on such issues. Lithuania still has room for improvement on this matter, starting with the fact that it has not yet ratified the Charter for Minority and Regional Languages. Taking such a step would ensure the protection of the rights of minorities at the level set down by the Council of Europe. And it would also bring national legislation in line with the Council of Europe's legal framework on this issue, thereby resolving the issues faced by the Polish (and also the Russian and Belarusian) minorities in the matter of being able to properly write their names on official documents. Such a step would also allow for topographical names to be written in minority languages in regions where minorities constitutes majorities, and would further establish minorities' freedoms to operate educational systems in their respective languages. Again, we must emphasise that Lithuania's first step towards making such progress rests in it signing and ratifying the European Charter for Minority and Regional Languages.

Therefore, we may conclude that despite the fact that minorities have repre-sentatives in Lithuanian political and cultural life, there are serious shortcomings in Lithuanian national legislation. Indeed, the existence of such a situation sug-gests that the minority-related policies in Lithuania may be the result of nationalis-ing processes that occurred in the country.

Minorities' external homelands in Lithuania and Slovakia – active participants or observers?

In the preceding section, we presented evidence that suggests the relevance of Brubaker's thesis on nationalising processes, to the newly-reframed states of Slovakia and Lithuania. His theory has been borne out by our analysis of relevant constitutional legislation, which despite its recognition of minorities, its acknowl-edgement of their cultural needs, and even its formal compliance with the pan-European standards of minority protection, pursues policies that can be viewed as assimilatory. These policies range from delimiting where minority languages can be used to those imposing additional loyalty-related measures upon members of minorities.

In Brubaker's scheme, the role played by external national homelands is seen as one of monitoring the circumstances their co-ethnics experience, and of helping to defend their co-ethnics' interests (Brubaker 1995: 109–10). Thus, within this scheme, the external homelands might act as a potential counterbalance to government discrimination, helping enable higher standards for minority protection in certain nationalising states. Commercio (2008), however, criticises Brubaker for overestimating external homelands' political and economic capacities for effectively protecting their co-ethnics in nationalising states – suggesting that the external component of Brubaker's 'triadic nexus' is not always effective. This section provides an analysis of the role external homelands play in these situations – investigating the rationale of Commercio's critique – in the context of the inter-ethnic policies of Lithuania and Slovakia.

Hungarians in Slovakia – when the past predetermines the contemporary

For the purposes of our analysis, it is important to note that Hungarians exist as an ethnic majority in the southern parts of Slovakia, in the regions directly adjacent to Hungary. Hungary's attempts to reconcile its relations with Slovakia, and the formal settlement of the issue are embodied principally in the bilateral Friendship Treaty. Currently, the Hungarian minority in Slovakia is politically represented, territorially concentrated, and socially mobilised – factors that allow Slovak Hungarians to have representatives not only at the local or national levels, but also at the European level. The Slovak majority uses the Hungarian issue to achieve its political goals and, more importantly, the Hungarian topic remains crucial to Slovak identity. Despite its formal compliance with European standards, the country's current legislation seems to single out minorities by imposing further obligations on them – requiring them to pledge additional loyalty to the Slovak state.

Indeed, the development of bilateral Slovak-Hungarian relations shows that the bilateral Friendship Treaty – signed on the 19th March 1995 in Paris – *should* have served to promote historical reconciliation between the two nations. Under the then-Prime Minister, Gyula Horn, Hungary had called for a 'historic reconciliation' with Slovakia in 1994 (Fowkes 2002: 125). This treaty aimed to establish Hungary as a new democratic power in the eyes of its neighbours – one that had completely abandoned its interwar imperialist policies and any irredentism. Thus, Hungary recognised the territorial integrity of Slovakia and the existing borders between the two nations were declared inviolable. Another important aspect of the treaty was its inclusion of protections for the Slovak minority in Hungary, meaning that the Slovak side would have to implement similar cultural and linguistic rights for citizens of Hungarian ethnicity (Rupnik 2003: 40) and these rights would be in full compliance with international standards of minority protection (Fowkes 2002: 125). Importantly, this 'historic reconciliation' was made 'in Europe's name' and both parties saw it as a way of obtaining future membership of the European Union (Rupnik 2003: 40). Thus, considering the above-mentioned minority-related legislation in Slovakia, we can conclude that formally, it is consistent with the major international and European standards of minority protection. Indeed, the

Hungarian minority has received the main rights and freedoms under the treaty and takes an active part in Slovakia's political life.

This treaty did not change prevailing attitudes towards ethnic Hungarians in the Slovak political establishment, however. This was revealed by the adoption of a new, eight-region administrative system (the *kraje*, in Slovak) from which only two regions (Trnava and Nitra) qualified for minority rights protection (Fowkes 2002: 125). According to Fowkes, the Mečiar government did nothing to implement minority protection provisions, while his ally in the SNS, Jan Slota, declared this act 'unfortunate'. In fact, the inclusion of the Hungarian Coalition Party in the Dziurinda's government proved an effective – although only an intermediate – solution. On the one hand, there still exists no rule or obligation demanding the inclusion of representatives of the Hungarian minority in the ruling coalition in Slovakia; on the other hand, such inclusion has enabled the adoption of higher standards for minority protection, and brought Slovakia into more active regional cooperation (something that was important in the context of the country's EU accession). However, despite this intermediate solution and the country's accession to the EU, anti-Hungarian sentiments did not vanish from Slovak politics and, in fact, remain, one of the central characteristics of Slovak political identity. The formation of the present government coalition – the Fico-Slota-Mečiar triangle – attests to this fact. Furthermore, accession of both countries to the EU did not bring about any real reconciliation; on the contrary, several conflicts have since appeared. It seems unnecessary to quote each conflict involving the Hungarians in Slovakia, but we will briefly name some elements of the nationalising policies pursued by Bratislava, that illustrate the overarching situation. First, when the Hungarian Coalition Party proposed a draft of a new law on moral and financial compensation in 2007 – one that would aid Hungarians who had suffered from the Beneš decrees – all of the ethnic Slovak MPs voted to confirm the validity of the Beneš decrees. Secondly, the new version of the State Language Law, adopted in 2009, dictates that only the Slovak language can be used in most public offices and institutions. Despite various protests from Hungarians in Slovakia, and Hungarian and international intellectuals, the OSCE, via its High Commissioner on National Minorities, Knut Vollebæk, judged that 'the Law does not (and cannot) imply a restriction of the linguistic rights of persons belonging to national minorities' and thus does not breech any of Slovakia's international obligations (EU Inaction on Minority Rights 2009). A third example can be seen in the ban that prohibited the Hungarian president, Laszlo Solyóm, from visiting the city of Komárno/Komárom, on the invitation of the local authorities.

Hence, it is clear that the issue of the Hungarian minority's status in Slovakia goes beyond the scope of the Slovak domestic problem, and beyond the scope of bilateral Slovak-Hungarian relations. It remains bound to the past of both nations and represents an important part of the state's national identities – particularly on the Slovak side. However, Hungary's attempts to act in the service of the Hungarian minority in Slovakia have proved neither effective nor consistent.

Autochthonous Slavs in Lithuania – political pragmatism at the expense of minorities?

This latter sentiment, concerning the efficacy of Hungarian involvement in minority-related issues in Slovakia, also proves true with regard to the relations between Lithuania and the two kin states of the country's autochthonous Slavs. Even though the Lithuanian-Polish relations and particularly Lithuanian-Belarusian relations were initially harsher than those between Slovakia and Hungary, the nature of their current relationship appears to be based on pragmatism.

Despite its concerns over the situation of the Polish minority, Poland was one of the main proponents of Lithuanian independence. Thus, as early as January 1992, during the visit of the then-Polish Minister of Foreign Affairs, Skubiszewski, a joint declaration was issued 'which gave an impulse to the preliminary works concerning the Polish-Lithuanian Friendship and Cooperation Agreement'. The agreement was concluded on the 26th April 1994 (Lopata 1998: 60). While this treaty recognised the territorial integrity of its parties, it also secured the application of 'international principles and standards regarding the prevention of the minority rights, namely Poles in Lithuania and Lithuanians in Poland' (Lopata 1998: 60–1). Thus, the agreement may be viewed as milestone for the present political, military, economic and cultural cooperation between Poland and Lithuania. Consequently, Lithuanian-Polish relations have evolved into a strategic partnership within the context of the Europeanisation of both the states and their integration into the European Union. Thus, as of the 1st May 2004, bilateral relations between Lithuania and Poland became an element of the cooperation within the EU.

This was not the case with Belarus. Lithuania and Belarus had very different backgrounds from the beginning. If one analyses the political relations between them in the first half of the 1990s, one notices that, despite the fact that countries recognised each other as early as 1991, by 1994 their 'bilateral relations were not distinguished by great intensity and some special achievements' (Gricius 1998: 153). Moreover, Belarus was the only one of Lithuania's neighbours that presented formal territorial claims to Lithuania. On February 25, the *New York Times* reported that, at a meeting of the representatives of the European Communities, the then-Foreign Minister of Belarus, Piotr Kraučanka, stated it was necessary to raise the issue of the revision of the Belarusian-Lithuanian border. These claims negatively affected economic relations between the two countries. Thus, we can conclude that, due to its territorial claims to Vilnius County, Belarus 'may prefer to avoid close economic relations with Lithuania' – something that was manifested in the decision to use the Polish port of Gdynia, instead of the nearest Lithuanian port of Klaipeda (Burant 1993: 407, 417). The reactivation of bilateral relations between Belarus and Lithuania is largely connected with the election of Aliakandr Lukašenka as president. Lithuanian officials participated in his inauguration, sending a signal of renewed cooperation – and subsequently, the two countries finalised two important agreements during Lukašenka's visit to Vilnius in early 1995. The Agreement on Cooperation and Good Neighbourliness, as well as the Agreement on the State Border between Lithuania and Belarus, settled the border between the two states for the first time in history, making it legally recognised by both parties, and resolving many difficult territorial issues, some of which reached back to the Soviet era (Gricius 1998: 154). However, it may also be that the personality of the Belarusian president had an impact on the Belarusian minority in Lithuania, and notably on their public organisations, which became bitterly split in their attitudes towards the political regime of Aliaksandr Lukašenka (Daugela no date). Indeed, Daugela provides an eloquent illustration of this: one of the political wings, led by Chviedar Niuńka, passed a resolution welcoming the Lithuanian accession to NATO and the EU, and simultaneously condemned the regime of Aliaksandr Lukašenka. Another group of representatives, led by Leanid Muraška, responded by expressing the sentiment that Niuńka's group was not entitled to speak on behalf of all Lithuanian Belarusians. While relatively unimportant to the Lithuanian majority, this conflict was of considerable importance to the Belarusian minority. Another important development came in the form of Lithuania declaring support for the Belarusian opposition, a development that was not warmly welcomed by Minsk. In light of this situation, it seems that the split in the Belarusian minority is a highly politicised one and may thus become an obstacle to its normal functioning. Moreover, the Belarusian authorities have been somewhat reluctant to intervene in the problems of their ethnic kin in Lithuania – an issue that the Belarusian minority in Lithuania has raised with notable insistence.

Thus, we may conclude that the participation of Poland and Belarus in situations involving their ethnic kin in Lithuania is much more moderate than the corresponding situation of Hungary and its ethnic kin in Slovakia. Moreover, the popular perception of Lithuania as a success story is one based on its accommodation of minorities, but its minorities are almost completely subject to the authority of official Vilnius, thus proving the rationale of Commercio's criticism of Brubaker, i.e. the overestimation of the role external homelands play in such minority-related issues.

Nationalising Slovakia and Lithuania *vis-à-vis* the EU – 'triadic' or 'quadratic' nexus?

One of the major aspects of Brubaker's critical scheme comes in its omission of international organisations as a factor, notably the European Union. According to Smith (2002: 10, 14), the EU's democratic values should have a positive influence on trends in minority treatment in Central and Eastern Europe. And thus, he holds that minority policies in this region should be treated as functioning within a 'quadratic nexus', as opposed to Brubaker's 'triadic' one. Smith's amendments to Brubaker's scheme are based on the EU's positive influence over minority policies in Estonia, which he expects to be equally effective in all of the CEE EU member-states. The following section aims to analyse the role of the EU in inter-ethnic relations in Slovakia and Lithuania, in light of the limited efficacy of external homelands' involvement in minority-related issues in nationalising states, as described above.

The EU and Slovak minority policies – a mediator that keeps the status quo

In the previous section, we showed that the status of the Hungarian minority in Slovakia is more than a domestic issue, even though Hungary's attempts to influence the situation of ethnic Hungarians in Slovakia have largely failed. Since both countries are parties to the European Union, the problem of ethnic Hungarians in Slovakia goes beyond bilateral relations between Slovakia and Hungary. At the same time, the inter-ethnic Slovak-Hungarian relations are largely viewed through the prism of their respective histories, which constitute an important component of these countries' national identities both sides of the border. Despite the active involvement of ethnic Hungarians in the political life in Slovakia, and despite Slovakia's EU accession, substantial anti-Hungarian sentiments persist and remain one of the central issues for Slovak politics.

The inter-ethnic conflicts between the Slovak majority and Hungarian minority in Slovakia, as described above, suggest that the historical legacies of these countries still exert a huge impact on the people of Central Europe. It seems, furthermore, that the issue of 'Europeanisation' has little relevance in this case.

At this point, it is necessary to revisit the bilateral Friendship Treaty between Hungary and Slovakia of 1995, and to analyse its 'European' dimension. As we have mentioned, this treaty was intended to achieve a 'historic reconciliation', and was made 'in Europe's name' (Rupnik 2003: 40). Both parties saw the treaty through the lens of providing for their eventual future membership in the EU. Moreover, the treaty might have been seen as an intermediate solution for the protection of the Hungarian minority in Slovakia, since after the dissolution of Czechoslovakia, Prague stopped acting as a neutral judge in cases of Slovak-Hungarian tensions over the treatment of minorities. Indeed, the Hungarian minority in Slovakia was left basically under the authority of official Bratislava. Furthermore, this treaty should have been a guarantee that minority-related legislation in Slovakia would formally be brought in compliance with the major international and European standards for minority protection. In the light of the EU membership perspective, Brussels should have replaced Prague as a neutral judge in inter-ethnic relations in Slovakia, in cases involving the country's ethnic Hungarian citizens.

The reality, however, is that Brussels usually does not go beyond acting as an observer; on rare occasions, the EU acts as a mediator. During the accession period, the EU's official role was to oversee the 'appeal of membership and the requirements of accession criteria to temper some of the historical legacies in Central and Eastern Europe by attempting to bring the region in line with what it promoted as "European" norms and standards for minority protections' (EU Inaction on Minority Rights 2009). Its present inability to offer any comprehensive solution under the rather high standards of minority protection that exist in the EU suggests that the Central European region's past remains of considerable importance, notably in matters of Slovak-Hungarian relations and the status of Hungarians in Slovakia. While advocating relevant legislation and urging its member states to protect and respect rights of national and ethnic minorities, the European Union does not possess a mechanism for the effective control of the realisation of such aims. The case of Hungarians in Slovakia reveals that the implementation of minority protection standards was more effective during the accession period than it was in the period after membership was granted – something that may be the case in other, similar contexts. This development suggests that the role played by the EU in the case of the Hungarian minority in Slovakia was one that essentially maintained the status quo, while occasionally acting as a mediator. This suggests that, on the one hand, the accession of the nationalising Slovakia to the EU did not have a significant impact on the standards of its treatment of the Hungarian minority. On the other hand, it suggests that the application of the 'quadratic nexus' offered by Smith reveals the limited influence that external factors have over inter-ethnic relations between the Slovak majority and Hungarian minority in Slovakia.

The EU and Lithuanian minority policies – a supervisor but not a referee

Along lines similar to those seen in the case of the Hungarian minority in Slovakia, historical legacies still exert strong influence on inter-ethnic relations in Lithuania; likewise, the role of Europeanisation has little relevance there.

In some sense, bilateral relations between Lithuania and Poland have evolved into a strategic partnership and, after the 1st May 2004, became an element of their cooperation within the European Union. Furthermore, the enhanced protection given to the minority's personal rights points to the presence of higher standards for the general protection of human rights in Lithuania. In the matter of the EU's role in the case of minorities in Lithuania, Brussels has taken over the function that, during the Soviet times, was performed by Moscow – however, acting as a supervisor instead of a referee.

But even though Lithuania is often considered a success story in terms of its accommodation of minorities, one may emerge with a somewhat more complex impression when viewing the country's minority relations within the context of Europeanisation. A relevant quotation can be found in the analysis of European MP Waldemar Tomaszewski, reported by *Delfi.lt* on 2nd March 2010. Tomaszewski stated that Lithuania is presently confronting the possibility of regression, in the matter of the treatment of its minorities. In his view, it may be assumed that some representatives of the Lithuanian ruling elites are in fact combative towards na-tional minorities. Because of this, he suggests that the EU pay more attention to the protection of national and ethnic minorities' rights throughout the Union, and that the EU demand such observance from its member states so that EU practices may serve as positive examples for other states. The lack of strong commitment to these aims on the part of the European Union is perhaps best expressed by claims made by Polish minority members, during Jerzy Buzek's visit to Vilnius in autumn 2009. Indeed, at this time, the representatives of the minorities appealed, 'Europe, protect our rights!'

Thus, similar to the case of Hungarians in Slovakia, the usage of Smith's 'quadratic nexus' confirms the limited capacity external factors have in influencing inter-ethnic relations in Lithuania between the Lithuanian majority and autochthonous Slavic minorities. Moreover, this case also proves that the role of the EU as an external factor in minority-related issues in its member states is also a limited one.

Conclusion

The portraits we have presented here – of the Lithuanian and Slovak societies – are similar in many ways, and the circumstances surrounding the states' autochthonous minorities have much in common. Indeed, in both cases, the autochthonous minorities are territorially concentrated, politically represented, and culturally developed. The mobilisation capacity of the Hungarians in Slovakia seems to be more efficient than that of the Poles and (in particular) the Belarusians in Lithuania. This puts the Slovak Hungarians in a somewhat advantageous position compared to the autochthonous Slavs in Lithuania. Two additional advantages may also be found in Hungary's commitment to its ethnic kin in Slovakia, and in the Slovak government's more efficient legislation. The relative efficacy of the latter may be judged on the basis of the fact that – in contrast – Lithuania has neither signed nor ratified the Charter for Minority and Regional Languages.

In both cases, the past plays a very important role – historical legacies and their attendant narratives have a huge impact on the peoples of Central Europe; in the cases described above, they create an environment in which the issue of 'Europeanisation' has little relevance. This so-called Europeanisation, in both cases discussed here, brought about a more formal protection for individuals than it did for collective groups, such as national minorities. Another obstacle can be seen in the European Union's position on the situation of minorities in these countries. While it has implemented relevant legislation, and urged its member states to protect and respect the rights of national and ethnic minorities, the EU lacks a mechanism to effectively promote the realisation of these aims. In the case of the Hungarian minority in Slovakia, the EU's minority protection standards proved effective during the accession period, but less so after membership had been granted. However, in case of the autochthonous Slavs of Lithuania, such a pattern could not be confirmed. Overall, it can be said that the two case studies presented here suggest that Brubaker's model *does* have its shortcomings – and that it likely overestimates the role that external homelands play in these processes. However, the expansion of his theory to a 'quadratic nexus' – as suggested by Smith – seems to overestimate the role of the EU in minority policies in these countries, since the Europeanisation of national minority policies does not prove equally successful across all EU member states. Finally, these case studies – of the Hungarians in Slovakia and the autochthonous Slavs in Lithuania – prove that the major interactions in inter-ethnic relations in these states occur at the domestic level, between the ethnic minorities and the nationalising states. By contrast, the impact of external factors – that of the external national homelands and international organisations (here, the EU) – is rather limited and thus largely overestimated, even if important in some regards.

Bibliography

Author unknown. 'National minorities in Lithuania and Estonia, 2009', *The Mercator European Research Centre on Multilingualism and Language Learning*, June, no date. Online. Available /www.mercator-research.eu/research-projects/endangered-languages/national-minorities-in-lithuania (accessed 13 May 2011).

'Belarus official lays claim to Lithuanian border lands', 1992. *The New York Times*, 25 February. Online. Available http://query.nytimes.com/gst/fullpage.html?res=9E0CE4DA1E38F936A15751C0A964958260 (accessed 12 May 2011).

Brubaker, R. (1995) 'National minorities, nationalizing states, and external national homelands in the New Europe', *Daedalus*, 124(2): 107–32.

Burant, S. R. (1993) 'International relations in a regional context: Poland and its eastern neighbours Lithuania, Belarus, Ukraine', *Europe-Asia Studies*, 45(3): 395–418.

— (1997) 'Belarus and the "Belarusian irredenta" in Lithuania', *Nationalities Papers*, 25(4): 643–58.

Commercio, M. E. (2010) 'Systems of partial control: ethnic dynamics in post-Soviet Estonia and Latvia, Studies', *Comparative International Development*, 43(1): 81–100.

Data Assessment for Hungarians in Slovakia (2006) *Minorities at Risk Project.* Online. Available /www.cidcm.umd.edu/mar/assessment.asp?groupId=31701 (accessed 13 May 2011).

Daugela, L. (no date) 'Diaspora: belorusy pasportnye i jazykovye' ['Diaspora: Belarusians by passport and by language'], *Birzha Informatsii.* Online. Available /www.gazeta.grodno.by/233/t72.html (accessed 12 May 2011).

Eriksonas, L. (2004) *National Heroes and National Identities*: *Scotland, Norway and Lithuania*, Brussels: PIE Lang.

'EU inaction on minority rights', 2009. *EU Reporter*, 14 September. Online. Available. http://www.eureporter.co.uk/story/eu-inaction-minority-rights (accessed 13 May 2011).

'Evrodeputary: vlasti Belarusi nedalnovidny, situatsiya s Soyuzom poliakov slozhnaya' ['MEPs: Belarusian authorities are blear-eyed, situation of the Union of Poles is difficult'], (2010). *Delfi.lt*, 2 March. Online. Available http://myep.delfi.lt/archive/article.php?id=29537157 (accessed 13 May 2011).

Fowkes, B. (2002) *Ethnicity and Ethnic Conflict in the Post-communist World*, Basingstoke and New York: Palgrave Macmillan.

Gricius, A. (1998) 'Vliyanie "belorusskogo faktora" na vneshniuju politiku Litvy i stabilnost v Baltiyskom regione' ['The impact of the "Belarusian factor" on Lithuania's foreign policy and Baltic region's stability'], in S. Garnet and R. Legvold (eds) *Belarus na pereputje [Belarus at the crossroads]*, Moscow: Carnegie Center, pp. 139–62.

Hanák, P. (1994) 'A national compensation for backwardness', *Studies in East European Thought*, 46(1/2): 33–45.

Kaścian, K. (2008) Die litauische Verfassung und die Auslegung des Begriffs "Volk" in historischer Perspektive, *Osteuropa-Recht*, 54(5): 290–7.

Kirchbaum, S. (1995) *A History of Slovakia: The struggle for survival*, New York: St. Martin's Press.

Kusý, M. (1997) 'The state of human and minority rights in Slovakia', in S. Szomolanyi and J. A. Gould (eds) *Slovakia: Problems of democratic consolidation and the struggle for the rules of the game*, Bratislava: Slovak Political Association, pp. 169–86.

Lanstyák, I. and Szabómihály, G. (2005) 'Hungarian in Slovakia', in A. Fenyvesi (ed.) *Hungarian Language Contact Outside Hungary: Studies on Hungarian as a minority language*, Amsterdam: John Benjamins, pp. 47–88.

Lithuania (no date) *The Euromosaic Study*. Online. Available /ec.europa.eu/education/languages/archive/languages/langmin/euromosaic/lith_en.pdf (accessed 13 May 2011).

Lopata, R. (1998) *National Question in Lithuania: Acculturation, integration or separateness?*, Vilnius: *NATO* Research Fellowship Programme 1996–1998. Online. Available /www.nato.int/acad/fellow/96-98/lopata.pdf (accessed 12 May 2011).

Mackiewicz, J. (2002) *Prawda w oczy nie kole [Home Truths Are Hard to Swallow]*, London: Kontra. Online. Available /www.nasz-czas.lt/Fundacja/Biblioteka/Prawda_w per cent20oczy.html (accessed 13 May 2011).

Rupnik J. (2003) 'Joining Europe together or separately? The implications of the Czecho-Slovak divorce for EU enlargement', in J. Rupnik and J. Zielonka (eds) *The Road to the European Union: The Czech and Slovak Republics*, vol. 1, Manchester: Manchester University Press, pp. 16–50.

Smith, D. J. (2002) 'Framing the national question in Central and Eastern Europe: a quadratic nexus?', *The Global Review of Ethnolopolics*, 2(1): 3–16.

Snyder, T. (2003) *The Reconstruction of Nations: Poland, Ukraine, Lithuania, Belarus, 1569–1999*, New Haven and London: Yale University Press.

Spiesz, A. (2006) *Illustrated Slovak History: A struggle for sovereignty in Central Europe*, Wauconda: Bolchazy-Carducci Publishers.

Stein, E. (*1997) Czecho/Slovakia: Ethnic Conflict, Constitutional Fissure, Negotiated Breakup*, Ann Arbor: University of Michigan Press.

Topidi, K. (2003) 'The limits of EU conditionality: minority rights in Slovakia', *Journal on Ethnopolitics and Minority Issues in Europe*, 2003(1): 1–38

Zaprudnik, J. (1975) 'Belorussia and the Belorussians', in Z. Katz (ed.) *Handbook of Major Soviet Nationalities*, New York: Free Press, pp. 49–71.

chapter six | nationalising states and nationalising policies in southeast asia – malaysia and indonesia

Karolina Prasad

Introduction

This chapter investigates state-minority relations in two post-colonial Southeast-Asian countries, Malaysia and Indonesia, in the context of the concept of 'nationalising states'. On the surface, these countries may look dramatically different in terms of their state ideologies. However, by looking beyond the notion of an Indonesian 'civic nation' and a Malaysian 'ethnic nation', I shall demonstrate how both nations implement similar patterns of policies towards their indigenous and immigrant minorities. At the start of this chapter, I will dissect the nation-building policies of the two states according to Brubaker's framework: identifying the elements of a 'nationalising state' in Malaysian and Indonesian politics. And, in addition to the main focus on the Chinese minority's situation in both states – something that resembles the Jewish diasporas in East and Central European countries before World War II, as has long been recognised (see Chirot and Reid 1997), I will also strive to shed some light the countries' policies towards indigenous ethnic minorities, especially in Malaysia. In this way, I hope to draw clear distinctions between the states' treatment of indigenous and non-indigenous minorities, along the lines described by Brubaker in his discussion of Poland post-World War I (Brubaker 1996: Chapter Four).

Malaysia and Indonesia are two states that came into existence after colonial rule. Neither one was preceded by a pre-colonial state that corresponded in shape and/or content to the newly-created political entity. And in both cases, there was no particular common cultural identity shared by their respective citizens. As is true of most post-colonial states, they emerged with territorial polities whose residents, as a whole could not be equated with any coherent ethno-national group. Therefore, to use Brubaker's concept, they emerged as '*polity-based, nation shaping (or nation-promoting)* nationalisms that aim to nationalise an existing policy' (Brubaker 1996: 79, original emphasis). Malaysia and Indonesia faced this issue in its fullness, and have been striving until today to conceptually design their 'nations' and, even more so, to materialise them.

In the first part of the chapter, Malaysia's and Indonesia's policies will be contrasted against the backdrop of Brubaker's theory of a nationalising state. Over the course of this investigation, I will pay particular attention to the legal and ideological framework of the 'core nation' in each of the two states, along with policies intended to help realise each core nation's interests. In the second part, I will take on the problem of a possible correlation between authoritarianism-democracy dynamics and nationalising policies. In order to shed some light on this correlation, I will proceed to catalogue historic moments that represent shifts towards authoritarianism in both states, and the return to democracy in Indonesia. In the mid- to late 1960s, democracy retreated in both countries; simultaneously, the two states entered a phase in which their nationalisation policies escalated in intensity. The core nations' 'political hegemony' dimension became of extreme concern to the increasingly authoritarian governments. While common sense suggests that a decline in political freedoms is generally likely to result in the curtailing of minority rights, two important questions remain: (1) Could nationalising ideas serve to legitimise a non-democratic government? (2) What role (if any) did disadvantaged minorities play in democratisation processes? Consequently, the question is then: if a regime moves towards the democratic end of the regime scale, does it necessarily result in renouncing nationalising policies? In other words, neither 'democracy' (compare Tilly 2008) nor 'nationalising state' are (0, 1) value phenomena. An ideal democratic regime would stand in stark contradiction to nationalising policies, but a dynamic 'democratising regime' might or might not include ethnic equality initiatives into its liberalising reforms. In the analysis of these two cases, I hope to shed some light on this issue.

Indonesia – after three decades of tight rule under Suharto – became a democracy again in late 1990 and, to date, three consecutive free general elections have been held. Indonesia is now considered a stable democratic state, and I can comfortably draw conclusions based on this status. Malaysia, by contrast, can be said to have only just embarked on the path toward democratisation. To assume that the recent events in Malaysia represent initial steps on the state's way to democracy is undoubtedly a risky endeavour, however. Simply put: what I present here as democratising dynamics may not result in Malaysia's successful democratic transition – and may instead be categorised as a period of weakness in the history of the dominant ruling coalition. Nevertheless, despite its potential to be premature, my analysis of the Malaysian 'democratisation process' may yield high returns, due to the strong ethnic factor present in the events in question.

The focus here, as dictated by the theory that frames this study, is on the excluded minorities: specifically, their positions under their respective non-democratic regimes, and their roles in the struggle against the status quo. The Indonesian case points to the Chinese minority's lack of active participation in democratisation processes and, by contrast, to their enormous but passive role as the catalyst of the events. The Malaysian case is radically different. The role of the Chinese in politics is very prominent due to ethnically-defined political parties, both in the ruling coalition and, in the opposition. Moreover, nationalising policies are in Malaysia at the centre of contention, making it a very compelling case. Therefore, while the conclusions can only be tentative, it is interesting to have a closer look at the dynamics of the process even before seeing its results.

Malaysia and Indonesia as nationalising states

The 'core nations' and state policies towards the minorities

The events of World War II and the Japanese occupation of the Dutch East Indies intensified ongoing debates among local intellectuals about what shape an independent Indonesian state might take. As a result of these debates, Indonesian nationhood was conceived as an umbrella for hundreds of ethnic groups. The Malay language, at that point the lingua franca of the archipelago, was adjusted to accommodate local borrowings from the Dutch, and its standardised version was labelled as *Bahasa Indonesia*, or 'the Indonesian language'. The national language was promptly promoted as a token of unity and as a practical solution for facilitating nation-wide education and media. The Javanese language was never seriously considered as an option for national language (despite being the native language of over 40 per cent of the population, as compared to 3 per cent in case of Malay) to avoid the dissent of Indonesians in the outer islands ('the inner islands' being Java and Madura). The national motto of Indonesia, *Bhinneka Tunggal Ika* (in Old-Javanese, literally 'many yet one', commonly translated as 'unity in diversity'), reflects the idea of Indonesia as a multi-ethnic state.

Islam, professed by the vast majority of Indonesians, was seen as the chief unifying and identity-bolstering factor. However, institutionalising Islam as the national religion was expected to spark discontent among followers of other faiths, whose concentrations in remote eastern parts of Indonesia could have made them prone to secessionist movements (Indrayana 2008: 13–17). As a result, the concept of *Pancasila* was coined, establishing 'belief in One and Only God' as one of the five pillars of *Pancasila* ideology.[1] The state originally recognised five religions based on this 'one-God' principle, namely Islam, Catholicism, Protestantism, Buddhism and Hinduism. Therefore, in its cultural form, Indonesian nationhood was conceptualised as speaking Indonesian, embracing *Pancasila* and following one of the five recognised religions. According to Sukarno, who conceptualised 'Indonesianness' in its early years, the Chinese – and in particular those who were born in Indonesia – were simply one of many *suku* (ethnic groups) that constituted the nation (Suryadinata 2009: 4).

While these facts could be used to portray Indonesia as a 'civic nation', i.e. as 'state of and for all citizens, irrespective of their ethnicity' (Brubaker 1996: 105), a detailed look at the country's citizenship rights and at some administrative actions that targeted the Chinese, does not substantiate such a claim. The Indonesian Constitution of 1945 addressed the question of citizenship thus: 'Citizens are

---

1. According to the Preamble of the Indonesian Constitution of 1945, the principles of *Pancasila* are as follows: '[...] the belief in the One and Only God, just and civilised humanity, the unity of Indonesia, democracy guided by the inner wisdom of deliberations amongst representatives and the realisation of social justice for all of the people of Indonesia' (Indrayana 2008: 420). Notably, in cases of Buddhism and Hinduism, the 'One and Only God' criterion can hardly be applied.

native Indonesian persons and persons of other nations who have acquired legal status as citizens.' Such a division, between 'native Indonesians' and the 'persons of other nations', corresponds to the conceptual distinction that Brubaker describes between an 'imagined "core nation"' and other citizens or residents of the state. This constitutional distinction is also reflected in the terminology used: one the one hand, the constitution describes *pribumi* (native) Indonesians and, on the other, *Warga Negara Indonesia* (literally 'Indonesian citizen', shortened as WNI) – those who are not native and merely hold Indonesian citizenship. The 'persons of other nations' in Indonesia were mostly Chinese, and comprised two important groups. The first, called *peranakan*, were predominantly descendants of early immigrants, and mostly of mixed parenthood. The second, called *totok*, were less numerous but more visible: less assimilated recent immigrants from China, prone to marrying within their own group.[2]

The conditions and procedures for acquiring the citizenship were left to be regulated outside of the constitution; settling this issue, both internally and internationally, took fifteen years. This lengthy period was a result of a claim made by the People's Republic of China's (PRC), which held that all Chinese people living abroad were PRC citizens. Such an interpretation was perceived as problematic since it would have allowed for dual Chinese and Indonesian citizenship if a Chinese person also acquired Indonesian citizenship (dual citizenship was *not* acceptable to the Indonesian Republic or to Communist China at this time). Eventually, in 1954, both parties negotiated a treaty to resolve this sticking point. However, it was not until 1960 that documents were ratified by the parliaments of both countries, opening a formal channel for Indonesian Chinese to become citizens. As a result of this fifteen-year absence of formal regulations, polarisation increased between 'native Indonesians' and the Chinese. And in this manner, both the terminology of the constitutional regulation and the conditional citizenship rights accorded by that regulation, positioned the Chinese outside of the 'core nation'. At the same time, the cultural, religious and linguistic provisions embedded in *Pancasila* were inclusive enough to contain 'Chineseness', indeed, they allowed for a nation that could contain all of the other culturally, religiously and linguistically distinct groups of the Archipelago.

The Indonesian quasi-civic nation represents just one of many possible institutional forms a nationalising state may take. Consideration is now given to the Federation of Malaysia, which presents another example of a nationalising polity. Malaysia's constitutional views of citizenship and the legal positions of ethnic groups were decided *before* the state formally came into existence. Before the British ceased to hold power and granted independence to Malaya (current West Malaysia), a commission was established in 1956 to investigate the preferences of the different 'races' (as Malaysians commonly refer to their different ethnic groups). It sought the views of the Malays, the Chinese and the

---

2.   William Skinner estimated that in 1950, there were about 2.1 million Chinese in Indonesia, roughly 1.5 million (or 70 per cent) of whom were born in Indonesia (Purcell 1965: 383).

Indians on what institutional shape the future independent state should have, particularly with respect to rights and privileges of its different ethnic groups. Based on the findings of the commission, a compromise was struck between the economically-underprivileged Malays and the relatively better-off Chinese and Indians. Although this *quid pro quo* arrangement is not specifically mentioned in the constitution, its terms are reflected in articles 14 to 18, which pertain to citizenship rights, granting them to all residents of Malaya, indiscriminately of race. Furthermore, article 153 guarantees specific privileges for Malays. According to the constitution (article 153), *Yang di-Pertuan Agong* (i.e. the monarch) 'is also obliged to safeguard the special position of the Malays'. This 'special position' is further explained as including reserved positions in public service, the existence of scholarships, and access to permits and licences for the operation of any trade or business that requires such documents. Moreover, symbols of the Federation of Malaya are designed according to Malay traditional symbols. Additionally, the national language (Malay), the religion (Islam)[3] and the position of the sultans and the *Yang di-Pertuan Agong* all reflect the 'Malayness' of the state. Thus, the idea of 'polity of and for the core nation', as conceptualised by Brubaker, is explicitly reflected in the constitution of the Federation of Malaya.

The creation of Malaysia blurred this clear-cut vision of the Malay state, however. When the British decided to withdraw from Singapore, Sarawak, and North Borneo (now called Sabah) in the early 1960s, they proposed a merger of the three entities and the Federation of Malaya to create the Federation of Malaysia.[4] Another commission was established to investigate the preferences of people in the two Bornean states (Sarawak and Sabah), regarding the imminent political transition. And although the commission's findings were inconclusive,[5] the merger was finalised in 1963. At this point, the constitution was amended to accommodate the new members of the Federation. The state was to be called the Federation of Malaysia, or Malaysia (in both Malay and English), and Malay privileges were to be extended to all indigenous peoples in Sarawak and Sabah (most of whom were non-Muslims). The policy established a period of ten years for completing a full transition from the English language (*lingua franca* in the new territories) to Malay. And religious provisions for the state as a whole remained unchanged, despite Muslims being a minority in the new states. Notably, without Sarawak and Sabah, the Singaporean Chinese would have shifted the ethnic composition of the Federation to the advantage of the Chinese; the mathematics of the merger suggests that Sarawak and Sabah were welcomed by the Malays to the Federation in order to counterbalance the demographic 'Chineseness' of Singapore. Many

---

3. The exact wording of article 3 is, 'Islam is the religion of the Federation; but other religions may be practiced in peace and harmony in any part of the Federation.'

4. The Sultanate of Brunei was originally included in the scheme, but opted very early on for its own separate state.

5. Compare with Leigh (1974: Chapter Two). Singapore held a referendum in 1962 in which citizens were asked to state their preferences on the conditions of the merger; being against the merger was not an option in the referendum.

people in Singapore strongly opposed the idea of 'Malay Malaysia', with special privileges for indigenous peoples that excluded the Chinese and Indians, something that is unsurprising, given the proportions of ethnic groups in Singapore (75 per cent Chinese, 15 per cent Malays and 7 per cent Indians). The issue proved unsolvable, however, and after two years of attempts to find a compromise between indigenous and non-indigenous interests, Singapore was expelled from the Federation.

Thus, since 1963, Malaysia has had two institutionalised categories of citizens: the *Bumiputra* ('sons of the soil', or the natives) and the non-*Bumiputra*, i.e. Chinese and Indians. It is important to emphasise, however, that the *Bumiputra* comprise two distinct groups: Muslims (mostly Malays, but also converts from animism, notably the Melanau in Sarawak); and non-Muslims (chiefly the indigenous peoples of Sarawak and Sabah, who are predominantly Christian). Significantly, Malay is defined in the Malaysian constitution (article 160) as having three elements: professing Islam, habitually speaking the Malay language, and following Malay customs, converting from Islam, in this light, means ceasing to be Malay. Similarly, speaking the Malay language, following Malay customs, and converting to Islam are conditions that must be fulfilled by any Malaysian citizen who wishes to become Malay (and enjoy the constitutional reservations accorded to the *Bumiputra*). This definition opens a way to become 'Malay', and in situations where there is a disadvantageous proportion of Malays to non-Malays (as is the case in particular regions), certain incentives can be introduced to attract desirable groups to *become* Malays. In this way, the demographic position and political hegemony of the 'core nation' can be secured – two elements that, according to Brubaker's definition, reflect the nationalising character of a state.

Early on, the strong economic position of the Chinese in Malaysia and Indonesia prompted both states to take action regarding Chinese dominance in trade and manufacture. In 1959, President Sukarno issued a decree (known as Presidential Decree No. 10, or PP 10) that banned alien trade outside of cities and towns across Indonesia. Existing businesses in rural areas were to be moved to the nearest towns; and while, officially, the ban should have only affected alien traders, all of the Chinese were forced to move, since the vast majority of them still had not been able to obtain the necessary documents to prove their Indonesian citizenship. The retail ban resulted in over 100,000 Chinese people leaving Indonesia permanently.[6] In the long run, however, the Indonesian state knew that it needed to provide stability and health for its economy. In fact, President Suharto (who took power in 1965) and his administration actually made a point of confining the Chinese within their traditional entrepreneurial activities, keeping them away from politics, the civil service and armed forces. Chinese businesses expanded, and the president enjoyed the material benefits that grew out of a well-cultivated nexus between Chinese entrepreneurs and the top political players. While Suharto shifted to support more indigenous business in the 1980s, this did not significantly

---

6. For details, see Mackie (1976).

hinder the well-established Chinese tycoons (Suryadinata 2009: 5). However, it is important to note that, while the incidence of poverty among the ethnic Chinese remains low compared to that of the *pribumi*, and while the bulk of *Tionghoa* (as the Chinese are habitually called in Indonesia) constitutes the Indonesian middle class, the economic prominence of a small number of the Chinese created a far-reaching impression that 'all Chinese are rich' – a statement that is too general to be true.

In Malaysia, the reservations granted by the constitution served to promote the core nation's economic welfare (i.e. that of the Malays). K. S. Jomo (1997) suggests that these privileges were introduced in order to eliminate economic disparities between races, and not because of the Malays' status as indigenous to Malaysia. Jomo's conclusion is based on an originally proposed constitutional provision that stipulated that the reservations were to be reviewed after fifteen years, i.e. after enough time had passed for Malays to progress economically, and be more on par with other ethnic groups. The sunset clause was not, however, included in the final text of the constitution (Means 1976: 178), and Malays (and, since 1963, other natives of Malaysia) still enjoy what Brubaker called a 'remedial' or 'compensatory' action: policies that favour the core nation, in order to counterbalance previously existing advantages held, in this case, by the Chinese (and, arguably, the Indians). While reliable and comprehensive data is not available, there are reasons to believe that the aims of this affirmative action (reduction of relative economic disparities) have long since been achieved (Jomo 1997). The fact that these policies have not been repealed would seem to indicate that the justification of the economic privileges they accord is rooted in the 'nativeness' of the Malays, rather than in their relative poverty.

I have described above the privileged positions held by the core nations, relative to immigrant minorities, in Malaysia and Indonesia. In the case of Indonesia, I noted how the government's practical legal solutions to the 'Chinese issue' stood in contradiction to the general ideological framework of the country as conceptualised as a 'civic nation'. In the case of Malaysia, I described how the various disadvantages faced by the Chinese were a consequence of the country's design as an 'ethnic nation', i.e. as a nation of and for Malays.

Assimilation versus dissimilation

During Indonesia's first decade of independence, the Indonesian Chinese community entered into its own discussions of whether assimilation or integration should be the community's preferred modus vivendi. Two institutions were created, each promoting a different one of these two strategies. To articulate the community's interests during the Sino-Indonesian citizenship negotiations, the Chinese elite established an institution called *Badan Permusjawaratan Kewarganegaraan Indonesia* (Consultative Body for Indonesian Citizenship, or the BAPERKI). The BAPERKI championed the idea of citizenship rights irrespective of ethnicity or origin, and promoted the integration of the Chinese into Indonesian society, as opposed to assimilation. The BAPERKI also aimed to contest the upcoming first legislative election in 1955 and provide the Chinese community with coherent representation. During the Sukarno era it was not unusual to see ethnic Chinese in prominent positions in Indonesian politics; several ethnic Chinese figures became members of the cabinet in early 1950s, and three were reappointed as ministers after the violent anti-Chinese attacks in Bandung in 1963 (Wibisono 2009). The BAPERKI also ran schools and opened a higher-education institution that served graduates from Chinese-medium schools who could not enter Indonesian-medium state-run universities. This area of activity was particularly important after 1957, when most Chinese-medium schools were closed. Most of these schools were attended by the *totok* children – but, since these institutions provided a better education, many *peranakan* children, began receiving instruction there as well (Suryadinata 1972). The organisation, which was very popular among the community, had strong leftist inclinations, and many Chinese were believed to sympathise not only with the Communist Party of Indonesia, but with be clandestine supporters of PRC-sponsored communism as well.

A Chinese-oriented state-sponsored organisation, *Lembaga Pembinaan Kesatuan Bangsa* (the Institute for Promotion of National Unity, LPKB) promoted a different route for the Chinese to establish themselves in the Indonesian nation: assimilation. While conversion to Islam represented a sound means of assimilation into Indonesian culture, most Chinese were not attracted to this solution. Even LPKB activists who had opted for expunging the 'Chineseness' from Chinese life in Indonesia – in order to become more Indonesian – opposed conversion, since most of them were of Christian background (Suryadinata 1997: xix). Assimilation also faced a practical challenge in the fact that in a multi-ethnic state there is no clear cultural model to which one can subscribe. Furthermore, as will be shown below, assimilationist goals were soon curbed by state policies. The ideological differences between these two organisations, the BAPERKI and the LPKB, speak not only to the heated, ongoing debates taking place within the Chinese community at this time (more among the *peranakan* than the *totok,* though), they also indicate the intellectual and political freedom that the minority enjoyed within the Indonesian state in the first decade after independence – during which it worked to define itself within the framework of the nationhood promoted by the state. The inclusiveness of the notion of *Pancasila* and the relatively democratic character of the state allowed space for the Chinese to decide upon their own course (with the exception of the trade limitations mentioned above, and the closing of Mandarin-language schools discussed below). At this stage, however, 'Chinese policies', such as they existed, were rather fluid.

A process of 'dissimilation by assimilation' began in 1965 with Suharto's rule; the army general's anti-communist, anti-religious and anti-pluralistic attitude quickly spread throughout the country's ruling elite. The remaining Chinese-medium schools were closed and there were no state-run schools that would accept alien Chinese children; only years later, in 1969, did the government allow the opening of eight privately-sponsored institutions to offer education to these children (Suryadinata 1972: 70). In addition, Suharto's administration forced the assimilation of the *Tionghoa*; made the display of Chinese characters forbidden;

forced ethnic Chinese to change their names into Indonesian-sounding ones; and shut down all Chinese-medium newspapers. Suharto's decree of 1967 banned Chinese cultural, linguistic and religious activities.

Enforced assimilation was not accompanied by the administration's equal treatment of the Chinese. Indeed, Chinese identity documents included a code that indicated their ethnicity, and no administrative procedure could be completed without producing a document called the 'Certificate of Indonesian Citizenship'[7] as well as the documents required from native Indonesians. While they were suppressed culturally, the Chinese *were* allowed to prosper in business; more precisely, their professional activity was confined to the fields of trade and manufacture. The output of Chinese-owned enterprises amounted to a significant share of the Indonesian economic activity overall; without these enterprises, the dynamic economic development of the Suharto era would not have been possible.

These ethnic and professional distinctions contradicted the purpose of assimilation, however. And as a result, while the cultural attributes of 'Chineseness' effectively disappeared from the public sphere, the *Tionghoa* were subjected to strong differentiation, especially when dealing with the administration and seeking employment. Native ethnic groups that did not fit into the mainstream of Indonesian society for whatever reason (e.g. Christians, upland tribes of Borneo, Muslims of more extreme extractions, the Timorese, Acehnese or Papuans) were subjected to straightforward assimilation and discrimination (as opposed to discrimination by neglect or omission), especially in matters concerning nominations for political and administrative positions. The Timorese and Acehnese were intensively 'Indonesianised' in a manner analogous to that experienced by the Belarusians and Ukrainians in post-World War I Poland. The assimilation of the Chinese, by contrast, was seen as both unlikely and undesirable.

In Malaysia, the assimilation of the natives and the dissimilation of the Chinese and Indians happened in a more formalised way. While the indigenous peoples of Borneo were granted *Bumiputra* status, making them equal with Malays, they were denied the language and education privileges enjoyed by the Chinese and Indians. Malay, labelled *Bahasa Malaysia*[8] ('the Malaysian language'), was to replace English in official use in education and the media, in both West Malaysia and in Sarawak and Sabah – although the constitution allowed for some flexibility in the first years of the transition. Education in Mandarin and Tamil-medium schools were not affected by the language provisions. In fact, Chinese schools came to be renowned for the quality of the education they provided. Parents may freely

---

7. The *Surat Bukti Kewarganegaraan Republik Indonesia*, or SBKRI was introduced in 1958 before the citizenship question was resolved by the treaty with China; by any logic, the document should have become redundant and obsolete upon formal acquisition of citizenship and possession of an identity card.

8. Between 1986 and 2007, the official term was once again established as *Bahasa Melayu*. However, in 2007 'the Cabinet felt that reverting to the term Bahasa Malaysia would help inculcate a sense of belonging for all citizens irrespective of race', according to the then-Information Minister (Wong, C. W. and Edwards 2007).

choose a school for their children, and there are cases of Malay children attending Chinese-medium schools. However, the indigenous peoples of Borneo were not given the option of operating their own, vernacular-speaking schools; after the merger, they opted to use English as a language for instruction, believing that this would be the only way to progress quickly and without impediments to their advancement in the society.

At the time of the creation of the Malaysian Federation, Sarawak 'accepted Malay as the national language' (Leigh 1974: 89), but opted for a ten-year clause allowing the use of the English language for official purposes. However, the Malay elites of West Malaysia pressured the Bornean states to introduce Malay as the official language, and as the language of instruction in schools, much sooner in order to boost national unity. It is worth noticing though that Malay speakers constituted a minority in Sarawak and Sabah, while the natives (the Dayaks in Sarawak and the Kadazan-Dusun in Sabah) spoke multiple languages/dialects. In particular, the first Sarawak government took a strong stand on language and education policy. Given that 'the Dayak literacy rate in English (1960) was three times the Dayak literacy rate in Malay' (Leigh 1974: 89), it was thought to be more crucial for the natives to expand their literacy in English, than to switch entirely to Malay (Leigh 1974: 93). Practical reason for this insistence on English education lay in the fact that, at the time, there were no schools in Sarawak teaching in the Malay medium; Mandarin had been the language of instruction in Chinese primary schools, while the rest of the existing primary and secondary schools used English, or some vernacular, in lower primary levels (Milne and Ratnam 1974: 46). These strong arguments fell on deaf ears in Kuala Lumpur.

Similarly, Sarawak[9] opted to extend the services of the British civil service on its territory. As the argument went, Sarawakians (especially the native Dayaks) needed time to train their own administrative staff, and they did not wish to replace the British with West Malaysians (i.e. Muslims). The central government rejected this proposition, arguing that colonial officers should not remain in service in an independent state. As a consequence, it was mostly Malays and Chinese who replaced the British officers, since there were not enough qualified Dayaks to compete for the positions. The non-Muslim natives of Sarawak and Sabah were (and are) apprehensive of the growing influence of the Muslim community. And while religious freedoms are generally upheld, two recent controversies – one over a ban of the use of the word 'Allah' by non-Muslims and another over the government's impounding of Bibles using the word 'Allah' – have provoked public outcry over the government's alleged violation of freedom of religion. Anti-Christian regulations are very controversial, since they alienate the Christian *Bumiputra* communities in Sarawak and Sabah.[10] Similarly, although traditional native law and courts

---

9. The cooperation between the Sabahan and the central governments was much smoother at that crucial time; according to Leigh (1974: 100–1), this was due to the composition of Sabahan cabinet, which included many strong supporters of the nation-wide ruling coalition.

10. Throughout 2010 and 2011, the issues of Christian rights, freedom of speech and the position of

(functioning under the so called *adat* law or traditional) were incorporated into Malaysian legal system, the state has encroached on the traditional social institutions of the indigenous tribes. In the 1970s, for example, village chiefs – hitherto elected or appointed according to each community's particular *adat* stipulations – became civil servants (with meagre pay) and local district officers were granted veto power, allowing them to nullify a village's decision on who should be the chief.

Sabah's astonishingly fast-growing Malay-*Bumiputra* population (Fernandez 2010) presents another case in point. Sabah (with the support of the central government) has been accepting significant numbers of Muslim immigrants from the Philippines. Based on the constitutional definition of a Malay, the moment these immigrants acquire the language they can legitimately claim to be (or, be claimed as) Malays. Often times, having fulfilled this criterion, they find few or no obstacles to acquiring citizenship. Increasingly, large numbers of Dayak and Kadazan-Dusun (Christian) children are also being registered as Malays, without the knowledge or consent of their parents. Striving for a higher proportion of Muslims in Sarawak and Sabah serves multiple purposes: first, it underscores the idea of Malaysia being 'a polity *of* and *for* Malays'; secondly, it helps legitimise Malay dominance in politics at both the central and regional levels; and, thirdly, it maintains and perpetuates this dominance.

In the preceding paragraphs, I endeavoured to contrast Malay and Indonesian policies towards the Chinese with the same countries' policies towards indigenous minorities. In both countries, the Chinese were systematically differentiated from the 'core nation', while 'indigenous' or other groups deemed desirable were continuously assimilated, in order to induce their convergence with the 'core nation'. Cumulatively, the first part of this chapter has presented the elements of Malaysian and Indonesian governmental policies that reflect their status as 'nationalising states'. With these elements established, the next discussion concerns the interweaving dynamics of nationalisation and regime change.

The nationalising chronology – political change and nationalisation

Since their independence, both of the states analysed here have shifted along the 'democracy-authoritarianism' scale significantly, and in different directions. Working in this context, I set out to determine if these regime changes have significantly influenced the nationalising properties of the states. Following Brubaker, I look carefully at the 'political hegemony of the core nation' (Brubaker 1996: 83) with regard to understanding the dynamics between political freedoms and nationalising policies. Given the clearly authoritarian nature of the Suharto regime in Indonesia, and what is, at best, a facade of democracy in Malaysia under the *Barisan Nasional* (The National Front (BN)), it is only natural to examine the

---

Christianity and Islam in Malaysia have been the subject of daily headlines of major newspapers and web portals.

means by which these respective administrations have maintained their hegemony, both in practical terms of power consolidation and in the ideological dimension (which helps control public discourse). I will propose a timeline describing the dynamics of the changing nationalising policies, in order to demonstrate:

- the role of nationalising ideas in legitimising non-democratic practices; and
- how democratisation processes cannot be reconciled with the continuation of nationalising policies.

Within the period under study (from independence to the present), Indonesia has made a full circuit from parliamentary democracy (1950–7) and 'Guided Democracy' (1957–65) to 'undemocracy' (Tilly 2008) (in 1965) and back to democracy (1998) (see Figure 6.1). Malaysia started off with democratic institutions, and these institutions have been upheld to a certain extent. But over the course of time, the independence of the country's media, judiciary, and election commission has declined significantly, and patronage's role in politics has increased tremendously – to the extent that, since 1969, Malaysia has merely been an 'electoral democracy'. I will now analyse three phases in Malaysia's and Indonesia's post-independence history.

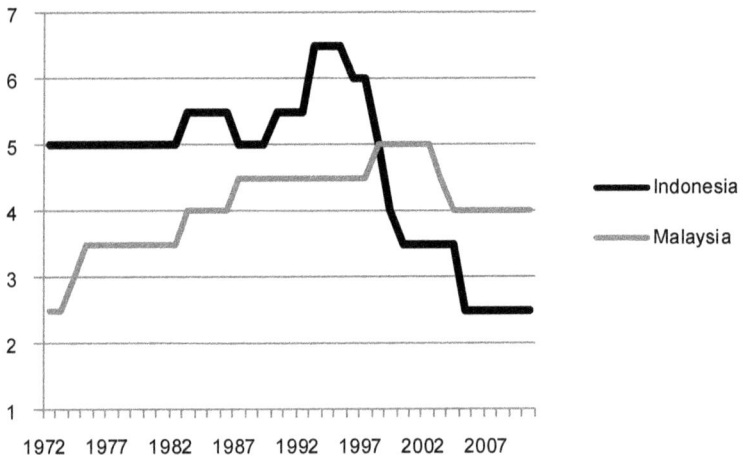

Figure 6.1: Indonesia and Malaysia according to Freedom House report on political freedoms, 1972–2010

Source: Author's compilation based on Freedom House 2011; score 1.0 to 2.5 means 'free'; 3.0 to 5.0, 'partly free'; and 5.5 to 7.0 'not free'.[11]

---

11. The graph is to provide the reader with a general overview and needs to be treated with caution, as in the case of all quantitative aggregate data (compare Munck and Verkuilen 2002). For the period prior to 1972, Polity IV data may be consulted (Polity IV Country Reports 2010).

The first phase covers a time when basic freedoms in both countries were up-held and ethnic categories were still being defined, and in which some space re-mained for their redefinition. The second phase comprises the time in which the two countries fell into the 'undemocratic' category, with both states being scored in Freedom House rankings as 'partly free', and Indonesia entering the 'non-free' category between the years of 1993 and 1997. The third phase covers a time of re-newed democratisation/democracy, commencing at the end of 1990s in Indonesia, and in the early 2000s in Malaysia. In this part of the chapter, I will emphasise le-gitimisation strategies, ethnic distribution of power, and the intensification/decline of nationalising policies during the analysed periods.

Phase I: after independence

Indonesia's parliamentary democratic period lasted from 1949, when the Netherlands recognised the former colony's independence, until 1965, when General Suharto took power. During these 'democratic' years, however, only one election took place (1955) and the composition of the elected parliament (which was decided by a proportional electoral system) had no stable majority. President Sukarno was the first to become overtly impatient with the inefficient assembly, and in 1959 he declared that Indonesia would be governed via 'Guided Democracy' with himself as 'the guide'. The Guided Democracy period proved to be a halfway stop between the democracy of the earlier years, and the 'authoritarianism-proper' that was established under Suharto. Sukarno's legitimisation was rooted in his popularity as a founding father of Indonesia and in the post-independence eupho-ria of the time in which he ruled; the natives' struggle for political hegemony was not yet present in Indonesia's public discourse. The Chinese, for their part, were seen merely as an 'economic issue', not a political one, partly due to the fact that many of them, as aliens, did not have electoral rights.

Throughout the period leading up to 1965, the country's nationalising policies largely took the form of economic and legal regulations. The Chinese (and 'na-tive minorities') presence in politics at different levels was hardly limited, and, as indicated earlier, the *Tionghoa* community took this opportunity to seek out their own modes of coexistence in society and in the polity. The BAPERKI competed in the 1955 elections and won one of the nine seats reserved for the Chinese minor-ity. Likely for want of a better political aegis, many Chinese drifted towards the Communist Party of Indonesia, which was then a popular and influential political force. The Communist Party was an important pillar of Sukarno's rule, and com-peted with the army and Muslim organisations for the leading role in the state. In the eyes of the right wing, the nexus between the President, the Communists, the PRC and the Chinese (which was likely more perceived than real) was slowly becoming unacceptable.

Malaysia's party system and power relations originated during its pre-inde-pendence years, and have changed little over the intervening decades. Since 1957, the composition of the ever-ruling *Barisan Nasional* coalition[12] has reflected a West Malaysian racial composition, while its ideological framework and power distribution have both incorporated something of a trade-off. The three main West Malaysian ethnic groups (the Malays, Chinese and Indians) are represented by their respective parties and, through these parties, also participate in the government. However, the United Malay National Organisation holds unquestionable dominance in the ruling coalition (*Barisan Nasional*) and, consequently, in the cabinet. The Malaysian Chinese Association and Malaysian Indian Congress (as well as several smaller and state-level parties) hold limited-at-best influence on the policy making and overall ideology of both the coalition and the state. The position of prime minister and the head of UMNO are always held by the same person and the prime minister has final say on the seat allocation of component parties, and over the candidates to be fielded in each constituency. Over time the *Barisan Nasional's* component parties had consolidated – and there has been less and less reason to view the *Barisan Nasional* as a coalition. Indeed, the BN is registered as a party (as all of its components are); direct membership to the BN is allowed (i.e. it's not necessary to be a component-party member to be a BN member), and the organisation's ideological and structural coherence all indicate that it is more suitable to see the BN as a single party rather than as a coalition.[13]

Both ideologically and in terms of its practical organisation, the BN has been based on the idea of power-sharing between communal groups. All of its ethnic components are represented in the legislature, and all of them enjoy at least some positions in the executive. The entity's concept of power-sharing rests, rather precariously, on the assumption that each of the ethnic groups supports its respective BN-component party. If one of the communities turns against its communal party, then the BN is in a position to lose its legitimisation as a coalition of all races. The first and most prominent case of such a configuration occurred in the 1969 general election; the Chinese voters in Kuala Lumpur cast more votes for Chinese opposition parties – the Democratic Action Party (DAP) and the Gerakan – than for the MCA. Riots broke out after a triumphant march of Chinese voters, which aggravated local Malays. Over the subsequent weeks, several hundred people were

---

12. The coalition of the three main component parties dates back to pre-independence; until 1973 it was called The Alliance.

13. The BN component parties do not compete against each other (except on an unofficial basis, against the leadership); inter-ethnic electoral competition is rare. Seats are labelled according to the ethnic majority in the constituency and, except for a few mixed seats with no clear majority, candidates who contest them, both from BN and the opposition, tend to be of the same ethnic background as the majority constituents. Therefore, ethnic composition of the parliament remains fixed and communal-based representation is perpetuated. After 1963, Sarawak and Sabah political parties gradually evolved towards the communal-based party system, with the Muslim-component party enjoying the dominant position. The UMNO entered Sabah in 1991 and secured the position of the Muslims, despite strong claims for political dominance from the local Christian Kadazan-Dusun ethnic group. In Sarawak, Muslim interests are represented by a local party *Pesaka Bumiputra Bersatu* (United Traditional *Bumiputra* Party or PBB), which exercises power similar to the UMNO in West Malaysia and Sabah.

killed in the resulting street violence. The parliament was suspended for two years after the riots and debate over the rights and privileges of different ethnic groups was reopened.

The first dozen years of independence presented important tests for the institutions and ethnic policies of Malaysia and Indonesia. During this period, the political freedoms extended to ethnic minorities allowed them to express their political preferences. And while the state imposed economic disadvantages upon the Chinese, it did not attempt to curtail their participation in positions of power in the state. The ideological atmosphere left enough of a margin for minorities to establish their own parties and organisations. But this was soon to change.

Phase II: shift towards authoritarian rule

Suharto came to power in 1965 after a group of army officers attempted to stage a coup; as a top general, he personally commanded the anti-rebellion action, and became the President several months later.[14] The Communist Party of Indonesia was accused of masterminding the coup and was banned, along with several other leftist organisations, including the BAPERKI; many activists were arrested and sentenced to prison for alleged conspiracy against the government. In the months that followed, 500,000 people died in a massive outburst of violence, whose primary target included communists, or persons perceived as such. While many ethnic Chinese people were victims of violence, and some were among the casualties, 'their numbers [as targets of persecution] were disproportionately low' (Coppel 2003: 327). Based on the small size of their population in Indonesia, the Chinese could not have posed a serious political threat. However, exercising their influence via a powerful organisation, e.g. the Communist Party, or a few individuals in top positions, did not seem unimaginable. This kind of reasoning seems to have informed Suharto's attitude towards the minority. The new right-wing administration accused the People's Republic of China of having backed the coup via the Communist Party and in 1967 Suharto broke diplomatic ties with China.

The New Order, as the Suharto rule is known, did involve elections, but there was no actual political competition. Three political parties were allowed to exist, of which only the *Golongan Karya* (or the *Golkar*, 'functional groups') held power. During the thirty-two years of the New Order, political pluralism was curbed and party politics became insignificant. Elections were rigged to ensure the *Golkar*'s continuous power, and the *Golkar* in turn served as a machine for mobilising mass support for Suharto. This setup, according to Suharto, was intended to serve political stability and unity, which were also secured, in any case, by the strong position of the military, both in politics and in administration. Public discourse on inter-ethnic, religious and race issues (referred to as SARA issues) was forbidden

---

14. For a detailed account of these events, including evidence against the official version of the coup, see Anderson and McVey (1971). According to the authors, the Communist Party of Indonesia had no involvement in the coup.

beginning in the early 1970s and *Pancasila* was deployed with increased force to fill the void of discussion. The ethnic Chinese disappeared from politics. Indeed, the only ethnic Chinese minister ever nominated joined the final Suharto cabinet, and served for only two months (Wibisono 2009).

This intensification of nationalising policies was made possible by Suharto's ability to penetrate the society he governed; indeed, his *Golkar* succeeded in reaching all corners of the country and in absorbing people of all walks of life. State institutions, agencies and organisations were invariably committed to serve the goals of the New Order, one of which was to eliminate the Chinese from the public sphere. This community was stigmatised by its earlier ties to an outlawed organisation, the Communist Party. At the same time, an omnipresent state ideology eliminated alternative discourses of 'Chineseness' or, for that matter, of 'Indonesianness'. The alleged coup of 1965 and the subsequent period of political and social instability legitimised the government, which had invented itself as the guardian of peace and stability. And the above-mentioned SARA topics were deemed too seditious to be open to public debate, since inter-racial relations were implied to be a source of social unrest. As argued above, the Chinese now became a special category of citizens due to a combination of assimilationist and differentialist policies. Having already been excluded from the 'native' category, they could hardly dream of striving for public positions, which were only available through the *Golkar* and the army machinery – two institutions with strong nationalist (and nationalising) backgrounds.

In Malaysia, further efforts were made to guarantee Malays their privileged position, as a consequence of the May 1969 elections and riots. The constitutional reservations were now extended, in the form of the nation's New Economic Policy (NEP). Under these measures, a quota was established for Malays and other *Bumiputra* for university admissions, and a goal was set to have 30 per cent the country's equity capital in Malay hands by 1990. Government contracts were to be granted only to *Bumiputra*-owned companies. The main ideologue of the NEP – the Prime Minister of Malaysia between 1981 and 2003, Mahathir Mohammed – did not use euphemisms when explaining the principle of the NEP: 'The only thing to do is to admit that in giving the Malays their place in the sun, there must be denial for some non-Malays. Some non-Malays will have to be sacrificed in order to bring the Malays up' (Khoo 2004: 6).

Furthermore, the constitution was amended in 1971 to impose restrictions on freedom of speech; the constitutional articles 152, 153 and 181 (*Bumiputra* privileges) were deemed off-limits for public discourse. And so were religion and language matters. Open questioning of inter-ethnic, linguistic and religious regulations came to be considered seditious, and punishable under the Sedition Act (originally imposed by the British in 1948; if it were not for the 1971 amendment, the Act would be in conflict with constitutionally-guaranteed freedom of speech). Arrests under the Sedition Act were and remain frequent, and it is safe to assume that the Act imposes widespread self-censorship.

In the years after 1969, the *Barisan Nasional* monopolised public discourse on inter-ethnic relations. The propaganda, which was very effective due to the government's tight control of the mass media, emphasised the BN's role as the sole safeguard against ethnic tensions. In early 1970s, both the Gerakan party and Sarawak United People's Party[15] – two Chinese-based organisations that had previously been in the opposition – joined the BN; as a result, the number of alternative voices in Malaysian politics declined significantly. After this point, unity and harmony were attributed only to the BN's power-sharing apparatus, while (according to the BN logic) any party standing in opposition to the status quo presented a threat to the peaceful coexistence of ethnic and religious groups. Thus, in the government-controlled media, the Pan-Malaysian Islamic Party (the PAS, an opposition party) has often been presented to Chinese voters as one that will forbid eating pork, drinking alcohol and gambling, and even introduce *sharia* law. Similar antagonising rhetoric is used to scare the Muslims: BN-sponsored media and BN electoral campaigns warn them that a win for the Chinese party will affect the position of Islam in Malaysia.

The UMNO, as a Muslim party, has always been involved in a competitive outbidding with the PAS. During the Mahathir's reign (1981–2003), the outbidding became very prominent, revealing how difficult it was for the UMNO to be a partner in a multi-ethnic coalition while also remaining attractive to more traditional Muslims. The events of September 2001 shed some light on the immense contradictions inherent in the ideas embedded in this nationalising state, and in the power-sharing scheme that the *Barisan Nasional* tries to maintain in Malaysia. The PAS – at the time the strongest opposition party in the parliament – promoted policies that would have resulted in Malaysia becoming an Islamic state. In response to the PAS' propositions, Prime Minister Mahathir, 'then made a calculated move to steal the PAS's thunder and bait it toward extremism by trumpeting his claim that there was no need to build an Islamic state, since Malaysia *already* had become one, thanks to him' (Wong, C. H. and Chin 2009: 73). This statement was mere rhetoric, since Malaysia could in no way be categorised as an Islamic state. Still, it reflects the then-prime minister's confidence in his ability to ignore the UMNO's coalition partners and to make a statement they would never corroborate. In general, the Chinese and Indian components of the *Barisan Nasional* are very obedient partners and hardly represent the interests of their respective communities; the well-being of Malays' (or what is understood by the UMNO as such) is, in any case, a priority.

The religious disposition of the UMNO presents a challenge for its coalition partners in much the same way that the PAS's Islamic ambitions represent a challenge for *its* allies. The PAS has the longest record of denying the BN rule in individual state governments – most notably those of Kelantan and Terengganu – and most of its support comes from rural conservative Malay areas. The party criticises the BN (specifically the UMNO) for not being Islamic enough, and denounces the BN's policies for not benefiting poor Malays. The original agenda of the PAS – to

---

15. Sarawak United People's Party (SUPP) was not only in opposition to the BN, but also to the merger with Malaya in the first place; compare Leigh 1974.

turn Malaysia into an Islamic state – put them in opposition to the Democratic Action Party and the *Parti Keadilan Rakyat* (People's Justice Party, PKR), the latter having ambitions to be the first truly multi-ethnic party in Malaysia. Despite these programmatic differences, the three opposition parties (the DAP, PKR and PAS) came to an understanding before the general elections of 2008, which they entered into as a coalition (called *Pakatan Rakyat*, or People's Pact) – meaning they did not field candidates against each other. Subsequently, the PAS dropped the Islamic state element from its campaign. Nevertheless, the PAS's Islamic inclinations make the *Pakatan Rakyat* vulnerable to similar contradictions as the BN: the Islamic agenda is ultimately irreconcilable with a programme of a multi-ethnic party coalition.

The 'undemocratic' period of Indonesia and Malaysia had a visible effect on minority rights. The suppression of freedom of speech was particularly intense on religious and ethnic issues, as the government placed a priority on keeping these issues out of the public sphere. The political and economic position of the Chinese was deemed non-negotiable. Both states made use of past violent episodes to empower law enforcement at the expense of democratic procedures, and the threat of ethnic conflict was invoked frequently in order to legitimise authoritarian rule.

Phase III: democracy/democratisation

The end of the Suharto era came with the 1997–8 financial crisis in Southeast Asia. In May 1998, the country's dire economic situation and the unstable political climate turned inner-city mobs against the Chinese middle class. Rapes, killings and arsons of Chinese estates drove dozens of thousands of Tionghoa out of the country for fear of their lives. Many Chinese had come to believe that they were accepted by the *pribumi* as compatriots, since they spoke the national language, used Indonesian-sounding names and also made attempts to integrate into Indonesian society. Nevertheless, their economic status – a result of Suharto's policies – made them textbook scapegoats. Even if he had acted on it, Suharto would have lost the authority necessary to order the protection of the Chinese by the armed forces.

The president was under pressure to step down, and did. Interim president Habibie's administration paved the way for the first free elections held in Indonesia since 1955. A swift-running process of democratising Indonesian political life began and, over the subsequent years, resulted in far-reaching constitutional changes, as well as the decentralisation of power and renewed ideological pluralism. However, Habibie did not take immediate action to reach out to the traumatised Chinese. In the first months of his administration he stated that it was more important to empower the *pribumi* economically than to try to convince the Chinese to come back to Indonesia (Suryadinata 2009: 9). He was soon proven wrong; it became clear that without Chinese entrepreneurs, the Indonesian economy would collapse entirely. The president promptly changed his attitude, reaching out to the key representatives of the Chinese business elite, and promising to investigate the riots that specifically targeted the Chinese.

In recent years, the Chinese have successfully regained a place on the Indonesian political scene. Three parties were formed by the *Tionghoa* after 1999, though none of them survived the strong party competition in elections.[16] Since 1999, the Chinese vote has been split between several parties, although there are multiple ethnic Chinese in the parliament (indeed, there are three from West Kalimantan province alone). Kwik Kian Gie was the first *Tionghoa* to be appointed a minister during *Reformasi* ('Reformation', as the current period of political transformation is called). The vice-governor of West Kalimantan, elected in direct elections along with a Christian governor, is an ethnic Chinese; in the same province, a Chinese is mayor in the Chinese-dominated city of Singkawang.

Pancasila still serves as the ideological basis for national harmony, as the moral common denominator between the religious groups, and as the government-promoted, all-encompassing guideline for political parties and public personae. Although SARA issues remain politically taboo, religious organisations and parties have re-emerged. Regional parties are forbidden by law,[17] and this regulation also extends to ethnic indigenous parties. Article 6 of the Constitution, which had hitherto stipulated that the president must be 'a native Indonesian citizen', was amended in 2001 and now reads: 'Candidates for the President and Vice-President must have been Indonesian citizens since birth, must never have taken other citizenship of their own accord [...]' (Indrayana 2008: 422). Furthermore, during B. J. Habibie's administration, Abdurrahman Wahid's administration, and Megawati Sukarnoputri's administration, the majority of the country's anti-Chinese regulations were abolished. The SBKRI is no longer needed and there are no limitations on Chinese cultural, religious or linguistic activities. The Chinese press and other Mandarin-medium media are readily available and many public schools offer Mandarin lessons. Since 2006, Confucianism has been listed among the state's officially-recognised religions (i.e. it is included in *Pancasila*). The first year in which the Chinese New Year was celebrated as a public holiday was in 2003. Each year the celebrations have grown larger and *Imlek* (as the festival is known in Indonesian) is now an important date in Indonesia's calendar of celebrations. Politicians participate in public events related to the occasion, seizing it as an opportunity to gain popularity among the Chinese voters.

Unlike Indonesia under Suharto, Malaysia has always held frequent and competitive – albeit not fair – elections; according to the Freedom House, Malaysia has been 'partly free' for nearly the entire period from 1972 to the present (with short 'free' spells) and has systematically scored as 'more free' than Indonesia (compare Figure 6.1). The revolutionary mode of democratisation seems unlikely

---

16. Forty-four parties competed in the 2009 polls, of which only nine won seats in the parliament

17. Except for the province of Aceh, where regional parties are allowed. In the 1999 elections, the requirements for a party to compete included: having branches in one third of Indonesia's former twenty-seven provinces, and offices in more than half the districts or municipalities within each of the provinces where the party claimed to have branches. The 2004 election laws introduced even stricter regulations: new parties needed branches in two-thirds of all provinces and municipalities within those provinces.

to take hold in Malaysia, but rising support for the opposition parties since 2004 informs the basic assumption of the next paragraphs: *Barisan Nasional* rule may be approaching its end. The 2008 General Election marked the biggest defeat of the ruling coalition since 1969. In this development, the BN was denied a two-thirds majority in the parliament, and in five states opposition parties won; governments in these states were taken over by opposition parties. The DAP won more seats than the MCA, the BN Chinese party (as they had previously done in 1969); the PKR won the most seats among opposition parties,[18] and its centrist programme and multi-ethnic composition seemed to have resonated with voters. The BN not only lost seats in parliament, but it also lost its monopoly as the only political organisation overtly promoting peaceful cooperation between ethnic groups. Tellingly, the ever-ruling coalition was defeated even in ethnically-mixed constituencies, which theretofore had been *strongly* behind the BN (Wong, C. H. and Chin 2009: 80). Indeed, it seems that fear of inter-ethnic conflict no longer loomed so strongly over the country, and that the BN's rhetoric – based on safeguarding peace and harmony – could no longer legitimise its rule.

The events that have taken place in the state of Perak after the 2008 election reflect some very practical contradictions between the democratically-expressed will of the people and the country's nationalising policy. Although the DAP won the most seats in the State Assembly of Perak, the *Menteri Besar* (Chief Minister) was not nominated from among the DAP assemblymen, since there was no Muslim state representative from the DAP. According to a constitutional regulation, the *Menteri Besar* must be a Muslim, and only the Sultan could waive this requirement – which he did not in this case (the Rulers, whose position is safeguarded by the constitution, are traditionally behind the ruling coalition). The PAS' assemblyman (a Muslim) became the *Menteri Besar* despite the party having secured only six seats in the assembly (against the DAP's eighteen and PKR's seven in the fifty-nine-seat Perak state assembly (Ong 2008).

The 2008 election cost Abdullah Ahmad Badawi the position of prime minister, and Najib Tun Razak took his place. In 2009, the new prime minister launched the '1Malaysia' campaign, which – though vague in its rhetoric and not yet backed up by any practical or legal instruments – attests to an intellectual shift in the conceptualisation of Malaysia.[19] The official website – set up to promote the ideas of '1Malaysia' – explains its aims as follows:

> 1Malaysia is intended to provide a free and open forum to discuss the things that matter deeply to us as a Nation. What makes Malaysia unique is the diversity of our peoples. 1Malaysia's goal is to preserve and enhance this unity

18. PKR won thirty-one seats, DAP twenty-eight and PAS twenty-three.

19. Earlier, during Mahathir Mohamad's tenure as Prime Minister, the term 'Bangsa Malaysia' ('Malaysian Nation') was used in a document called Vision 2020; the substantial contents of the term 'Bangsa Malaysia' are difficult to discern, since it was never further elaborated. The short-lived term was received positively by the Chinese and widely criticised by UMNO (compare Lim 2007).

in diversity which has always been our strength and remains our best hope for the future saying.[20]

While this appeal (which is personally attributed to Prime Minister Najib) also refers to a '1Malaysian identity', there is no further description of what, explicitly, this identity is. If this campaign was to be followed up with legislation reflecting the spirit of 'Malaysia' in its current state (which, at the time of this writing, remains to be clarified), it would be tantamount to renouncing the nationalising policies.

The opposition coalition *Pakatan Rakyat* openly debates the idea of eradicating quotas for the *Bumiputra*. It also proposes need-based social assistance programmes (as opposed to the existing, ethnic-based ones), and campaigns for the political equality of all races. During an electoral rally in Sarawak, an ethnic Chinese DAP Member of Parliament from Kuala Lumpur compared Muslim domination in Malaysian politics to white domination in American politics before Martin Luther King. The MP, after recalling Rosa Parks' story and fast-forwarding to Obama's win in the most recent US presidential election, went on to ask whether a non-Muslim would be able to become the Prime Minister of Malaysia.[21]

The recently concluded elections in Sarawak confirmed that the DAP is more popular than the local Chinese-based BN component – the Sarawak United People's Party, which had represented the Chinese community in Sarawak for decades.[22] Indeed, the DAP won twelve out of the fifteen seats it contested; amongst the ones it won, all but two were urban Chinese-majority seats (the two others were ethnically-mixed seats). The multiple-term incumbent Deputy Chief Minister of Sarawak – the highest-ranking Chinese person in the state BN – was defeated.

The SUPP's relatively poor performance in previous state elections, and the growing Chinese discontent in West Malaysia, had made the BN quite apprehensive. Therefore, before the elections, the BN issued warnings that insufficient Chinese support for the SUPP and BN would result in the absence of Chinese ministers in the state cabinet. The threat had little influence on voter's preferences, however, and put the Sarawak Chief Minister in a difficult position when the SUPP was visibly defeated. An influential Muslim organisation from West Malaysia had demanded that the Chinese be excluded from the Sarawak state government, when such a move would defy the BN's claim of serving all communities and offering due representation for all. In response, one of the three Chinese SUPP representatives was immediately appointed to join the cabinet.[23]

---

20. 1Malaysia: The Personal Website of Dato' Sri Najib Razak, Online. Available /www.1malaysia.com.my/about/about-1malaysia/ (accessed 11 February 2012).

21. Teo Nie Ching's speech at the DAP rally in Kuching/Batu Kawa on the 13th April 2011.

22. The SUPP also contested several non-Muslim *Bumiputra* seats; the party managed to win all of these and currently has more non-Chinese than Chinese elected representatives in the state legislative assembly.

23. Surprisingly, the SUPP criticised this decision by the chief minister, arguing that the non-Chinese assemblymen of this party deserve to be appointed to the cabinet.

The opposition's recent gains in popularity opened up a public space for discussion about the role in politics of the Chinese, about legal stipulations regulating the holding of top government positions by non-Malays, and of the true nature of inter-ethnic relations in the state. However, first and foremost, the BN's weakened control of the media, especially the Internet, has given rise to broad discussions on the nature of the state, electoral flaws, patronage and corruption. The strong position of the Chinese-based party in the opposition enables the *Barisan Nasional* and its satellite organisations to draw connections between the notions of 'opposition' and 'Chinese politics'. And calls for the further political exclusion of minorities, typically made in Malay-extremist quarters, have not ceased – on the contrary, they have become more vocal. The Malacca Chief Minister recently demanded that an activist of Indian descent be stripped of her Malaysian citizenship (Lee 2011). This was his response to the fact that the organisation she chairs was planning to organise a rally to protest against electoral inequalities. Preparations for the rally also prompted the police to pre-emptively arrest several people. And a president of a pro-government organisation threatened that, if the rally was indeed to take place, the Chinese community 'should stock up on food' because 'anything could happen' (Sipalan 2011).

Conclusion

This chapter has aimed to tackle two questions: first, whether Brubaker's concept of a 'nationalising state' can inform our understanding of Indonesia's and Malaysia's policies towards their minorities; and secondly, whether nationalising policies are compatible with democratic and authoritarian regimes.

The answer to the first question has proven to be 'yes': in both states, there is a 'core nation', or more accurately, an 'imagined core nation', whose members are believed to be disadvantaged in comparison to non-native residents. In Indonesia, this core nation had originally been designated in ethnically-neutral, or civic, terms. Nevertheless, 'native' versus 'other nations' categories were introduced into the nation's constitution; and the ownership of the polity by the natives was underscored by citizenship stipulations in the constitution. The culturally-discriminating policies of the New Order era completed the picture of Indonesia as a nationalising state. However, the democratisation processes of the late 1990s and 2000s opened up debate over equality and civil liberties. And subsequently, all anti-Chinese laws were abolished; Confucianism (a religion professed exclusively by the Chinese) was included in the national ideology of *Pancasila*; and the Indonesian 'nation' – legally and ideologically – changed to include the Chinese minority.

Malaysia's core nation was originally defined as 'Malays'; after 1963, this was expanded to include the natives of Borneo, and the new category was labelled *Bumiputra*. Recently the notion of a 'Malaysian nation' was proposed, although it never became more than an intellectual experiment, both in its practical aspect and in a cultural sense. The exclusion of the country's non-indigenous groups (the Chinese and Indians) remains a constitutionally-sanctioned and everyday reality, despite, paradoxically, the fact that the two groups enjoy political representation proportional to their numbers. Malaysian nationalising policies are most prominent in the country's economic context: the New Economic Policy and its later versions limit the scope of non-*Bumiputras* in business. However, education policies do not restrict the rights of the Chinese or Indian communities to speak their own languages or practice their own cultures.

The second part of this chapter attempted to find a correlation between regime change and nationalising policies. A chronological analysis of nationalising dynamics in the two countries suggests that changes in policy took place in close relation to power shifts in both states. In late 1960s, Indonesia and Malaysia moved towards authoritarianism, and visibly limited the opportunities of the Chinese to participate in policy and discourse shaping. The curtailing of political freedoms during this period was accompanied by stricter regulations towards the ethnic minorities. And violent events in Indonesia in 1965, and in Malaysia in 1969, were traumatising moments for both societies. In both cases, the new regimes skilfully depicted these events as ethnically fuelled. Fear of bloodshed – actual, but also partly induced – yielded necessary legitimisation for Suharto's administration and for the *Barisan Nasional*. In this fashion, nationalising policies were shown to be highly compatible with non-democratic governments.

The political developments of recent years in Indonesia and Malaysia have offered empirical evidence as to whether a nationalising state can fully democratise and reconcile political liberties with the continued exclusion of minorities. In the introduction to this chapter, we had argued the answer to be negative. And indeed, after the end of the New Order, Indonesia renounced all discriminatory policies against the ethnic Chinese, and did away with legal solutions of a nationalising character introduced during pre-New Order times. Within the renewed political pluralism of democratic Indonesia, there is now a place for ethnic Chinese politicians – both in the legislative and executive. More interestingly, however, is the fact that minorities have proven to be an important, if not central, element of the events leading to the transformation. Minorities' status as a catalyst was evidenced both in their passive role in the events, e.g. as victims of violence invoked by mass frustration (Indonesia) and verbal attacks and threats (Malaysia), and in their active role as advocates for change. In Indonesia, the Chinese were excluded from the public sphere during the New Order, and the revolutionary and violent character of the early phase of the transformation deterred them from taking a clear stand. In Malaysia, by contrast, Chinese and Indians are present and active in political life, and they are among the most vocal critics of the power abuses of the current regime. While their real influence within the ruling coalition is at best limited, they nevertheless represent strong and daring forces in the ranks of the opposition. As a result, calls for the democratisation of the polity and for the revision of ethnic-based policies come most often from these opposition quarters. Slow but steady increases in the opposition parties' representation in national and state legislatures, which could ultimately lead to a final power shift via electoral ballot, seem the most likely scenario for Malaysia's democratisation process. However, whether and how quickly nationalising policies would be renounced under a new government remains to be seen. Any revision of ethnic-based regulations under the *Barisan Nasional* rule seems unlikely.

References

Anderson, B. R. O. and McVey, R. T. (1971) *A Preliminary Analysis of the October 1 1965 Coup in Indonesia*, Ithaca: Cornell University Press.

Brubaker, R. (1996) *Nationalism Reframed: Nationhood and the national question in the new Europe*, Cambridge: Cambridge University Press.

Chirot, D. and Reid, A. (eds) (1997) *Essential Outsiders: Chinese and Jews in the modern transformation of Southeast Asia and Central Europe*, Seattle: University of Washington Press.

Coppel, C. A. (2003) 'Special issue foreword', *Asian Ethnicity*, 4(3): 327–36.

Fernandez, J. (2010) 'Who, really, are the "Malays"?', *Malaysiakini*. Online. Available /*malaysiakini*.com/news/149777 (accessed 11 February 2012).

Freedom House (2011) 'Freedom in the world: country rating and status'. Online. Available /www.freedomhouse.org/sites/default/files/inline_images/FIWAllScoresCountries1973-2011.xls (accessed 13 February 2012).

Indrayana, D. (2008) *Indonesian Constitutional Reform, 1999–2002: An evaluation of constitution-making in transition*, Jakarta: Kompas Book Publishing.

Jomo, S. K. (1997) 'A specific idiom of Chinese capitalism in Southeast Asia: Sino-Malaysian capital accumulation in the face of state hostility', in D. Chirot and A. Reid (eds) *Essential Outsiders: Chinese and Jews in modern transformation of Southeast Asia and Central Europe*, Seattle: University of Washington Press.

Khoo, B. T. (2004) 'Managing ethnic relations in post-crisis Malaysia and Indonesia: lessons from the new economic policy?'. Online. Available /www.unrisd.org/unrisd/website/document.nsf/%28httpPublications%29/22E1E0E487E13A1F80256B6D005786B7?OpenDocument (accessed 25 November 2011).

Lee, R. (2011) 'Ali Rustam wants Ambiga's citizenship revoked', *Malaysiakini*. Online. Available /www.malaysiakini.com/news/168707 (accessed 11 February 2012).

Leigh, M. B. (1974) *The Rising Moon*, Sydney: Sydney University Press.

Lim, K. S. (2007) 'National education blueprint – first official document to abandon "Bangsa Malaysia" concept/objective', *DAP Malaysia*. Online. Available /www.dapmalaysia.org/english/2007/jan07/lks/lks4160.htm (accessed 11 February 2012).

Mackie, J. (1976) 'Anti-Chinese outbreaks in Indonesia: 1959–68', in J. Mackie (ed.) *The Chinese in Indonesia: Five essays*, Honolulu: University Press of Hawaii.

Means, G. P. (1976) *Malaysian politics*, 2nd ed., London: Hodder and Stoughton.

Milne, R. S. and Ratnam, K. J. (1974) *Malaysia – New States in a New Nation: Political development of Sarawak and Sabah in Malaysia*, London: Frank Cass.

Munck, G. L. and Verkuilen, J. (2002) 'Conceptualizing and measuring democracy', *Comparative Political Studies*, 35(1): 5–34.

Ong, A. (2008) 'PAS Nizar is new Perak MB', *Malaysiakini*. Online. Available / www.malaysiakini.com/news/79710 (accessed 11 February 2012).

Polity IV Country Reports (2010). Online. Available /www.systemicpeace.org/
   polity/polity06.htm#asia (accessed 13 February 2012).
Purcell, V. (1965) *South and East Asia since 1800*, Cambridge: Cambridge
   University Press.
Sipalan, J. (2011) 'Ibrahim Ali hauled up for alleged sedition', *Malaysiakini*.
   Online. Available /www.malaysiakini.com/news/168129 (accessed 11
   February 2012).
Suryadinata, L. (1972) 'Indonesian Chinese education: past and present',
   Indonesia, 14: 49–71.
—   (1997) *Political Thinking of the Indonesian Chinese, 1900–1995: A
   sourcebook*, 2nd edn, Singapore: Singapore University Press.
—   (2009) 'The ethnic Chinese issue and national integration in Indonesia'.
   ISEAS. Online. Available /www.iseas.edu.sg/trends992.pdf (accessed 11
   February 2012).
Tilly, C. (2008) *Democracy*, reprinted edn, Cambridge: Cambridge University
   Press.
Wibisono, C. (2009) 'Learning from Malaysia's mistakes', *Inside Indonesia*, 95.
   Online. Available /www.insideindonesia.org/edition-95-jan-mar-2009/
   learning-from-malaysia-s-mistakes-11011166 (accessed 11 February
   2012).
Wong, C. H. and Chin, J. (2009) 'Malaysia's electoral upheaval', *Journal of
   Democracy*, 20(3): 71–85.
Wong, C. W. and Edwards, A. (2007) 'Back to Bahasa Malaysia', *The Star*, 4 June.
   Online. Available http://thestar.com.my/news/story.asp?file=/2007/6/4/
   nation/17923478&sec=nation (accessed 3 February 2012).

chapter seven | nationalising discourse versus minorities' political demands – the case of the palestinian minority of israel

Sharon Weinblum

Introduction

Since the establishment of the state of Israel, discussions over the identity of the regime have consistently been prominent in the political arena, with Israel being alternately or concomitantly promoted as a 'Jewish state', a 'Jewish and democratic state', a 'state of all its citizens' or a 'bi-national state'. Since the mid-1980s, Israel has been officially defined as both Jewish and democratic, which are the terms set down in the nation's major Basic Laws.[1] Beyond the Jewish and democratic motto, however, one may wonder what role the identity dimension of the regime plays in Israel and what impact it has on Israel's non-Jewish minorities, particularly on the 20 per cent minority of Palestinian citizens living in Israel.[2] Many studies have tackled the question of the identity of the state of Israel and many of them have also described the discriminatory policies of Israel toward their non-Jewish minorities. Drawing on Brubaker's model of nationalising state (Brubaker 1996), this contribution addresses a considerably less-studied dimension of this issue, namely the discourse produced by the Israeli elite on the question of the regime identity and its relation to the Palestinian minority.

More precisely, the first objective of this chapter is to assess whether the discourse produced by the Israeli central elite can be characterised as a 'differentialist nationalising discourse'. The second and more specific objective of the chapter is to capture to what extent does the central elite's discourse leave room to the Palestinian national minority's political expression. Working in a similar vein to other contributions to this book, the issue at the core of this chapter also pertains to the broader question of the compatibility between a nationalising state and the fulfilment of democratic goals.

---

1. In 1985, the Basic Law on the Knesset was amended to include an article defining Israel as the state of the Jewish people and as a democratic state. Since 1992, it has defined Israel as a Jewish and democratic state, along with the Human Dignity and Liberty Basic Law (1992).

2. There is no consensus on the denomination of the one million Palestinians who enjoy Israeli citizenship. While the 'Israeli Arab' denomination is seen as part of the authorities' discourse aimed at separating this population from its 'kin nation', the 'Palestinians of Israel' is obviously a normatively loaded descriptor as well. I have nevertheless chosen to use this expression, not to assert a political stance, but because this is the most common way in which the minority elite defines itself today.

On the basis of a discourse analysis, this chapter argues that, when confronted with tangible political expressions presented by the Palestinian minority, the Israeli central elite, with the exception of a small part, tends to employ a 'differentialist nationalising discourse' that characterises the minority as both a security threat and a danger to the state identity. My conclusion is that, under such circumstances, the possibility of *real* inclusion of the minority in the polity is greatly minimised, if not absent. On the methodological level, the research question is investigated by means of an analysis of the Israeli central elite's discourse, namely the political actors who dominate the legislative arena, and whose positions are reflected in the legislation. The analysis is based upon primary sources including legal documents, parliamentary debates and political speeches accounted for by the press.

Structurally, this chapter is divided in three parts. In a first part, I give a brief introduction on Israel and some specifics of the debate over the state identity both in the academic and political arenas. I also clarify and rationalise the choice to mobilise the notion of 'nationalising discourse'. In the second part, I investigate the way the central Israeli elite has discursively articulated the Palestinian minority's political expression. I show that the dominant discourse has framed it as a threat both to the state and to the state's identity, hence leaving little space for the Palestinian minority to express a position on the political regime, and to promote its own vision of the polity. Finally, I present two competing and marginal discourses, which have been articulated by the Israeli central elite concomitantly with the dominant nationalising discourse: the first reinforces the differentialist nationalising patterns present in the dominant discourse, whereas the second one articulates an alternative to the differentialist nationalising discourse.

The conceptual fight over the identity of Israel – a new outlook

The definition of the Israeli state has never been consensual across the entire Israeli political elite. Most obviously, the Zionist project—following the nation-state model of the epoch—was founded out of a desire to create a Jewish state that would also be based on democratic values. The Israeli declaration of independence stated that:

> we [...] by virtue of our natural and historic right and on the strength of the resolution of the UN General Assembly, hereby declare the establishment of a Jewish state in Eretz-Israel, to be known as the State of Israel [...] that will be open for Jewish immigration and for the in-gathering of the exiles; it will foster the development of the country for the benefit of all its inhabitants; it will be based on freedom, justice and peace as envisaged by the prophets of Israel; it will ensure complete equality of social and political rights to all its inhabitants irrespective of religion, race or sex [...]

In order to promote the 'in-gathering of the exiles', the Israeli legislature passed a law allowing every Jewish person to immigrate to Israel and to become full citizen of the state (Law of Return 1950; Law on Citizenship 1952). Later, several Israeli Basic laws – which may be seen as the constitutional basis of the state in the absence of a constitution – were amended in order to define Israel as 'the state of the Jewish people', and as a democratic state (Basic Law: the Knesset 1985 version) or as a 'Jewish and democratic state' (Basic Law: the Knesset present version, Basic Law: Human Dignity and Liberty 1992).

However, the definition of the state of Israel, or the 'essence dilemma' (Peleg 2004), remains the subject of heated debate (Peleg and Waxman 2011) as revealed in the discussions that took place during the legislature's most recent failed attempt to draft a constitution for the state (Kenig and Cavari 2008; Lerner 2009). While some political groups (mostly Palestinian and far-left groups) advocate removing the reference to Israel's Jewish character – thereby yielding a more 'neutral' definition of the state – others champion the reinforcement of the Jewish dimension, as understood in a religious sense (the ultra-orthodox groups) or in an ethnic sense (this is especially the case of the nationalist parties Israel our Home and Jewish Home). For the dominant stream that adheres to the 'Jewish and democratic' definition of the state (comprised mainly of the centre-left and centre-right groups), the exact balance between the two dimensions remains unclear.

The intensity of the political debate over the nature of Israel is reflected in the academic arena, where the issue has generated much discussion. Scholars have offered numerous analyses of a regime often presented as being very specific, if not unique. A first conceptual perspective has drawn on the democratic regime definition and has described Israel as a liberal democracy, albeit an 'imperfect' one. This imperfect character would arise from four key discrepancies: the lack of a constitution, the occupation of Palestinian territories, the diminished status of the Palestinian-Arab minority and the lack of secularisation of the state (Neuberger 1998: 8). Besides, the notion of 'ethnic-democracy' has been introduced by Smooha (1989) to refer to 'a system in which two contradictory principles operate: the democratic principle, making for equal rights and equal treatment of all citizens, and the ethnic principle, making for fashioning a homogenous nation-state and privileging the ethnic majority' (Smooha 1997: 200). Building on this discussion, scholars have further elaborated on the ethnic character of the state and offered different models to characterise the state of Israel, including the 'exclusive ethnic state' (Rouhana 1997) or the 'ethnocracy' model, understood as a state that 'promotes the expansion of the dominant group in contested territories and its domination of power structures while maintaining a democratic facade' (Ghanem 2011; Yiftachel 2006: 3).

By applying Brubraker's concept of 'nationalising state' to the case of Israel, this chapter may be seen as a contribution to the academic debate on the definition of the Israeli regime. Despite the hesitancy of Israeli academics to mobilise the notion of a 'nationalising state', aside from Kaufman's recent contribution,[3] the mobilisation of Brubaker's model seems however appropriate for at least two

---

3. Quite surprisingly, the notion of nationalising state elaborated by Brubaker has rarely been used in the Israeli literature to tackle the question of its Jewish character. In his book *Ethnocracy*, Yiftachel explains the concept only to invalidate its usefulness in the Israeli case (Yiftachel 2006: 21) and Smooha only refers to it explicitly in a footnote (Smooha 1997: 200). Recently, Kaufman did mobilise the notion of nationalising state and Brubaker's triadic model in a study of the Palestinian minority's political relations with their 'kin state' and Israel (Kaufman 2010).

reasons. On the one hand – in opposition to most of definitions proposed by Israeli academics – the idea of nationalising processes is less normatively oriented than either a critique or ratification of the Israeli Jewish and democratic model. On the other hand – in contrast to the terms of ethnocracy or ethno-democracy, which generate a reification of the regime – mobilising the notion of 'nationalising' state implies both the idea of an on-going process, *and* of contingency, a path that seems much more appropriate if we want to understand the dynamic and evolving construction of the state and its relations with its national minorities.

More specifically, this chapter focuses on the discursive dimension of the nationalising state concept, i.e. the discourse produced by the central national elite, and asks two related questions:

(1) To what extent can the discourse formulated by the central elite in Israel be characterised as a 'differentialist nationalising discourse'?

(2) What effect does such discourse have on the minority's capacity for political expression and participation in the polity?

The notion of 'differentialist nationalising discourse' is understood as a specific form of nationalising discourse that is defined as a discourse emphasising the following: (1) the existence of a conceived core nation (here the Jewish people); (2) for which the polity exists; (3) but is not perceived as fully realised or is conceived as being threatened; (4) a perception that pushes the elite to take actions; (5) which are also often justified by previous discriminations (Brubaker 1996). In contrast to an 'assimilationist nationalising discourse' that aims to eradicate differences, the 'differentialist nationalising discourse' takes difference as axiomatic and foundational and leads to the reinforcement of the barrier between the 'core nation' and the others. As Brubaker and, subsequently, Kymlicka have shown, such differentialist nationalising discourse has quite frequently gone hand in hand with a discourse of suspicion toward the minority that is perceived and presented as potentially disloyal to the nation-state (Brubaker 1996; Kymlicka 2004). The following analysis shows that most of the Israeli elite has indeed articulated a differentialist nationalising discourse when addressing the relationship between the state and its national minority, a discourse often associated with a threat discourse reinforcing the 'us and them' approach.

The defensive nationalising state versus the political expression of the Palestinian minority

In the following sections, I give an account of the manner in which a dominant political discourse has been articulated *vis-à-vis* the Palestinian minority's political expression. A first section focuses on the reactions to the first political expressions of the Palestinian minority in the political arena. Subsequently, my analysis turns to the years after 2000, which were marked by a series of events, including the second Palestinian uprising – the *intifada*. Finally, I scrutinise how, in the present discursive context, the attempts of the Palestinian minority to influence the regime definition are constructed by the central elite.

The Palestinian minority as a threat and the formulation of the defensive (Jewish) democracy

After the first Israeli-Arab war of 1948 and the establishment of the Israeli state the same year, the Palestinian minority was put under military administration. Because of their historical, social and cultural proximity to an enemy state, the so-called Israeli Arabs were perceived as a potential internal fifth column (Smooha 1993). Though most of them were granted citizenship in the early 1950s, military rule was maintained for security reasons until the end of the 1960s (Hofnung 1996). Politically speaking, having military rule in place during the first years of the state severely constrained the Palestinian minority's capacity of expression and association. At the time, the only political channels open to the Palestinian citizens of Israel were the Jewish-Palestinian Communist Party and the 'minority lists' that worked under the tutelage of Zionist lists. From the mid-1960s, due in part to the softening of military rule and to the occupation of Gaza and the West Bank, the minority's political mobilisation grew stronger, with the reinforcement of a Palestinian consciousness and identity[4] – a process often referred to as 'Palestinisation' (Rouhana 1989: 45).

As a consequence of these processes, the Socialist Party emerged in 1965 as the first political group to define itself as a Palestinian party (Peled 1992). The Palestinian characteristic of the party was very pronounced in its platform, which emphasised the identity of the minority as part of the Palestinian people and also officially supported the Palestinian side in the Israeli-Palestinian conflict by advocating 'a just solution for the Palestinian problem as a whole, and as an indivisible unit'(McDowall 1989). When the party applied to run for the Knesset (the Israeli Parliament) elections that same year, the Central Elections Committee (CEC), a body composed of members of the Knesset (MKs) and headed by a Supreme Court Justice, made the decision to disqualify the list. The disqualification was based on the grounds that the party's objectives were seen as a threat to Israel's integrity (Cohen-Almagor 1997; Peled 1992: 463) and on the fact that a subset of its members was affiliated with Al Ard, a group previously banned for endangering state security (Navot 2008). When the list petitioned the Supreme Court to challenge this decision, the Court maintained the disqualification of the party on the basis of:

> […] the most elementary right of every state to defend its freedom and very existence against enemies from without and against their followers at home […] I call this self-defending democracy (*Yeredor v. the Chair of the Electoral Committee of the 6th Knesset* 1965).

After this landmark Supreme Court ruling, no Palestinian party attempted to run in elections until 1984. Nevertheless, the process of 'Palestinisation' and of politicisation of the Palestinian minority was now underway (Rouhana 1989) – a shift evidenced most clearly in the early 1980s by the collective affirmation of three core beliefs:

---

4. For more details on the links between identity and political action, see Rouhana (1989); Ghanem (2002).

(1) the Arab minority was part of the Palestinian people whose suffering it shares;

(2) the Palestinian people of the occupied territories had the right to self-determination; and

(3) the Israeli Palestinians should be granted individual rights equal to those accorded to Israeli Jews (Ghanem 2002; Rouhana 1989).

It is in that spirit that the Progressive List for Peace (PLP) was established in 1982 and introduced its candidacy to run in the Knesset elections (Rouhana 1989: 48). Confronted with this Palestinian list, on a similar basis as in 1965, the CEC disqualified the PLP – together with a Jewish far right party, Kach[5] – on the grounds that sympathisers of Israel's enemies were on the PLP's list, as well as on the basis that there were subversive elements in some of the groups affiliated with the list. Nevertheless, the Supreme Court overruled the decision owing to the lack of appropriate legal grounds upon which to uphold such a measure, and pushed the Knesset to pass a law dealing with the issue of participation in elections.

As a consequence, the government introduced in the same year, a bill that amended the Basic Law: the Knesset. This law clearly establishes and institution-alises the link already implicit between security and identity. It states that:

'A list may not take part in the national elections if its goals or action include, implicitly or explicitly, one of the following:

Negation of Israel's right to exist *as the state of the Jewish people*

Negation of the state's democratic nature

Incitement to racism' (article 7a).

As in the previous discussions that were held in the CEC and in the Supreme Court, the debates expressed in the Knesset over this amendment reflect a two-fold worry, wherein an anxiety over the preservation of the state's integrity com-mingled and overlapped with anxiety over the preservation of the state's Jewish identity. The speech of the Minister of Justice, who drew on the 1965 words of the Supreme Court Justice, was especially striking in this respect:

[…] not only is Israel a sovereign state, independent and freedom-loving and characterised as a regime governed by the people, but it was founded as the state of the Jewish people in Eretz-Israel and the fact of this establishment was a consequence of the natural and historical right of the Jewish people to live like all other people, in his own authority in his sovereign state. It's an act that realised the aspiration of generations of the Israel Diaspora. And if we don't say that, the wars that Israel has waged would make no sense. It would be an

---

5.   Kach had one deputy in the Knesset, its founder, Meir Kahane. The core element of its platform was to strengthen and assure the Jewish dimension of the state, by transferring the Arab popula-tion out of the Israeli borders, so as to preserve a Jewish majority (see Pedahzur 2002: 36–7).

absolute contradiction to the history of the Jewish people and its yearning, and a contradiction to the fact that the state was created after the Holocaust when millions of Jews in Europe were slaughtered, and which has proven again the necessity of solving the problem of a people lacking a homeland by establishing the Jewish state in Eretz- Israel (Minister of Justice Nissim, first reading of the Basic Law: the Knesset 1985).

It is safe to say at this stage, that the Palestinian minority's first attempts at political expression were received by the political elite in Israel with substantial fear. Interestingly, the dominant discourse that developed contained all the elements of the differentialist nationalising discourse: the representation of the minority as a potential threat due to the minority's supposed links to the enemy; the mingling of the notions of the minority being a threat to the state and to the Jewish identity; the reaffirmation of the identity of the state through legislation and the reference to past sufferings to legitimise these processes.

The years 2000 and the reinforcement of the defensive nationalising discourse

In contrast to the first decades of the state, the context of the late 1980s and 1990s witnessed the relaxation of obstructions to the political expression of the minority and gave rise to a series of political movements and political parties that worked from the three principles mentioned above (common identity, support of a Palestinian state, and quest for equality) (Kaufman 1997). The outbreak of the second Palestinian *intifada* (end of September 2000), the consequent terror attacks within the country, and the participation of Palestinian citizens of Israel in demonstrations in favour of the uprising that led to the death of twelve Palestinians in October 2000, however, provoked a shift in the elite's overarching stance on the Palestinian minority's political expression (Kaufman 2011). Not only did these events generate the reinforcement of the threat and suspicion discourse already present, but they also reinforced the discourse that conflated both the 'security threat' and threat to the identity of the state. In the area of political participation, these concerns were especially clearly articulated and institutionalised in the law regulating elections, which was amended twice in order to further delimit participation in electoral competition.

The first of these changes was an amendment introduced one year after the start of the *intifada*, which added a new criterion for disqualifying a political list from the Knesset: 'support to terrorism and identification with the enemies' (article 7a).[6] Following the war in Lebanon and the 'Bishara affair',[7] a second 'security amendment' was added to the law in 2008. According to the amendment, a visit to 'enemy states' – a category then comprising Syria, Lebanon, Iraq, Saudi Arabia,

---

6. At the same time, a law was passed that made incitement to terrorism a new criminal offence.

7. The Bishara affair commonly refers to several visits made by MK Bishara, to Syria and Lebanon between 2001 and 2006 where the MK issued messages of support for Hezbollah, in its struggle against Israel (Kaufman 2011; Navot 2008: 96–7).

Yemen, Iran and Gaza – made without ministry permission, would be seen as tantamount to supporting armed struggle against the state of Israel. Consequently, a candidate making such visit up to seven years prior to an election is not allowed to take part in those elections (Basic Law: the Knesset 2008).

Again, the official arguments mobilised in the bills and during the debates that justified the amendments were articulated in a security-oriented manner, with the Palestinian minority framed as a threat. In the proposition, the initiator of the bill, for instance, very clearly justified the amendment by portraying the Israeli Arabs' participation in the demonstrations, referred to as a 'radicalisation process of a part of the political leadership among Arabs of Israel, and of parliament members that incite to rebellion against the state of Israel and against Jews and that express support to terrorist movements' (Bill on the Basic Law: the Knesset 2001).

As in 1985, the debates that followed presented a clear interrelation between the construction of the minority as a threat to security and as a threat to identity. While most of the speakers emphasised the security argument by describing the minority's support for the Palestinian cause as either 'parliamentary terrorism' (MK Zeev, first reading of the Basic Law: the Knesset 2001) or as an act of disloyalty on the grounds that supporting 'my enemy, [means that] you are my enemy' (MK Orlev, *ibid.*), several speakers established a clear link between the supposed threat to the state and its citizens, and to the Jewish identity of the state. Such a position was expressed in the speech of a Likud majority member who suggested:

> […] to the Arab MKs that they find a way to be citizens of the state of Israel, which is the state of the Jewish people and of its Arab citizens. But this requires loyalty to the state of Israel as a Jewish state (MK Eytan, first reading of Basic Law: the Knesset 2001).

In a similar vein, in 2008, an initiator of the amendment banning visits to enemy states asserted that 'the problem of the Arab MKs' visits is that they call for opposing and destroying the state of Israel as a Jewish state. It is the principal objective of these visits' (MK Orlev second and third readings of Basic Law: the Knesset 2008).

This discourse intermingling concerns for security and for the identity of the state was also to be seen in the practices of the Central Elections Committee during the same years. In 2003 and then 2009, with article 7(a) already amended, the CEC decided with an overwhelming majority to ban the three Palestinian political lists as well as individual members, from taking part in the national elections.[8] The rationale for the disqualification referred to the position of the parties on the question of Israel regime identity. All parties' platform demanded that Israel becomes a 'state of all its citizens', which according to the MKs who took part in the decision was in contradiction to the Jewish pattern of the state of Israel, and hence

---

8. Those disqualified included MK Bishara and the Balad Party; MK Tibi and Hadash-Ta'al; MK Bishara and the United Arab List (see Shamir and Weinshall-Margel 2004). Balad, Ta'al and the UAL were disqualified in 2009 (see Kaufman 2011).

in contradiction to the Basic Law on the Knesset. Several MKs also asserted that the Jewish character of the state should be seen as a prerequisite for its democratic objective, and that any attempt 'to kill Israel (character) as a Jewish and democratic state' should be prevented (Glickman 2009). In both 2003 and 2009, the Supreme Court nevertheless overruled the CEC's decisions, and the political parties were eventually able to take part in the elections with their political platforms unchanged.

While the formal representation and political expression of Palestinian political parties have not been effectively limited since the introduction of the three amendments to the law on elections, the discourse expressed by the dominant elite since 1965 has systematically entailed differentialist nationalising dimensions. These patterns were reinforced particularly strongly in the years after 2000, which witnessed a growing sense of distrust towards the minority. The dominant discourse portrayed the minority's public support to the Palestinian cause as a potential threat, a threat which was seen not only as a danger to the state of Israel in a physical sense, but also to its core essence, i.e. to its Jewish identity.

In light of the dominant differentialist nationalising discourse, the next section scrutinises how the Palestinian minority's attempts to propose alternative models to the nationalising state have been perceived by the central elite. As I will show, the dominant nationalising discourse has not only contributed to the limitation and de-legitimisation of the Palestinian political expression, but it has also led to obstructing its political participation in the stewardship of the political regime definition.

Responding to the Palestinian minority's demands – excluding the minority from defining the polity

While the Israeli Parliament launched a constitutional process in 2003 aiming to draft a constitution for the 60-year anniversary of the state, different attempts to participate in the definition of the state were formulated inside and out of the Knesset by individual MKs, political parties and non-governmental organisations of the Palestinian minority. Among the attempts made in the Knesset, the Palestinian minority mobilised two channels to participate in the debate. Whereas Palestinian parties mostly boycotted the constitutional process and rejected the draft constitution proposed in 2006,[9] some suggestions pertaining to the status of the minority in the state were made during this process. While a few of them proposed granting the minority a certain level of autonomy, at least in cultural affairs, others suggested formally recognising Arab citizens as a minority with rights equal to those held by Jews (MK Whbee, discussions on the Constitution project

---

9. The arguments invoked were the fear that the constitution process would not do enough for the minority's rights and for basic rights in general. See Consitution, Law and Justice Committee protocols 21 June 2005 and 24 December 2006. For these reasons, the Palestinian MKs were mostly out of the discussion process and voted against the constitution draft in the Knesset. See Knesset Protocols 13 February 2006.

26 June 2005; bills amending the Basic Law: Human Dignity and Liberty). The responses to these claims were all negative. The first rationale to deny these claims was based on reasoning that there should be no collective rights in a democratic state 'promoting individual rights' (Minister of Justice Sheetrit, preliminary reading of the amendment of the Basic Law: Human Dignity and Liberty 2001; MK Chayne, discussions on the Constitution 26 June 2005; preliminary reading of the amendment on the Basic Law: Human Dignity and Liberty 2004). The second motive to disqualify the demand was that granting the Palestinian people both a state in the future and collective rights inside the Israeli state would provoke an imbalance and injustice for the Jewish people (discussions on the Constitution 26 June 2005).

The minority's political positions on the constitutional process were more strongly articulated *outside* of the political realm, in the form of four 'vision documents'.[10] Drafted by part of the elite of the Palestinian minority, these documents offered alternative models for the regime, all of which challenged to some extent the dominant notion of a 'Jewish and democratic state'. Despite their divergent conceptions of the practical measures that should be implemented, all of these documents displayed three common characteristics (Waxman and Peleg 2008). First, they defined the minority as part of Palestinian people. Second, they offered a counter-narrative on the establishment of the Israeli state, presented as a '*nakba*' (catastrophe) rather than as an independence day. Finally, they introduced material propositions for improving Palestinians' minority status in the state of Israel. In this regard, one of the constitutional projects advocated a 'state for all its citizens', while other propositions pushed for the creation of a 'consociative' state, where the minority would not only enjoy cultural autonomy, but also political autonomy.

To say the least, these documents were received with great reserve in the Israeli elite, including the media and academic elite (see Abulof 2008; Susser 2009). The documents were presented by some as acts of confrontation, and even as a 'declaration of war' (Tal 2006). Interestingly, one of the most potent messages was issued by the security services, warning the government about a 'strategic danger for the existence of the state', describing the groups that had drafted the documents as 'subversive entities seeking to harm the character of the state' (Stern 2007). Besides, in this context, a series of political initiatives were soon introduced, which further reinforced the nexus between political expression of the minority, security and identity of the state. The Hebrew bill introduced in 2008 and that called for the establishment of Hebrew as the sole official language was for instance justified publicly on the grounds that:

> Precisely in these times, when there are radical groups of Israeli Arabs trying to turn the state of Israel into a bi-national state, it is most urgent to put into law the unique status of the language of the Bible – the Hebrew language (Minister Livnat quoted by Shahar 2008).

---

10. *The Future Vision of the Palestinian Arabs in Israel* 2006; *An Equal Constitution for All?* 2006; *The Democratic Constitution* 2007; *The Haifa Declaration* 2007.

In a same vein, the association law, which was passed in March 2011 with the support of the government, can be seen as another articulation of the minority-security-identity nexus. Under the law, associations that commemorate the day of the creation of Israel as a mourning day can have their funding cut by the state. In order to justify the bill, its initiators asserted the following:

> the principle of 'defensive democracy' will be brought into action [...] The reason for this is the existence of Israel as a Jewish state. This nature is central to its existence, and we should not allow organisations, which are supported financially by the state budget to finance or to provide sponsorship of activities that deny the existence of the Jewish state, among which the commemoration of the independence as a mourning day (Bill on Association Law 2009).

Under those circumstances, not only has the minority's participation in the design of the regime been disqualified, but the minority's expression of its own narrative on the history of the regime has also been de-legitimised. Hence, if the differentialist nationalising discourse has very rarely led to the formal silencing of the minority's political expression (at the exception of 1965), the nationalising elements of the Israeli central elite's discourse have clearly left very limited space for real participation by the Palestinian minority in the elaboration of the definition of the polity.

Two marginal discourses on the Palestinian minority

In the previous sections, I described the discursive link made by the central Israeli elite between the Palestinian minority political expression, the security of the state of Israel and the threat to the state's identity as a Jewish state. Along with this dominant differentialist nationalising discourse, the central elite has also developed two competing discourses on the minority's place in the polity. The first one has reinforced the differentialist nationalising patterns of the dominant discourse by articulating the Palestinian minority in the form of a demographic threat. The second one has been grafted onto liberal and democratic values and can be seen as a competing discourse striving to reconcile the Jewish identity of the state and its democratic dimensions by including the minority's voice in the polity. The first alternative discourse has gained legitimacy and weight in recent years, while the second competing discourse remains marginal.

Reinforcing the differentialist nationalising discourse – the demographic issue

The desire to protect and/or reinforce the Jewish character of the state has led some part of the Israeli central elite to express a discourse articulating the minority as a threat, not only due to its political expression, but also because of its demographic weight in the country. Expressed previously in a very radical version by Kach's transfer project in the 1980s, this 'demographic threat' discourse seems to have gained new legitimacy after the second *intifada*.

In the recent years, the demographic issue has been articulated publicly by major members of the government and the parliament. Among them, in one notable speech, given at the annual strategic conference in Herzliya (December 2004), Netanyahu, then in charge of the Finance Ministry, explicitly mobilised the notion of a 'demographic threat' in reference to the Palestinian minority. The minister later justified his statement to the Knesset on the basis that the first condition for the Jewish and democratic state to exist is that there be a Jewish majority (Minister Netanyahu, Knesset plenum, 21st January 2004). The demographic threat was also articulated in a similar fashion during the 2004 and 2005 debates over the extension of the Citizenship and Entry into Israel law limiting the granting of visas and residence permits to residents of the Palestinian territories. On that occasion, a series of MKs, both religious and secular, from the opposition and the majority, asserted similar views, arguing, for instance, that:

> we are a Jewish state by definition, as it has been defined at the independence. And with all due respect and sympathy, there exists a basic right to every son of the Jewish majority, to conserve and protect the state identity, namely its national, cultural identity, its public structure and its security. This decision is right even if it goes – and this is the case – against human rights (MK Golan, second reading of the Citizenship and Entry into Israel Law 2005).[11]

In its more radical version, the discourse on the demographic threat has led to the articulation of what Lieberman, the Minister of Foreign Affairs and head of Israel our Home (at the time of writing) has named a 'territorial exchange plan'. This project entails two dimensions. First, it calls for a redefinition of the borders between the states (the Israeli state and the future Palestinian state) – one that would follow the 'natural ethnic borders' separating the Palestinian minority from the Jews.[12] Secondly, it suggests the establishment of a loyalty oath that would oblige any aspiring citizen to uphold the state and its Jewish symbols (Saban 2008; Waters 2008). While the first part of the plan has not been discussed since Lieberman's accession in the government, several loyalty oath bills have been placed on the agenda of the cabinet (though without success, as of this writing).

Interestingly, the demographic issue has also been articulated by centre and left

---

11. For a more in-depth analysis of the debates on this law, see Weinblum (2010).

12. It is important to note that, in contrast to the transfer project of the Kach list, Lieberman's project does not imply a call for ethnic cleansing but rather a transfer of sovereignty (see Waters 2008 on that topic).

wing political actors, although in another form. Some political leaders on the left have indeed stressed the need to stop the occupation in order to preserve the Jewish state, i.e. 'a state where the majority is Jewish and that defines itself as Jewish' (MK Avital, interview 2008). Recently, leaders of the centre party, Kadima, have also presented a similar discourse. These figures suggest, for instance, that: 'There is no Jewish state without the guarantee of a Jewish majority for generations to come and this majority does not exist in Greater Israel. The conclusion is clear: two states for two peoples' (Prime Minister Olmert, speech in the Knesset, 30th March 2009).

In this instance, the nationalising discourse is articulated in an even more exclusive form than in the dominant discourse. Regardless of the actual political stance of the minority toward the state and its identity, the demographic discourse unambiguously characterises the minority as a problematic issue for the Jewish and democratic state, not only because of the security threat it could represent, but also due to its mere presence as an 'other' on Israeli the territory. Framed in this manner, the nationalising discourse both reinforces the 'us and them' barrier already present in the dominant discourse, and sometimes advocates the complete exclusion of the Palestinian minority from the Israeli polity.

Recognising the minority's own narrative and reconciling the Jewish and democratic dimensions of the state

Along with the development of the dominant differentialist nationalising discourse and the more marginal demographic discourse, another competing discourse has also been continuously present in the political spectrum. While supporting the Jewish and democratic slogan, it has attempted to articulate both dimensions as crucial to the liberal spirit. This discourse has been expressed most prominently by the Supreme Court, on the occasion of its ruling on parties' rights to take part in Knesset elections, in which it stated that 'Israel's democracy is strong and can tolerate irregular cases and alternative voices' (quoted by Alon and Ettinger 2003). In the central political elite, this idea was conveyed most strongly by left wing political actors. In reaction to the above-mentioned laws, and to the right's harsh critiques of the constitutional documents proposed by the minority, a renowned left wing MK avowed in the press, for instance, that: 'Israel is a sovereign state, which is still considered to be a democracy. In other words, it is a state for all of its citizens. Therefore it must not demand of the Palestinians to recognise it as a Jewish state' (Aloni 2007).

Noteworthy enough, several right-wing political actors have also recently called for the recognition of a legitimate alternative narrative and conception of the regime identity. MK Rivlin, for instance, then chairman of the Knesset, publicly declared in the press that:

> the establishment of Israel was accompanied by much pain and suffering and [has been] a real trauma for the Palestinian [...]. Many of Israel's Arabs, who see themselves as part of the Palestinian population, feel the pain of their

brothers across the green line, a pain they feel the state of Israel is responsible for (MK Rivlin quoted by Haaretz Service 2009).

Such discourse has also been voiced by other members of the current government. The formulation of such discourse by cabinet members is what led to the softening of the Nakba law, from its original proposed form.[13] It is also on the basis of this discourse that the passing of a 'loyalty oath' on the symbols of the state was hindered on the grounds that: 'The majority doesn't need to remind the minority that it is in fact a minority all the time' (Deputy Prime Minister Meridor quoted by Ravid 2019; Deputy Prime Minister Meridor, interview 2010). By reconciling the national and democratic patterns of the state, this discourse may be seen as a move towards a possible legitimisation of the Palestinian voice and, more largely, as a potential alternative to the differentialist nationalising discourse. However, this discourse is clearly marginal with regard to the central elite at the time, with most of those articulating it expressing a nationalising discourse concomitantly.

Conclusion

This chapter represents a contribution to a larger reflection on the compatibility between the affirmation of the nation-state model and the integration of national minorities in the polity. Besides offering a definition of Israel as a nationalising state, the focus on the nationalising discursive processes of the state offers a dynamic picture of the relationship between the central elite and the Palestinian national minority. Hence, in contrast to other prisms of analysis used to study the relationship between the Israeli state and its minority, focusing on the discursive dimensions helps to account for the internal complexity of the processes at play.

Ultimately, the analysis leads to conclude that the central political elite in Israel tends to articulate a discourse that comprises most of the characteristics of a differentialist nationalising discourse. This discourse indeed conceives of the existence of the polity for a core nation, the Jewish people; it presents the polity as threatened by a minority different from the core nation; which justifies measures aimed at protecting the state and its identity often framed as a unique reality. As I presented, this nationalising discourse has been articulated by a dominant political elite, from centre-left to right, and by religious and secular groups, who have been quick to present the Palestinians' political demands as dangerous to the state and its identity. The differentialist nationalising discourse has been pushed even further in the form of the demographic threat discourse, which is present in the country's various political streams, even if the nationalist far right has articulated it most clearly. In this discourse, the Palestinian minority is not only conceived as a threat due to its political expression, but because of its sheer presence in the polity; hence, it is seen as imperilling the core nation simply by its presence. Interestingly, part of the elite that developed the nationalising discourse has *also*

---

13. The original bill provided that the commemoration of the nakba would become a criminal offence (bill p/18/1403).

articulated yet another discourse competing with, and tempering the differentialist nationalising discourse. Voiced by a small fringe of the centre-left and centre-right political actors, this discourse acknowledges the legitimacy of diverging narratives on the polity and accepts the existence of different positions on the Israeli regime. Nevertheless, this discourse has remained marginal among the central elite while being mainly expressed by far-left parties and the Palestinian minority itself.

In a context where the differentialist nationalising discourse combined with the increasingly strong demographic discourse prevail, room for real inclusion of the minority in the polity appears to be greatly reduced, if not completely absent. Although the Palestinian minority has not been denied political expression so far (with the exception of the 1965 elections), each time the minority has attempted to contest the 'Jewish and democratic' state definition and tried to offer alternatives to the nationalising model, their demands have been labelled as a threat or as disloyal, and thus de-legitimised or legally banned. Under such circumstances, any attempt by the minority to formulate new propositions of regime definition that would allow their integration within the polity seems to be doomed to disqualification, unless the discourse mitigating the differentialist trends of the nationalising discourse was to become dominant.

References

Abulof, U. (2008) 'Back to the future': A comparative ethical look at Israeli Arab future visions documents', *Israel Studies Forum*, 23(2): 29–54.

Alon, G. and Ettinger, Y. (2003) 'Election Committee disqualifies MK Bishara and Balad list', *Haaretz*, 1 January.

Aloni, S. (2007) 'Still a democracy?' *Haaretz*, 15 November.

Brubaker, R. (1996) *Nationalism Reframed: Nationhood and the national question in the new Europe*, Cambridge: Cambridge University Press.

Cohen-Almagor, R. (1997) 'Disqualification of political party lists in Israel: 1988–1996', *Emory International Law Review*, 11(1): 67–109

Ghanem, A. (2002) 'The Palestinians in Israel: political orientation and aspirations', *International Journal of Intercultural Relations,* 26(2): 135–52.

— (2011) 'The expanding ethnocracy: Judaisation of the public sphere', *Israel Studies Review*, 26(1): 21–27.

Glickman, A. (2009) 'Arab parties win disqualification appeal', *Y net*, 21 January.

Haaretz Service (2009) 'Knesset speaker: establishment of Israel caused Arabs real trauma', *Haaretz*, 3 August.

Hofnung, M. (1996) *Democracy, Law, and National Security in Israel*, Aldershot and Brookfield: Dartmouth.

Kaufman, I. (1997) *Arab National Communism in the Jewish state*, Gainesville: University Press of Florida.

— (2010) 'Escalating minority claims: the Arab "visions documents" of 2006–2007 in Israel', in A. Lecours and L. Moreno (eds) *Nationalism and Democracy: Dichotomies, complementarities, oppositions*, London and New York: Routledge, pp. 184–208.

— (2011) 'Les dynamiques d'opposition dans les situations de conflit: les partis arabo-palestiniens d'Israël', *Revue Internationale de Politique Comparée*, 18(2): 29–43.

Kenig, O. and Cavari, A. 'Israel's long and winding road to a constitution: main issues, actors and political balance', paper presented at ECPR Joint Sessions, Rennes, April 2008.

Kymlicka, W. (2004) 'La justice et la sécurité dans la prise en compte du nationalisme minoritaire', in A. Dieckhoff (ed.) *La constellation des appartenances*, Paris: Presses de Science Po, pp. 181–222.

Lerner, H., (2009) 'Entrenching the status quo: religion and state in Israel's constitutional proposals', *Constellations*, 16(3): 445–61.

McDowall, D. (1989) *Palestine and Israel*, London: Tauris.

Navot, S. (2008) 'Fighting terrorism in the political arena: the banning of political parties', *Party Politics*, 14(6): 745–62.

Neuberger, B. (1998) *Democracy in Israel: Origins and development*, Tel Aviv: Open University.

Pedahzur, A. (2002) *The Israeli Response to Jewish Extremism and Violence: Defending democracy*, Manchester and New York: Manchester University Press.

Peled, Y. (1992) 'Ethnic democracy and the legal construction of citizenship: Palestinian-Arab citizens of the Jewish state', *American Political Science Review*, 86(2): 432–43.

Peleg, I. (2004) 'Israeli foreign policy under right-wing governments: a constructivist interpretation', *Israeli Studies Forum*, 19: 1–14.

Peleg, I. and Waxman, D. (2011) *Israel's Palestinians: The conflict within,* New York: Cambridge University Press.

Ravid, B. *et al.*(2009) 'Ministers reject Yisrael Beiteinu's loyalty oath bill', *Haaretz*, 1 June.

Rouhana, N. (1989) 'The political transformation of the Palestinians in Israel: from acquiescence to challenge', *Journal of Palestinian Studies*, 18(3): 38–59.

—   (1997) *Identities in Conflict: Palestinians in an ethnic Jewish state*, New Haven: Yale University Press.

Saban, I. (2008) 'Citizenship and its erosion: transfer of populated territory and oath of allegiance in the prism of Israeli constitutional law', *Law and Ethics of Human Rights*, 2(2): 1–32.

Shahar I. (2008) 'MKs: Make Hebrew the only official language', *Haaretz*, 19 May.

Shamir, M. and Weinshall-Margell, K. (2004) 'Disqualifications of political party lists and candidates for the Knesset: were the 2003 elections unique?', in A. Arian and M. Shamir (eds) *The Elections in Israel 2003*, New Brunswick and London: Transaction Publishers, pp. 101–23.

Stern, Y. (2007) 'Arab leader air public relations campaign against Shin Bet', *Haaretz*, 6 April.

Susser, A. (2009) 'Partition and the Arab Palestinian minority in Israel', *Israel Studies*, 14(2): 105–19.

Smooha, S. (1989) *Arabs and Jews in Israel*, vol. 1 and vol. 2, Boulder: Westview Press.

—   (1993) 'Part of the problem or part of the solution: national security and the Arab minority', in A. Yaniv (ed.) *National Security and Democracy in Israel*, Boulder and London: Lynner Rienner Publishers, pp. 105–27.

—   (1997) 'Ethnic democracy: Israel as an archetype', *Israel Studies*, 2(2): 198–241.

Tal, A. (2006) 'This is a declaration of war', *Haaretz*, 8 December.

Waters, T. W. (2008) 'The blessing of departure: acceptable and unacceptable state support for demographic transformation: the Lieberman plan to exchange populated territories in Cisjordan', *Law and Ethics of Human Rights*, 2(1): 1–65.

Waxman, D. and Peleg, I. (2008) 'Neither ethnocracy nor bi-nationalism: in search of the middle ground', *Israel Studies Forum*, 23(2): 55–73.

Weinblum, S. (2010) 'Beyond the security vs. liberty paradigm: an analysis of "security" politics in Israel', in Y. Peled, N. Lewin-Epstein, G. Mundlak and J. Cohen (eds) *Democratic Citizenship and War*, London and New York: Routledge, pp. 54–73.

Yiftachel, O. (2006) *Ethnocracy: Land and identity politics in Israel/Palestine*, Philadelphia: University of Pennsylvania Press.

Official documents

An Equal Constitution for All? Mossawa Center, Position Paper, May 2006.
EA 1/65 *Yeredor v. the Chair of the Electoral Committee of the 6th Knesset* (1965).
Constitution, Law and Justice Committee protocols, 26 June 2005. Summary in English at: http://huka.gov.il/wiki/index.php/The_Jewish_State_and_the_Rights_of_Minorities (accessed 14 February 2012).
Prime Minister Ehud Olmert's Speech at the Special Knesset Session Marking 30 Years Since the signing of the Peace Accord with Egypt, 30 March 2009.
Statement of Finance Minister Benjamin Netanyahu at the Herzliya Conference, 21 January 2004.
The Democratic Constitution, Adalah Center, March 2007.
The Haifa Declaration, Mada al-Carmel, May 2007.
The Future Vision of the Palestinian Arabs in Israel, The National Committee for the Heads of the Arab Local Authorities in Israel, 2006.

Knesset protocols related to Basic Law: the Knesset

Amendment 12, first reading, 7 May 1985.
Amendment 12, second and third readings, 31 July 1985.
Bill p/2262, amendment 35, 30 October 2000.
Amendment 35, first reading of the law, 5 November 2001.
Bill p/17/2506, amendment 41, 7 May 2007.
Amendment 41, first reading of the law, 26 May 2008.
Amendment 41, second and third readings, 30 June 2008.

Bills on equality

Private bill, Basic Law: Human dignity and Liberty, amendment on equality, p/2556, first reading, 23 January 2002.
Preliminary reading on the private bill on Basic Law: Human dignity and Liberty, amendment on equality, 21 March 2001.
Preliminary reading on the private bill on Basic Law: Human dignity and Liberty, amendment on equality, 21 January 2004.
Private Bill on Basic Law: equality and full citizenship, p/2197, 24 March 2004.

Citizenship and entry into Israel Law (Temporary provision), 2003

Government bill, 4 June 2003.
First reading of the law, 17 June 2003.
Second and third readings of the law, 27 July 2003 and 31 July 2003.
Plenary debates 20 July 2004, 21 July 2004.

First reading of the law, 25 May 2005.
Second and third readings of the law, 27 July 2005.
Plenary discussions, 19 December 2006 and 15 January 2007.

The Association (Nakba) law

Bill p/18/1403, 6 July 2009.
Second and third reading, 22 March 2011.

The National languages bill

Bill p/17/3723, 26 May 2008.

All Knesset documents have been found on the Knesset website, online protocols, bills and committee protocols (in Hebrew) at:
/www.knesset.gov.il/divrey/qform.asp (accessed 14 February 2012); and
/www.knesset.gov.il/privatelaw/plaw_display.asp (accessed 14 February 2012).

Interviews

Interview with MK Colette Avital (Labour Party), Jerusalem, Knesset, 25 August 2008.
Interview with Deputy Prime Minister Dan Meridor (Likud), Jerusalem, office of the Prime Minister, 28 July 2010.

the legacy of the nation-state
building process – minority
politics in greece and turkey

Fulya Memisoglu

Introduction

In an attempt to investigate how nationalising states approach issues involving minorities, this chapter considers the minority policies of Greece and Turkey, and their development over time. Generally speaking, Turkey is a predominantly Muslim nation, while Greece has an overwhelmingly Orthodox-Christian population. As will be argued here, these demographics can be traced directly to policy continuities that have existed since the early twentieth century: ones guided by a dominant ideology focused on creating nation-states with homogenous societies. In both countries, the dynamics of change and transformation reflect some of the key features outlined by Brubaker (1996) in his landmark study of nationalising states, which described how understanding minorities and minority politics can offer insightful analytical perspectives on the nations they reside in. From this angle, this study intends to devote particular attention to the primary subjects of the minority policies under consideration, namely the so-called 'Lausanne minorities', who were granted legally-recognised status under the 1923 Treaty of Lausanne. In the case of Turkey, the Greek-Orthodox community and the Armenian and Jewish communities fall under this category. And in the case of Greece, the Muslim-Turkish minority of Western Thrace belongs under this heading.[1] The status of

---

1. The Armenians of Turkey constitute the largest legally-recognised minority group, with a population of approximately 60,000–65,000. The Jews of Turkey are mostly Sephardic Jews, who originally migrated to the Ottoman Empire from Spain and Portugal towards the end of the fifteenth century. Their population has considerably decreased since the foundation of Israel in 1948, and today there are approximately 25,000 Jews in Turkey. The Greek-Orthodox community of Turkey has had a centuries-long presence in Asia Minor. Following the compulsory exchange of populations between Greece and Turkey in 1923, approximately 110,000 Greeks continued living in Istanbul and the islands of Gokceada [*Imvros*] and Bozcaada [*Tenedos*]. Deteriorating Greek-Turkish relations since the early 1960s and growing emigration in the following decades have left a shrinking population of 1,500–2,000 Greeks in Turkey. The exchange of populations between Greece and Turkey also considerably diminished the Muslims population in Greece, with the important exception of the Turkish/Muslim minority of Thrace (Tsitselikis 2007: 1). The majority of this community still lives in the border region of Western Thrace, the north-eastern part of Greece. The region is one of the least developed regions of the European Union. Almost 80 per cent of their population works in the agricultural sector. Apart from being the only legally-recognised minority group, their strategic location between Greece, Turkey and Bulgaria also make their small population of approximately 120,000 politically significant (Triandafyllidou and Anagnostou 2007).

these groups as recognised legal entities also implies that any international and regional human rights instruments to which Greece and Turkey have become parties directly concern the conditions and protection of these minorities.

The small number of recognised minority populations[2] in both countries, combined with the presence of established legal mechanisms to protect their rights, might lead one to assume that their accommodation has been relatively efficacious. Working from a perspective of historical institutionalism, however, this chapter sets out to describe how domestic policies and the formation of rigid policy patterns have *negatively* affected the conditions of these minorities. In both countries, attempts to strengthen the concept of equal citizenship have been hindered by discriminatory policies, which have threatened to make members of these minorities second class of citizens (especially from the point of view of the minority members). The disruption of the democratisation process by military interventions, the periodic rise of nationalist movements, and fraught bilateral relations between Greece and Turkey have been some of the key factors holding back the effective protection of the minorities concerned.

Limiting the scope of analysis to legally-recognised minorities also serves a practical purpose. The societal structure of the two case studies makes it extremely difficult to compile a detailed analysis of the conditions of every group that could conceptually be described as a national minority. Since the early years of modern Greece and Turkey, various measures and practices aiming to homogenise the societies have been employed as a means to establish nation-states. And yet – much as in most of the other new nation-states of the interwar period – the nations to be built were perceived as 'trans-ethnic' or 'supra-ethnic', meaning, they did not treat ethnicity as a major component of the nationalisation process (Brubaker 1996: 413). Accordingly, the tripartite criterion employed under the League of Nations to define minorities in racial, linguistic and religious terms was limited in Turkey to the recognition of 'non-Muslims', and in Greece to 'Muslims'. Turkey, in particular, presents a highly-complex case due to its large population and ethnic structure. As the successor to a multi-ethnic empire, the modern Turkish state has included over 30 ethnic groups since its founding.[3] In forging a national identity, the republican regime originally subscribed to a definition of 'Turk' that was based on culture, not race (Oran 2007). In turn, the ethnic identities of most groups have become sub-identities under the supra-identity of being Turkish. Thus, Muslim citizens with ethnic and linguistic characteristics that are different from the majority are not classified as minorities in Turkey. The situation in Greece has been more or less similar. The Greek nation's self-perception is based on Greek Orthodoxy and

2. The provisions of the Lausanne Treaty explicitly refer to the legal protection of 'non-Muslims'. However, apart from Armenians, Jews and Greeks, there are other groups who may be eligible right-holders in accordance with the provisions of Lausanne Treaty. For a detailed discussion, see Baskin Oran (2004).

3. According to a study undertaken by Alfrod Andrews, there are forty-two ethnic groups in Turkey (1992 cited Oran 2004: 47).

upon a somewhat ambivalent conception of 'racial continuity' (Tsitselikis 2007: 1).

This chapter employs the process tracing method for its analysis of Greece and Turkey and the cases of minority groups in the two countries. Semi-structured in-depth interviews were conducted with thirty-three individuals from Turkey, and thirty-one individuals from Greece. In accordance with the process tracing technique, both positional and reputational criteria were taken into account in the selection of respondents. The selection of interviewees involved the non-probability sampling methods of purposive sampling and chain-referral/snowball sampling. While the respondents comprise a heterogeneous group in terms of gender, ethnicity and educational background, the majority ranged between twenty-five and sixty-five years of age. Most respondents had some knowledge of minority politics in Greece and Turkey. Among the minority members, individuals from various backgrounds were selected, who were mostly active in their community's economic, social, political and cultural life. The respondents also include members of the Turkish Parliament, members of the Greek Parliament, policy-makers and policy experts, members of non-governmental and human rights organisations, academics, and journalists from Greece and Turkey.[4] The interviews mainly aimed to assess respondents' views and perceptions of individual actors, and to evaluate how these actors viewed the socio-economic, political and legal conditions of minorities.[5]

The format of the chapter is as follows. The first part highlights the plausibility of borrowing from historical institutionalism by introducing some of its key concepts, such as initial policy choices, path dependency and critical junctures. The second part elaborates on the formal and informal procedures embedded in the 1923 Treaty of Lausanne, which was subsequently institutionalised within the minority rights systems of both Greece and Turkey. We shall argue that the treaty's key element – the principle of reciprocity – not only affected domestic actors' initial policy choices, but that it has also created a path-dependent policy pattern in the area of minority rights, by virtue of its implementation within the bilateral context of Greek-Turkish relations. This section focuses on certain key events that resulted in critical junctures in the treatment and conditions of minorities. As is often stressed in various analytical platforms, despite the specificities of each country's minorities, minority-related issues in both Greece and Turkey are interlinked and multifaceted. Accordingly, this chapter aims to present the conditions of minorities as an outcome of the strikingly similar policy patterns created by the Greek and Turkish states within a framework of historical institutionalism.

---

4. Some of the interviews in Greece were conducted in conjunction with EUROREG, a research project coordinated by the Hellenic Foundation of European and Foreign Policy (ELIAMEP). Funded under the EU's Sixth Framework Programme, the EUROREG project mainly explores the links between European economic integration and ethnic minority mobilisation in EU member states and accession countries. EUROREG, Contract no: CIT2-CT-2003-506019

5. For an extensive analysis of minorities in Greece and Turkey, which also covers the reform process since the 1990s, see Memisoglu (2009).

Conceptualising path-dependent policy patterns – creation of normative orders?

Historical institutionalism defines the state as a set of potentially autonomous institutions that structure power relations and competition between actors (Lecours 2000: 513). Institutions are seen as a critical contextual variable that shape the behaviour of actors through strategic interaction, by providing 'greater or lesser degrees of certainty about the present and future behaviour of other actors' (Hall and Taylor 1996: 7). To assess how institutions affect the behaviour of actors, historical institutionalism suggests focusing on their initial policy choices as a key starting point. The operative forces that shaped these initial policies will be mediated by the contextual features of subsequent situations – thus influencing subsequent policy choices (Peters 1999), which may lead to a path-dependent policy pattern.

The concept of path dependence refers to the dynamics of 'self-reinforcing or positive feedback processes in a political system' (Pierson and Skocpol 2000: 6). Path-dependent processes lead actors to take into account existing patterns in a policy area when making their ensuing choices. After all, once certain economic, social and political arrangements are in place, Alexander (2001: 254) argues, they appear to generate patterns of costs and benefits in which actors will typically prefer to maintain the status quo. When actors undertake a particular policy path for a period, they are likely to find it highly difficult to reverse their action, since political alternatives that were once plausible may become obsolete (Pierson and Skocpol 2000: 6). Nonetheless, actors consistently calculate the probable benefits of change from the status quo in the long run (Alexander 2001: 254). This is why advocates of historical institutionalism place such strong emphasis on the timing and sequence of particular events within path-dependent processes, since certain events may create 'critical junctures' for actors. As Mahoney (2001: 113) defines them, critical junctures are choice points that present an alternative to path-dependent policies; not all choice points represent critical junctures, however, since only those choice points that close off important future outcomes should be treated as critical junctures. The choices given at a critical juncture are shaped by a wide range of factors, including agency discretion (Collier and Collier 1991: 27), the costs and benefits of rejecting initial policy choices, and by the impact of institutional arrangements. Moreover, many critical junctures occur in contingency situations, in which unforeseen events may have an important impact (Mahoney 2001: 113). Thus, events or processes that occur during and immediately after critical junctures are also important, in that they may have a causal impact on the consequences of later developments (Pierson and Skocpol 2000: 6). As will be further elaborated, this theoretical rationale is particularly useful in understanding how the implementation of the reciprocity principle in minority politics created path-dependent policy patterns in Greece and Turkey. The concept of critical junctures offers a powerful analytical tool, by focusing researchers' attention on key choice points. This enables one to find a 'meaningful beginning point of analysis' (Mahoney 2001: 113) for understanding policy shifts at the domestic level in the area of minority rights.

Furthermore, characterising the relationship between institutions and actors as 'non-symmetrical' means assuming that institutions may place some actors in a more advantageous position in the pursuit of particular interests, resulting in disproportionate access to the decision-making process (Hall and Taylor 1996: 9; Rothstein 1992: 52). Consequently, institutions often reinforce power disparities, although disadvantaged actors continue to adapt, either by working within the existing framework in pursuit of goals or looking for alternative choices (Thelen 1999: 385). These analytical points carry particularly strong significance in the context of minority-state relations in Greece and Turkey, which were institutionalised by the 1923 Treaty of Lausanne. The formal and informal procedures embedded in this treaty created a minority rights system that has elevated disparities between dominant and non-dominant groups within the highly-centralised state structures.

The legacy of nationalisation and minority politics

Initial policy choices

Both Greece and Turkey demonstrate some of the key, common features of nationalising states as presented in Brubaker's study. These include the existence of a polity owned by a core nation or nationality; whose specific interests include language, culture, demographic majority; and whose economic wellbeing and political supremacy are actively protected and promoted by the formal/informal practices and policies pursued by the autonomous institutions of the state (Brubaker 1996: 415–16). The compulsory 1923 exchange of populations between the two countries reflects the impact such nationalisation dynamics can have on minorities. Greece and Turkey signed the Convention on the Exchange of Populations in 1923 as a constituent part of the Lausanne Peace Conference – setting down conditions for transferring property and compensation, while exempting the Greek populations living in Istanbul, the islands of Gokceada (Imbros) and Bozcaada (Tenedos) and the Turkish population living in Western Thrace from the exchange process (Hirschon 2003: 7). The exchange of populations institutionalised the homogenisation of Turkish and Greek populations (Akgonul 2008: 20), forcing people to leave their homeland because of their exclusion from the newly-established nation-states of Greece and Turkey (Barutciski 2003: 24).

As far as the consequences of the population exchange are concerned, most scholars argue that they have been asymmetrical, with Greece more heavily affected than Turkey, especially when the numbers of refugees and social consequences are taken into account (Keyder 2003; Kontogiorgi 2003; Veremis 2003). As Keyder notes (2003: 43), the returning Greek migrants constituted almost a quarter of Greece's existing population, whereas the newcomers to Turkey amounted to less than 4 per cent of Turkey's population. Considering the gravity of the influx to Greece, this resettlement proved a particularly great burden to the Greek economy, which was forced to resort to dependence on foreign financial aid

(Hirschon 2003: 17). However, it may also be observed that Greece was successful in transforming this situation into a socio-economic, political and cultural asset in the long run (Voutira 2003: 147), since the returning refugees were mostly skilled entrepreneurs, traders and craftsmen who contributed positively to Greece's economic development (Kontogiorgi 2003: 64). Besides, the Greek government also took effective measures to invest in the rural economy, in order to promote settlement in the less developed northern region of the country (Voutira 2003: 148). By contrast, Turkey did not seek financial assistance, since the Turkish refugees did not pose any financial distress; indeed, they were mainly peasants, who were easily adapted to the agriculture-based economy of Turkey. The country's economy suffered for a longer period from the departure of Greeks, who controlled vital sectors of economic life such as trade, industry and export-import. Turkey lost its most economically-skilled population, necessitating long years of structural modification and readjustment in its economy (Aktar 2003: 79).

The exchange of populations between Greece and Turkey had a severe social impact on both of the communities forced to migrate, and on those exempted from the exchange. According to Barutciski (2003: 25), population exchanges typically emerge as a political option in times of crises; decisions to undertake them are usually made very quickly, without fully understanding the long-term consequences they may have on the 'targeted minorities'. In the case of Greece and Turkey – even though population exchange led to short-term stability in their relations – it caused considerable human suffering and led to long years of mistrust between the people of the two societies. More significantly, in the context of Greek-Turkish relations, those who were exempted from the exchange became 'the pawns in the endless Greek-Turkish chess game' (Bahceli 1990: 174), since the system created under the Treaty of Lausanne gave precedence to state interests over the rights of individuals (Barutciski 2003: 27). As Aktar argues (2003: 94), despite granting citizenship to those who were exempted under the Treaty, these exempted minorities were, nevertheless, treated as outsiders in many aspects of social life in both countries, which made their integration into the national community highly problematic. Soner's (2005) study on the development of citizenship and minorities in Turkey demonstrates how centuries-old cleavages, confrontations and prejudices have continued to play an important role in shaping citizenship policy practices, jeopardising possible grounds for the creation of equal coexistence between the Turkish-Muslim and non-Muslim sections of population. Indeed, the author describes how the 'national otherness' of minorities has led to the infringement of the Lausanne commitments, and how no compromise could be achieved between the 'principles of citizenship equality and the disparate treatment on the part of the non-Muslim minorities' (Soner 2005: 298).

From the minorities' perspective, their treatment as 'second-class citizens' not only caused fearful and insecure feelings towards the majority and the state, but also complicated their socio-economic and political integration into society. As a number of minority members from different communities in Turkey have asserted, such integration problems have become more evident in later years, with the de facto exclusion of Lausanne minorities from undertaking roles in the state administration.[6] It has been argued that such discriminatory measures have played a crucial role in shaping the socio-economic and political conditions of non-Muslim minorities in later decades. In the words of a minority member who now works as a vice-president at a municipality:

> Yes, we are Turkish citizens, but in the past we have always been excluded from the state administration, we can neither be a police officer, nor a judge or an attorney. We could not work at the prefecture; in fact we could not even work as a cleaner at any state office. However, I should also emphasise that since the late 1990s, local governance gained significant importance in Turkey. Thus, a number of minority members get elected in local elections these days and work for the municipalities (Interview T007 2007).

Overall, Greek and Turkish governments used the exchange of populations as a method to create cultural and ethnic homogeneity within their borders without giving much consideration to the implications it would have for either the people who left or for those who stayed. In fact, troubled minority-state relations in the intervening decades corroborate Claude's (1955: 91) comment that 'this policy [that resulted in the exchange of populations] is not a way of solving the minority problem, but eradicating it by the alteration of ethnographic conditions that gave rise to it'.

Centrality of the principle of reciprocity

From 1923 onwards, minority rights policies were largely shaped by nationalist policies (Soner 2005: 298) and by the implementation of the reciprocity principle between Greece and Turkey. The Treaty of Lausanne established the minority rights protection system, taking the principle of reciprocity as its basis and defining both countries 'as custodians that could monitor and intervene in the affairs of their kindred minority across the border' (Anagnostou 2005: 38). Nonetheless, the absence of an effective multilateral mechanism to assure the implementation of new minority rights created a 'sense of bilateralism' between Greece and Turkey; thus, the wellbeing of minorities was sustained as long as Greek-Turkish relations were good, as was the case during the rapprochement periods in the 1930s and early 1950s (Alexandris 2003: 117; Niarchos 2002: 9). Considering the fact that Greek-Turkish relations have suffered from a series of bilateral disputes over the past decades, their respective minorities have become the target of retaliation,

---

6. Although there is no statistical or legal evidence to support claims of discrimination concerning equal employment opportunities, Turkey has constantly been criticised on various grounds by the European Union institutions and other human rights organisations for the absence of effective anti-discrimination legislation or a state-level monitoring body. See reports released by the European Commission Turkey Progress Reports SEC (2005) 1426-COM (2005) 561final, SEC (2006) 1390-COM (2006) 649 final, SEC (2007) 1436-COM (2007) 663 final; (ECRI) European Commission against Racism and Intolerance (2005) 'Third Report on Turkey' CRI (2005) 5; US Bureau of Democracy, Human Rights and Labor 'International Religious Freedom Report 2006'; Human Rights Watch Turkey Reports 2007 and 2008.

with the Turkish minority in particular encountering 'physical, economic, social, educational and religious repression' (Niarchos 2002: 2).

In fact, the implementation of the reciprocity principle as a policy tool has been so effective that it has transcended its status as a solely legal concept within this context. As Akgonul (2008:152) notes, it is found in everyday life, as well as in the minds of the minority groups. Indeed, the people in each group set their standards by the status of the opposite group. While the Muslims of Thrace widely believe that the Greeks of Turkey have a wealthier and happier life (Akgonul 2008: 152), the minorities of Turkey regularly refer to the advantageous status of Muslims in Greece, due to their larger population. The implementation of the reciprocity principle did not lead to the emergence of social cooperation between minorities. According to a former member of the Greek parliament:

> I think the Ottoman history demonstrates that Greeks and Turks can live together in peace despite different religious beliefs. Yet, reciprocity has created a different mentality in which mutual understanding somehow lost its importance. As a minority member, you are preoccupied with your own minority's problems. You constantly compare your 'bad' conditions with the 'good' conditions of the reciprocal minority, but empathy rarely becomes a part of this process. Thus, there has never been strategic cooperation between the minorities of the two countries (Interview G019 2005).

Our findings also indicate that the implementation of the reciprocity principle affects not only the Greek minority of Turkey, but also the other Lausanne minorities. As was suggested by a number of minority members of non-Greek origin in Turkey, even though Greece is not their kin-state, worsening Greek-Turkish relations in the past have also made them targets of retaliatory policies. According to a member of the Armenian minority from Turkey:

> The Greek and Armenian communities do not really live together and they are not that integrated. Yet, the government policies towards both communities are very much alike. Just to give an example, there was an interview in *Hurriyet* [a Turkish newspaper] with a former member of the parliament sometime ago.[7] The interviewer says that the reciprocity rule and arrangements between the Greek minority in Turkey and the Turkish minority in Greece are reasonable, but then asks why the implementation of these rules includes the Armenian minority of Turkey. The answer of the MP is quite interesting – disappointing as well – 'it is too difficult to divide them after all these years of similar policy implementation. Yes, the wet also burns with the dry [a Turkish expression]'. This is a statement given by a MP, which I think very much explains the situation (Interview T001 2006).

Thus, the notion of reciprocity in minority policies has not only been internalised

---

7. See, *Hurriyet* newspaper (1997), Ersin Kalkan's interview with Former State Minister Metin Gurdere, 12 October.

by minority members (Yagcioglu 2008: 103), but also by *state* institutions and political actors. Indeed, some political actors argue that the reciprocity principle has been a useful policy tool for defending the rights of their respective minorities abroad. In the words of a current member of the Turkish Parliament:

> Yes, the members of the Turkish minority of Western Thrace are Greek citizens. But for decades, they have regarded the Turkish state as the primary guarantor of their rights. Most families have sent their children to study in Turkey due to poor socio-economic and education standards in Western Thrace. So, if we abolish the principle of reciprocity, what would be the legal basis to defend their rights? And the same logic applies for the Greek state. I do not think that the Greek authorities would ever want to give up the reciprocity principle for the sake of the Greek minority living in Turkey (Interview T023 2007).

According to some political actors, the Turkish state's desire to safeguard the principle of reciprocity has mostly been a by-product of the 'ineffectiveness of the international community' in preventing the violations of the Muslim minority's rights until recent years. As expressed by a member of the Human Rights Commission of the Turkish Parliament:

> We first need to assess whether there is a more effective protection system than the implementation of the Lausanne Treaty. I am referring to an international system that would adopt a more 'genuine' approach, a system that would be applicable to all states, not just 'particular ones', because its current approach differs from one country to another. The Turkish minority of Greece still cannot freely elect their own religious leader; this is a well-known problem. Their freedom of association is also disputed. Yet, the international community's response has been inadequate to such violations of minority rights in Greece. Let's just assume that the Turkish parliament adopts a new legislation tomorrow, which would bring similar restrictions on the elections of the Greek or the Armenian Patriarch in Turkey. Such a radical decision would draw all the attention of the international media, international organisations and the EU officials would immediately criticise Turkey. And yes, this should be the proper reaction, but such external pressures should also be strong in the case of Greece (Interview T025 2007).

Political actors from Greece also emphasise the political salience of the reciprocity principle for the Greek state and its institutions. Some respondents consider the country's static approach towards the major issues faced by the Muslim minority – such as the Greek state's refusal to recognise the minority's ethnic identity – as an indicator of the prevailing importance of the reciprocity principle. As one policy-maker noted:

> From a legal perspective, the Lausanne Treaty granted subjective rights to the Greek minority of Istanbul and the Muslim minority of Thrace. Yet, the major issue about these minorities has been a very acute political issue. It is mostly a matter of policy, not law. I mean, it is mostly a matter of 'political will', not

law. When you look at previous policies, one can easily observe the political impact of the relationship between Greece and Turkey, the conflict between Greek-Turkish nationalism and the impact of reciprocity principle in shaping policies towards minorities (Interview NG027 2007).

Some other respondents, in contrast, draw attention to the reciprocity principle's diminishing impact on the Greek state's policies towards the Western Thracian minority. According to a political adviser to the former Greek government:

> When we look at Greece, the negative implications of the principle of reciprocity on the Thracian minority have considerably diminished since our country became more democratic as a result of domestic dynamics and the EU membership. Now the Greek government adopts a number of policy measures to improve the standards of the Muslim minority, regardless of its counterpart's [Turkish state] policies. The university quota for Muslim minority students is just one example; and such positive discrimination does not exist for the Greek minority students studying in Turkey (Interview G028 2007).

Some also highlight how certain state institutions have become less resistant to change, as a result of the growing importance of minority rights in international law. For example:

> Even though the courts in Greece were reluctant to accept changes brought by the obligations of international treaties, this is gradually changing due to the impact of international law, because international courts adopted a more sensitive approach to the issue of minority rights (Interview G025 2007).

According to other political actors, the principle of reciprocity has diminished in importance in line with the shrinking population of the Greek minority of Turkey. In the words of a member of the EU parliament:

> The Greek minority's survival depends on Turkey, because it is not a matter of reciprocity anymore. It requires the Turkish state's positive discrimination to ensure that such a historic community does not go extinct. That is why I am in favour of Turkey's membership in the EU, because in my view it would promote democracy and rule of law, which would create a more peaceful environment for the protection of small minorities (Interview B003 2006).

Most of the narratives we encountered indicated a strong perception that the Treaty of Lausanne both formally and informally institutionalised minority rights protection in Greece and Turkey, through the implementation of the reciprocity principle. By defining the two countries as the custodians of their respective minorities, the Treaty of Lausanne established the legal and political basis for each state to monitor and intervene in the affairs of its kin-related minority across the border, thereby integrating minority affairs into the larger context of Greek-Turkish relations (Rozakis 1996: 105). Robert Keohane's conceptualisation of reciprocity sensibly fits into this context. According to Keohane (1986 cited in Kamouzis 2007: 50):

Reciprocity refers to exchanges of roughly equivalent values in which the actions of each party are contingent on the prior actions of the others in such a way that good is returned for good, and bad for bad. If either of two parties practicing specific reciprocity begins with a malign move, cooperation can never be achieved as long as both persist in this strategy.

While some respondents perceived reciprocity as having a negative connotation, others viewed it as the *sine qua non* for the protection of minorities subject to the Lausanne minority system in both countries. Overall, it can be said that the principle of reciprocity represents one of the core elements that shaped the initial policy choices of domestic actors, and its implementation has had major socio-economic, political and cultural implications for the conditions of minorities.

Critical junctures and the formation of path-dependent policy patterns

While the above findings reflect actors' various perceptions of the principle of reciprocity, it is also essential to assess the reciprocity principle's impact on policy practices involving the Lausanne minorities. Three major events in recent Turkish history the collection of wealth tax in the 1940s, the Istanbul Riots in 1955,[8] and the expulsion of thousands of Greeks in 1964 – merit particular attention. These events shed light on the nationalist tendencies[9] demonstrated by the core nation in its nationalisation process and attest to the formation of path-dependent policy patterns. In accordance with the conceptual framework developed by Collier and Collier (1991), Pierson (2004) and Capoccia and Kelemen (2007), these turning points can be referred to as critical junctures, since they precluded alternative options and led to the establishment of institutions that generate 'self-reinforcing path-dependent processes' (Capoccia and Kelemen 2007: 341). Furthermore, by placing these events within the general context of Greek-Turkish relations, and taking into account responding policy measures taken by the Greek state, we may better understand the prevalence of 'reciprocity principle' in domestic policy-making. While this study does not intend to provide an extensive historical account on these events,[10] a brief overview helps to inform our general discussion, since these turning points decisively changed the socio-economic and political conditions of minority populations.

---

8. Also known as the Istanbul Pogrom in English, Σεπτεμβριανά [Events of September] in Greek, and 6–7 Eylül Olaylari [Events of 6–7 September] in Turkish.

9. Soner (2005: 298) also highlights how demographic, linguistic, cultural and economic policies of nationalism – which became prevalent during the single-party period in Turkey (1923–50) – advanced at the expense of non-Muslim minorities' ethno-cultural, demographic and economic presence in the country.

10. See, Akar (2006) and Aktar (2006).

The first turning point, as mentioned above, came in the form of the wealth tax (or capital tax) that the Turkish government collected from the non-Muslim population during the 1940s, in the hope of reducing the financial burden that World War II had placed on the Turkish economy. According to official figures, 350 million Turkish lira was to be collected from taxpayers – of which 289 million would be taken from non-Muslim taxpayers.[11] In his comprehensive study on that period, Akar (2006) describes the wealth tax as an economic genocide, and argues that no other measure or event concerning the non-Muslim minority was as extensive or systematic as the policy implemented during the collection of the wealth tax. While this policy measure did not result in any economic improvements in the long run, it was remembered subsequently as a discriminative policy (Akar 2006: 59). A recent work conducted by journalist Yahya Kocoglu, comprised of interviews with fifteen elderly members of Greek, Armenian and Jewish minorities who lived through this period, sheds light on 'this dark episode of Turkish history' (Akyol 2007). While most commentators pointed out the immense financial distress the tax inflicted on the non-Muslim communities, others described examples of family members who were deported to labour camps in the eastern part of Turkey (Kocoglu 2003); 1,229 out of the 1,440 taxpayers who were sent to labour camps were Lausanne minorities living in Istanbul.[12] Also, as noted above, many minority members – the Greeks of Istanbul in particular – had to sell their properties and leave the country (Niarchos 2002: 9; Ustundag 2003: 6).

The second turning point came with the outbreak of riots in Istanbul in 1955 – triggered by false speculation that the house in Thessaloniki, Greece, where Ataturk was born, had been bombed. The riots primarily targeted the Greek minority, but soon enough were directed at the Armenian and Jewish communities. During the two-days of rioting, minority businesses, schools, churches and houses were severely damaged and destroyed, causing the deaths of several individuals from the Greek and Armenian communities, as well as numerous injuries. The estimated economic cost of the riots has been variously estimated at between US$25 million and US$150 million (Interview T010 2006). Just before the riots, the Greek community's population was 135,000, a number that declined to 70,000 after a significant post-riot emigration flow (Interview T010 2006).

The third and final turning point came with the outbreak of inter-communal violations in Cyprus, which escalated Greek-Turkish tensions over a period of several years. For the Greek minority in Turkey, the immediate consequences of this situation involved the departure of more than 30,000 Greeks who held Greek citizenship (Niarchos 2002: 11; Tsitselikis 2008: 82). After the 1930 Turkish-Greek agreement of residence, some Greeks had returned to Istanbul with Greek nationality, a development that ensured the survival of the Greeks of Istanbul until the 1960s (Akgonul 2008: 23). But then, as a consequence of the Cyprus problem,

---

11. See, *Salom* Newspaper (2011) Varlik Vergisi, 6 July. Online. Available /www.salom.com.tr/news/ detail/18806- Varlik-Vergisi-Gercegi.aspx

12. See, *Salom* Newspaper (2011) Varlik Vergisi, 6 July.

these Greeks were once again forced to leave the country, along with thousands of Turkish-nationality Greeks who had constituted the real Greek minority of Turkey (Akgonul 2008: 23).

In the wake of these events, the minority education system became a major target and was subject to numerous restrictions. Indeed, minority schools were mostly shut down during the hostile Greek-Turkish relations in the 1960s (Oran 2004: 109). Tsitselikis (2008) describes how education became one of the key areas in which both Greece and Turkey adopted mutually-exact measures in the name of reciprocity during the troubled relations. These included mutual prohibitions of Greek and Turkish textbooks – their redistribution being on an entirely reciprocal basis – along with the firing of Muslim teachers from their posts as a countermeasure in response to the dismissal of Greek teachers in Turkey[13] (Tsitselikis 2008: 84–5). Although freedom of religion had not thus far been a principal target as such, there *have* been indirect limitations, whereby the opening of new churches, the establishment of religious charities and the education of clerics in religious schools has proven highly problematic (Oran 2004: 111). Macar (2008:146), however, has argued that the Greek Patriarchate in Istanbul has been a victim of reciprocity, due to its negative image as a 'foreign institution', since it was considered to be a part of the opposing side during the 1955 riots, and during the Cyprus conflict of the 1960s. Indeed, the official discourse during that period confirms the Patriarchate's status *vis-à-vis* the principle of reciprocity. In the words of the spokesperson for the Ministry of Foreign Affairs:

> Turkish-Greek relations are based on the balance established by the Lausanne Treaty. By means of comparison, the Cyprus Question, Dodecanesian Turks, Greeks living in Istanbul and the Patriarchate would be regarded as within that equilibrium (*Milliyet* newspaper 1965, cited in Macar 2008: 146).

One immediate policy restriction involved the closure of the Theological School of Halki [Heybeliada] in 1971. As Baloglu (2000:11) notes, the two institutions (the School of Halki and the Patriarchate) have served as important 'trump cards' in the resolution of Turkish and Greek problems. It should also be noted that the two issues have been on the political agenda since Turkey's relations with Greece and the European Union rose to prominence in the late 1990s. The EU Commission progress reports on Turkey have repeatedly emphasised the importance of improving standards of freedom of religion by reopening the Theological School and respecting the international recognition of the Patriarchate.[14]

---

13. For a detailed assessment of the impact of reciprocity principle on education, see Tsitselikis (2008).

14. See, European Commission (2006): 'As concerns freedom of religion, freedom of worship continues to be generally respected [...] Furthermore, a number of other problems remain [...] Restrictions on the training of clergy and on foreign clergy to work in Turkey remain. Turkish legislation does not provide for private higher religious education for these communities. The Greek Orthodox Halki [Heybeliada] seminary remains closed. The public use of the ecclesiastical title of Ecumenical Patriarch is still banned.'

Some scholars argue that the Muslim minority in Greece did not encounter problems as severe as those faced by their counterparts in Turkey because the policies adopted by the Greek state were less hostile and assimilating (Niarchos 2002: 25). Indeed, several minority members from Turkey share the general belief that, despite experiencing difficulties as a minority group, their counterparts in Greece have always held a more advantageous status, largely the result of their sizeable population and, especially, due to their status (as of the 1980s) as citizens of an EU member state. While both governments are restrictive and discriminative in nature, it could be argued that the subsequent Greek governments did not employ an approach towards minorities that was as intensely interventionist as that of Turkey's government during the period under analysis. Nevertheless, our findings draw attention to the long-standing problems of the Muslim/Turkish minority in Greece and their isolation as a community, along with poor economic conditions and living standards in the region (Oran 2004: 28). Accordingly, the actions of Greek policy-makers from the 1920s to the 1980s could perhaps be better understood as 'a policy of benign neglect' (Alexandris 2003: 128). The long-standing isolation of the Muslim minority, combined with their poor economic conditions and living standards, has its roots in earlier negligent policies pursued by the Greek governments. And while the Greek government undertook certain measures to facilitate the settlement of newcomers from Asia Minor, no such measures were adopted for the integration of the Muslim community. This 'intended or unintended' neglect led to the emergence of a severe educational and socio-economic gap between the Muslim minority and the Christian majority, which continued to widen throughout the following decades. Until the early 1990s, discriminative legal and administrative measures undertaken by subsequent Greek governments obstructed Muslims' full enjoyment of citizenship rights, including freedom of movement and equal rights in business and professional life. As stipulated in Decree 1366/1938, land transactions in border areas had to be authorised by the prefecture, which largely blocked Muslims from buying and selling of real estate property in Western Thrace (Interview G030 2007). 'It was almost impossible for minority members to buy and sell property, except if they were selling property to an Orthodox Christian, which was a bit more easy' (Interview G025 2007).

Perhaps more significantly, article 19 of the Greek Citizenship Code had severe implications for the Muslim minority, implicitly rendering them second-class citizens (Triandafyllidou and Anagnostou 2007: 9). The article had initially addressed the citizenship of Slavic-Macedonians (Interview G030 2007) and the communists during the Civil War years, but was later expanded to address the Muslim-Turks, in the wake of deteriorating Greek-Turkish relations during the mid-1960s (Interviews G001 2005; G030 2007). Subsequently, it became a means of balancing out the demographic decline of the Greek population in Turkey following the critical junctures discussed above (Triandafyllidou and Anagnostou 2007: 9; Tsitselikis 2008: 82–3). As Anagnostou (2005: 339) notes:

The deprivation of citizenship on the basis of article 19 was part and parcel of a broader set of informal but widespread restrictive measures instituted by Greek governments appealing to the need to balance out the demographic decline of the Greek population in Istanbul.

Following the implementation of the article, 46,124 Muslim-Turks were stripped of citizenship as a result of going abroad, and approximately 600 people became stateless despite the fact that they did not leave the country during these years.[15]

Legal experts from the Greek majority described further restrictive measures that negatively impacted on minority members' daily life, such as rules requiring licenses to build or rebuild houses. Licences to practice professions or run businesses were also almost impossible to obtain due to bureaucratic difficulties. In the words of one lawyer:

> What is interesting to note here is that minority members were driving without driving licences. The policemen were issuing tickets when they stopped them for violating a traffic rule, and also for not having a driver's licence. But there was some sort of a 'silent agreement' between the minority members and the local politicians. They [local politicians] were saying, 'Don't worry, I am going to delete these tickets'. But of course, these discriminatory policies had more serious ramifications: the Muslim minority neighbourhoods turned into ghettos and there are still various ghettos in Thrace now (Interview G025 2007).

One minority member, who is currently working at the Prefecture Council in Komotini, described how he had to wait for nineteen years after graduating from university to obtain permission to practice his profession as a veterinarian and to sell veterinarian medicine (Interview G023 2005). While such examples help illustrate the conditions experienced by the Muslim-Turkish minority in pre-1990s Thrace, several minority members described the implementation of such measures as an extension of the Greek state's policy towards minorities at the time, which was aimed, in their opinion, at driving away the educated members of the minority and assimilating the rest (Tsitselikis 2008: 83). Indeed, widespread discriminatory measures against the minority – which resulted in their social and economic isolation in the region – led to large-scale emigration to Turkey, Germany and to the urban centres of Athens and Thessaloniki (Triandafyllidou and Anagnostou 2005: 13).

Moreover – just as in the case of the minorities of Turkey – the Muslim community in Greece became a target of retaliation in times of troubled bilateral relations. Since the outbreak of the Cyprus conflict in the 1960s, and particularly in the aftermath of 1974, the Greek population became increasingly prejudiced and distrustful towards the Muslim community, a development that was also reflected in the state policies towards the minority at that time (Triandafyllidou and Anagnostou 2005: 7; Tsitselikis 2008: 79). Indeed, as was the case in Turkey, nationalist tendencies also appear to have affected the policy choices of Greek

---

15. See, Council of Europe (2006).

policy-makers.[16] Triandafyllidou and Anagnostou (2005: 7) elaborate further on the broader pattern of national politics in this period, arguing that:

> thoroughly misconstruing the principle of reciprocity, Greek authorities sought retribution by disenfranchising the latter [the minority in Thrace]. Depicting it as a 'fifth column' of Turkey, a danger to national unity and territorial integrity that had to be assimilated or defended against, also served a powerful nationalising function domestically.

In the context of the Muslim-Turkish minority, the impact of Greek-Turkish relations can be seen most clearly in the sporadic recognition of the minority's ethnic identity. Up until the early 1950s, the Muslims of Thrace – made up of individuals of Turkish origin, Gypsies (Roma) and Slav-speaking Pomaks – were characterised as a religious community sustaining the main element of the Ottoman millet system (Triandafyllidou and Anagnostou 2007: 4). In the post-World War II period, the Greek state's policy towards the minority, and its implementation of the Lausanne Treaty provisions, fluctuated in response to the ebb and flow of Greek-Turkish relations (Rozakis 1996: 105). In 1951–2, the official label used for the Thracian minority was briefly changed from 'Muslim' to 'Turkish', arguably as a goodwill gesture to Turkey during a brief period of rapprochement, during which the two countries joined NATO (Anagnostou 2001: 102). Minority schools and other associations were denominated as 'Turkish' and the teaching of the Turkish language was also made mandatory for Pomaks, contributing to their linguistic and cultural homogenisation in the long run. As a result of their education in bilingual Greek-Turkish schools, alongside ethnic Turks, Pomaks have also come to speak Turkish and have developed significant affinities with ethnic Turks. However, the official term was changed back to 'Muslim' when relations between the two countries deteriorated in the 1960s, particularly after the installation of the military regime in Greece in 1967 (Triandafyllidou and Anagnostou 2007).

Thus, the recognition of a common ethnic identity became highly problematic in the context of minority-Greek state relations. Indeed, in this case nationalising forces were also accompanied by what Brubaker (2000) has referred to as 'transborder nationalism' or 'homeland nationalism' – a force that leads to the emergence of minority nationalism, linked to the accidental diasporas. As Brubaker (2000: 5) elaborates: 'minority nationalist stances involve a self-understanding in specifically "national" rather than merely "ethnic" terms, a demand for state recognition of their distinct ethnocultural nationality, and the assertion of certain collective, nationality-based cultural or political rights.'

As a consequence of the escalating Greek-Turkish conflict in the period from the 1960s onward, the spread of a Turkish identity among minority members became a primary concern, making the 'promotion of religion as the collective

---

16. As Tsitselikis (2008: 81) argues, the decline in the number of Greeks of Turkey and the relatively stable number of Turks/Muslims in Thrace fuelled nationalistic and ideologically-oriented discourses aimed at the preservation/extinction of 'our'/'their', 'race'/'nation' on a given territory.

identity' a central element of the Greek minority rights policy. Because national/ ethnic origin, language and religion are no longer included in censuses in Greece, different sources provide different numbers for the 'exact' populations of minority groups living in Western Thrace (Koutroubas 2001: 13; Rozakis 1996: 98). Based on independent sources, the population of the Western Thrace minority represents approximately 30 per cent (120,000) of the total population of the region; ethnic Turks constitute the dominant community (70,000), followed by Pomaks (30,000) and Muslim Gypsies (20,000). It has been argued that, since there is no linguistic and ethnic homogeneity within the minority group, the strongest bond its members share is their religious affiliation (Koutroubas 2001: 13) – though some scholars claim that the spread of the Turkish language and identity among the non-Turkish Muslim minority became more prevalent during the late 1980s (Poulton 1993). The spread of the Turkish language was to be expected, since it has been taught in all of the minority schools of Western Thrace following the 1951 and 1968 Turkish-Greek educational agreements (Koutroubas 2001: 15). By contrast – excluding the short-lived rapprochement (1947 –53) between Greece and Turkey – the Greek state has refrained from referring to the minority group of Western Thrace as 'Turkish', and instead uses the term 'Muslim' (Human Rights Watch 1999).

It has also been argued that encouraging ethnic awareness within the Turkish-speaking minority, particularly within the Pomaks, has been an important aspect of the Greek state's minority policy in recent years, and part of a wider programme of actions meant to control the spread of Turkish identity (Demetriou 2004: 97). As Oran (2003: 104) notes, the Turkish community's three main civil society organisations were shut down in 1987, on the grounds that by referring to the Muslim minority as 'Turkish' in their titles, they presented a threat to public order. Subsequently, in 1990, the Greek High Court officially prohibited of the use of the word 'Turk' in reference to the Muslim minority (Koutroubas 2001: 17). Nonetheless, despite the Greek government's counter efforts, most minority members define themselves as being of 'Turkish-origin' – a phenomenon that has only grown since the 1980s (Triandafyllidou and Anagnostou 2005). According to Koutroubas (2001: 11), such insistence on defining the minority as a religious entity rather than recognising their ethnic difference, earns Greece reprimands from the European Convention on Human Rights and other human rights organisations

Conclusion

In order to explicate developments in policy practices in the area of minority rights, this chapter has explored the historical context of minority issues in Greece and Turkey. By elaborating on the evolution of minority rights protection in the early twentieth century, the first section stressed the institutionalisation of minority politics in both countries under the 1923 Treaty of Lausanne. The treaty's key element, the principle of reciprocity, was revealed to have shaped not only the initial policy choices of the domestic actors involved, but was shown – *vis-à-vis* its implementation within the bilateral context of Greek-Turkish relations – to have created a path-dependent policy pattern in the area of minority rights. The concept of path dependency is a key analytical tool of historical institutionalism, which refers to the dynamics of 'self-reinforcing or positive feedback processes in a political system' (Pierson and Skocpol 2000: 6). Path-dependent processes lead actors to bear in mind existing patterns in a policy area.

In the context of Greek and Turkish policy-makers, the strategies and goals of their counterparts also demonstrated a substantial impact on policy choices as a result of the reciprocity principle. Accordingly, one major consequence of path-dependent policy patterns has been a considerable decline in minority populations in both countries, especially after the outbreak of inter-communal violations in Cyprus, following which both Greek and Turkish governments implemented countermeasures to diminish the populations of their respective minorities. Thus, it can be convincingly argued that the principle of reciprocity has repeatedly taken the form of 'negative reciprocity' in the administration of minority issues in both countries. Years of troubled bilateral relations, resulting from various factors, have turned the Greek minority in Turkey and the Turkish/Muslim minority in Greece into targets for retaliation; they can be seen as entrapped by the foreign policies of their kin-states and by the national antagonisms of their own countries. Indeed, the implementation of the reciprocity principle appears to affect not only these two minority groups, but also to have major implications on other non-Muslim entities – particularly in Turkey – who are also subject to the minority rights system established under the Treaty of Lausanne. While this chapter has focused on the formation of initial policy choices and the subsequent creation of path-dependent policy patterns, there is ample scope for further studies on the recent reform processes in Greece and Turkey to add to our understanding of the legacy of past policies in the area of minority rights.

References

Akar, R. (2006) *Askale Yolculari: Varlik vergisi ve calisma kamplari* [*On the road to Askale: The capital levy and the labour camps*], Istanbul: Mephisto Basim.

Akgonul, S. (ed) (2008) *Reciprocity: Greek and Turkish minorities law, religion and politics,* Istanbul: Bilgi University Press.

Aktar, A. (2003) 'Homogenising the nation: Turkifying the economy', in R. Hirschon (ed.) *Crossing the Aegean*, Oxford: Berghan Books, pp. 79–96.

—   (2006) *Varlik Vergisi ve Turklestirme Politikalari,* Istanbul: Iletisim Yayinlari [Iletisim Publications].

Akyol, M. (2007) 'The protocols of the elders of Turkey', *Washington Post*, 7 October.

Alexander, G. (2001) 'Institutions, path dependence, and democratic consolidation', *Journal of Theoretical Politics*, 13(3): 249–70.

Alexandris, A. (2003) 'The identity issue of the minorities in Greece and Turkey', in R. Hirschon (ed.) *Crossing the Aegean*, Oxford: Berghan Books, pp. 117–32.

Anagnostou, D. (2001) 'Breaking the cycle of nationalism: the EU, regional policy and the minority Western Thrace', *South European Society and Politics*, 6(1): 99–124.

—   (2005) 'Deepening democracy or defending the nation? The Europeanisation of minority rights and Greek citizenship', *West European Politics*, 28(2): 335–57.

Bahceli, T. (1990) *Greek-Turkish Relations since 1955*, London: Westview Press.

Baloglu, Z. (2000) *Grek Devleti, Patrikhane ve Rahipler Okulu* [*Greek State, the Patriarchate and the Theological School*], Istanbul: Harp Akademileri Komutanligi Yayinlari.

Barutciski, M. (2003) 'Population exchanges in international law and policy', in R. Hirschon (ed.) *Crossing the Aegean*, Oxford: Berghahn Books, pp. 23–37.

Brubaker, R. (1996) 'Nationalising states in the old "new Europe" and the new', *Ethnic and Racial Studies*, 19(2): 411–37.

—   (2000) 'Accidental diasporas and external "homelands" in Central and Eastern Europe: past and present', *Political Science Series*, 71 (October), Vienna: Institute for Advanced Studies.

Capoccia, G. and Kelemen, R. D. (2007) 'The study of critical junctures theory, narrative, and counterfactuals in historical institutionalism', *World Politics*, 59 (April): 341–69.

Claude, I. L. (1955) *National Minorities: An international problem*, Cambridge: Harvard University Press.

Collier, R. B. and Collier, D. (1991) *Critical Junctures, the Labor Movement, and Regime Dynamics in Latin America*, Princeton: Princeton University Press.

Council of Europe (2006) 'Follow-up report on the Hellenic Republic (2002–2005):

assessment of the progress made in implementing the recommendations of the Council of Europe Commissioner for Human Rights', CommDH (2006) 13, 29 March.

Demetriou, O. (2004) 'Prioritizing ethnicities: the uncertainty of Pomak-ness in the urban Greek Rhodoppe', *Ethnic and Racial Studies*, 27(1): 95–119.

Hall, P. A. and Taylor, R. C. (1996) 'Political science and the three new institutionalisms', Max-Planck-Institut für Gesellschaftsforschung (MPIFG) Discussion Paper, 96(6).

Hirschon, R. (2003) 'Unmixing peoples in the Aegean region', in R. Hirschon (ed.) *Crossing the Aegean*, Oxford: Berghan Books, pp. 3–20.

Human Rights Watch (1999) 'Greece: The Turks of Western Thrace', *Human Rights Watch Publications*, 1 January.

Kamouzis, D. (2007) 'Reciprocity or international intervention? Greek and Turkish minority policy, 1923–1930', in S. Akgonul (ed.) *Reciprocity: Greek and Turkish minorities law, religion and politics*, Istanbul: Bilgi University Press, pp. 49–69.

Keyder, C. (2003) 'The consequences of the exchange of populations for Turkey', in R. Hirschon (ed.) *Crossing the Aegean*, Oxford: Berghahn Books, pp. 40–52.

Kocoglu, Y. (2003) 'Gayrimüslim hayatlar [Lives of non-Muslims]', *Radikal Newspaper*, 29 January.

Kontogiorgi, E. (2003) 'Economic consequences following refugee settlement in Greek Macedonia, 1923–1932', in R. Hirschon (ed.) *Crossing the Aegean*, Oxford: Berghan Books, pp. 63–78.

Koutroubas, T. (2001) 'Trapped in enemy territory or pilots towards regional integration? A challenge for democracy in the South-Eastern Mediterranean', EUI Working Paper RSC No 2001/19, Florence: European University Institute.

Lecours, A. (2000) 'Theorizing cultural identities: historical institutionalism as a challenge to the culturalists', *Canadian Journal of Political Science*, 33(3): 499–522.

Macar, E. (2008) 'A victim of reciprocity: the Greek Patriarchate of Istanbul', in S. Akgonul (ed.) *Reciprocity: Greek and Turkish minorities law, religion and politics*, Istanbul: Bilgi University Press, pp. 143–50.

Mahoney, J. (2001) 'Path-dependent explanations of regime change: Central America in comparative perspective', *Studies in Comparative International Development*, 36(1): 111–41.

Memisoglu, F. (2009) *The European Union's Approach to Minority Rights and Its Impact on the Development of Minority Rights Protection in Greece and Turkey*, unpublished PhD thesis, University of Nottingham.

Niarchos, G. (2002) *Continuity and Change in the Minority Policies of Greece and Turkey*, London: London School of Economics.

Oran, B. (2003) 'The story of those who stayed: lessons from articles 1 and 2 of the 1923 Convention', in R. Hirschon (ed.) *Crossing the Aegean*, Oxford: Berghahn Books, pp. 97–116.

—	(2004) *Turkiye'de Azinliklar: Kavramlar, teori, Lozan ic mevzuat, ictihat, uygulama* [*Minorities in Turkey: Concepts, theory, Lausanne Convention, and its application*], Istanbul: Iletisim Yayincilik [Iletisim Publications].

—	(2007) 'Minority concept and rights in Turkey: the Lausanne Peace Treaty and current issues', in Z. F. Kabasakal Arat and R. Falk (eds) *Human Rights in Turkey*, Philadelphia: University of Pennsylvania Press.

Peters, B. G. (1999) *Institutional Theory in Political Science*, London: Pinter.

Pierson, P. (2004) *Politics in Time*, Princeton: Princeton University Press.

Pierson, P. and Skocpol. T. 'Historical institutionalism in contemporary political science', paper presented at the American Political Science Association Meeting, Washington, September 2000.

Poulton, H. (1993) *The Balkans: Minorities and governments in conflict*, London: Minority Rights Groups Publication.

Rothstein, B. (1992) 'Labor markets and working-class strength', in S. Steinmo, K. Thelen and F. Longstreth (eds) *Structuring Politics: Historical institutionalism in comparative politics*, Cambridge: Cambridge University Press.

Rozakis, C. (1996) 'The international protection of minorities in Greece', in K. Featherstone and K. Ifantis (eds) *Greece in a Changing Europe: Between European integration and Balkan disintegration*, Manchester: Manchester University Press, pp. 95–116.

Soner, A. (2005) 'Citizenship and the minority questions in Turkey', in F. E. Keyman and A. Icduygu (eds) *Citizenship in a Global World: European questions and Turkish experiences*, London: Routledge, pp. 289–311.

Thelen, K. (1999) 'Historical institutionalism in comparative politics', *Annual Review of Political Science*, 2: 369–404.

Triandafyllidou, A. and Anagnostou, D. (2005) 'Regions, minorities and European policies: a state of the art report on the Turkish Muslims of Western Thrace (Greece)', project report prepared for the EUROREG Research Project (CIT2-CT-2003-506019).

—	(2007) 'Policy brief: the Muslims of Western Thrace, Greece. Recommendations for regional development strategies', policy brief prepared for the EUROREG Research Project (CT-2003-506019).

Tsitselikis, K. '(2007) 'The pending modernisation of Islam in Greece: from millet to minority status', *Südosteuropa*, 55(4): 1–21.

—	(2008) 'Reciprocity as a regulatory pattern for the treatment of Greece's Turkish/Muslim minority', in S. Akgonul (ed.) *Reciprocity: Greek and Turkish minorities law, religion and politics,* Istanbul: Bilgi University Press, pp. 69–102.

Ustundag, E. (2003) *Changing Practices of Citizenship in Turkey: The case of Beyoglu*, Toronto: York University.

Veremis, T. (2003) '1922: political continuations and realignments in the Greek state', in R. Hirschon (ed.) *Crossing the Aegean*, Oxford: Berghan Books, pp. 53–62.

Voutira E. (2003) 'Refugees: whose term is it anyway? Emic and etic constructions of refugees in Modern Greek', in J. van Selm, K. Kamanga, J. Morrison, A. Nadig, S. Spoljar Vrzina and L. van Willigen (eds) *The Refugee Convention at Fifty: A view from forced migration studies*, Lanham: Lexington Books, pp. 65–80.

Yagcioglu, D. (2008) 'The internalization of reciprocity by many members of Greek-Orthodox and Turkish Muslim minorities: How can it be explained? some initial reflections', in S. Akgonul (ed.) *Reciprocity: Greek and Turkish Minorities Law, Religion and Politics*, Istanbul: Bilgi University Press, pp. 103–115.

Primary Sources (interview tape recordings in possession of the author)

G001 (2005) Interview with the author on 10th July 2005, Athens-Greece.

G016–G023 (2005) Interview with the author on 10th December 2005, Komotini-Greece, conducted on behalf of the EU- funded research project EUROREG, contract no. CIT2-CT-2003-506019.

G025–G030 (2007) Interview with the author on 13th April 2007, Athens-Greece.

B003 (2006) Interview with the author on 20th July 2006, Brussels-Belgium.

T001– T005 (2006) Interview with the author on 10th March 2006, Istanbul-Turkey.

T007 (2007) Interview with the author on 06th August 2007, Istanbul-Turkey

T010 (2006) Interview with the author on 10th March 2006, Istanbul-Turkey.

T022–T028 (2007) Interview with the author on 5th July 2007, Ankara-Turkey.

chapter nine | whose mobilisation? An ontological primer on the mobilisation of national minorities[1]

Christina Isabel Zuber

Introduction

'No political analysis can proceed in the absence of assumptions about political ontology. That such assumptions are rarely explicit hardly makes them less consequential' (Hay 2008: 81). This chapter argues that, prior to investigating the mobilisation of national minorities in nationalising states, we should establish whose mobilisation we are talking about. The key question we set out to answer is: What ontological perspective allows us to assume that mobilised national minorities actually exist? While research results in the field of comparative ethnic mobilisation studies are highly sensitive to the views researchers hold about the nature of ethnic groups and ethno-political collective action, ontological considerations have largely remained implicit in their research. This chapter seeks to discuss the ontological assumptions involved in studying minority mobilisation explicitly, and to show how they affect the answers to our research questions.

To provide proper context for this discussion, I posit that studying the 'mobilisation of national minorities' as a bounded phenomenon requires two assumptions – the first one concerning group formation on the basis of ethnic identification and the second concerning collective action on the basis of ethnically defined interests:

- A number of individuals *identify* predominantly with an ethnic category and form a bounded group that is recognised as a national minority by both members and non-members (I will refer to this as the 'ethnic identification assumption', or EI).

- Members of this group share an ethnically-defined collective *interest* and the group confronts the nationalising state with a collective, ethno-political *behaviour* to defend this interest (I will refer to this as the 'ethnic behaviour assumption', or EB).

---

1. My interest in exploring theoretical avenues beyond constructionism in the third section of this chapter was inspired by Sarah Jenkins' compelling talk at the 2011 ASN convention in New York. Constructionism was unable to account for the structurally stable meaning of ethnicity she found to be in place at the local level during her field research in Kenya. I thank her, as well as Christian Blum and Dominik Becker from the University of Cologne and the editors of this volume, for providing very helpful comments on this chapter. Needless to say, all remaining errors are my own.

Drawing on a huge range of research in social and cognitive psychology, Henry E. Hale (2008) has convincingly shown that EB is not implied by EI: ethnic identification at the cognitive level must be kept conceptually distinct from manifest interests and strategic choice that constitute the realm of ethnic politics. Nonetheless, many studies in the field of minority mobilisation still take EI to imply EB. The first section of this chapter argues that this is because the most straightforward ontological basis for treating minority mobilisation as a bounded phenomenon is an essentialist, primordial view of ethnic identity categories. Essentialism allows the researcher to assume the existence of national minorities as collective entities without further argument. This view is now considered untenable throughout a range of disciplines, although it survives *implicitly* in large-N empirical research on minority mobilisation. Indeed, it exerts a profound impact in all steps of the research process, from concept formation to operationalisation, from data collection to analysis and inference. In the last instance, an underlying essentialism determines the view a researcher will hold about the viability of multinational democracy, and encourages a scholarly tendency to overemphasise cases of inter-group conflict and neglect phenomena, such as intra-ethnic competition for diverse preferences of supporters, and mobilisation strategies that fall short of radical ethnic outbidding.

Social constructionists,[2] by contrast, have convincingly argued that working from an essentialist ontology about ethnic groups – or, in Brubaker's (2004: 2) words, a 'groupism' defined as 'the tendency to take bounded groups as fundamental units of analysis (and basic constituents of the social world)' – has serious limitations, and should be abandoned. Constructionism acknowledges that the identity categories of both elites and followers are manifold, and that membership in an ethnic category is defined by social practice, *not* by essential attributes. Thus, a researcher should not simply assume that a national minority exists as a social entity. Furthermore, the fact that people in a given society define themselves along a certain ethnic line (EI) does not imply that there will be coherent behaviour across the group (EB), since group elites may construct alternative categories in order to mobilise support. They might find it in their primary interest to mobilise other cross-cutting identities, rather than fight for representation of the minority group.

However, as I will discuss in the second section on social constructionism, empirical studies of ethnic mobilisation that draw on a constructionist ontology of social categories do have a key shortcoming. Rather than simply presupposing

---

2. The term 'constructivism' is used in many political science writings as an alternative to: 'social constructionism'. I stick to the term 'social constructionism' in order to underscore a theoretical perspective that views social facts as the result of discursive social practice in a given context. The term 'constructivism' is more adequately applied to the psychological construction of meaning at the individual level: 'Despite the many forms of social constructionism, virtually all those who identify themselves as social constructionists favor using the term "constructionism" rather than "constructivism". This distinction reflects the social constructionist's aversion to the notion of an isolated knower' (Raskin 2002: 17).

their subject of analysis to exist, they run the risk of losing the capacity to delineate ethnic mobilisation studies as a specific subfield at all. The pure construction
assumption regarding EI can lead to an overestimation of ethnic entrepreneurs'
capacity to strategically manipulate flexible – qua constructed – identity categories, and thus may be unable to account for the simple fact that 'in many parts of
the world humans on occasion behave differently towards those whom they regard
as co-ethnics' (Banton 2011: 187). A pure constructionist outlook on EI makes it
difficult to live up to the analytical expectation that 'it should therefore be possible
to devise a conceptual framework that facilitates the *comparison* and *explanation*
of *ethnic relations* in *different localities*, provided it takes account of the overlap
between ethnic relations and certain other kinds of social relation' (Banton 2011:
187, my emphasis).

Acknowledging this challenge, the third section of this chapter suggests a
third ontological path, in the form of a cognitively naturalised constructionism.
Presented by philosopher Ron Mallon as a potential means for reconciling natural-
ist and constructionist accounts of social categories (2007b),[3] this perspective is
inspired by social categorisation research in cognitive psychology. This research
finds a cross-cultural predisposition of the human brain to treat ethnic groups *as if*
they *were* natural kinds, though they are in fact social constructs (Gil-White 2001,
see also Brubaker *et al.* 2004). This perspective falls in line with recent empirical analyses in the field of mobilisation studies that present a more fine-grained
picture of EB, and present it as a result of the relationship between elites and
their supporters, in which the latter turn out to be both more heterogeneous than
acknowledged by essentialism, and more stable in their ethnic identification (EI)
than a pure constructionist might be willing to grant. While agreeing that EI does
not imply EB, I argue that naturalised constructionism can indeed explain actors'
cross-cultural predisposition to naturalise along ethnic and racial social categories,
better than conventional constructionism. In addition, drawing on the topic of this
volume I present an example that shows how the mobilisation of ethnic categories
can turn into a default option for elites of national majorities and national minorities in the socially unstable, insecure environment of regime change.

I conclude by arguing that naturalised constructionism is in a position not just
to spare researchers of the unattractive ad hoc explanations for the resilience of
ethnic categories they currently tend to apply when studying ethnic mobilisation,
but also to enable us to delineate ethnic politics as a distinct subject area – offering the potential to reconcile comparative, generalisation-seeking research with
interpretive, case-centred research.

---

3. A comprehensive discussion of the philosophical debate between constructionists and realists
    exceeds the scope of this chapter. I focus on the recent contributions of Ron Mallon (2007a;
    2007b) because they can solve the ontological impasse constructionist-minded political scientists
    encounter when they draw on ad hoc explanations to explain the stickiness of ethnic identity
    categories across socio-historical contexts.

Essentialist primordialism

The introduction to this volume states that 'recent national minority studies have mostly approached the question through the perspectives of social mobilisations, secessionism (Hale 2008 or Gurr 2011) or violence (Laitin 2007) without specifically anchoring these questionings in theories of nationalism' (see Chapter One). One direct consequence of dissociating minority mobilisation from the theories of nationalism that have long experienced their constructivist turn (see, seminally, Anderson 1991) is that many scholars studying mobilisation still employ the ethnic group as their primary unit of analysis, assuming that by virtue of belonging to the same ethnic group, ethnic elites and citizens can easily be merged into a collective actor with unified preferences. While social scientists have mostly used the term 'primordialism' to characterise a view that treats ethnic groups as naturally given and unchangeable social entities, philosophers have engaged with this perspective under the label of 'essentialism' and have more explicitly spelled out what an essentialist view on ethnic identity implies. An essentialist ontology provides the preconditions under which the ethnic identification assumption (EI) may function – allowing ethnic categories to have a core essence defined by a set of intrinsic, natural (biological) properties. 'Essences' are properties or sets of properties that define which individuals are part of the category – in this case, the ethnic minority group (those who possess the necessary properties defining the category) – and which are not (those who do not possess the necessary properties) (employing Mallon's definition of essentialism, 2007a: 148). In this manner, ethnic essences account for who is in and out of a bounded group, as defined by a set of necessary characteristics.

Primordialists go one step further at this point, assuming that ethnic essence implies the presence of manifest collective interests, as well as collective action to defend this interest. In Gil-White's (2001: 515, note 2) terms, they confound 'processes such as ethnic mobilisation with ethnogenesis'. The notion that EI implies the ethnic behaviour assumption (EB) is not necessarily entailed by an essentialist theory of ethnic categories, however, unless we stipulate that one of the necessary criteria for belonging to an ethnic group is a certain set of preferences. The classical outbidding model of ethnic politics (as a micro mechanism, explaining patterns of inter-ethnic conflict at the macro level) assumes precisely that. The ethnic outbidding model, whether expressed in materialist (Rabushka and Shepsle 1972) or socio-psychological (Horowitz 1985) terms, was developed in times when scholarly wisdom followed the primordial paradigm (Chandra 2005), for example:

> The primordial communities that partition the plural society [...] provide a natural base for political organisation and a source of divisiveness as well. And in the plural society, primordial sentiments are (by definition as well as by observation) manifest and politically salient (Rabushka and Shepsle 1972: 63).

The authors explicitly start from the notion of 'uniformity of preference within communities' (Rabushka and Shepsle 1972: 67) and assume that the radical elites that style themselves as the most authentic defenders of the group's collective interest will win the bulk of support among voters within each group. The outbidding model thus connects EI, collective interest and radical behaviour, and spells out the mechanism behind the general primordial view 'that ethnic conflict is inevitable; it is the "natural outlet" for primordial sentiments' (Green and Seher 2003 in portraying primordialism: 521). This account of ethnic politics offers a gloomy perspective for the peaceful accommodation of national minorities within nationalising states, predicting irreducible conflicts over values fuelled by outbidding elites.

By 2012, constructionism – implying a non-essentialist view on ethnic groups – has emerged as the sole winner of ontological debates about ethnic identity in the fields of nationalism studies and political anthropology (Lewellen 2003: 163). In a very recent article, Chandra, however, still summarises recent research practices in political science that presuppose EI to imply EB:

> Indeed, the assumption that ethnicity exerts a pull on individuals that is deeper than the pull of economic interests has become a premise driving not just the questions we ask about ethnicity but also the theories we formulate about other subjects. Thus, explanations for why class-based mobilisation does not succeed often fall back on the supposedly more fundamental pull of ethnicity (Chandra 2011: 153).

Primordialists might no longer publish articles as far as open theoretical debate is concerned (Gil-White 2001: 516), but they enjoy a vivid afterlife in empirical studies of ethnic mobilisation.

Large-N approaches, in particular, tend to take unified ethnic groups as their key unit of analysis and seldom examine preference formation at the intra-group level. To supply only one most recent example, the authors of the Ethnic Power Relations (EPR) dataset explicitly state that the dataset does not intend to account for the degree of representativity and for the possible heterogeneity of positions of different organisations claiming to speak for a mobilised group. An ethnic group is defined as politically relevant 'if at least one significant political actor claims to represent the interests of that group in the national political arena, or if members of an ethnic category are systematically and intentionally discriminated against in the domain of public politics' (Cederman *et al.* 2009, Coding rules EPR). The power distribution between the organisations recorded as representing the group is then supposed to have an effect on the conflict behaviour of the group. This causal connection can, however, only be made if the group is stipulated to be unified in its interest, as well as in its behavioural responses to state policies. At a meta-theoretical level, only presupposing EI, as well as the implication of EI $\Box$ EB, can justify this lack of effort to collect data below the group level.

Similarly, those seeking to prevent detrimental outbidding dynamics with the help of power-sharing institutions have in common the underlying assumption of unified groups and outbidding elites. In particular, Lijphart's (1977) 'consociational' model of democracy in plural societies relies heavily on the coherence of ethnic groups, and the capacity of unified elites to speak for their respective groups as a whole. This stipulation of externally divided, internally unified ethnic groups,

guided by comparatively cooperative, peace-seeking elites has, rather unsurprisingly, been criticised as somewhat paradoxical: 'Is accommodation an acceptable
strategy for followers? If so, why don't they change their positions? If not, why
don't they replace their leaders?' (Tsebelis 1990: 163). Nonetheless, academics
and policy makers still widely turn to this model – a phenomenon that is perhaps most visible in the post-communist nationalising states in Eastern Europe.
Inspired by one or more of Lijphart's (1977) four consociational principles, institutions have been installed to give national minorities in this region a stake in the
game, whether in the form of proportional representation in parliament through
guaranteed seats (Romania, Croatia), eased conditions for parties representing national minorities (Serbia), a minority veto (Macedonia), or the full range of all four
principles, ethnic quotas, territorial autonomy, mutual vetoes and a grand coalition
executive (as is the case in Bosnia and Herzegovina).

Social constructionism

Only recently has the study of minority mobilisation begun to experience its own
constructionist turn, driven, in part, by the various theoretical and empirical contributions of Kanchan Chandra and co-authors (Chandra 2004; 2005; Chandra
and Boulet 2005; Chandra and Wilkinson 2008). A small but growing range of
recent contributions now suggest that ethnic minority groups cannot be treated
as monolithic blocks with intransigent group preferences, and that minorities are
represented by their elites in democratic politics in a much more flexible way than
has traditionally been anticipated by conflict studies and the outbidding model
(see e.g. Birnir 2009; Chandra 2004; 2005; Mitchell *et al.* 2009; Stroschein 2001;
Zuber 2011). By the twenty-first century, many nationalising states have moved
beyond the initial challenge of post-independence ethnic mobilisation and polarisation. Constructionists who treat ethnic identities as fluid and multi-dimensional
(Chandra 2005: 236) now try to account for the empirically-given multi-dimensionality of ethnic identity: exploring the heterogeneity of preferences both across
and within groups and, consequently, the flexible patterns of representation and
participation of ethnic groups in multinational democracy (see e.g. Birnir 2009).

A constructionist account of ethnic identification is radically different from an
essentialist one. According to Mallon (2007a: 148):

> constructionist anti-essentialists are interested in replacing explanations
> of group differences that appeal to natural or biological differences among
> members of human categories with other explanations that hold that such
> differences are caused or constituted by relational (for example, social)
> differences.

In this manner, natural, intrinsic properties that justify group membership via
essentialist means are supplanted by relational categories, constructed through social practice. Since ethnic categories do not rely on essential, natural properties
and instead focus on social practice, they can be made and unmade by human
decisions. Thus, a key constructionist insight is found in the notion that 'ordinary

actors usually have considerable room for manoeuvre in the ways in which they use even highly institutionalised and powerfully sanctioned categories. They are often able to deploy such categories strategically, bending them to their own purposes' (Brubaker *et al.* 2004: 35).[4] On this account, ethnic groups are not naturally given biological facts; group formation is subject to human decision and cultural norms and constitutes a topic worth researching in its own right since multiple categories form the potential bases for the classification of groups. As a consequence, the variety of flexible identity categories available for political actors seeking to mobilise support, as well as for voters choosing whether to give this support, is diverse.[5]

This implies that we can neither presuppose the ethnic identification assumption (EI), nor take the convenient short cut from EI to the ethnic behaviour assumption (EB). If one works from an instrumentalist explanation of minority mobilisation, based on a constructionist ontology, strategic elites would be expected to mobilise those identity categories that best serve their interests, and these categories need not be the ethnic ones. A prime example of evidence for this constructionist line of argument in the field of mobilisation studies – and one that provides powerful evidence that EI does not imply EB – can be found in Posner's (2004) study of why cultural cleavages become politically relevant in some contexts but not in others. Posner shows that politicians choose whether to emphasise ethnic cleavages in Zambia and Malawi by following a simple 'logic of ethnic arithmetic' (Posner 2004: 539):

> If the purpose of mobilising the cultural cleavage is to build a coalition that can help them [the politicians] achieve political power, then it is natural for them to emphasise the cleavage that defines the most usefully sized coalitional building blocks and to ignore those that define groups that are too small to be politically viable (Posner 2004: 538).

Through a range of paired comparisons, he shows that the presence of identifiable cultural difference is neither a sufficient nor a necessary condition for the emergence of a salient political cleavage (Posner 2004: 543). In other words, group formation on the basis of ethnic categorisation does not entail mobilisation.

However, there is one problem with this conception of constructionism.[6] While the conventional mobilisation approach overstates the stickiness of group identity by fully essentialising the properties that an individual must have to be included

---

4. A perfect example of such 'bending' is the regionalist party 'Lega Nord' in Italy. The party succeeded in mobilising voters, constructing an ethnic identity on the basis of economic disparities.

5. This has implications for institutional design in divided societies: in light of constructionist accounts of ethnic identity, it is no longer self-evident why some attributes of ethnic identity mobilised at a particular point in time should be permanently advantaged over others that might be mobilised in the future; institutions that share power between currently mobilised groups have to be flexible enough to take this into account (Chandra and Boulet 2005).

6. This, and the critique that follows, is aimed at constructionist approaches within the field of mobilisation studies more narrowly – not at the paradigm per se.

in the concept of a particular ethnic group, the constructionist approach – at least in its elite-centred variant – overstates the capacity of actors to strategically bend identity categories to their purpose. It fails to account for the importance of local, cognitively-fixed identities and the stability of ethnicity compared to other identities over time (Jenkins 2011). Consequently, Lewellen (2003: 164), in his introduction to political anthropology, warns readers that 'constructivism, however, can easily be overstated' and reminds us of Milton Esman's argument that 'a cultural and experiential core must validate identity and make solidarity credible to potential constituents' (Esman 1994: 14, cited after Lewellen 2003: 164).

Elites cannot and do not choose any random category that is demographically large enough to grant them power. Indeed, they must choose categories that are cognitively stable enough to provide the basis for group coordination in at least the medium run otherwise their appeal will not resonate among the ethnic constituency to whom it is directed. Conversely, sometimes ethnic elites choose categories likely to yield only limited power over categories that have much higher power potential. From the perspective of Posner's findings, based on evidence collected in the context of Zambia and Malawi, elite behaviour in nationalising Eastern European states seems irrational: if a cleavage has to demarcate a group large enough to provide for a useful coalition, the spread of minority parties in Eastern Europe is puzzling if, like Posner, we assume politicians to be power seeking. Why should politicians engage in appealing to a group that only allows them to mobilise a maximum of 2 per cent of all voters? Why should they not seek to create larger blocks by emphasising a cleavage that incorporates a range of ethnic minorities against the majority group, thereby constructing an 'umbrella' minority identity? National minority identity categories can be too small, demographically speaking, to guarantee power positions, yet this does not stop elites from appealing to them.[7]

One simple way to skirt this conundrum would be to state that there are two kinds of constructionism: an instrumentalist and a historical version. Under this distinction, only the *first* kind – which postulates that elites create groups by successfully linking power and material gains to people's participation in an ethnically-defined group – is afflicted by the aforementioned problems. Green and Seher (2003) present only the latter kind under the label 'constructivism', and place the former under the label of 'instrumentalism'. However, both theories postulate that there are no groups to start with, and that there are no essential categories that define the nature of an ethnic kind. In both cases, groups are social constructs and only the 'constructor' differs: strategic elites in the first place and historical, external processes in the latter. Instrumentalism is not an ontological theory in its own right, but rather a specific, elite-centred *explanatory* theory of ethnic mobilisation that *presupposes* a constructionist ontology.

Historical constructionism focuses on historical processes that create groups as social constructs. It explores how the long-term historical institutionalisation of identity categories through states makes mobilisation of ethnic categories more

---

7. However, if we assume the goal of symbolic power, the choice to mobilise voters on the basis of a demographically-small identity category need not be irrational at all. I am indebted to the editors of this volume for pointing this out to me.

likely (Green and Seher 2003). The historical view does a better job of explaining how individuals come to take a construct for fact, suggesting that a construct is more likely to be institutionalised in a particular context if it persists for a sufficiently long period of time. In this manifestation, however, constructionism's predictions concerning minority behaviour are still problematic since they would be equivalent to those of a primordialist in the short run (and hence non-testable). Additionally, we would still lack an explanation for why *ethnic* categories are particularly resilient, and provide such a fruitful basis for elites' mobilisation strategies across such *different* historical contexts.[8]

Some constructionist political scientists, who are sympathetic to comparative, generalisation-seeking research,[9] try to solve this problem by differentiating between categories of self-classification that can be modified in the short run and those that are more rigid and can only be modified in the long run. From an overall constructionist perspective, Birnir (2009: 24) states that 'an ethnic group is defined by members of the group who consider themselves ethnically distinct from other groups in society. Furthermore, this identification centres on a characteristic that is difficult to suppress, such as language, location, or race'. Summarising political scientists' contemporary use of the term 'ethnic identity', Chandra (2006: 398), a constructionist, has suggested applying a definition based on 'descent-based attributes': 'ethnic identities are a subset of identity categories in which eligibility for membership is determined by attributes associated with, or believed to be associated with, descent'. Treating ethnic identity categories as relatively more rigid than others, and as descent-based distinctions, seems like an ad hoc explanation, however – a practice necessitated by the fact that ethnic categories play a role across contexts and one that appears more rigid than other social categories across contexts. In light of this, it seems that even a constructionist might be tempted to bring in essentialisms, when they prove most necessary, through the back door.

---

8. I agree with Colin Hay's assertion that ontological disputes ultimately cannot be solved empirically, since the facts each side will choose to accept as valid empirical evidence are themselves informed by potentially competing ontological commitments about whether reality can be independent of and observable by the researcher (Hay 2008: 82 and footnote 3). My more modest argument against a constructionist ontological basis for studying ethnic mobilisation is therefore that *if* we accept the findings in the field of mobilisation studies that point to cross-contextual similarities in the causes and effects of ethnic mobilisation as valid evidence, a constructionist ontology does not appear to be the best choice. In light of this, I seek an alternative in section three of this chapter, drawing on advances in cognitive psychology and philosophy.

9. This may seem like a contradiction in terms if we understand constructionism in the strong sense, as an anti-realist stance not only about social facts but also about scientific findings. However, constructionism can be more limited and emphasise merely that certain objects are better candidates for social construction than others, 'human kind' being among the former (Mallon 2007b: 97). Weak constructionism claims that there are *social facts* (constructed and ontologically subjective) and *brute facts* (real in an objective sense) (see, seminally, Searle 1995). Political scientists who are self-declared constructivists when it comes to ethnic identity – such as Birnir and Chandra – seem to be of the latter sort, since they engage in cross-national data collection and research, and work from a presupposition that their concepts defining ethnic groups, ethnic representation and ethnic competition can indeed travel across cultural contexts.

Naturalised constructionism

The nearly-universal success of constructionist over essentialist accounts of ethnic identity testifies to the idea that there are good reasons to grant that the content of ethnic categories is defined by social practice rather than biology – and, hence, differs across space and time (Mallon 2007b). However, as Brubaker (2004: 3) rightly states, this universal success bears with it the danger of preventing further improvements to the constructionist perspective, leaving 'complacent and clichéd constructivism' as a rather uninteresting analytical tool, 'too obviously right, too familiar, too readily taken for granted'. Brubaker *et al.* (2004) therefore present their own account, treating 'ethnicity as cognition'. A cognitive perspective, however, actually naturalises constructionism, treating not the content of the categories as essential, but the ethnic categorisation scheme as such (Mallon 2007b).

At the end of an overview on different strands of constructionism, Mallon presents an example of how constructionist and non-constructionist accounts of 'human kinds' (Hirschfeld 1996: 13) could be satisfyingly combined. He cites recent psychological findings from the study of race that also start from the tenet that biological, essentialist accounts of race are false. In explaining how 'folk racial theories' – or in our case, everyday primordialism – comes about, however, they do not simply resort to answers rooted in cultural framing and social practice. Instead, 'these psychologists posit a role for innate psychological propensities to categorise persons in particular ways' (Mallon 2007b: 103). Where Mallon himself states that constructionists have not taken much notice of this research, this is not the case for Brubaker *et al.* (2004), who cite the same psychological findings from the literature on categorisation as inspiration for the cognitive turn in their study of ethnicity.[10]

In his study *Race in the making: cognition, culture, and the child's construction of human kinds* (1996) anthropologist and cognitive scientist, Hirschfeld, started from the observation that 'humans appear to be ready to conceptualise the human world as composed of distinct types – what I call human kinds' (Hirschfeld 1996: 13), becoming the first to apply categorisation arguments from cognitive science to the *social* category of race. More importantly, from the perspective of this volume, Gil-White (2001) used a review of findings from the cognitive categorisation literature and his own field experiments in Mongolia to explore whether there existed a 'mental machinery specific to processing *ethnies*' (Gil-White 2001: 517, my emphasis). Based on his findings, he suggests that ethnic categories are processed *as if* they were natural, human kinds, or 'species,' because they look like species to our cognitive apparatus (which has – by his account – an innate tendency to categorise its environment in terms of natural kinds). In this view, category-based endogamy and descent-based membership meet our brain's criteria for classifying something as a 'natural kind' (Gil-White 2001: 532). This

---

10. To provide a short comparison: Mallon (2007b) refers to Hirschfeld (1996), Kurzban *et al.* (2001), Gil-White (2001), Machery and Faucher (2005); whereas Brubaker *et al.* (2004) focus on Hirschfeld (1996) and Gil-White (2001).

helps explain why we tend to 'essentialise' ethnic and racial, but not other social categories. In addition, Gil-White provides an evolutionary explanation for how this cognitive mechanism came about: applying our 'species-module' to ethnic categories likely evolved as a cognitive practice since it provided a double evolutionary advantage in ancestral times:

> (1) it allowed us to learn a lot about out-groups in a very inexpensive way, in particular by making inductive inferences about non-obvious properties, and (2) it made possible processes of discrimination that prevented us from incurring the costs of coordination failure (Gil-White 2001: 536).

If our predisposition to view the world in ethnic categories is itself ingrained in humans' cognitive make-up, then the following statement, made by Brubaker *et al.* (2004: 45), should be qualified: 'Race, ethnicity, and nationality exist only in and through our perceptions, interpretations, representations, classifications, categorisations, and identifications. They are not things in the world, but perspectives on the world – not ontological but epistemological realities'. In fact, if we take the findings cited seriously, the content of ethnic categories is *still* determined by our socially-shared perspectives on the world. But a perspective that categorises humans along ethnic lines is itself a fact – pertaining to a cognitive system that makes the construction (and naturalisation) of similarities between members of a society that belong to the same ethnic group much easier than the construction of perceived natural belonging among, for example, members of a society that all work in the same profession.

This naturalised constructionism, which operates at the intersection of culture and cognition (Hirschfeld 1996: 14),[11] has the potential to account for the fact that, independent of the specific content of ethnic categories in a specific socio-historical and institutional context, people tend to naturalise ethnic rather than other categories: 'people the world over appear to discriminate between members of their own and other ethnoraces in a unique way: they naturalise the difference. "Naturalisation" here involves the practice of conceptually identifying social differences with natural ones' (Hirschfeld 1996: 21). In the political realm, this seems poised to reasonably explain cross-cultural empirical findings about the role of ethnicity in politics, explaining, for example, why in situations of regime change and democratisation, ethno-national identities tend to be highly mobilised across contexts (Hechter 2000: 93). In the absence of other defined social categories, orientation along ethnic lines appears as a default option for the human brain. The 'groupness variable' (Brubaker 2004) takes on a higher value under conditions where other social categories have collapsed or are in the process of profound reconstruction. Peripheral elites take advantage of this window of opportunity to gain power and choose ethnic appeals to mobilise ordinary citizens who are now much more likely to categorise their social world in terms of human kinds. A

---

11. Hirschfeld (1996: 14) refers to his own approach both as a 'cultural psychological' or a 'universal constructivist account'.

shared perception of the social world as a space demarcated along ethnic lines helps solve the collective action problem for ethnic minority groups in new nation-states, where other categories are not yet discernible on the political scene.

In nationalising states in particular, an additional factor to consider is the idea that majority elites may already follow a strategy of nation-building. Rather than advertising 'cultural models that supersede in part our native intuitions' (Gil-White 2001: 535), majority elites in these contexts may concentrate on emphasising them. This, in turn, sets forth the ideal conditions for minority elites who seek to mobilise support. These minority elites can draw on the local importance of ethnicity on the ground, since EI has been solved for them by the cognitive default orientation. To go one step further and form a collective interest of the group as a basis for ethnic collective action (EB), they are primed to find an easy target: presenting the nationalising state (i.e. the state as constituted by the ethnic majority) as a threat to the survival of the identity of the national minority. Hence, shared interest is presented (i.e. constructed) as crucial to the self-preservation of the ethnic minority in the face of central nationalism. Naturalised constructionism can thus explain why ethnic mobilisation takes place under conditions of regime change across contexts without falling back on essentialist accounts of ethnic identity, since it leaves a decisive role for discursive social practice in filling the ethnic perspective with content. Indeed, the conditions for membership in each context depend on social practice and are relational, not natural. The fact that we have a predisposition to resort to ethnic categories when other information in our social environment is scarce is likely, at least according to the findings cited, to be innate.

Another empirical implication of the perspective of naturalised constructionism can be found in Birnir's (2009) comprehensive study of electoral politics in new democracies. She finds that, in new democracies where ethnicity is part of electoral competition, party systems stabilise more quickly than in circumstances where parties make no appeal to ethnic categories. At the micro level, she explains that voters who identify with an ethnic group, and have the opportunity to vote for an ethnic party, can cast their vote on the basis of information that is less costly than information on the programmes of parties based on less intuitive appeals. If no parties run on ethnic platforms, voters cannot use their cognitive default category to vote in a newly-developing multiparty system, and their voting patterns are hence less stable, due to a lack of information on the actual positions of parties that have only recently been formed.

Whether ethnic categories will lead to the subsequent formation of a collective interest associated with that category, and whether this will result in a conflictual or cooperative relationship between national minorities and majorities (EB), remains open to debate, since the answer still depends on political actors' choices as they attempt to garner the support of voters with multiple identity categories, under institutional restrictions. When making this choice, however, both elites and citizens are limited in their flexibility by the cognitive resilience of ethnic categories. This explains why multinational states can be expected to remain somewhat special in the long run, since cognitively-predisposed shared ethnic perceptions ease the formation of collective interests and collective action. Ethnic elites seeking to receive a mandate in representing the minority – *vis-à-vis* the nationalising state and within the state's institutions – can draw on the cognitive practices of individuals who identify with the same ethnic category. Since the content of these ethnic categories is not essentially fixed, however, elites may in the longer run redefine the social categories they include – and those they exclude – through their appeals.

Conclusion

In the introduction, I posited that studying ethnic minority mobilisation as a given phenomenon requires assuming both the collective ethnic identity of a bounded minority group (EI) and its coherent political behaviour (EB). And in my subsequent analysis, I have shown that an essentialist account of ethnic identity, traditionally embraced by primordialists, provides the most straightforward ontological basis for these assumptions. On this account, ethnic identification is a natural given, based on necessary and sufficient properties that define who is a member of an ethnic group (see Table 9.1 for a summary). When studying minority mobilisation, primordialists take an additional short cut assumption that is not itself implied by an essentialist ontology: stating that a unified group identity implies the presence of unified interests that contradict the interests of members associated with other essential categories, such as the national majority within the state. The most useful elite strategy for gaining as much support as possible within the group is thus most likely to be ethnic outbidding, wherein each competitor styles herself/himself as the most authentic defender of the manifest group interest.

Essentialism at the ontological level allows us to take the bounded, politically-cohesive group as a given and study minority mobilisation as such: a phenomenon at the level of bounded groups. Essentialism is now, however, widely accepted to be untenable, leaving the field to anti-essentialists and, above all, social constructionists, who treat ethnic categories as constructs caused by social practice. The beauty of this change of perspective is that it forces us to engage with minority mobilisation as a complex, compound phenomenon; and tackle research questions

Table 9.1: Theoretical perspectives on ethnic identification

Theory	Ontological status of ethnic categories
Essentialist primordialism	Essential (natural and intrinsic properties as necessary and sufficient conditions for membership)
Social constructionism	Constructed (relational properties contingent on social practice to define membership)
Naturalised constructionism	Constructed under cognitive predisposition (cognitive predisposition to naturalise ethnic categories; actual category defined by relational property-clusters caused by social practice in a given context)

such as how ethnicity is *made* and unmade through the drawing of social boundaries (Wimmer 2008); and how ethnic groups' collective preferences are *formed*
through interactions between competing elites and voters (Giuliano 2000).

I have also tried, however, to show that constructionists in the field of mobilisation studies struggle to explain the resilience of ethnic categories and therefore
often resort to ad hoc explanations of 'everyday primordialism' that force them
to give up a unified ontological assumption about the social world – one that is
somehow meant to be different for the researcher (constructed) and the participant
(caught within the primordial matrix). Additionally, when it comes to the more
specific topic of studying the strategies of elites, who often seek support by invok-
ing ethnically-charged issues, the flexible nature of constructed categories does
not correspond to the limits elites encounter on the ground when trying to change
the category they are appealing to. Treating the ethnic identification assumption
(EI) as the contingent result of context-dependent constructed categories fails to
provide theoretical concepts able to account for the fact that ethnic categories are
more stable than other categories – and that this holds true across time and space.

Constructionism's seemingly ad hoc definition of ethnic categories – as more
rigid than others – can be avoided under a third perspective that treats ethnicity as a cognitive, classificatory scheme (Brubaker *et al.* 2004; Gil White 2001),
whereby the fact that we classify by means of ethnic categories can be attributed
to an 'evolved [...] ethnic cognitive system' (Machery and Faucher 2006: 1029).
The exact nature of the cluster of properties associated with ethnic categories in
social practice can only be established *a posteriori*, however, through empirical
analysis (Mallon 2007a; 2007b). Following from this view, the resilience of ethnic
categories as a means for navigating our social environment is not a mere by-product of social practice within the institutional opportunity structures provided by
historically-contingent processes. Rather, reliance on ethnic (as opposed to other)
categories for social classification under conditions of insecurity can be thought
of as stemming from an innate cognitive predisposition to think in ethnic terms.
By contrast, the tangible attributes associated with an ethnic category are seen as
socially constructed in nature, and only careful study of classificatory practice and
the meaning of a category in a specific context can yield the set of properties that
define actual membership.

Reviewing the literature on social categorisation in 2005, Machery and Faucher
(2005: 1029) still cited Gil-White's (2001) findings and his argument in favour of
an ethnic cognitive system as an advance worth endorsing – suggesting that more
work needs to be done to highlight how social constructionist and cognitive-cum
evolutionary accounts (such as Gil-White's) can be further integrated. This is also
an important area for the future of studies of ethnic mobilisation. Taking the conditions for ethnic identification and mobilisation as both universal (ethnic categorisation as an innate cognitive mechanism) and context-specific (the cluster of
properties defining membership in the ethnic category as a social construct) should
open avenues in research. Working from this perspective, comparative research
aimed at generalisable knowledge on the role of ethnicity in political mobilisation
and context-centred, interpretive approaches seeking to extract the actual meaning

attached to specific ethnic categories in a given context can be *connected*, rather than inimically juxtaposed – an enterprise already being undertaken within this volume.

References

Anderson, B. (1991) *Imagined Communities: Reflections on the origin and spread of nationalism*, London and New York: Verso.

Banton, M. (2011) 'A theory of social categories', *Sociology*, 45(2): 187–201.

Birnir, J. K. (2009) *Ethnicity and Electoral Politics*, Cambridge: Cambridge University Press.

Brubaker, R. (2004) *Ethnicity without Groups*, Cambridge and London: Harvard University Press.

Brubaker, R., Loveman, M. and Stamatov, P. (2004) 'Ethnicity as cognition', *Theory and Society*, 33(1): 31–64.

Cederman, L.-E., Min, B. and Wimmer, A. (2009) 'Ethnic power relations dataset' and 'Coding rules EPR'. Online. Available http://hdl.handle.net/1902.1/11796 (accessed 15 July 2011).

Chandra, K. (2004) *Why Ethnic Parties Succeed: Patronage and ethnic headcounts in India*, Cambridge: Cambridge University Press.

— (2005) 'Ethnic parties and democratic stability', *Perspectives on Politics*, 3(2): 235–52.

— (2006) 'What is ethnic identity and does it matter?', *Annual Review of Political Science*, 9(1): 397–424.

— (2011) 'What is an ethnic party?', *Party Politics*, 17(2): 151–69.

Chandra, K. and Boulet, C. 'Ethnic cleavage structures, permanent exclusion and democratic stability', paper prepared for presentation at Conference on Alien Rule and its Discontents, Seattle, June 2005.

Chandra, K. and Wilkinson, S. (2008) 'Measuring the effect of "ethnicity"', *Comparative Political Studies*, 41(4/5): 515–63.

Gil-White, F. J. (2001) 'Are ethnic groups biological "species" to the human brain? Essentialism in our cognition of some social categories', *Current Anthropology*, 42(4): 515–54.

Giuliano, E. (2000) 'Who determines the self in the politics of self-determination: identity and preference formation in Tatarstan's nationalist mobilization', *Comparative Politics*, 32(3): 295–316.

Green, D. P. and Seher, R. L. (2003) 'What role does prejudice play in ethnic conflict?', *Annual Review of Political Science*, 6: 509–31.

Gurr, T. (2011) *People and States: Minorities at risk in the new century*, Washington: United States Institute of Peace.

Hale, H. E. (2008) *The Foundations of Ethnic Politics: Separatism of states and nations in Eurasia and the world*, Cambridge: Cambridge University Press.

Hay, C. (2008) 'Political ontology', in R. E. Goodin and C. Tilly (eds) *The Oxford Handbook of Contextual Political Analysis*, Oxford: Oxford University Press, pp. 78–96.

Hechter, M. (2000) *Containing Nationalism*, Oxford: Oxford University Press.

Hirschfeld, L. (1996) *Race in the Making: Cognition, culture, and the child's construction of human kinds*, Cambridge and London: The MIT Press.

Horowitz, D. L. (1985) *Ethnic Groups in Conflict*, Berkeley: University of California Press.

Jenkins, S. 'Ethnicity, violence and the "immigrant metaphor" in Kenya', paper presented at the ASN annual convention, New York, April 2011.

Kurzban, R., Tooby, J. and Cosmides, L. (2001) 'Can race be erased? Coalitional computation and social categorization', *Proceedings of the National Academy of Sciences of the United States of America*, 98(26): 15387–92.

Laitin, D. (2007) *Nations, States and Violence*, Oxford: Oxford University Press.

Lewellen, T. C. (2003) 'The politics of identity: ethnicity and nationalism', in *Political Anthropology: An introduction*. Westport: Praeger Publishers, pp. 159-179.

Lijphart, A. (1977) *Democracy in Plural Societies*, New Haven: Yale University Press.

Machery, E. and Faucher, L. (2005) 'Why do we think racially?', in H. Cohen and C. Lefebvre (eds) *Handbook of Categorization in Cognitive Science*, Amsterdam: Elsevier, pp. 1009–33.

Mallon, R. (2007a) 'Human categories beyond non-essentialism', *Journal of Political Philosophy*, 15(2): 146–68.

— (2007b). 'A field guide to social construction', *Philosophy Compass*, 2(1): 93–108.

Mitchell, P., Evans, G. and O'Leary, B. (2009) 'Extremist outbidding in ethnic party systems is not inevitable: tribune parties in Northern Ireland', *Political Studies*, 57(2): 397–421.

Posner, D. N. (2004) 'The political salience of cultural difference: why Chewas and Tumbukas are allies in Zambia and adversaries in Malawi', *American Political Science Review*, 98(4): 529–45.

Rabushka, A. and Shepsle, K. A. (1972) *Politics in Plural Societies: A theory of democratic instability*, Columbus: Charles E. Merrill Publishing Company.

Raskin, J. D. (2002) 'Constructivism in psychology: personal construct psychology, radical constructivism, and social constructionism', in J. D. Raskin and S. K. Bridges (eds) *Studies in Meaning: Exploring constructivist psychology*, New York: Pace University Press, pp. 1–25.

Searle, J. R. (1995) *The Construction of Social Reality*, Harmondsworth: Allen Lane The Penguin Press.

Stroschein, S. (2001) 'Measuring ethnic party success in Romania, Slovakia, and Ukraine', *Problems of Post-Communism*, 48(4): 59–69.

Tsebelis, G. (1990) *Nested Games: Rational choice in comparative politics*, Berkeley and Los Angeles: University of California Press.

Wimmer, A. (2008) 'Elementary strategies of ethnic boundary making', *Ethnic and Racial Studies*, 31(6): 1025–55.

Zuber, C. I. (2011) 'Beyond outbidding? Ethnic party strategies in Serbia', *Party Politics*, published online before print 25 July 2011, doi: 10.1177/1354068811410368.

chapter ten | ethnicity and strategic voting in the 1998 ukrainian elections

Julian Bernauer

Introduction

Having gained independence after the breakdown of Communist rule, Ukraine can be perceived as a nationalising state (see Brubaker 1996 and Wydra's contribution in Chapter Three in this volume). And within Ukraine, the presence of a considerable Russian minority provides an exemplary case of a confrontation between a nationalising state and a national minority. One of the various consequences of such a scenario can be observed in electoral politics (Selb 2012). Minorities who face nationalising policies on behalf of the majority population, also visible in (majority) party platforms, might have difficulties voting for a party that promotes such policies. Often, ethnic parties, or parties that appeal to ethnic minorities to a significant extent, are present in such political systems. If electoral rules are strict enough to prevent the electoral success of ethnic parties or parties attractive to ethnic minority voters, it stands to reason that less strategic voting for a party representing the 'Ukrainising' discourse should occur.

This research question becomes even more relevant in light of the fact that the persistency of wasted votes hinders the development of stable party systems and the consolidation of new democracies (Duch and Palmer 2002; Horowitz and Browne 2005). Strategic voting requires elites to coordinate their efforts to back promising candidates and parties, and requires voters to focus on viable alternatives. For ethnic minorities in particular, an inability to successfully vote strategically could lead to their permanent exclusion from representation – something that presents a further threat to political stability and peace (Alonso and Ruiz-Rufino 2007; Cohen 1997; Saideman *et al.* 2002; Schneider and Wiesehomeier 2008). When minorities refuse to vote for mainstream parties (on the basis of their failure to adopt minority issues), even when their preferred (minority) party fails to win seats, this equals the failure of political integration of ethnic minorities. This has particular serious consequences in nationalising states with salient ethnic cleavages. This chapter presents a rational choice perspective on the interplay between nationalising states and national minorities in the electoral arena.

With these issues in mind, this chapter explores whether Russians in Ukraine display distinct patterns in their strategic voting behaviour.[1] A strategic vote is

---

1. Here, ethnic minorities are defined as numerically non-dominant groups in a country's population whose identity is constructed along cultural, historic, linguistic or religious lines (see Weber 2002; Fearon 2003). The assumption of single and clear-cut ethnic identities is obviously simplifying, but analytically helpful.

defined as a vote for a party that is not the preferred one, motivated by the intention to affect the outcome of the election (Blais *et al.* 2005). My core arguments are:

(1) ethnic minorities are less likely than the majority population to vote strategically because when ethnic issues are politicised and thresholds for achieving representation are high, minorities that lack viable alternatives to their preferred ethnic minority party are more likely to waste their vote than support another party;

(2) spillover effects occur – meaning that, in districts with fractionalised populations, all citizens have limited alternatives and are likely to vote less strategically; and

(3) both the population shares of the minorities and the status of the trailing party interact in a non-linear fashion.

I argue that the share of Russians in the district has a varying mediating impact on the strength of strategic voting among the minority population. Starting from low shares of Russians, a rising share in an electoral district does not necessarily create more alternatives in the sense of viable, attractive parties for the Russian voters, and hence does not yield more possibilities to vote strategically. Within a certain range– up to about 50 per cent – this lack of alternatives might be even *stronger* since conflict could be more intense when the share of Russians is higher. Only after about 50 per cent, when the Russians constitute a clear local majority, does one expect levels of strategic voting to rise to higher levels relative to the rest of the population.

Ukraine provides a suitable example for my analysis, since it has a considerable Russian minority and ongoing tensions along ethnic lines (Bremmer 1994; Constant *et al.* 2006; Wilson and Birch 1999). The electoral structure at the 1998 parliamentary election features a mixed electoral system of the parallel type, with seats independently distributed in 225 single-member simple majority districts and one nation-wide 225-seats PR district (Bugajski 2002: 926; Tiemann 2006: 151; Wilson and Birch 1999: 1041). In the majoritarian tier of the electoral system, disproportionalities – and thus, incentives for strategic voting – occur. Furthermore, ethnic conflict carries over at least partially into vote choices. In some districts, the party preferred by the Russian minority in 1998 (the Communist Party) had little chance of winning a seat, while in other districts 'majority' parties (those preferred by ethnic Ukrainians) were trailing.[2] In sum, the Ukrainian political system is a productive locus for conducting an investigation into patterns of strategic voting, since we may compare the extent of strategic voting by considering whether the party potentially liable to be deserted strategically is a minority or a majority party.

This chapter's research design relies on district-level aggregate data. Second-to-first loser (SF) ratios are computed for each district, which indicate the extent

---

2. Additional analyses using individual-level data (not reported) confirmed that Russians have a high probability to vote for the Communist Party even after controlling for ideology.

of strategic voting. Descriptive analysis and beta-distributed regression models explore the strategic voting behaviour in electoral districts, paying particular attention to situations in which the party that may be deserted strategically is the Communist Party (preferred by ethnic Russians), to the influence of the population share of Russians in the district, and to non-linear interactive effects between these factors.

The body of the chapter is structured as follows. First, strategic voting is introduced as a concept rooted in rational choice literature, the theoretical expectations of strategic voting among ethnic minorities are elaborated in further detail, and the core argument is derived. Secondly, the research design, data and statistical models are introduced. A further section presents and discusses the results of the analysis. Finally, the last section sums up my conclusions.

Strategic voting and ethnic minorities

Following the definition set forth by Blais *et al.* (2005), a strategic vote is a vote for a party that is not the preferred one, motivated by the intention to affect the outcome of the election. Fisher (2004: 157) delivers a similar definition (for majoritarian systems): 'A tactical voter is someone who votes for a party they believe is more likely to win than their preferred party, to best influence who wins in the constituency.' This implies that two conditions must be met for strategic voting to occur. Not only do the first preference of the voter and the vote choice have to differ but, furthermore, the divergence must be of a strategic nature – because the chances of the most preferred party entering parliament (or winning another seat) are remote. In other words, strategic voting can be defined as the 'result of the total calculus of voting given preferences and beliefs on the probabilities of the relevant states of a specific electoral situation' (Shikano *et al.* 2009: 635).

My analysis of strategic voting is deeply rooted in the literature on rational choice (Cox 1997; Fisher 2004: 153), which suggests that – assuming short-term instrumental rationality – voters may maximise their utility by voting for a party other than their most preferred one. Cox (1997) further explicates the logic of strategic voting. According to his point of view, the central assumptions in play – in addition to short-term instrumental rationality – are that elites and voters have common expectations about the viability of candidates. Taking into account voter preferences and electoral system constraints, he holds that elites and voters will have strict preferences regarding alternatives (i.e. they are not indifferent) and that there will be at least some competitiveness in the electoral race.

For my purposes, short-term instrumental rationality and competitiveness are assumed for now, and it is assumed that electoral constraints are constant in single-member districts. Consequently, my focus is on the preferences of the voters and the viability of the candidates in play. According to the logic of strategic voting, strategic utilities determine the vote choice. These have two components (Myerson and Weber 1993):

(1) The ideological component describes the losses a voter would suffer if a party other than the preferred party were elected.

(2) The pivot probability component describes the probability that the vote for a party will make or break a seat-changing tie.

In sum, strategic utilities are based not only on preferences for parties like ideological utilities, but *also* take into account how likely it is that a vote for a party will change the outcome of the election.

If we follow the definition of strategic voting as a vote for a party other than the preferred one in order to influence the outcome of the election, the absence of strategic voting could be observed under two scenarios:

(1) Pivot probabilities do not encourage voting for another party, since the vote will no more likely make a difference than voting for the most preferred party.

(2) While voters might have an incentive to vote for another party because of pivot probabilities, they may also be so ideologically distant from the alternative parties that a strategic vote would not reflect an instrumentally rational short-term move.

Here, it is argued that the question of strategic voting is particularly relevant in ethnically-divided societies and nationalising states (see Introduction above). When ethnic issues are politicised, ethnic minority members will arguably have distinct preferences, in that there are only one or a few (ethnic minority) parties that fully represent their views, and 'mainstream parties' constitute a less attractive alternative. The dynamics of intra- and inter-ethnic competition in such a setting resembles parts of the ethnic outbidding model (Horowitz 1985; Rabushka and Shepsle 1972: 62–88; Saideman *et al.* 2002: 108). According to this model, ethnical divisions translate into inter-ethnic processes of out-mobilisation and intra-ethnic processes of radicalisation or outbidding, which in turn deepen the divide between ethnic groups.[3]

As a result, and also due in part to their smaller choice set as compared to the majority population, the likelihood that ethnic minority voters will find a suitable alternative party in situations where a vote for the most preferred party would be wasted is smaller than for voters from the majority population, leading to less strategic voting. Furthermore, in disproportional electoral systems, minority voters will be forced to choose between wasting their vote and voting for an alternative party relatively frequently, since they are by definition small electorates. Recent

---

3. This does not mean that the ethnic outbidding model has been fully adopted here. Some assumptions, such as diametrically-opposed preferences between groups and the absence of floating voters between ethnic groups, are inadequate for the purposes of this chapter. For explanations of the limitations of the ethnic outbidding model, see Chandra (2005) and Birnir (2007). These authors argue that ethnic parties can stabilise a divided polity. Still, the mechanism described in the ethnic outbidding model provides an explanation for deepened cleavages between ethnic groups.

empirical findings lend validity to such theoretical considerations. In a study of strategic adaption in Spanish electoral districts, Selb (2012) finds fewer instances of strategic voting in districts where ethnic conflict is intense, as well as a tendency towards less strategic voting when the party poised to be deserted is an ethnic one.[4]

Against this backdrop, one may a hypothesis on ethnic and strategic voting.[5] My primary argument holds that minority voters will be less liable to vote strategically than the majority population in situations involving potentially wasted votes, since other parties may offer unpalatable ideological alternatives (on the desired political dimension), or because of other reasons – such as the desire for descriptive representation despite the presence of ideological alternatives (Mansbridge 1999). This argument has several parts, starting with the relationship I have already described between the status of the trailing party and strategic voting. Thus, in situations with a trailing ethnic minority party, I argue that strategic voting should occur less often, and that *ethnic minority parties should not be strategically deserted by their voters as often as other parties*.

There are additional facets to my argument, however, which require further elaboration. Selb (2012) discusses a spillover effect, resulting in lower levels of strategic voting in districts where ethnic minorities are strong. If there are strong ethnic minority parties – something that is expected in districts with high shares of a minority population – these should be inherently unattractive for the majority population. Selb (2012), in his findings on the levels of strategic voting in Spain, even reports this effect of ethnic minority population share on strategic voting to be more clear-cut than that of trailing minority parties in general. In sum: large minority communities in electoral districts should be associated with lower levels of strategic voting even if the party to be strategically deserted is not an ethnic one.

However, these arguments on trailing minority parties and spillover effects refer only to situations in which the share of Russians remains below or around 50 per cent. Only in such cases is there reason to expect less strategic voting where an ethnic minority party is trailing, and spillover effects with rising shares of the minority population. *Above a minority population share of 50 per cent, the argument is turned on its head.* Under these circumstances, mainstream parties become

---

4. It is important to note that the absence of strategic voting under these conditions is not irrational. Quite the contrary; if the preference structure of minorities is as described, it is rational to refrain from strategic voting even when the probability that a sincere vote will influence the outcome of the election is close to zero. I will continue using the term 'strategic voting', since the definition I refer to here pertains to a 'vote for a party that is not the preferred one, motivated by the intention to affect the outcome of the election' (Blais *et al.* 2005). Under this rubric, minorities are generally not expected to be unable to vote, as compared to other voters given the same incentives structure. Rather, they are assumed to have different incentives that are less likely to lead to a strategic vote.

5. My argument refers to the aggregate level, even though strategic voting is an individual-level process (Alvarez and Nagler 2000: 61). A full analysis of strategic voting at the individual level is hampered, unfortunately, by the absence of information on vote choice in the relevant electoral districts (as opposed to the PR tier) for the 1998 parliamentary election, even in the CSES election study.

minority parties and the majority voters become minority voters – mirroring the situation for trailing minority parties in areas that have a 50 per cent or lower share of Russians. Hence, beyond spillover effects, which result in lower expected over-all levels of strategic voting in districts with a fractionalised population, a trade-off between the alternatives of minorities and majorities is expected. The share of minority members per district should alter the effect a trailing minority party has on strategic voting. Where minorities approach the status of local majorities, they may potentially have a local choice between several parties or candidates, and thus have more opportunities to vote strategically.[6] In the data at hand, the share of Russians goes up to about 70 per cent – and so, the argument is relevant. Thus, trailing ethnic minority parties should only be associated with lower levels of strategic voting when the share of Russians in a district is below 50 per cent. At the same time, while the share of Russians is *above* 50 per cent, trailing majority parties should be associated with *less* strategic voting. This is best captured by an interaction effect between the share of Russians and the status of the trailing party. Adding an argument on potentially lower levels of ethnic conflict given small population shares of minorities, the total effect resembles an U-shaped relation-ship between the share of Russians and strategic voting specific to the status of the trailing party. For example, for trailing minority parties, I hold that the share of Russians in the district has a varying mediating impact on the strength of strategic voting among the minority population. Starting from low shares of Russians, a rising share in the electoral district does not necessarily instantly create more alter-natives in the sense of viable, attractive parties for the Russian voters (and hence more possibilities to vote strategically). Within a certain range, up to about 50 per cent, the lack of alternatives could even become stronger at times, since conflict could be more intense where the share of Russians is higher. Only after about 50 per cent, when the Russians constitute a clear majority, should their levels of stra-tegic voting rise to relatively higher levels, as compared to the remainder of the population. In sum, the main argument of my analysis is as follows:

Hypothesis – The share of Russians in an electoral district interacts with the minority status of the trailing party in a non-linear fashion: When population shares are small, trailing ethnic minority parties are connected with less strategic voting than are trailing majority parties, but the effect diminishes or eventually turns into a positive effect when Russians constitute a local majority. The effect is non-linear since, given low shares of Russians in the district in question, low conflict levels might allow more strategic voting.

---

6. At the same time, such an interaction between minority population shares and the status of the trailing party means that the effect of the share of Russians in the district for non-minority voters (trailing majority parties) is automatically estimated. These are expected to display lower levels of strategic voting once the minority population share rises, drawing on the very same argument of limited choices in these circumstances that has been set forth for trailing ethnic minority par-ties.

Research design, data and model

A much-debated methodological issue comes into play when determining the ideal way to analyse strategic voting. The fundamental decision is one of establishing whether the strategic vote should be measured or modelled – or, in other words, whether it should be assessed 'directly' or 'indirectly' (Blais *et al.* 2005; Fisher 2004). In principle, there are at least two ways to measure strategic voting. First, individuals can be asked to state their intention or report their behaviour on strategic voting directly.[7] Secondly, strategic voting can be inferred from aggregate data, which is the strategy adopted here. Using individual-level data is often highly attractive, particularly for modelling vote choice while also incorporating strategic utilities, since strategic voting is an individual-level process (Alvarez and Nagler 2000: 61). Unfortunately, the most relevant survey data available – in this case, the Comparative Study of Electoral Systems (CSES) on the 1998 Ukrainian election – is not well suited to pursue such a strategy.[8] Therefore, for the purposes of this chapter, I rely on an aggregate measure of strategic voting: the SF ratio. Arguably, 'there is only justification for aggregate data studies in the absence of good quality individual-level data' (Fisher 2004: 159).

Cox (1994; 1997) convincingly demonstrates that strategic voting has observable implications in electoral results, and hence in aggregate data (see also Selb 2012). The SF-ratio, discussed in detail below, is the ratio of vote shares of the Second and the First loser in an electoral district. When there are M+1 viable candidates, where M indicates district magnitude, this ratio takes on values close to 0 if voters behave strategically, deserting candidates or parties that have little chance of winning a seat. For more than M+1 viable candidates, the ratio takes on values close to 1, since there is no reason to desert second losers in a close race. All values in between indicate the absence of strategic voting. Two clear advantages of the measure are that that it only relies on electoral results, and that it is applicable to a wide range of electoral systems.[9]

---

7. The approach of 'reported strategic voting' is strongly advocated by Fisher (2004). He favours employing a question used in the British Election Studies provided by Heath *et al.* (1991) offering voters the option, among others, to answer a question for vote motivation with the statement: 'I really preferred another party but it had no chance of winning in this constituency' (Fisher 2004: 160). Respondents choosing this item are asked to indicate which party they initially intended to vote for. To my knowledge, such a question is not available in any survey covering the 1998 Ukrainian election.

8. The 1998 CSES election study on Ukraine does not contain information about vote choice in the single-member districts; such information is available only for the PR tier of the mixed electoral system (Sum and Badescu 2008: 93).

9. Another body of literature chooses to *model* strategic voting instead of measuring it (Alvarez and Nagler 2000; Blais *et al.* 2005; Blais and Nadeau 1996). In particular, conditional logit or multinomial probit models offer a framework for analysing vote choices between a full set of alternatives as a function of individual and individual-choice specific factors (Alvarez and Nagler 1998; 2000; Adams *et al.* 2005 2005). Individual-choice specific factors are those that vary by both individual and alternatives. For example, the choice of transportation depends on factors specific to each individual and alternatives such as individual travel time and cost for taking the

The 1998 parliamentary election in Ukraine has been chosen for this analysis because it satisfies several useful conditions. In 1998, Ukraine had a parallel mixed electoral system with fully separate multi-member proportional and single-member majoritarian tiers (Bugajski 2002: 926; Tiemann 2006: 151; Wilson and Birch 1999: 1041).[10] The system allows no compensation for disproportionalities arising from the single-member districts (OSCE 1998).[11] The independence of the tiers is also reflected in the voting procedure. Voters cast two ballots, one for district candidates and one for party lists.[12] Therefore, analysing the SF ratios in single-member districts allows for the detection of patterns of strategic voting, since votes for losing candidates are wasted. The country has a considerable Russian minority, which holds some local majorities in electoral districts. Also, ethnic divisions are politicised and we can expect some ethnically-based voting from certain parties – although pure Russian minority parties are scarce (Wilson and Birch 1999: 1042). In sum, there are incentives for strategic voting in districts where the party to be deserted is a minority party, as well as in other districts.

The dependent variable for exploring strategic voting among majorities and minorities is the modified second-to-first (SF) loser ratio. It is calculated by dividing the votes for the second losing candidate by those of the first losing candidate. In cases of true Duvergian equilibriums, which occur when there are exactly two viable alternatives in a single-member district, the SF ratio takes on a value close to 0. In cases of non-Duvergian equilibriums, which occur when more than two viable alternatives exist and result in a close race between trailing candidates, the SF ratio takes on a value close to 1. As a consequence, values *both* close to 0 and close to 1 indicate strategic voting behaviour.

By contrast, when voters cast ballots for candidates who have minimal chances of obtaining a seat, the SF ratio takes on intermediate values, indicating *non-strategic* voting behaviour. To accommodate the possibility of a lopsided electoral race, where false non-Duvergian equilibriums could be indicated by the SF-ratio, a slight modification is used.[13] These cases are classified correctly when the lower of the second-to-first loser ratio and the first-loser-to-winner ratio is taken into

---

bus, car or bicycle (Liao 2006: 59f.). Equivalent, strategic utilities vary per individual and party, depending on the probability that the vote will alter the outcome of the election and the individual distance from alternative parties.

10. In the meantime, the electoral system has been changed to a pure proportional representation system.

11. The OSCE (1998: 5) election report states: 'This so-called mixed system is a clear compromise between a majoritarian system and a proportional system. The two elections are totally separate so that proportionality is not maintained in the Parliament.'

12. See the 'Law of Ukraine on the Elections of People's Deputies of Ukraine, 1997', Article 40/6. On-line. Available: /www2.essex.ac.uk/elect/database/indexCountry.asp?country=Ukraine&opt=leg (accessed 14 February 2012).

13. When the election is lopsided and candidates win, for example 90, 5, and 5 per cent of the votes, the unmodified SF ration would take on the value 5/5=1. However, there is little reason to perceive this situation as a non-Duvergian equilibrium, where two viable trailing candidates are engaged in a close race.

account. SF ratios are calculated using district-level election results from the Essex database.[14]

If strategic voting is more widespread among ethnic minorities, this should be visible in the SF ratio given a specific condition: in the SF ratio framework, the second loser is defined as the party that is to be deserted from a strategic point of view. If this party is less frequently strategically deserted when it is an ethnic one than when it is a mainstream party, we have evidence for the basic argument that minorities vote strategically less often. Wilson and Birch (1999: 1049) performed path analyses of their own survey data on the 1998 Ukrainian election for different parties. They present reasons for identifying the Communist Party as the party preferred by ethnic Russians in the 1998 parliamentary election: 'Ethnic Russians were twice as likely to vote for the party as ethnic Ukrainians, 32.3 per cent as opposed to 16.7 per cent' (Wilson and Birch 1999: 1049). From electoral results, the relevant parties are identified and the independent variable 'trailing minority party' is coded 1 when it is the Communist Party, preferred by Russians. The share of Russians per district is taken from official census results.[15]

My analysis explores differences in strategic voting between the ethnic minority and the majority population. The SF ratios used here for measuring strategic voting have the distinct feature of being bounded between 0 and 1. Furthermore, their distribution can be highly skewed, or even bimodal. For example, when most of the voters in our application are voting strategically, they either desert the relevant candidate, resulting in a SF ratio close to 0 – or, if the race between the two trailing contestants is too close to make clear who will win, both will receive similar proportions of the vote, resulting in a SF ratio close to 1. Intermediate values will be absent, resulting in a bimodal distribution of the SF ratio. Therefore, conventional regression models are unsuitable, since these can only model the mean of a distribution.

The possibility of bimodality renders the mean parameter rather uninformative, since both strategic and non-strategic behaviour could result in similar means. The dispersion of the distribution should be smaller, however, when voting behaviour is non-strategic and SF ratios are clustered around 0.5. Substantially, a SF ratio of 0.5 means that votes are wasted on an unpromising candidate, in a situation where there is neither a close race nor a candidate clearly leading. Since on average, and at least in non-consolidated electoral democracies,[16] strategic voting should result

14. Ukraine constituency data. Online. Available /www2.essex.ac.uk/elect/database/indexCountry.asp?country=UKRAINE&opt=con (accessed 14 February 2012).

15. Census statistics on the ethnic composition of the population of Ukraine. Online. Available /www. ukrcensus.gov.ua/eng/results/general/nationality/ (accessed 27 February 2010). Unfortunately, population shares are only readily available for the twenty-four regions, two cities, and the one autonomous republic of Ukraine. Therefore, ethnic conflict is assumed to be constant across the two (Sevastopol) to twenty-three (Donetsk) electoral districts within regions.

16. In consolidated democracies, where coordination between parties and voters works, strategic voting should more often result in SF ratios of 0 (Duvergian equlibriums), since there is only one

in SF value ratios of either 0 or 1, and non-strategic voting should result in inter-mediate values, the variance of the distribution of the SF ratio should be smaller given the absence of strategic voting. Therefore, the main test of my hypotheses on strategic voting relies on the effect of the covariates on the variance of the distribution of the SF ratio. Thus, beta-distributed regression models are used, since they can accommodate bounded distributions and allow for the modelling of both the mean and the variance or dispersion (or, turned on its head, the precision) of a distribution (see Appendix 10.A for a description of the model).

Results

Wilson and Birch (1999) present some evidence that the Communist Party was the primary choice of the Russian minority in the 1998 parliamentary election in Ukraine. The strategic voting behaviour of the Russian minority population is analysed in a first step and the SF ratio captures traces of strategic voting via elec-toral results. As discussed above, the ratio is bound between 0 and 1, with values close to 0 or 1 indicating the incidence of strategic voting, and intermediate values indicating the absence of strategic voting. Figure 10.1 displays the distribution of SF ratios by the status of the party to be deserted as either the Communist Party (minority) or any other party.

The visual evidence suggests that in both cases, a large share of the votes has been wasted. In both situations, the distribution peaks in the middle of the scale, indicating that votes were cast for candidates who did not have realistic chances of obtaining a seat. The trend is not more pronounced if the Communist Party is trailing, as shown on the right-hand side of Figure 10.1. The standard deviation of both distributions is about 0.21. In sum, there is no initial visual evidence for less strategic voting among ethnic minorities, but at the same time, strategic voting is generally not very pronounced, as we would typically expect in new democracies.

As discussed above, the logic of strategic voting in divided societies could be more complicated than is captured by Figure 10.1. Therefore, the relationship between the status of the trailing party as a minority or majority party and strategic voting is analysed using a beta-distributed regression model introducing covari-ates (see Table 10.1 in Appendix 10.A for results).[17] As argued above, in newly-established democracies, non-Duvergian equilibriums (where more than two can-didates have chances of obtaining a seat in single-member districts) are as frequent as Duvergian equilibriums, resulting in SF ratios close to 1 in addition to close to 0, with both indicating strategic voting behaviour. Such a data structure is reflected in the visual analysis above. Thus, we are mainly interested in the

---

viable alternative candidate in single-member districts. Following from this line of reasoning, the mean of the SF ratio can then be modelled, with higher values indicating the absence of strategic voting, since values of 1 for close races between second and first losers are absent.

17. In Table 10.1 (Appendix 10.A), the mean (without specifying a hypothesis) and the precision (inverse of the variance) of the SF ratio are modelled As implied by the theoretical expectations, no effects are observed for the model of the mean.

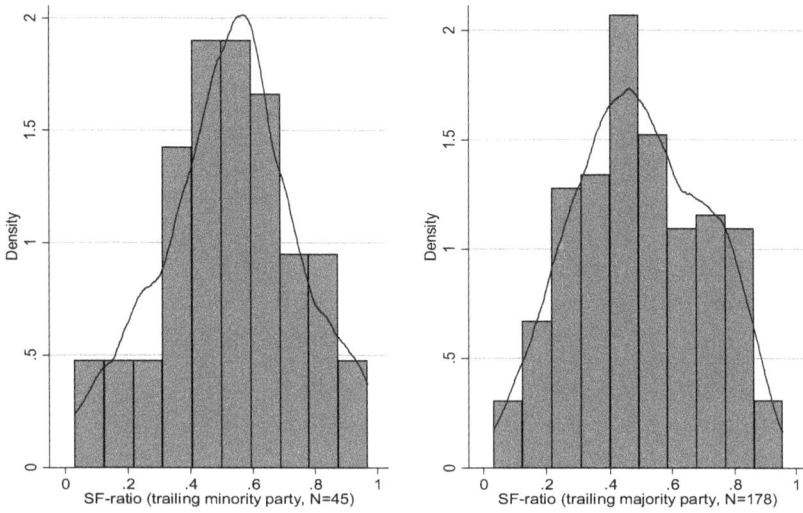

Figure 10.1: Distribution of SF ratios by type of trailing party

variance of the distribution of the SF ratio, which is smaller in the absence of strategic voting, when SF ratios cluster around the middle of the scale

A series of beta-distributed regression models has been estimated for testing the focal hypothesis and some simpler specifications (see Appendix 10.A). The first model (Model 1 in Table 10.1 in Appendix 10.A) features just one explanatory variable and does not indicate systematically less strategic voting in districts where the Communist Party's candidate should be strategically deserted. There is no statistically significant difference in the distribution of SF ratios – and thus no difference in strategic voting – when trailing parties are ethnic minority parties or not. The sign of the variable 'trailing minority party' is even negative. Therefore, in a naïve model specification, a trailing majority party even results in slightly less strategic voting when the party to be deserted is a majority party.[18]

---

18. Two further models present partial versions of the focal argument. Model 2 (see Table 10.1 in Appendix 10.A) adds the ethnic context and tests the implications of the U-shape argument of shares of Russians in the district on strategic voting. The share of Russians and the square of the share of Russians are included in the model for this purpose. The argument is that spillover effects lead to the lowest levels of strategic voting overall in fractionalised settings where the population shares of Russians and Ukrainians are roughly equal, while one group has more opportunities for strategic voting in more homogenous settings. Model 2 reports no evidence for a U-shaped relationship in this partial implementation of the focal argument. Model 3 (Table 10.1 in Appendix 10.A) features an interaction between 'trailing minority party' and 'share of Russians' in isolation. The expectation is that trailing 'minority' parties only result in lower levels of strategic voting when the minority population really is a numeric minority. The results of the linear interaction model do not support this expectation. But, the model does not take into account the potential U-shaped relationship described above.

The final model (Model 4 in Table 10.1 in Appendix 10.A) tests the fully elaborated hypothesis.[19] The results largely support the focal argument.[20] The effect of trailing minority parties on strategic voting depends on the share of Russians in the district, in a non-linear fashion. For low shares of Russians, trailing minority parties may even translate into more strategic voting (see effect on 'trailing minority party'). Once the share of Russians rises, less strategic voting occurs given a trailing ethnic minority party (see effect on 'share of Russians*trailing minority party'). However, as the effect on 'share of Russians squared*trailing minority party' indicates, this trend is countered by one in the direction of more strategic voting again, when Russians constitute a local majority. For trailing majority parties, a similar, yet reversed, U-shaped relationship to strategic voting is observed as expected, conditional on the share of Russians in the district. The effects are slightly less pronounced, though (see constant term and variables capturing the share of Russians without interactions in Model 4, Table 10.1, Appendix 10.A).

To facilitate interpretation, Figures 10.2 and 10.3 use the results of Model 4 to provide meaningful marginal effects and standard errors for the U-shaped interaction and employ the model's predictions to illustrate the net effect the included variables have on strategic voting.[21] Figure 10.2 illustrates the changing effects a trailing minority party has on strategic voting (captured by the variance of the SF ratio) discussed above. For trailing minority parties, strategic voting is slightly more pronounced given low population share of Russians, but the effects are not statistically significant for most situations. This runs counter to the expectation that majority voters should display more strategic voting behaviour than minority voters given small minority populations. Once the population share of Russians rises, less strategic voting is observed for trailing ethnic minority parties – a result that is in line with the argument that larger but non-majoritarian shares of Russians in a district translate into stronger conflict.[22]

---

19. Model 4 introduces the more flexible, non-linear U-shaped interaction between population shares of Russians and trailing minority parties. This model fully allows spillover effects and trade-offs to operate. For each group, an effect of having their party trailing – depending on the share of Russians in the district – is estimated, providing for the possibility of trade-offs. Furthermore, the non-linearity of the estimation in the form of squared terms allows for spillover effects to enter the picture, resulting in lower overall levels of strategic voting given intermediate population shares of Russians. The non-linear form can also capture situations, such as low conflict levels, given small shares of Russians, potentially resulting in relatively high levels of strategic voting.

20. For the interpretation of the coefficients, remember that they report effects on the precision of the distribution of the SF ration, where low precision indicates strategic voting.

21. Using the variance in the figures – instead of the precision, as in the regression models – yields the advantage of a more natural interpretation, since higher variance translates into more strategic voting.

22. For population shares of about 19 per cent, which is close to the sample mean of 18 per cent, the variance of the SF ratio is 0.025 smaller, indicating more votes 'wasted' on candidates who lack realistic chances for being elected. Given the overall variance of the SF ratio of about 0.044, this reflects a considerable difference, of more than 50 per cent.

Marginal Effect of 'Trailing Min. Party' on 'Variance of SF-ratio' As 'Share of Russ.' Changes

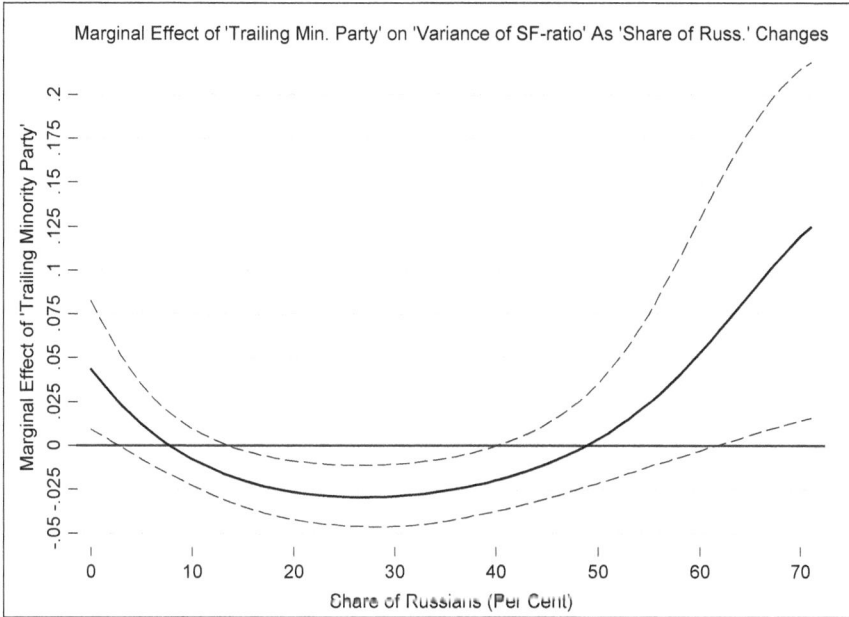

Figure 10.2: U-shaped interaction effect of trailing minority party moderated by share of Russians

However, the negative effect of a trailing minority party on strategic voting only lasts until the population share of Russians reaches approximately 50 per cent. The range in which a trailing ethnic minority party's statistically significant negative effect can be observed is between about 15 and 40 per cent Russians in an electoral district. Beyond this point, the effect of a trailing 'minority' party turns positive, and, with a large standard error, even statistically significant after a population share of about 60 per cent. In these situations, trailing 'minority' parties do not lead to less, but rather to *more* strategic voting – something that makes intuitive sense, given that in such cases 'minority' voters constitute a local majority.[23]

The varying effect of a trailing minority party is the result of two non-linear curves of strategic voting for trailing minority and trailing majority parties, estimated across the range of the share of Russians. Figure 10.3 shows the levels of strategic voting (in terms of predicted variances of the SF ratio) for these two instances, demonstrating the origin of the non-linear interaction effect described. Figure 10.3 also mirrors the observation made above, which holds that for very

---

23. The empirical range of the share of Russians is limited to about 1 to 70 per cent. Therefore, no situations of small 'majority' population shares are observed, where a slight increase in strategic voting among the smaller ethnic group due to low levels of conflict would be expected.

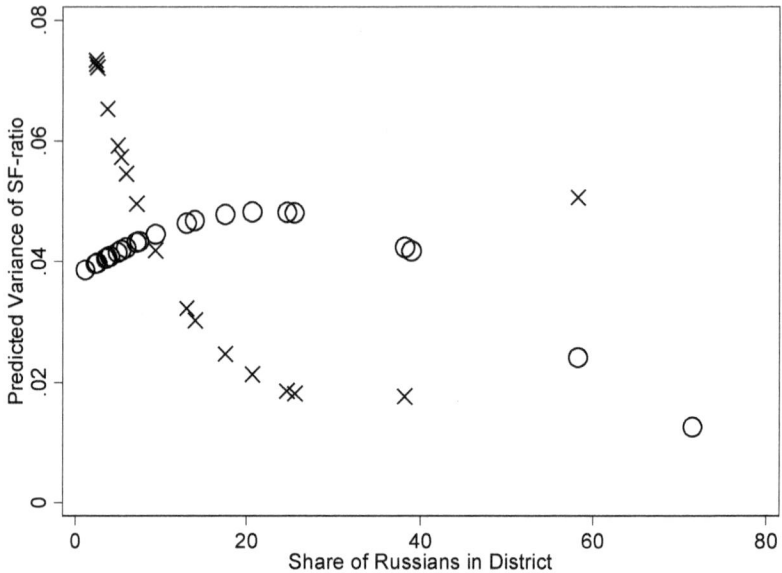

Figure 10.3: Predicted variance of SF ratio based on Model 4. ('X' indicates trailing minority parties; 'O' indicates trailing majority parties.)

low shares of Russians, trailing minority parties le.ad to more strategic voting than trailing majority parties, contrary to expectations. Still, and particularly in cases with intermediate Russian population shares, the expectation of a group-specific non-linear relationship between the share of Russians and strategic voting is confirmed.

Conclusion

Working within the context of the Ukrainian Russian minority's response to a nationalising state in the electoral arena, this chapter has analysed patterns of ethnicity and strategic voting in the 1998 Ukrainian parliamentary election. To this end, a beta-distributed regression model was used to analyse SF ratios in the electoral districts. SF ratios are defined as the ratio between the second and the first loser of the election, and reflect whether candidates who have little chance of obtaining seats are deserted strategically. Within this framework, two scenarios are possible:

(1) If two top-runners in a single-member district exist, strategic behaviour would imply a sharp decline of votes between the first and second loser, and the SF ratio would take on values close to 0.

(2) If a close race between three top-runners in a single-member district occurs – resulting in the kind of non-Duvergian equilibrium that is likely to exist in new democracies – strategic behaviour would predict similar vote shares for the second and first loser.

If such strategic voting behaviour occurs, the SF ratio takes on values close to 1. Values close to both 0 and 1 thus indicate strategic voting behaviour, while intermediate SF ratio values indicate the absence of strategic voting. In other words, strategic voting is indicated by a SF ratio distribution with larger variance, while the absence of strategic voting is indicated by distributions with smaller variances. As the ratio is bounded between 0 and 1, and likely to be non-normally distributed, its variance can be analysed using a beta-distributed regression model to explore the effect of ethnicity on strategic voting behaviour.

Departing from these preliminaries, the research subsequently asked whether trailing ethnic minority parties are deserted less frequently by their voters, since the voters may arguably have less attractive alternative parties to vote for, compared to the majority population. Strategic voting is defined as voting for a party other then the most preferred one, and assumed to be determined by ideological utilities and pivot probabilities (the perceived chances of candidates). Using the SF ratio, the aggregate-level consequences of strategic voting are analysed. Depending on pivot probabilities, and assuming sufficient levels of information and coordination, rational voters should vote for a viable candidate, resulting in either SF ratios close to 1 or 0. If intermediate values are observed, it would seem that information on pivot probabilities is insufficient or ambiguous – or that there are other reasons, such as a lack of sympathy towards viable parties. This latter aspect is the focus of the present analysis, since sympathy towards alternative, viable parties or candidates is assumed to be lower for ethnic minority voters.

My argument has also been refined further. First, I noted that spillover effects could occur, resulting in low overall levels of strategic voting in ethnically-heterogeneous electoral districts. Secondly, I noted that 'minority' voters – in this application, the Russians in Ukraine – were only expected to have a limited choice set when they constitute a local population minority. In cases where Ukrainians were the minority, trailing minority parties were expected to be related to higher levels of strategic voting. This implies an interaction between the status of the trailing party and the share of Russians in the electoral district. Furthermore, non-linear effects of the interaction were allowed, as homogenous districts might have lower levels of conflict, something that makes it easier for minorities to vote for mainstream candidates.

The results verify these expectations to a large extent. There is no naïve effect of a trailing minority party on strategic voting, and no evidence of simple spillover effects. But the effect of a trailing minority party on strategic voting clearly depends on the share of Russians in the district. Contradicting expectations, minority voters tended to vote even more strategically than majority voters in districts with very low population shares of Russians. The main result was that, especially in districts with Russian population shares of between about 15 and 40 per cent, trailing minority parties are clearly related to less strategic voting than trailing majority parties. At population shares of about 50 per cent and above, the effect turns *positive* towards increased strategic voting, in line with the logic that after that point, 'minorities' constitute a local majority.

As far as the substantial implications for ethnicity and strategic voting are concerned, the conditional effect of a trailing minority party confirms that, depending on the context, minority voters (given that they really constitute a local minority) have difficulties voting for a mainstream party that has a greater chance of obtaining a seat – likely due to doubts about the party's ability to represent these voters' views. Furthermore, the effect appears to be non-linear: The lack of strategic voting, at least for trailing minority parties, is more pronounced given, for example, 20 per cent Russians in the district as opposed to, say, 5 per cent – perhaps reflecting a more salient ethnic conflict in more heterogeneous districts.

The unexpected result that trailing majority parties are related to even lower levels of strategic voting in districts with low Russian population shares requires further explanation. Although the differences are close to being non-significant, my hypothesis predicted a clear *positive* effect to be apparent in these situations. The result I observed could be explained by the context of the election, which occurred in the early phase of Ukraine's democratic consolidation.[24] To wit, the 1998 parliamentary election in Ukraine was conducted in a situation of newly-established democratic rule and with a population demonstrating little attachment to political parties (Bugajski 2002: 924). It was only the second free election after Ukraine attained independence (Bugajski 2002: 923ff.). Many independent candidates were running in the single-member districts. In such situations, as Birnir (2007: 9) argues, 'ethnic identity serves as a stable but flexible information shortcut for political choices', which could give ethnic minorities an advantage over a majority population that may be confused by the offers emanating from the political parties. Minorities might be better equipped to identify their political demands and the parties promising to meet them. This could explain why trailing minority parties are related to higher levels of strategic voting, at least in situations with low levels of ethnic conflict. Once districts become more fractionalised, the argument of ethnic shortcuts applies to both the minority and the majority population, as the saliency of ethnicity is likely to increase.

These findings underscore the importance electoral system design can have in preventing the exclusion of ethnic minorities, who appear to have difficulty voting for alternative candidates. Pure majoritarian electoral systems do not offer incentives for moderation between groups, such as alternative vote systems might do (Horowitz 1993). In particular, in nationalising states with salient ethnic cleavages, the exclusion of ethnic minorities is a threat to political stability and peace (Alonso and Ruiz-Rufino 2007; Cohen 1997; Saideman *et al.* 2002; Schneider and Wiesehomeier 2008). In this sense, the analysis performed in this chapter also provides a rational choice perspective on the electoral interplay between majorities and minorities in nationalising states. Following from this line of logic, the move to full PR after the 2002 election would seem likely to have reduced the probability of ethnic conflict, as long as there has been no ethnic outbidding. As of today, ongoing tension which are not easy described in purely ethnic terms, lacking power sharing and issues with democratization appear to overshadow such theoretical effects.

---

24. Furthermore, the Communist Party has not been a clear-cut ethnic minority party.

In the years around the Orange Revolution, the 'dormant' (Wilkinson and Birch 1999: 1049) ethnic-regional cleavage was rekindled. And for this reason, an analysis of additional elections could help us assess our research question in more definitive terms. Only the 2002 election offers such a possibility, however, since the electoral system was changed to full PR thereafter.[25] Furthermore, despite the possibilities for analysing the connection between ethnicity and strategic voting at the aggregate level, appropriate individual-level data for modelling vote choice – which would allow for the incorporation of individual strategic and ideological utilities – remain among the most urgent research desiderata.

---

25. Sub-national level data for the 2002 election was not readily available.

Appendix 10: Methodology and results of the beta regression model

The class of beta-distributed regression models accommodates such distributions (Ferrari and Cribari-Neto 2004; Paolino 2001; Smithson and Verkuilen 2006).[26] The beta distribution is very flexible and can produce densities with very different shapes (Ferrari and Cribari-Neto 2004: 800), including bimodal ones. In its most convenient version, beta-distributed regression has two parameters, which are modelled separately. The parameters decide the location (mean) and the precision (influencing variance) of the distribution. The actual shape of the distribution depends on both factors, as very small or large means imply abrupt borders of the distribution close to the mean when responses are bounded (Smithson and Verkuilen 2006: 58). Nevertheless, both factors can be modelled separately. The sub-model for location reads (see Smithson and Verkuilen 2006: 59):

$$ln \frac{\mu_i}{1 - \mu_i} = \beta X_i$$

Where the logit transformation of the location parameter $ln \frac{\mu_i}{1 - \mu_i}$ provides a link function that guarantees predicted values between 0 and 1. Location is a function of a vector of covariates X_i with a vector of coefficients β. The precision submodel is given by:

$$\ln(\phi_i) = \delta W_i$$

The log link function of the precision parameter $\ln(\phi_i)$ ensures a positive prediction, appropriate for a variance. Precision is a function of a vector of covariates W_i with a vector of coefficients δ. Important for interpretation, larger precision indicates smaller variance.[27] As discussed above, both location and precision influence the variance of the distribution $Var(y)$. The link is (Smithson and Verkuilen 2006: 58):

$$Var(y) = \frac{\mu(1 - \mu)}{1 + \phi}$$

From this equation, it also becomes apparent that larger precision results in smaller variance, as the precision parameter is added to the denominator. The predicted values of the location parameter μ_i and the precision parameter ϕ_i are:

$$\mu_i = \frac{\exp(X_i\beta)}{1 + \exp(X_i\beta)}$$

and

$$\phi_i = \exp(W_i\delta)$$

---

26. See Selb (2012) for a discussion of the beta-distributed regression. Selb also provides an extension of the model into a dynamic multilevel version, modelling developments (learning curves) of strategic voting over several elections in Spain in different context (electoral districts).

27. Smithson and Verkuilen (2006) provide a discussion of the useful reparametrisation of the model. Their parametrisation does however differ from most implementations in statistical software packages such as Stata in that they model dispersion, not precision of the variance. This has consequences for interpretation: When dispersion is modelled, larger dispersion intuitively translates into larger variance. Larger precision translates less intuitively into smaller variance. To ensure consistency with regression outputs, the model is discussed in terms of precision here.

Table 10.1: Beta regression of strategic voting (dependent variable: SF ratio; mean and precision)

	Model 1	Model 2	Model 3	Model 4
Location sub-model				
Trailing minority party	0.104 (0.144)		0.027 (0.214)	−0.004 (0.305)
Share of Russians		−0.007 (0.010)	−0.002 (0.004)	0.004 (0.010)
Share of Russians squared		−0.000 (0.000)		−0.000 (0.000)
Trailing min. party X Share of Russ.			0.004 (0.007)	0.010 (0.026)
Trailing min. party X Share of Russ. Squared				−0.000 (0.000)
Constant (mean)	−0.009 (0.062)	−0.029 (0.113)	0.033 (0.094)	−0.027 (0.117)
Precision submodel				
Trailing minority party	−0.155 (0.213)		−0.240 (0.295)	−1.149 (0.416)***
Share of Russians		0.004 (0.018)	0.005 (0.007)	−.0028 (0.019)
Share of Russians squared		0.000 (0.000)		0.001 (0.000)*
Trailing min. party X Share of Russ.			0.006 (0.011)	0.155 (0.044)***
Trailing min. party X Share of Russ. squared				−0.003 (0.001)***
Constant (precision)	1.563 (0.097)***	1.433 (0.178)***	1.477 (0.156)***	1.734 (0.204)***
N (districts)	223	223	223	223

Notes: ***p <0.01, **p <0.05, *p <0.1. Standard errors are reported in parentheses. The beta-distributed regression model was computed with the beta fit command in Stata 10 using maximum likelihood estimation. The results of interest refer to the precision sub-model.

References

Adams, J. F., Merrill III, S. and Grofman, B. (2005) *A Unified Theory of Party Competition: A cross-national analysis integrating spatial and behavioral factors*, Cambridge: Cambridge University Press.

Alonso, S. and Ruiz-Rufino, R. (2007) 'Political representation and ethnic conflict in new democracies', *European Journal of Political Research*, 46(2): 237–67.

Alvarez, M. R. and Nagler, J. (1998) 'When politics and models collide: estimating models of multiparty elections', *American Journal of Political Science*, 42(1): 55–96.

—— (2000) 'A new approach for modelling strategic voting in multiparty elections', *British Journal of Political Science*, 30(1): 57–75.

Birnir, J. K. (2007) *Ethnicity and electoral politics,* Cambridge: Cambridge University Press.

Blais, A. and Nadeau, R. (1996) 'Measuring strategic voting: a two-step procedure', *Electoral Studies*, 15(1): 39–52.

Blais, A., Young, R. and Turcotte, M. (2005) 'Direct or indirect? Assessing two approaches to the measurement of strategic voting', *Electoral Studies*, 24(2): 163–76.

Bremmer, I. (1994) 'The politics of ethnicity: Russians in the new Ukraine', *Europe–Asia Studies*, 46(2): 261–83.

Brubaker, R. (1996) *Nationalism reframed: Nationhood and the national question in the new Europe,* Cambridge: Cambridge University Press.

Bugajski, J. (2002) *Political parties of Eastern Europe: A guide to politics in the post-communist era*, Armonk: Sharpe.

Chandra, K. (2005) 'Ethnic parties and democratic stability', *Perspectives on Politics* 3(2): 235–52.

Cohen, F. S. (1997) 'Proportional versus majoritarian ethnic conflict management in democracies', *Comparative Political Studies*, 30(5): 607–30.

Constant, A., Kahanec, M. and Zimmermann, K. F. (2006) 'The Russian-Ukrainian political divide', *IZA Discussion Paper*, 2530.

Cox, G. W. (1994) 'Strategic voting equlibria under the single nontransferable vote', *American Political Science Review*, 88(3): 608–21.

—— (1997) *Making Votes Count: Strategic coordination in the world's electoral systems*, Cambridge: Cambridge University Press.

Duch, R. M. and Palmer, H. D. (2002) 'Strategic voting in post-communist democracy?', *British Journal of Political Science*, 32(1): 63–91.

Fearon, J. D. (2003) 'Ethnic and cultural diversity by country', *Journal of Economic Growth*, 8(2): 195–222.

Ferrari, S. L. P. and Cribari-Neto, F. (2004) 'Beta regression for modelling rates and proportions', *Journal of Applied Statistics*, 31(7): 799–815.

Fisher, S. D. (2004) 'Definition and measurement of tactical voting: the role of rational choice', *British Journal of Political Science*, 34(1): 152–66.

Heath, A., Jewell, R., Curtice, J., Evans, G., Field, J. and Witherspoon, S. (1991) *Understanding Political Change: The British voter 1964–1987*, Oxford: Pergamon Press.

Horowitz, D. L. (1985) *Ethnic Groups in Conflict*, Berkeley: University of California Press.
—— (1993) 'Democracy in divided societies', *Journal of Democracy*, 4(4): 18–38.
Horowitz, S. and Browne, E. C. (2005) 'Sources of post-communist party system consolidation: ideology versus institutions', *Party Politics*, 11(6): 689–706.
Liao, T. F. (2006) *Interpreting Probability Models: Logit, probit, and other generalized linear models*, Thousand Oaks: Sage.
Mansbridge, J. (1999) 'Should blacks represent blacks and women represent women? A contingent "yes"', *Journal of Politics*, 61(3): 628–57.
Myerson, R. B. and Weber, R. J. (1993) 'A theory of voting equilibria', *American Political Science Review*, 87(1): 102–14.
OSCE (1998) 'Republic of Ukraine parliamentary elections 29 March 1998', *OSCE Election Reports*.
Paolino, P. (2001) 'Maximum likelihood estimation of models with Beta-distributed dependent variables', *Political Analysis*, 9(4): 325–46.
Rabushka, A. R. and Shepsle, K. A. (1972) *Politics in Plural Societies: A theory of democratic instability*, Columbus: Merrill.
Saideman, S. M., Lanouc, D. J., Campenni, M. and Stanton, S. (2002) 'Democratization, political institutions, and ethnic conflict: a pooled time series analysis, 1985–1998', *Comparative Political Studies*, 35(1): 103–29.
Schneider, G. and Wiesehomeier, N. (2008) 'Rules that matter: political institutions and the polarization–conflict nexus', *Journal of Peace Research*, 45(2): 183–203.
Selb, P. (2012) 'Strategic adaption to new electoral systems', *European Journal of Political Research*, 51(5): 583–606.
Shikano, S., Herrmann, M. and Thurner, P. W. (2009) 'Strategic voting under proportional representation: threshold insurance in German elections', *West European Politics*, 32(3): 634–56.
Smithson, M. and Verkuilen, J. (2006) 'A better lemon squeezer? Maximum-likelihood regression with Beta-distributed dependent variables', *Psychological Methods*, 11(1): 54–71.
Sum, P. E. and Bădescu, G. (2008) 'Ideological voting: a cross-national analysis of left-right orientations on voting behaviour', *Studia Universitatis Babes Bolyai Politica*, 53(1): 52–73.
Tiemann, G. (2006) *Wahlsysteme, Parteiensysteme und politische Repräsentation in Osteuropa*, Wiesbaden: VS Verlag für Sozialwissenschaften.
Weber, M. (2002) [1922] *Wirtschaft und Gesellschaft: Grundriss der verstehenden Soziologie*, Tübingen: Mohr.
Wilson, A. and Birch, S. (1999) 'Voting stability, political gridlock: Ukraine's 1998 parliamentary elections', *Europe–Asia Studies*, 51(6): 1039–68.

chapter eleven | on fissions and fusions of ethnic minority parties[1]

Edina Szöcsik and Daniel Bochsler

Introduction

In many Central and Eastern European countries, the transition towards democracy was linked to important political challenges faced by ethno-national minority groups. In the former Yugoslavia, Czechoslovakia and in the Soviet Union, the breakdown of communist regimes also meant the end of multi-ethnic federations – whether the process occurred in an ordered and peaceful manner or a chaotic and violent one – and the creation of new nation-states, which required minorities to find their place within a new political space. In states with unaltered borders (Albania, Bulgaria, Hungary, Poland, Romania), political liberalisation was accompanied by an awakening of old nationalism and revisionist ideas, along with the reactivation of links to external minorities. Furthermore, the new political geography, along with the changing political situations in neighbouring states, also altered the relation of the states to their minorities. Hence, both domestic factors and relations to neighbours have fundamentally changed ethnic relations during this period (Brubaker 1996).

The politicisation of ethnic relations was also reflected in the creation of ethnic minority parties in all of the countries of the region. Divisions along ethnic lines were not only one of the most common, but also one of the most stable denominators of party systems in Central and Eastern Europe (Moser 2005).

Because of this, ethno-national minorities' political exponents needed to balance different ways and strategies to establish minority rights in the new states. They were either attracted by their kin states, or reliant on external support for growing political demand; at the same time they also felt the need to voice concerns and demands, in light of the threat of a new or redefined nationalising state.

Much of the literature on this subject deals with ethnic minorities as united, homogeneous actors, neglecting the fact that many minority groups are politically fragmented (e.g. Rabushka and Shepsle 1972). An important strategic decision for the political mobilisation of ethnic minorities, however, involves their internal organisation. This chapter endeavours to shed light on the principle conflict between unity and political differentiation.

1. We are grateful to Julian Bernauer and to Christina Zuber and the three editors for very helpful comments on earlier versions of this chapter. Daniel Bochsler thanks especially his interviewees and the Political Science Institute at the University of Belgrade for a research stay, which enabled parts of this study. Edina Szöcsik thanks to the Forum Minority Research Institute in Šamorín/Somorja and the Jakabffy Elemér Foundation in Cluj-Napoca/Kolozsvár that enabled a research stay.

In quite a few cases in the region, there has been intense competition among rival parties of ethnic minorities. This is the case for Albanian minorities in Serbia, Macedonia, and in Montenegro; for the parties of the Hungarian minorities in Romania, Slovakia and in Serbia; and also for the parties of the Bosniak minority in Serbia (Bochsler 2012a). In many countries in the region, ethnic minority parties – which emerged in the early 1990s – are not only those with the most stable party history, but also those with the most loyal electorate. In several countries, this has changed suddenly, as parties of several significant minorities have very recently been challenged by rival parties.

Still, the pluralism of political interest organisations within minority groups is beginning to be acknowledged, though relatively few studies have turned their attention to the determinants and effects of intra-ethnic party competition. Empirically speaking, in the present chapter we will investigate ethno-national minority groups whose political organisations have changed. More specifically, we will consider four cases in which ethnic minority parties have recently experienced new intra-group divides, or alternately have recently merged.

These cases focus, in particular, on Hungarian minorities, which are most numerous in Romania, Slovakia and in Serbia. After the democratic transition, these groups were confronted with the Hungarian state's push for new ties to its external minorities, and with revived notions of Hungarian irredentism – factors that also affected the policies of the neighbouring states that were targeted by this agenda. All of the host states of the Hungarian minorities also developed or revived their own nationalistic movements in the 1990s.

Slovakia, after the split of Czechoslovakia, had a new ethnic majority and the new state was mainly identified with the Slovaks and their language. For the first time, the ethnic Hungarians of Slovakia found themselves in the position of being the largest minority and, in the first period, in the position of being excluded from government. After joining the national government in 1998, the Party of the Hungarian Coalition (SMK) was in power for eight years, a period during which internal tensions in the government became apparent. When ousted from government in 2006, the party changed its leadership. It split apart in 2009 and since then it has been challenged by a new, moderate, self-declared multi-ethnic party, Most-Híd (Slovak and Hungarian for bridge). Most-Híd receives its main support from the Hungarian minority, and has even credibly threatened the survival of the Party of the Hungarian Coalition in first national elections.

In Serbia, the Hungarian minority's situation was no less challenging, since the dissolution of Yugoslavia gave rise to the increasing domination of political institutions under Serbian political leadership guided by Slobodan Milošević. Those minorities within Serbia – most importantly ethnic Hungarians and the Bosniaks of the Serbian Sandžak – experienced the shrinking of Yugoslavia and the realisation of the Serbian nation-state within the state borders. In both cases, this led to a multitude of minority parties competing for votes and offices. As of 2008, however, the parties of the Hungarian minority formed a political alliance, and have since run jointly in national and provincial elections. Since 2008, the Hungarian Coalition has participated in government – a novelty, considering the history of

Hungarians' political representation in Serbia. However, it broke up as a consequence of internal tensions and its relationship to the Democratic Party, which presently leads the government coalition.

In contrast, Serbia's Bosniak population experienced an important political reformation only a few years later. In early 2011, the new Bosniak Democratic Community (BDZ) of the main *mufti* (Muslim religious leader) entered the competition, and may well be poised to become the most powerful party of the community after winning a plurality of votes in the elections for newly-formed minority councils. The party is politically radical and a serious threat to the two main incumbent parties, which both moderated their radicalism in the 2000s when they entered the national government.

Romania is certainly not a new nation-state. But nevertheless, the Hungarian minority's political situation has changed dramatically in Romania since 1989. It had to confront a new, nationalist wave of politics in Hungary and contend with the nationalising pressure that was then growing on the Romanian political scene. Indeed, internally, Romania experienced a wave of nationalism in the 1990s that coincided with a period in which Hungarian politics towards its external minority changed. Furthermore, Moldova – which has a sub-population that is culturally oriented towards Romania – also became independent at this time. After functioning under a nationalist government (which lasted until 1996) the organisation of the Hungarians in Romania (UDMR) was then brought into the government, and stayed there – or was closely supporting the government –for over twelve years. This relationship has led to increasing intra-ethnic pressure from dissidents, who formed the new Hungarian Civic Party (PCM) in 2007, as well as from other political interest organisations, focusing on making more radical ethno-national claims.

In this chapter, we will analyse the causes of the recent fissions and fusions within the political parties of these four national minorities in the three aforementioned countries. In particular, we will focus on the role of government participation, especially as it relates to the following research question: *what influence does government participation have on the fragmentation and, respectively, the unity of the political representation of ethnic minorities?*

We argue that two logics of political representation account for the emergence of intra-group competition. As a starting point, we argue that when ethnicity becomes politically salient, and members of the group have diverse political preferences, this generates a genuine need for *political pluralism* within the group. The basic divide takes place between moderates and radicals within a group, to the extent that members of these divisions favour minority rights. Pragmatic and office-seeking politicians might opt much more strongly for moderation, for instance, which typically better allows them to join government coalitions; however, they are likely, then, to be challenged by more radical, opposition-oriented actors. Bearing this in mind, we argue that *government participation* puts the political unity of ethnic minority groups at stake and accelerates internal divides or sharpens competition between existing rival organisations within minorities.

This chapter will proceed as follows. In the next section, we will develop our arguments pertaining to the effect government participation has on the form of political representation pursued by national minorities. Our arguments will be illustrated by an analysis of the parties of four minority groups in Central and Eastern Europe, with specific attention paid to the changing roles of government and opposition, and the resulting fissions and fusions. In particular, we will discuss the emergence of new parties that challenge the previously dominant Hungarian parties in Slovakia and in Romania, the creation of a third political bloc of the Bosniaks in Serbia, and an attempt made by the three most important Hungarian minority parties in Serbia to come together.

Theory on intra-ethnic party competition

Intra-ethnic competition is largely a neglected topic in ethnic politics. Most common large-N quantitative studies in the field of ethnic politics still analyse on the level of ethnic groups (MAR 2009; Cederman *et al.* 2009). Research on elections in divided countries often assumes that minority groups are politically-homogenous units. Hence, the plurality of their political organisations and the political positions held by these organisations are not accounted for. When dealing with intra-group competition, the literature mainly argues that such competition leads to a race to extremes, with each competitor striving to position itself as the most credible representative of minority interests – something that typically involves a presentation of more and more radical arguments, and thus eventually undermines democratic stability (Gormley-Heenan and Macginty 2008; Horowitz 1985; Mitchell 1995; Rabushka and Shepsle 1972). Recently, however, research has emerged that investigates the circumstances that lead ethnic parties radicalise. Radicalisation appears to be only one among many strategies that may be chosen by parties engaged in political competition (Coakley 2008; Zuber 2011; Bochsler 2012b). Flexible institutions and intra-ethnic plurality may also create varying majorities over time, intercepting the radicalisation of a group (Chandra 2005; Gormley-Heenan and Macginty 2008; Mitchell *et al.* 2009).

This chapter proposes a demand-driven and an institution-driven argument in order to explain plurality in the political representation of ethnic minorities.

The demand for political pluralism within the ethnic group

Institutional constraints influence and delimit the forms of political representation available to an ethnic minority. This is particularly so in cases where the ethnic minority constitutes a rather small portion of the population and where electoral laws are restrictive at the national level; here such groups face incentives to pursue unified political representation in order to secure the national representation of the group. Thus, particularly restrictive electoral rules (e.g. those with high electoral thresholds) prevent small and dispersed minority political groups from fragmenting – hindering the fission of ethnic minority parties and the emergence of alternative breakaway parties (Barkan 1995; Bochsler 2011; 2012a).

However, the members of an ethnic group almost inevitably have diverse interests and these typically lead to a drive for politically-plural representation of the minority. For instance, there may well be different economic interests or different views on cultural liberalism within the group. Additionally, once ethnicity becomes a politically salient category, diverse political preferences emerge related to the ideal (co-)existence of the diverse ethnic groups in the country in general, and to the preferred extent and types of special rights for ethnic minorities in particular. Furthermore, within ethnic groups, there may also be a demand for amendment to political elites. This creates a demand for political pluralism regarding the representation of the ethnic group. The possibility of plural representation of minority groups depends, most crucially, on the size and the territorial concentration of the ethnic groups. Indeed, these factors determine the extent to which a minority group may be focused or powerful enough to win entry to the national parliament with a plurality of parties. In addition, the demand for internal differentiation is likely to be particularly high if a minority dominates political life in a municipality, city or region. In such cases, local politics is an intra-ethnic matter, and local political competition happens within the minority group. Thus, in such cases, there is a greater demand for the plural representation of ethnic minorities (Bochsler 2012a).

In sum, we argue that members of an ethnic group have diverse political preferences; therefore, there is likely to be genuine demand for diverse political representation. The character of the ethnic minority group's political representation (i.e. whether it is unified or fragmented) is shaped by that group's interaction with institutions (i.e. electoral rules, and the structural features of the group, such as size and territorial concentration). Regardless of the type of political representation in place, intra-ethnic competition may occur either within the unified party or between the multiple ethnic and multi-ethnic parties competing for the vote of ethnic minority.

Argument 1: Members of ethnic minorities have diverse political preferences related to a wide range of issues and interests, including cultural, socio-economic and ethno-political topics. Yet the interaction of the relative size and degree of the territorial concentration of the ethnic minority with the electoral system might be a barrier to the representation of such diverse interests by a plurality of parties.

The role of government participation

The inclusion of minority groups in national political institutions might spur internal differences within these groups (Robotin and Salat 2003; Mitchell *et al.* 2009). The minority party in opposition to or as part of the governing coalition is under cross-pressure.

To investigate this phenomenon in more detail, we look at situations in which an ethnic minority group is represented by one political party – something that is often the case in restrictive electoral systems, which frequently do not allow for multiple parties representing minorities to enter parliament. This is especially the case in situations where legal thresholds for party recognition as a percentage of the population are almost as high as the relative size of the ethnic minority groups in question.

Minority parties are not systemically different from other political parties, despite having different policy goals; ultimately, *all* parties strive to attain both a maximum of votes, to effect policy change, and to obtain offices (Strøm 1990; Sartori 2005).[2] United parties – which aim for the representation of an entire minority group – may include exponents who are more or less moderate or radical (relative to their central ethno-political claims) and who weigh the goals of office-seeking and policy-influence differently.

It should be noted, however, that these different goals are more or less easily accessible, dependent on the party's role in the political system and on the specific point in time of the political cycle. Government participation might help parties bring some of their goals into the coalition programme. And an oppositional role gives parties the potential to maintain and campaign for radical changes, and to keep the pressure for policy moves. During elections, radical claims are typically more strongly rewarded by the electorate than moderate ones – whereas between elections, it is typically most efficacious to obtain rewards by working inclusively with political institutions, by seeking offices and/or influence over policy.

We argue that, while moderates profit from government inclusion – which provides access to offices and requires a moderation of the party line – radicals might be less liable to agree to compromises that enable the formation of coalitions with opposition partners. These differences are somewhat limited in degree, and *do* often allow cooperation. In certain situations, however, the trade-off between policy influence and benefits from office holding – and the conflict between moderates and radicals – becomes vital and irreconcilable:

- At times of government formation, coalition partners must accept compromises; these typically include concessions to programmes. Both moderates and office-seekers may be willing to make the necessary policy moves, and this might accentuate intra-party divisions between radicals and policy-seekers, who might be reluctant to give up long-standing demands.

- During the governing period, decisions on the most controversial issues might require new compromises and concessions, and the more sweeping promises to the minority party may well remain unfulfilled. Such situations accentuate the tensions between the more pragmatic and more radical elements within the minority party, and may ultimately lead to the more radical elements agitating for departure from the governing coalition.

- After enjoying incumbent status within the government for a long time, and then becoming a part of the opposition, a party may experience fragmentation, as the difference between moderates and radicals becomes more pronounced. When suddenly placed in the position of opposition, moderates

---

2. Sartori (2005) speaks of idea-promotional groups, spoils-power groups and career-seeking politicians.

no longer enjoy office-related private gains. In such cases, they are liable to lose political influence, and radicals may be free to demand that the party change course to a more radical direction.

Such situations fuel conflict between those who are more or less moderate, and between those who weigh the goals of policy influence and office-holding differently. If the minority is organised within one party and is operating in a restrictive institutional setting, then the conflicts that emerge within that party can occasionally lead to splits within the minority party itself. Yet, if the party has not formerly represented all minority interests, it is possible that a new political party will emerge, completely outside the framework of the party.

Argument 2: Within unified ethnic minority parties, competition takes place between radicals and moderates and between office-seekers and policy-seekers. The conflict over whether to proceed by participating in government or by staying in opposition can exacerbate this conflict, and may even lead to the division of the party. This provides the opportunity for radicals to mobilise and outbid the governing party, by making more extreme demands.

Discussion of the cases

Our empirical investigation analyses four cases of party changes in which governmental participation played a key role. We discuss how the inclusion in national government contributed to fissions and fusions of minority parties in the regions in question. For the purposes of this study, we focus only upon fissions and fusions displaying the most relevant consequences, such as when new parties emerged and competed independently in elections, or were able to win offices, or otherwise presented a credible threat to the incumbent parties. We selected four minority groups that had experienced major changes in the form of political representation in recent years. And in all four cases, analysis over time allowed us to distinguish between situations in which minority parties were both in opposition and in the government, and the effect of governmental inclusion.

Our use of various available sources allowed us to grasp the different aspects and perspectives of minority politics, as well as the party fissions and fusions. For the purpose of this chapter, we combined our own interviews, conducted with experts and with important actors of minority politics, with analyses of party documents (manifestos, etc.), newspaper articles and relevant secondary sources.

A new, radical challenger to the Hungarian minority organisation in Romania

After its foundation at the end of 1989, the Democratic Alliance of Hungarians in Romania (UDMR) acted as an umbrella organisation, spanning internal ideological differences, as well as those of the diverse organisations of the Hungarian minority in Romania. Since its founding it has fulfilled the functions of a Hungarian political party and was working with the government – if not as part of it –

throughout the period from 1996–2008. Given the 6.6 per cent[3] relative share of the Hungarian minority in Romania, and the legal threshold of 5 per cent that was enacted for national elections in 2000, there has been a strong incentive for a unification of political organisations in order to successfully compete in elections.

During the period in which the National Salvation Front (FSN) was in government (1990–6), the UDMR was in opposition. After some initial achievements involving the reintroduction of high schools providing education in the Hungarian language, members of the UDMR grew increasingly suspicious of the ethno-nationalist discourse of the FSN – a situation that first became notable in 1991 – and became even more significant after two ultra-nationalist Romanian parties joined the government in 1992 (Horváth 2004). Isolated in opposition, internal dissonances in the UDMR first became manifest *vis-à-vis* the question of autonomy. Following the party platform of the Reform Bloc – the most radical platform of the UDMR – autonomy (both cultural and territorial) was held up as an indispensable right of the Hungarian minority. By contrast, the party leadership wanted to align with the mainstream opposition alliance, and rather hoped to achieve autonomy through government participation and step-by-step negotiation with the parties of the majority society (Horváth 2004).

In 1996, the UDMR entered an over-sized government coalition consisting of the centre-right Democratic Convention of Romania (CDR) and Democratic Party (PD). While no formal agreement specifying the result of the coalition negotiations existed, it is speculated that the UDMR had to make concessions to its programme in order to be included in the coalition, especially on the matter of territorial autonomy (Horváth 2004; Kántor and Bárdi 2000).

Governmental inclusion, along with the concessions to its programme, intensified the party's internal struggles, however. Ever since, the Reform Bloc has remained suspicious of the UDMR's participation in the government, because of the informal coalition agreement. Furthermore, the UDMR's continued failure to both establish a public Hungarian university and to promote the hiring of Hungarian faculties at public universities have caused heated debates on the purpose of government participation within the party.

After the 2000 elections, the UDMR's ongoing participation in government led to the first visible signs of serious internal divisions. As the Romanian Social Democrats (PSDR) came to power, UDMR supported their new minority government. As it became increasingly entangled with the PSDR, the UDMR's claim for cultural or territorial autonomy had completely disappeared from its political agenda. The Reform Bloc, meanwhile, was pushing for a less conciliatory strategy, and the UDMR underwent its first internal splits, which lead to a multitude of organisations: A rival Hungarian political organisation, the Civic Association for Oderheiu (UPE), ran in the 2000 local elections in the Hungarian-dominated town of Odorheiu Secuiesc, supported by the Reform Bloc and the conservative party in

---

3. Census 2002. National Institute of Statistics of Romania. Online. Available /www.insse.ro/cms/ files/RPL2002INS/vol5/tables/t16.pdf (accessed 15 March 2010).

Hungary, Fidesz (Udvardy 2006). In 2004, several local Hungarian associations, lead by the UPE, formed the Hungarian Civic Union (UCM) under the leadership of a member of the radical wing of the UDMR, the mayor of Odorheiu Secuiesc, Jenő Szász. After failing to register as a party, the UCM entered candidates in the national and district elections on the list of the non-ethnic People's Action Party (PAP) in two predominately Hungarian counties (Bakk *et al.* 2004). In 2003, a significant portion of the UDMR departed to establish the Hungarian National Council of Transylvania (CNMT) and the Szekler National Council (CNS), outside the framework of the UDMR (Mandel 2004), with the main aim of establishing Hungarian autonomy (Eplényi 2006). The common denominator of the new rival political organisation was the claim for autonomy for the Hungarian minority, with an emphasis on the territorial autonomy of the Szekler Land.

These first intra-ethnic splits made the position of the UDMR more difficult and it reacted by making more pronounced demands. After the 2004 elections, the UDMR once again changed its allegiance and joined the centre-right minority coalition in government, led by the National Liberal Party (PNL). This legislative period was dominated by plans to promote Hungarian minority issues put forward by the UDMR and rival alternative Hungarian organisations. The UDMR reacted to the intensified intra-ethnic competition and to the increased mobilisation based on the claim for autonomy, by launching a law on minorities that entailed cultural autonomy and a law on the reform of development regions – while UDMR representatives who were sympathetic to the new alternative Hungarian organisations submitted a plan for the territorial autonomy of the Szekler Land. All of these plans were rejected by the Romanian mainstream parties, but it is important to observe that the Hungarian groups' internal struggles also impeded the success of each of the propositions.

The Hungarian Civic Union (UCM) became a serious challenger to the UDMR in 2007, when it registered as the Hungarian Civic Party (PCM). It ran with own candidates in the local elections, and supported independent candidates in the national elections in 2008 (Kántor and Pászkán 2009). After its rather weak electoral performance, and internal disputes over its president, the PCM was slowly replaced by the Hungarian National Council of Transylvania (CNMT) as the main challenger to the UDMR, with the latter continuing to rely on a very popular president. However, none of these vehicles for UDMR dissidents successfully established itself as a strong political option. Subsequently, the demand for autonomy became of lower priority on the political agenda of the UDMR. Whether the UDMR can be challenged by a more radical Hungarian party remains to be seen. In the 2012 elections, it will probably have to compete with the CNMT, which is likely to convert to a party (EMNT 2010).

The case of the UDMR in Romania illustrates how a unified ethnic minority party participating in government moderated its course by giving up some policy goals in exchange for offices. The UDMR largely abandoned the claim for a number of collective rights and, in particular, gave up its claim for territorial autonomy. This was as the most controversial and radical demand of the Hungarian minority, one that is still not accepted by the Romanian majority parties. The UDMR pronounced its more moderate demands with regard to education in Hungarian and the use of language, which especially served the interests of Hungarians dispersed across Transylvania. However, any success by the UDMR on this front failed to have much impact in the historically core settlement of the Hungarians, the Szekler Land. One outcome was the emergence of a rival party – the Hungarian Civic Party – based in the heart of the Szekler Land. Additionally, internal, more radical dissident factions founded alternative political organisations, which meant the end of the homogenous representation of the Hungarian minority in Romania. The new Hungarian political organisations now compete for the support of the Hungarian minority by focusing on the establishment of a comprehensive system of autonomy for the Hungarian minority in Romania.

A multi-ethnic split-off of the Hungarian minority of Slovakia

The Hungarian minority of Slovakia constitutes some 9.7 per cent of the population,[4] living mostly in the south, along the Hungarian border. After the regime transformation in 1989, the emerging political representation of the Hungarian minority splintered into three main and two minor parties. The largest of these (the Hungarian Civic Party, MOS) entered the government in this first governing period – at this time, the Czechoslovakian and the Slovak government, from 1990–92 (Öllös 2004) – but after 1992, all Hungarian parties remained in opposition. The government of Vladimír Mečiar (1994–8) enacted legislation that reduced the rights of the Hungarian minority – and even modified the electoral law – incrementally reducing the possibility of plural political representation of the Hungarian minority. It introduced a legal threshold of 5 per cent in national elections, in 1994, which led to the formation of an alliance of two Hungarian parties (since independently, they would probably have failed to cross the threshold). Four years later, the threshold was increased, resulting in the merging of the Hungarian minority parties to form the Party of the Hungarian Coalition (SMK).

After the 1998 elections, the unified SMK joined the new pro-democratic government of Prime Minister Mikuláš Dzurinda (Öllös 2004) and remained in government until the new nationalist government of 2006 was formed. Some of the SMK's demands were successfully introduced into the government programme, but it abandoned the claims that were the most controversial in Slovak politics, such as the abolition of the Beneš decrees,[5] the foundation of an independent Hungarian university, and territorial autonomy on the basis of ethnicity (Szarka 2002). The SMK's overall success at achieving its goals was mixed. Some of the regulations of the Mečiar government were repealed (Hamberger 2004; Némethová and Öllös

---

4. According to the last available census data, 2001, Statistical Office of the Slovak Republic. Online. Available /portal.statistics.sk/files/Sekcie/sek_600/Demografia/SODB/Tabulky/Tabulky_AJ_SODB/tab11.pdf (accessed 15 March 2010).

5. The Beneš decrees were issued by the government of Czechoslovakia in exile during the German occupation in the Second World War. Germans and Hungarians were collectively punished for their alleged collaboration. Today these decrees hinder the restitution or reclaiming of properties and citizenship taken away from Germans and Hungarians between 1945 and 1948.

2003) and a Hungarian University was opened during the second period of the coalition government (Hamberger 2004).

The failure to create a region with a Hungarian majority during the administration reform in the first term of the Dzurinda government was seen by some internal critics as a failure caused by the participation in government of the SMK. This notion has fuelled internal debate over the moderate programme of the party, and over governmental inclusion. This debate intensified even more when the economic left wing and nationalist parties (Smer, SNS, HZDS) formed a new government coalition in 2006, putting the SMK in opposition. Béla Bugár, the president of the SMK since its formation, was replaced. Many partisans disapproved of the moderate direction of Bugár, and when the SMK was returned to opposition, the demand for new leadership and a more pronounced position on minority issues increased. The new leadership of the SMK reacted by pursuing a confrontational course, and reopened the discussion on sensitive issues such as the Beneš decrees. Unsurprisingly, this triggered heated internal debates, and incited friction with former coalition partners. Under the leadership of former party president Bugár, a large number of representatives of the SMK established a new party, Most-Híd (bridge) in the summer of 2009, and took part in the regional elections in the autumn of 2009. Most-Híd describes itself as the party of cooperation between Slovak and the Hungarian and any other national minority. While the SMK programme focuses on minority rights in cultural, educational and local matters, Most-Híd emphasises propositions in favour of reconciliation between Hungary and Slovakia – something that would also decrease tensions between the communities within Slovakia. Under its programme, it views Slovakia as a multi-ethnic, multicultural and a multilingual state. In the first series of elections (regional elections in autumn 2009, local and national elections in 2010), Most-Híd made massive gains and won 8.1 per cent of the votes in the national elections. These votes came largely from Hungarian areas, and presumably from former SMK voters. The SMK, in contrast, failed to cross the 5 per cent threshold with only 4.3 per cent of the vote.[6] Ultimately, it would seem that the SMK's radicalised course during the four years of opposition, and its campaign to brand Most-Híd as a betrayer of the Hungarian minority failed.

After the elections, Most-Híd joined the centre-right government coalition under the leadership of the SDKÚ-DS. Since only half of the 14 parliamentarian representatives of the Most-Híd were ethnic Hungarians and the other half ethnic Slovaks, the SMK had a rather easy time in its continued questioning of Most-Híd's capacity and will to defend Hungarian interests in the new government. Most-Híd, however, managed to have included in the government programme a considerable portion of its demands on minority issues, including regulations concerning double citizenship and the use of minority languages. It remains to be seen how effective Most-Híd's government participation will be, and what kind of a strategy the SMK will deploy in opposition.

---

6.   Statistical Office of the Republic of Slovakia. Online. Available /app.statistics.sk/nrsr_2010/sr/ tab3.jsp?lang=en (accessed 2 September 2011).

In contrast to the case of the Hungarian minority party in Romania, in Slovakia the new challenger party became more *moderate* than the old one. However, government participation of the unified Hungarian minority party can explain this, as in the case of the UDMR. Similarly, internal tensions emerged about the purpose and the gains of being in the government when painful policy concessions had to be met. As Slovakia is a new nation-state, demands that challenge the current territorial setup or the historical foundations of the country are perceived as more controversial by the majority society here than in Romania. Yet, the SMK fell back into opposition after eight years of government participation, followed by the replacement of its moderate leadership. In opposition, the new leadership turned to controversial issues that were seen as taboo when in the government. This, however, led to the breakup of the party under the lead of the former, more moderate party president.

A new political head of the Bosniaks in Serbia

Serbia, like the countries in the two cases above, is a multi-ethnic country. But instead of having one 'major' minority, it is home to several minority groups of roughly similar size. While Roma (an estimated 6 per cent of the population[7]) do not have strong political organisations, the Bosniak minority (1.8 per cent, according to the 2002 census) living in the Sandžak region in southern Serbia, the Hungarian minority (3.9 per cent) living in parts of the Vojvodina province, and the Albanians (0.8 per cent) in the Preševo Valley in South Serbia depend on minority parties, which were formed during the first transition of 1990.

In the 1990s, the most important political manifestation of the Bosniak minority was a pro-autonomy plebiscite organised by the non-recognised Muslim National Council of Sandžak in 1991, which resulted in a 99 per cent showing in favour of autonomy among the 70 per cent of the voters who turned out. The plebiscite was backed by the political leaders of the Bosniak minority, Sulejman Ugljanin and Rasim Ljajić. Regional autonomy was the most important political claim of the political organisations of the Bosniak minority and the core of the programme of the first Bosniak party, the Party for Democratic Action (SDA), founded by Ugljanin and Ljajić in 1990 as the Serbian branch of the SDA of neighbouring Bosnia and Herzegovina. While the SDA was led by Ugljanin, a rather right-wing leaning politician, the left-winger Ljajić split off in 1995. He offered a slightly more conciliatory political option for the Bosniaks organised under the Sandžak Democratic Party (SDP), which adopted a more pragmatic strategy; it was also the first to participate in a Serbian government after the country turned towards democracy in 2000.

Additional parties were mushrooming at this time (Zuber 2011), but these were essentially just satellites of the parties run by Ugljanin and Ljajić. In some cases,

---

7.   UNHCR. Online. Available /www.unhcr.org/refworld/country,,MRGI,,SRB,,49749cb137,0.html (accessed 6 June 2011).

their creation was motivated by laws that granted each parliamentary party a flat-rate subsidy. While Serbian mainstream parties supposedly had few supporters among Bosniaks, the pro-European and anti-nationalist Liberal Democratic Party (LDP), founded in 2005, recruits personnel – and, allegedly, also voters – in the Sandžak region, drawing form a pool with a considerable number of Bosniaks.[8]

The relationship between the two party alliances lead by Ugljanin and Ljajić can be characterised as bitter rivalry: hateful, extremely adversarial, and occasionally violent. Cooperation was never possible, and in local politics, the two leaders typically found it easier to form coalitions with ultra-nationalist Serbian parties, rather than cooperating (International Crisis Group 2005).

Since the beginning of 2000, the two Bosniak parties have enjoyed inclusion in the Serbian institutions – but they have also increasingly abandoned the (controversial) core demands they had championed in the 1990s, namely (asymmetric) regional autonomy. At the national level, Ljajić cooperated closely with the moderate Democratic Party (DS) and became minister in the government of Zoran Đinđić (2000–3), whereas Ugljanin temporarily threw his support to the government led by the nationalist-conservative Democratic Party of Serbia (DSS), which operated under the leadership of Vojislav Koštunica (2005-7) (Bochsler 2010). In 2008, in view of a very narrow majority, president Tadić included both Bosniak minority leaders in his governing coalition, supported by pressure from the European Union and of Turkey. Today, both parties emphasise opportunities for regional development in the upcoming decentralisation process, but insist that all Sandžak municipalities should be attributed to the same region, which is currently not the case. It is not just the demands of the parties that have become more moderate, partisan struggles in the Sandžak have also calmed somewhat.

The arrival of mufti Muamer Zukorlić – the religious head of the Sandžak Bosniaks – on the political scene in 2010 has turned the political situation of the Sandžak upside down. The economic hardships of the Serbian periphery and the widespread feeling that the two minority leaders were achieving little regional benefit (if any) and were instead emphasising their personal interests, created a opportunity for the mobilisation of a despairing Bosniak electorate. Being in government and deeply enmeshed with the parties of the Serbian majority, none of the Bosniak parties could play the card of representing anti-Belgrade opposition and being the defender of the Bosniak interests.

In the elections of the newly-established National Minority Councils in 2010, Zukorlić ran with his own electoral list, which unexpectedly won a plurality of all votes and seats for the Bosniak Council (48 per cent, although the turnout, of 56 per cent was low). Together with two members who switched from their own list, Zukorlić's followers were able to form a majority in the Council. Although no electoral lists in those elections were declared as adopting a partisan approach, all of them were closely linked to political parties – and Zukorlić's followers became a new political force. In January 2011, his movement was registered as a political

---

8. Congruent statements by several interview partners.

party: the Bosniak Democratic Community (*Bošnjačka Demokratska Zajednica* (BDZ)). The national government, however, did not recognise the BDZ or dissolve the Bosniak National Council, which contributed to even stronger tensions in the region.

There are also some other peculiar developments that have led to fissures in the Bosniak community and contributed to tensions with central government. Particularly noteworthy are tensions concerning the organisation of the religious community. Sandžak Bosniaks (Muslims) are predominantly organised in the Islamic community in Serbia, led by the Sandžak-based mufti Zukorlić. Several Serbian governments have contributed to conflict within the Islamic community, arguably trying to weaken the role of Zukorlić. The government of Vojislav Koštunica (2004–8) recognised the rival Islamic community of the Belgrade-based mufti Adem Zilkić, who had close contact with several former Belgrade governments – including the one of Slobodan Milošević – as the official Islamic community (Stanić 2009; Džihić 2011). The government of Tadić-Cvetković (2008 to present) confirmed its recognition of Ziklić's Islamic community of Serbia as the second Islamic group in the country. This provoked turmoil within the Bosniak community. The conflict pertains not only to issues involving the recognition of the second community, but also to the property rights of these religious communities, the non-equal treatment of these groups as compared to the Serbian Orthodox Church, and other issues linked to religious education in school and the registration of Zukorlić's private university in Sandžak.

Formally, Zukorlić's younger brother-in-law, Emir Elfić, acts as party president, while Zukorlić himself aims to become the future religious leader in Sarajevo for all Bosniak Muslims (not only those in Sandžak).[9] In the meantime, he plays a crucial political role in the Sandžak, by positioning his party as political opposition to the other Bosniak parties – which are included in government – and by using a radicalising strategy. On the one hand, Zukorlić and Elfić both criticise Ugljanin and Ljajić for pursuing 'only personal interests' in the current government. On the other hand, they consistently position their party at the radical side of the Bosniak minority, taking the more pronounced positions on all relevant issues compared to the other Bosniak parties. Their core programme is a copy of parts of Ugljanin's and Ljajić's programme from the 1990s, demanding the 'stepwise territorial autonomy for the Sandžak region, as a constitutional region of Serbia'.[10] Yet, the history of the party is short, and it still lacks a consolidated programme and direction. In addition, the claims of the informal party leader Zukorlić vary considerably, depending on the audience and the venue, and undoubtedly, parts of his communication are strategic in nature – aimed at increasing political tensions, at alarming the international community, and generally causing commotion in national politics.[11]

---

9. Speculations were further promoted by his statement of April 2011 (B92 2011).

10. Interview with Muamer Zukorlić, Novi Pazar, 19 January 2011.

11. The BDZ aims at more international attention, as this might put also pressure the Serbian government to change its priorities in the relations to the Sandžak. The BDZ opens issues that foreign

Therefore, it is hard to evaluate how radical the BDZ actually is. On some occasions (such as in Emir Elfic's interview with us),[12] Zukorlić highlights issues that are in line with other analyses, and of the SDA and SDP's outlook on the situation in the region, e.g. speaking of the economic neglect of the region by the national government, of the non-realised rights of Bosniaks in education, and of religious rights.

Elsewhere (and, indeed, in a speech made only a few days after our interview), he has discoursed on much more sensitive issues – ones that can only contribute to the deterioration of Bosniak-Serb relations. He has spoken, for instance, of several genocides perpetrated by Belgrade against the Bosniak minority in Serbia (Biševac 2011). In many aspects, the BDZ is an offshoot of the two established parties in the Sandžak. Party president Elfić was a former SDP cadre in Novi Pazar, the informal capital of the Sandžak, while Zukorlić has used his religious and economic authority to mobilise voters in the Sandžak. In the 1990s, he stood close to Ugljanin, and in the 2000s, close to Ljajić's SDP.[13] This also gave him political recognition, particularly with Prime Minister Zoran Đinđić (2000–3), who regularly met with Zukorlić when visiting the Sandžak.

The case of the BDZ is particularly helpful in illustrating the two arguments we have put forth about the logic of political representation, in this paper. Our first argument concerned the inherent need for representation of the plurality of the political preferences of a minority group. In the case of the Bosniak minority, political plurality among the Bosniaks – with two clearly distinguishable, even hostile political options, plus myriad satellite parties – existed long before the establishment of the BDZ. However, the rare occurrence of all the relevant minority parties being simultaneously included in the governing coalition provides an exceptional situation, where the arguments of internal plurality and governmental inclusion may be empirically separated. In the cases of the SMK and UDMR, the internal plurality of the Hungarian minority was mapped within the party so that government participation had an impact on the tensions within these parties.

Our second argument – on the effect of government participation – is illustrated by the emergence of a political vacuum in which an oppositional Bosniak party could come into existence, created through the governmental inclusion of both main Bosniak parties. The moderation of the SDA and SDP, the ongoing unequal employment opportunities in state institutions, various economic problems, and conflicts about the education of the Bosniak minority, and of the recognition of religious institutions created the basis of Zukorlić's characterisation of Belgrade's policy as discriminatory against the Bosniak minority.

---

analysts read as a threat of radicalisation and a threat to the stability of the Bosniak community in Serbia (Džihić 2011), a threat which Zukorlić himself frequently expresses explicitly. Zukorlić implicitly threatens to destabilise the region if his local power should not be recognised. On the other hand, the BDZ presents radical claims (compared to the incumbent Bosniak parties), but in the view of independent analysts these claims are not exaggerated, as they reflect the neglect of the region by Serbian politics (International Crisis Group 2005).

12. Similar: interview with Emir Elfić, Belgrade, 21 January 2011.

13. Interview with Zukorlić; several other interlocutors made similar statements.

There are also policy issues that might explain the BDZ's entry, but these alternative explanations do not seem very plausible. The economic problems experienced in the Sandžak are described in reports as early as the mid-2000s (International Crisis Group 2005), so the timing of the BDZ's entry in 2011 can best be explained by the SDA and SDP's simultaneous inclusion in the coalition government, and the subsequent creation of a political vacuum in which it was possible to mobilise Bosniaks, based on their long-standing feeling of being neglected and discriminated against. Apart from Zukorlić's personal motivation to regain influence in politics, this development can also be explained by the fact that the Belgrade government cut its ties to Zukorlić after 2003, choosing instead to rely on Ugljanin and Ljajić. Zukorlić himself does not deny that the conflict around the Islamic community was a trigger for the creation of the new party – though this was not the sole driving force. The government-opposition logic was also underlined by Zukorlić's links to the pro-European liberal opposition in Serbia, the Liberal Democratic Party (LDP) of Čedomir Jovanović (who politicises in the footsteps of Đinđić).

As things stand, both established party blocs must react to this new challenge, since many of their voters might leave in favour of the new political option. On their parts, Ugljanin and Ljajić have intensified negotiations over local coalitions in several Sandžak municipalities – something that would have been unthinkable before the entry of the BDZ.[14] As early as twelve years before Zukorlić's entry, he had started to transform his party into a non-ethnic Social Democratic Party, addressing both the Roma and economically-disadvantaged Serbian voters (*Politika* 2007). It remains to be seen, however, whether this new electorate will replace those voters who break away to the BDZ in future parliamentary elections.

How Hungarian minority parties in Serbia failed to find unity

Hungarians, at 3.9 per cent, constitute the largest national minority in Serbia, living predominantly in Vojvodina, where they are presently 14.3 per cent of the population. They are the majority in two municipalities in Northern Vojvodina, and also the largest group in the town of Subotica. In 1990, the Democratic Fellowship of Vojvodina Hungarians (DZVM) was established as the first and only Hungarian party in Serbia. Over time, two further parties have split off from the DZVM – the Alliance of Vojvodina Hungarians (SVM) in 1994 and the Democratic Party of Vojvodina Hungarians (DSVM) in 1997. Apart from these three parties, there are now two minor Hungarian parties as well: the Hungarian Civic Alliance (GSM) (founded in 2006) and the radical right Hungarian Hope Movement (PMN) (founded in 2009).

After the democratic revolution of 2000, the SVM was the most important party of ethnic Hungarians in Serbia. Among the three major parties, it was generally the most pragmatic and the most open towards cooperation with the democratic forces

---

14. Interview with Safeta Biševac, Belgrade, 11 January 2011

of the Serbian majority. It joined the broad pro-Democratic DOS coalition in 2000, and the SVM leader József Kasza served as vice prime minister in the Đinđić government, in charge of minority affairs and local governments (Jenne 2004). In the 2003 elections, however, the SVM ran in a coalition comprised mainly of other minority parties (Together for Tolerance), and failed to cross the 5 per cent threshold to enter parliament. The other two Hungarian minority parties did not participate in these elections (Bochsler 2008). In the 2004 elections to the provincial parliament of Vojvodina, the SVM took part independently and obtained 8.8 per cent of the votes, whereas the DSVM ran in a coalition and won a seat in one of the single-seat districts. The DZVM did not participate in the provincial elections. In the 2007 national elections, the SVM won 1.3 per cent of the votes and three seats, and joined the opposition in parliament, while the two other Hungarian parties ran in a coalition, but did not manage to enter the parliament (Bochsler 2008).

In 2007, before the presidential elections, the SVM initiated the nomination of a joint Hungarian presidential candidate. The DSVM and DZVM followed the call of the SVM and agreed to support the new president of the SVM – István Pásztor, who had been appointed following the SVM's disappointing results in the 2007 national elections – as a presidential candidate. Pásztor's programme was not focused on the pragmatic course of the party, but instead emphasised a need for dialogue and cooperation with other Hungarian political organisations in Vojvodina – a platform that was embraced by both the DSVM and DZVM. In 2008, in the national, provincial and municipal elections, this cooperation was pursued under the banner of the 'Hungarian Coalition'.

The formation of an electoral alliance became possible because the SVM, as the strongest party among the three, agreed to campaign with the most radical claim – the parties elaborated a joint autonomy plan that included territorial autonomy for the Northern part of Vojvodina, where Hungarians make up the majority of the population (VMSZ et al. 2008). The SVM was rather supportive of personal autonomy and the autonomy of the multi-ethnic Province Vojvodina, as well as of territorial autonomy. The Hungarian Coalition was also supported by the Fidesz and its leader, Viktor Orbán, who personally campaigned at the side of the Hungarian Coalition in Vojvodina (Népszabadság online 2008). Fidesz, which was the main national conservative party in opposition in Hungary at this time, was actively seeking out alliances with strong Hungarian minority parties abroad.

The Hungarian Coalition won only 1.8 per cent of the national votes and four seats in 2008 – so only the SVM entered parliament (Konitzer 2009). As in previous years, many ethnic Hungarians voted for Serbian mainstream parties, particularly the Democratic Party (DS), or for regional parties. The strategy of mobilising Hungarians with radical campaign promises of territorial autonomy did not pay off (Tanács 2008). The agreement between the parties in the Hungarian Coalition provided for the first four seats to go to the SVM, as the largest party, with the remaining seats to be allocated between the DSVM and the DZVM (Fazekas 2008).

Since then, the Hungarian Coalition has supported the DS-lead governing coalition, although without being part of the government. The (secret) cooperation agreement between the Hungarian Coalition of the SVM and the DS was negotiated and signed only by the SVM. According to Pásztor, of the twelve claims of the Hungarian Coalition towards the Democratic Party only one – the claim for territorial autonomy of Northern Vojvodina – was rejected by the DS (Ternovácz 2008a).

In the provincial elections in Vojvodina, the Hungarian Coalition also received 7.4 per cent of the votes, but the SVM continues to dominate the other Hungarian minority parties, and cooperates closely with the DS.

The coalition of the three Hungarian parties broke apart after the elections since; among them, only the SVM managed to enter the national parliament and gain political power and access to offices. The main concession, ceding the claim to territorial autonomy, was carried off easily by the SVM. Nevertheless, to stress its independent role as a protector of Hungarian and regional interests, and its independence from the government, the SVM fought with the government over the budget, demanding more financial resources for the Province Vojvodina (Sebestyén 2009; Vajdaság MA- Délvidéki Hírportál 2010).

In the area of minority rights, the SVM championed the adoption of the law on National Minority Councils in 2009, and the Statute of the Autonomous Province of Vojvodina – a distinctly multi-ethnic region of Serbia (Ternovácz 2009). Both the DSVM and DZVM questioned the importance of these two achievements. In their view, neither was far-reaching enough and they criticised the handling of voter lists for the elections of the national minority councils[15] and the autonomy status of Vojvodina, which they saw as not sufficiently generous (*Magyar Szó* 2009; Diósi 2010). They perceived the SVM's attitude as being much closer to that of the governing DS party than to their own (Ternovácz 2008b; Ágoston 2009); they therefore adopted a strategy of outbidding the claims of the SVM.

Conclusion

For national minorities, the aftermath of the political transition in Central and Eastern Europe gave rise to important political challenges. Changing borders, the creation of new nation-states, and the re-establishment or change of national attitudes across the region all contributed to the status of ethnicity as an emerging (or, indeed, re-emerging) political category. Foremost on the political agenda of the national minorities were promoting minority rights, gaining political autonomy, and promoting the economic development of the regions' dominant minority populations. These changes can also be seen in the different forms of political participation adopted by the minorities. While external actors – such as kin states, and the European institutions – were important in the debates on minority rights, minority parties came into being on the domestic political scene in many Central and Eastern European countries. After an initial period of political isolation, they gained access to government.

---

15. Voter lists were elaborated upon voluntary registration of citizens who needed to document that they belong to a national minority. The parties favoured an automatic inclusion of voters.

In the past, the interaction between nationalising states and ethnic minority groups has been studied mainly from the perspectives of radicalisation and conflict. This chapter, however, has striven to investigate the importance of *governmental participation* on the political organisation of ethnic minorities. And while the existing literature on ethno-political conflicts has often assumed that ethnic minorities are homogeneous actors, we have explored the dynamics within minority groups – focusing on the internal conflicts between different players within minorities, distinguished by moderate versus radical positions on ethno-nationalist issues, and by policy versus office-seeking orientations. The aim of this chapter is also to discuss the role of government participation on the political plurality – and, respectively, unity – of national minorities.

Very recently, in three cases in Central and Eastern Europe (concerning the Hungarian minorities in Romania and Slovakia, and the Bosniak minority in Serbia) government participation led to the fracturing of stable national minority parties. These parties were divided between more pragmatic office-seeking actors, who favoured government participation, and those who viewed government participation as a largely unsuccessful strategy for seeking policy influence, or who were dissatisfied with the parties in government and wanted to mobilise voters behind a more assertive position. In a fourth case, the long-standing rival parties of the Hungarian minority in Serbia made an attempt to unite forces. Their cooperation failed, since only one of the coalition parties managed to enter parliament. Upon entering the government, that party decided to *support* the government, leaving the other two parties to endorse a confrontational course from outside the government, outbidding their former coalition partner. In all of these cases, it has become clear that the internal dynamics of minority parties, and their inclusion in national governments, are closely connected – participation in government represents a chance for ethnic minority parties to influence policy. However, as we have seen, it might well *also* intensify intra-ethnic conflicts, highlighting different goals and favoured strategies for establishing minority rights. Under the right circumstances, this can intensify the divide between radicals and moderates, and between office- and policy-seekers – and finally lead to fissions within dominant minority parties.

References

Ágoston, A. (2009) 'A Demokrata Párt és a vajdasági magyarok [The Democratic Party and the Hungarians in Vojvodina]', *Vajdaság MA – Délvidéki hírportál,* 27 January.

B92 (2011) 'Zukorlić možda reisul-ulema u BiH?', *B92,* 19 April.

Bakk, M., Szász, Z. A. and Székely, I. G. (2004) 'Parlamenti és elnökválasztás Romániában 2004 novemberében [Parlamentarian and presidential elections in November 2004 in Romania]', *Magyar Kisebbség,* 9: 1–43.

Barkan, J. D. (1995) 'Elections in agrarian societies', *Journal of Democracy,* 6(4): 106–16.

Biševac, S. (2011) 'Tražili ste - gledajte', *Danas,* 25 January.

Bochsler, D. (2008) 'The parliamentary elections in Serbia, 21 January 2007', *Electoral Studies,* 27(1): 151–90.

— (2010) 'Regional party systems in Serbia', in V. Stojarová and P. Emerson (eds) *Party Politics in the Western Balkans,* Abingdon: Routledge, pp. 131–50.

— (2011) 'It is not how many votes you get, but also where you get them. Territorial determinants and institutional hurdles for the success of ethnic minority parties in post-communist countries', *Acta Politica,* 46(3): 217–38.

— (2012a) 'When two of the same are needed: A multi-level model of intra-group ethnic party competition', *Nationalism and Ethnic Politics,* 18(2): 216–41.

— (2012b) 'Radicalizing electoral system effects on support for nationalist hardliners in Serbia', *Nations and Nationalism,* published online before print 13 November 2012, doi: 10.1111/j.1469-8129.2012.00558.x.

Brubaker, R. (1996) *Nationalism Reframed: Nationhood and the national question in the new Europe,* Cambridge: Cambridge University Press.

Cederman, L. -E., Wimmer, A. and Min, B. (2009) 'What makes ethnic groups rebel? New data and new analysis', *World Politics,* 62(1): 87–119.

Chandra, K. (2005) 'Ethnic parties and democratic stability', *Perspectives on Politics,* 3(2): 235–52.

Coakley, J. (2008) 'Ethnic competition and the logic of party system transformation', *European Journal of Political Research,* 47(6): 766–93.

Diósi, Á. (2010) 'A VMDK es a VMDP a nemzetitanácsválasztásokról "szánalmasan kialakított névjegyzék" [TheVMDK and the VMDP on the elections for the national councils "the miserably constructed voters list"]', *Magyar Szó,* 8 May.

Džihić, V. 'Inter-ethnic relations as an indicator of democratic stability: Sandžak (Serbia) in 2010', paper presented at the 16th Convention of the Association for the Study of Nationalities, Columbia University, April 2011.

EMNT (2010) 'Autonómiát, politikai érdekképviseletet, nemzeti közösséget. Határozat az Erdélyi Magyar Néppárt létrehozásáról [For autonomy, political interest represantion and national community. Resolution on the formation of the Hungarian People's Party of Transylvania]', 4 December.

Eplényi, K. (2006) 'Székelyek és autonómia - tervek a mérlegen (2003–2006) [Drawing up the balance: an overview of the projects on Szekler autonomy in Transylvania (2003-2006)]', *Regio*: 61–80.

Fazekas, L. (2008) 'MTI-elemzés: Felbomlott a Magyar Koalíció [MTI-analysis: The break-up of the Hungarian Coalition]', *Vajdaság MA – Délvidéki hírportál*, 26 September.

Gormley-Heenan, C. and Macginty, R. (2008) 'Ethnic outbidding and party modernization: understanding the Democratic Unionist Party's electoral success in the post-agreement environment', *Ethnopolitics*, 7(1): 43–61.

Hamberger, J. (2004) 'A Magyar Koalíció Pártja a szlovák kormányban [The Hungarian Coalition Party in the Slovak Government]', in J. Fazekas and P. Hunčík (eds) *Magyarok Szlovákiában (1989–2004). Összefoglaló jelentés. A rendszerváltástól az Európai Uniós csatlakozásig [The Hungarians in Slovakia. Recapitulatory report. From the regime change to the European Union accession]*, Somorja-Dunaszerdahely: Fórum Kisebbségkutató Intézet, Liliom Aurum Könyvkiadó, pp. 105–24.

Horowitz, D. L. (1985) *Ethnic Groups in Conflict,* Berkeley: University California Press.

Horváth, I. (2004) *Facilitating Conflict Transformation: Implementation of the recommendations of the OSCE High Commissioner on National Minorities to Romania, 1993–2001*, Hamburg: Centre for OSCE Research.

International Crisis Group (2005) *Serbia's Sandžak: Still Forgotten*, Belgrade and Brussels: Crisis Group.

Jenne, E. (2004) 'A bargaining theory of minority demands: explaining the dog that did not bite in 1990s Yugoslavia', *International Studies Quarterly*, 48(4): 729–54.

Kántor, Z. and Bárdi, N. (2000) 'Az RMDSZ a romániai kormányban, 1996–2000 [The RMDSZ in the Romanian government, 1996–2000]', *Regio*, 150–87.

Kántor, Z. and Pászkán, Z. (2009) 'Parlamenti választások és kormányalakítás Romániában [Parlamentarian elections and government building in Romania]', *MKI-Tanulmányok*, 2: 1–21.

Konitzer, A. (2009) 'Parliamentary elections in Serbia, May 2008', *Electoral Studies*, 28(1): 141–71.

Magyar Szó (2009) 'A VMDP elégedetlen [The VMDP is not satisfied]', 29 September.

Mandel, K. (2004) 'Az RMDSZ oktatáspolitikája 1990–2003 között [The education politics of the RMDSZ between 1990 and 2003]', in K. Mandel and E. Blénesi (eds) *Kisebbségek és kormánypolitika Közép-Európában (2002–2004). [Minorities and government policies in Central Europe (2002–2004)]*, Budapest: Gondolat Kiadó-MTA Etnikai-nemzeti Kisebbségkutató Intézet, pp. 85–108.

MAR (2009) 'Minorities at risk dataset', College Park, MD: Center for International Development and Conflict Management.

Mitchell, P. (1995) 'Party competition in an ethnic dual party system', *Ethnic and Racial Studies,* 18(4): 773–96.

Mitchell, P., Evans, G. and O'Leary, B. (2009) 'Extremist outbidding in ethnic party systems is not inevitable: tribune parties in Northern Ireland', *Political Studies,* 57(2): 397–421.

Moser, R. G. (2005) 'Ethnicity, elections, and party systems in postcommunist states', in Z. Barany and R. G. Moser (eds) *Ethnic Politics after Communism,* Ithaca: Cornell University Press, pp. 108–39.

Némethová, D. and Öllös, L. (2003) 'Hungarians in the Slovak government', in M. Robotin and L. Salat, L. (eds) *A New Balance: Democracies and minorities in post-communist Europe,* Budapest: Open Society Institute, pp. 113–39.

Népszabadság online (2008) 'Magyar csalódás a Vajdaságban [Hungarian disappointment in the Vojvodina]', 27 May.

Öllös, L. (2004) 'A magyar pártok programjai [The programs of the Hungarian Parties]', in J. Fazekas and P. Hunčík (eds) *Magyarok Szlovákiában (1989–2004). Összefoglaló jelentés. A rendszerváltástól az Európai Uniós csatlakozásig [The Hungarians in Slovakia. recapitulatory report. From the regime change to the European Union accession],* Somorja-Dunaszerdahely: Fórum Kisebbségkutató Intézet, Liliom Aurum Könyvkiadó, pp. 51–77.

Politika (2007) 'Tema nedelje: Šta žele stranke nacionalnih – Ne predstavljam samo Bošnjake', 23 December.

Rabushka, A. and Shepsle, K. A. (1972) *Politics in Plural Societies: A theory of democratic instability,* Columbus: Merill.

Robotin, M. and Salat, L. (eds) (2003) *A New Balance: Democracy and minorities in post-communist Europe,* Budapest: Open Society Institute.

Sartori, G. (2005) *Parties and Party Systems: A framework for analysis,* Colchester: ECPR Press.

Sebestyén, I. (2009) 'VMSZ DS-es megregulázása? [Did the VMSZ put the DS in its place?]', *Vajdaság MA – Délvidéki hírportál,* 23 December.

Stanić, R. (2009) 'Interviju: Zukorlić-Čiplić', *Politika,* 25 May.

Strøm, K. (1990) *Minority Government and Majority Rule,* Cambridge, New York: Cambridge University Press.

Szarka, L. (2002) 'Administrative reform and the minority problem. The Slovak administrative reform and the plan of the Party of the Hungarian Coalition', *Minority Research: Minority Politics and Minorities Right,* 4: 122–34.

Tanács, I. (2008) 'Jólét vagy autonómia? [Wealth or autonomy?]', *Népszabadság online,* 29 May.

Ternovácz, I. (2008a) 'Együttműködési megállapodás [Cooperation argreement]', *Vajdaság MA – Délvidéki hírportál,* 4 February.

—   (2008b) 'A VMDK csalódottsága. Mit ró fel Páll a nagyobbik koalíciós partnernek [The disappointment of the VMDK. What Páll reproaches the bigger coalition partner with]', *Vajdaság MA – Délvidéki hírportál*, 23 September.

—   (2009) 'Ez már autonómia [This is already autonomy]', *Vajdaság MA – Délvidéki hírportál*, 3 August.

Udvardy, F. (2006) 'A romániai magyar kisebbség történeti kronológiája 1990-2003 [The historical chronology of the Hungarian minority in Romania]'. Online. Available http://udvardy.adatbank.transindex.ro (accessed 23 September 2012).

Vajdaság MA – Délvidéki Hírportál (2010) 'VMSZ-es szavazatokkal elfogadták a büdzsé kiigazítását [The adjustment of the budget was adopted supported by the votes of the VMSZ]', 30 November.

VMSZ, VMDP and VMDK (2008) 'A Magyar Koalíció autonómiakoncepciója [The autonomy concept of the Hungarian Coalition]', Online. Available /www.vajma.info/docs/MK_autonomiakoncepcio_2008_03_17.pdf (accessed 2 December 2009).

Zuber, C. I. (2011) 'Beyond outbidding? Ethnic party strategies in Serbia', *Party Politics*, published online before print 25 July 2011, doi: 10.1177/1354068811410368.

Appendix 11: List of the parties

English	Romanian/Slovak/ Serbo-Croatian	Hungarian
Hungarian minority parties/political organisations in Romania		
Democratic Alliance of Hungarians in Romania	Uniunea Democrată Maghiară din România (UDMR)	Romániai Magyar Demokrata Szövetség (RMDSZ)
Hungarian Civic Party	Partidul Civic Maghiar (PCM)	Magyar Polgári Párt (MPP)
Szekler National Council	Consiliul Naţional Secuiesc (CNS)	Székely Nemzeti Tanács (SZNT)
Hungarian National Council of Transylvania	Consiliul Naţional Maghiar din Transilvania (CNMT)	Erdélyi Magyar Nemzeti Tanács (EMNT)
Hungarian minority parties in Slovakia		
Hungarian Civic Party	Mad'arská obcanská strana (MOS)	Magyar Polgári Párt (MPP)
Coexistence	Spolužitie	Együttélés
Party of the Hungarian Coalition	Strana maďarskej koalície (SMK)	Magyar Koalíció Pártja (MKP)
'Bridge' party	Most-Híd	Most-Híd
Bosniak minority parties in Serbia		
Party for Democratic Action	Stranka demokratske akcije Sandžaka (SDA)	
Sandžak Democratic Party	Sandžačka demokratska partija (SDP)	
Bosniak Democratic Community	Bošnjačka demokratska zajednica (BDZ)	
Hungarian minority parties in Serbia		
Alliance of Vojvodina Hungarians	Savez vojvođanskih Mađara (SVM)	Vajdasági Magyar Szövetség (VMSZ)
Democratic Party of Vojvodina Hungarians	Demokratska stranka vojvođanskih Mađara (DSVM)	Vajdasági Magyar Demokrata Párt (VMDP)
Democratic Fellowship of Vojvodina Hungarians	Demokratska zajednica vojvođanskih Mađara (DZVM)	Vajdasági Magyarok Demokratikus Közössége (VMDK)
Hungarian Hope Movement	Pokret mađarske nade (PMN)	Magyar Remény Mozgalom (MRM)
Hungarian Civic Alliance	Građanski savez Mađara (GSM)	Magyar Polgári Szövetség (MPSZ)

conclusion | what's in a comparison? some remarks about the analysis of recurrent processes

Antoine Roger

Introduction

While looking through the chapters making up this volume, the reader has met with questions regarding the definition of the Moldovan nation, the Israeli nation, the Belarusian and German minorities in Poland, the Polish and Belarusian minorities in Lithuania, the Hungarian minorities in Slovakia, Romania and Serbia, the Bosnian minority in Serbia, the Russian minorities in Ukraine and Kazakhstan and the Chinese minorities in Indonesia and Malaysia. In some contributions, several cases are directly linked and treated in an explicitly comparative perspective. In others, a single case is studied in depth, but conclusions are reached about its specifics and an implicit comparison is offered. Having read through this volume, each of us may be tempted to home in on some of the analyses presented here and apply them to another area. In all these cases, questions emerge about the very status of such comparisons. How can we be sure that the cases are comparable? Can the differences identified between the cases be linked to a single variation principle? Do the cases studied here enable us to formulate universal rules of causality?

In comparative politics, the most basic orientation consists in taking ethnic or national minorities as primary realities and evaluating the opportunities and constraints that favour or inhibit the formulation of their claims. In order to determine the points of similarity and difference between the cases being studied, favourable factors and obstacles are always characterised in the same way and related to one and the same measurement scale. In this 'substantialist' perspective, comparison is limited to establishing the variable importance of one factor or another in space or time (Stanfield 1993). This approach has hardly been adopted at all in this volume. Instead, contributors have attempted to characterise fluid contexts of action.[1]

---

1. This approach can be characterised as 'constructionist' (on this point, see the contribution by Christina Isabel Zuber in Chapter Nine of this volume). Julian Bernauer's analysis is an exception here; adopting an argument couched in terms of rational choice and concentrating on the 'strategic vote' of 'members of ethnic minorities', the author tends to consider this membership as a primary data element that determines 'interests' and 'preferences'. He thus continues a research tradition inaugurated by Donald Horowitz: according to this author, an 'ethnic party' is called upon to serve the interests of a 'group' which pre-exists it. The contours of this group are clearly defined, in a manner independent even of political competition. All intellectual effort is directed towards those parameters which may facilitate or obstruct the orientation of the 'ethnic vote' towards those organisations which covet it (Horowitz 1985).

They have taken pains to specify the processes and modes by which a minority theme ends up being regarded as of central importance in a given context. In other terms, their common aim has been to account for the processes by which ethnicity and nationality become modes of classification that are perceived as legitimate and functional, and to shed light on the mechanisms which help to institutionalise them. This approach requires that great attention be paid to the historical relationships between the protagonists being studied as well as to the particular contexts in which discourses emphasising ethnicity and nationality are formulated. There is thus a risk of restricting oneself to isolated case studies and renouncing any ambition of attempting comparisons. A rejection of substantialism may in fact afford an intellectual alibi to researchers who wish to spare themselves the discomfort of more in-depth reflection on the overall reach of their conclusions.

If we are to avoid setting up a simple binary contrast between the schematic nature of substantialist contributions and the deep understandings offered by monographs, we would do well to return to the classic theses put forward by Rogers Brubaker, which are extensively discussed in this volume. In proposing a relational reading, Brubaker invites us to consider 'nationalising states', the 'national minorities' which are identified within them and 'external homelands' claiming to support them.[2] Each of these inputs should be analysed as a force field, and not as a rigid entity whose properties might be defined in a universal way – or which could be identified by a minimal list of common attributes (Brubaker 1996). Thus conceived, the comparative approach enables a break to be made with 'groupism' – with the propensity to think about ethnicity and nationality on the basis of rigid units whose terms are comparable on a unit-by-unit basis. It also marks a distancing from the radical formulations of 'social constructivism', inspired by the *linguistic turn* – i.e. with the postulate that social reality is entirely constructed by discourse, with any recurrence itself based on a sham lexical unification and with comparison becoming an intellectual operation with no foundation.

According to Brubaker (2004), the researcher's attention should be directed towards the origins of these discourses and the mechanisms that compel recognition of ethnicity and nationality as principles on which to perceive and segment the social world; this makes it essential to consider the relationships formed between socially-situated agents. Following the precepts of structural constructivism (Kauppi 2005), comparisons can be developed on precise foundations. The units compared are not 'nationalising states', 'national minorities' and 'external homelands' in themselves, but the structures of power relations and the relationships observed both within them and between them – the boundaries of each category being themselves the subject of disputes. From this point of view, the fact of adding a fourth force field (Smith 2002) or of considering that one of these has been overestimated (Commercio 2010) modifies the content of the analysis, but not the way the comparison is conceived.

---

2.   According to the definition put forward by Rogers Brubaker (1996: 5), 'a state becomes a national "homeland" when cultural and political élites construe certain residents and citizens of other states as co-nationals, as fellow-members of a single transborder nation'.

Although the form of reasoning proposed by Brubaker offers support to the comparativist, ambivalence can be detected in those works that make reference to it. The analyses presented in this volume should help us shed light on this and to formulate some proposals for finding a solution. This involves re-examining the epistemological bases of comparison.

As a first step, we shall see that comparativists may be tempted to make Brubaker's relational framework serve the ends of the search for a universal variation principle; in this case, they remain attached to a *positivist* approach – in searching for recurrences in the forms of relations within and between force fields, they claim to identify causal explanations with a universal scope. It is possible to substitute for this approach a comparison guided by the principles of *critical realism*. This is a matter of characterising 'causal mechanisms' on a theoretical level and then studying their complex and evolving combinations in case studies which cannot be reduced one to another. In this perspective, comparison does not aim to insert relational analysis into a scheme of linear causality, but instead to provide an accurate picture of 'causal constellations'.

Having made these distinctions, as a second step we can look again at the causal mechanisms identified in Rogers Brubaker's framework. We shall attempt to redraw its boundaries so as to widen the spectrum of comparison, without distorting the form of reasoning. Looking again at the studies in this volume, we can identify some combinations of mechanisms – which need to be supplemented by other comparative studies.

Basing comparison on critical realism

Rogers Brubaker (2004: 11) invites us to consider the principles of ethnic and national identification as 'practical categories, situated actions, cultural idioms, cognitive schemas, discursive frames, organisational routines, institutional forms, political projects, and contingent events'. Following this analysis, comparativists must detach themselves from native demarcations and distinctions, those espoused by the agents being studied, denaturalise them and substitute their own analytical categories. The units being compared are not 'ethnicities' or 'nations' but relational structures that preside over the adoption and mobilisation of these referents (Brubaker 1994):

> We need to be cautious about organizing comparative work around nation-states, ethnic groups, races, or cultures of any kind as taken-for-granted units of analysis. For it is precisely the 'unitness', 'entitativity', or 'groupness' of such units of analysis that is at issue. We don't want to presuppose that entitativity or groupness by inscribing it into the very terms in which we pose our research questions (Brubaker 2003: 5).

At each stage of research, one should 'decouple the study of nationhood and nationness from the study of nations as substantial entities' (Brubaker 1996: 16). The difficulty is, however, intensified by the fact that agents are themselves prone to making 'vernacular' comparisons in their relational activity of constructing ethnicity and nationhood. The researcher has to take this comparative activity itself as an object of comparison – it is:

> the study of vernacular comparisons that will enable us to see which vernacular explanatory schemas will be drawn on in what circumstances, without imposing our own analytical explanatory schemas on those whom we are studying (Brubaker 2003: 4, 6).

On further examination, these specifications are only very inconsistently respected by those authors who make reference to the work of Rogers Brubaker. In hidden ways, comparisons often tend to refer back to 'substantial unities' now constituted not by the distinctive traits of 'national' or 'ethnic' groups but by fixed and predictable relationships in and between the force fields identified. This methodological divergence can be explained by a propensity to search for linear causality and a universal variation principle. In order to avoid this, we need to explore the epistemological foundations of comparison.

Following the analyses proposed by George Steinmetz, we can make a distinction between two types of comparative activity which are often confused or intermingled within sociological discussions: the comparison of 'generative causal mechanisms' and the comparison of 'empirical-level events'. Critical realism leads to an emphasis on the first of these options. Two principles have been articulated as the basis for this. Firstly, a distinction is made between the levels of the empirical and the real: reality is not located in 'observable phenomena' but in 'underlying causal mechanisms'.

Secondly, and as a consequence, the objective is one of identifying 'constellations' that present a 'non-recurring' and 'conjunctural' character: it must therefore be accepted that 'a multiplicity of mechanisms typically will combine in conjunctural ways to produce any given event'(Steinmetz 2004: 377, 392).[3] On this basis, causal mechanisms may be found in the work of Rogers Brubaker and in developments arising from it: it is possible to include in this repertory the dynamics of the claims made by minorities, those made by nationalising states and those made by external national homelands – the list may be lengthened by other mechanisms, such as the effects produced by interventions made by international organisations (Smith 2002).

---

3. In support of the work by the British epistemologist Roy Bhaskar, partisans of critical realism refuse to look for causality in a 'model of regular successions of events' evidenced 'by gathering data on regularities, repeated occurrences'. This approach could only be relevant in a 'closed system', i.e. in the equivalent of a laboratory where 'causal power is stable and the external situation in which it is situated are constant'. Faced with an open system, the researcher should resolve to study 'interacting causal mechanisms that produce an event', constantly sharpening his or her understanding of interactions by having recourse to comparison. Identification of causal mechanisms itself stems from a perpetual to and from movement between abstraction and empirical studies. A search should be made for 'multidimensional accounts based on a synthesis of major significant elements, each of which is analysed abstractly and then combined in a movement back towards the concrete, tracing their evolution and interaction over time and space'. The information gathered enables the conceptualisation to be made more dense and for the properties of the 'various elements actually articulated' to be characterised (Sayer 2000: 10–27).

Thus conceived, critical realism enables a challenging of two orientations commonly adopted in works of comparative politics. Traditional positivism constitutes the most obvious target. Its followers flout the first principle set out above by adopting an 'actualist' form of reasoning: they situate causality at the very same level as the observable data, simply seeking to correlate each with the other. No 'underlying structure' is taken into consideration. The only discussion is of the reliability of techniques of observation. Quite logically, the second principle of critical realism is also denied: the problem is not one of shedding light on contingent constraints between several mechanisms, but rather to plot empirical regularities that lead to the formulation of definitive sociological laws. Another difference from 'positivist realism' should be pointed out. In more insidious forms, this latter option reproduces an unimaginatively causalist way of thinking. Following the first principle, 'underlying mechanisms' are indeed this time distinguished from observable phenomena. However, they are related to them through the mechanism of 'causal invariance', which marks a divergence from the second principle. The objective is not to delimit a constellation but to establish a 'universal conjunction'. There is still a search for general laws: the issue is one of showing that in the presence of mechanism A, event B occurs in all cases. In other terms, 'social processes [are] construed as connections between thing-like "variables"'. The sole aim of the researcher is to identify 'intransitive social realities' (Steinmetz 2004: 377–9).

All those comparativists who follow Rogers Brubaker's model, or who seek to amend it, condemn the first option and distance themselves from traditional positivism; nonetheless, many implicitly accept the second option and lapse into positivist realism. The designation of a common adversary has the effect of creating the illusion of a unified approach: routine attacks against traditional positivism hide the cleavage between uses of Brubaker's framework that are anchored in critical realism, and those that divert it towards positivist realism. All researchers who claim to respect this framework denounce those authors who think it enough to identify correlations between the empirical data collected in different case studies – who in other terms are concerned to identify regularities in the attributes of national and ethnic 'groups' in order to make causal inferences, plot the independent effect of a variable and from this draw explanations with universal pretension. But this denunciation does not prevent comparison being based on positivist realism principles: researchers who follow this path go looking for stable relationships in and between the fields under consideration, with the aim of identifying a single variation principle. Their analytical framework is well defined at a theoretical level, on the basis of multiple criteria. However, each time that the environment meets these criteria, it is supposed that the social movements being studied all follow the same trajectory. A universal conjunction is established between given institutional forms and one type of ethnic or national mobilisation.[4]

---

4. A prefiguration of this approach can be found in the framework for comparison proposed by Charles C. Ragin and Jeremy Hein. These two authors openly endeavour to identify 'causal regularities' (Ragin and Hein 1993: 255).

By drawing on critical realism, the researcher can turn his or her back on positivist comparisons without having to resort to a purely monographic approach. Comparative analyses conceived in this form take on board the fact that 'mechanisms are never related to events in a universal way'. They aim to accurately portray a 'plurality of conjuncturally interacting mechanisms' (Steinmetz 2004: 383–84). In other words:

> The elements that constitute causal constellations may vary from case to case. And even if we do find recurrent empirical patterns, these can never be assumed to be universal or to be determined by the same set of mechanisms in each case. Comparison thus can focus on the differing empirical effects of a single mechanism, or on the differing conjunctures leading to similar outcomes (Steinmetz 2004: 392).

The comparativist is enjoined to come up with 'individual explanatory histories': the ambition is not to isolate causal laws but to relate various different constellations in order to characterise 'the differing empirical effects of a single mechanism' or 'the differing conjunctures leading to similar outcomes' (Steinmetz 2004: 394; see also Bergene 2007).[5]

By distancing the relational framework of Brubaker from positivist realism and basing it epistemologically on critical realism, it is possible to offer constructivist analyses without limiting oneself to monographs: it is a matter of considering that the components identified combine with one another in multiple ways across space and time. Comparison does not consist of isolating a principle of linear causality. On the contrary, it takes on a 'modular' form (Goswami 2002) and leads to the characterisation of the multiple combinations of the same components – it being accepted that one component may play a very small role in certain cases without that invalidating the comparative scope of the model.[6]

In order to ensure that Brubaker's framework remains securely tied to critical realism – to avoid any uncontrolled lurches towards positivist realism – we must avoid restricting its field of application. If the mechanisms are specifically related to one clearly delimited 'field' (the post-Soviet states and the states of Central and Eastern Europe) and if they serve no purpose beyond this, the temptation towards positivism inevitably makes itself felt once more: by restricting the terrain on which the mechanisms may come into play, the belief arises that we can isolate a limited number of combinations and draw out from these a definitive causality

---

5. The analyses which Rogers Brubaker offers in this volume converge with the conception of comparison that we are defending. The very fact that the author has to expend effort on this clarification clearly indicates that his comparative framework is often subject to misuse.

6. As Rogers Brubaker reminds us in this volume: 'the concept of nationalizing states is not a device for classifying states as nationalizing or non-nationalizing; or for ranking states as more or less nationalizing; or still less for assessing the legitimacy of their policies and practices. It is not a device for posing yes-or-no questions like "is Ukraine a nationalizing state?" or "is Latvia more or less nationalizing than Estonia?".'

principle.[7] In order to prevent this temptation, it is preferable to define the mechanisms more widely, going beyond any excessively contextual identification with nationalising states and external national homelands. On the basis of mechanisms whose field of application is not delineated *a priori*, we ought to be able to widen the bounds of comparisons and multiply the possibilities for combination.

Widening the bounds of comparisons

We can retain the spirit of the framework devised by Rogers Brubaker and remain faithful to critical realism at the same time as we reconsider causal mechanisms. In order to enable comparisons beyond the area originally delimited, five generic mechanisms may be characterised within policy instruments, political representation operations, academic inputs, external inputs and everyday practices.[8]

Policy instruments include all official and codified instruments of action which enable an administration to establish identification criteria: statistics; demographic and registry office records; administrative documents; linguistic policies; education policies, etc. These are used to enshrine ethnic or national affiliations as a relevant category. This does not mean that administrative departments are monolithic blocks; between and within them, disputes can be observed over the delimitation of relevant groups (Noiriel 2006; Peterson 1987; Starr 1992).[9]

Political representation operations are formed and run by self-appointed spokesmen and women who delimit and give shape to the 'groups' that they claim to represent (political parties, trade unions, associations, interest groups, etc.). Through the discourses and the symbols that they deploy, they contribute towards elevating ethnicity or nationality as a relevant principle for demarcating and grouping. Within each of these, factions may struggle to maintain or redefine the boundaries of the group represented. Competition between political representation

---

7. As Brubaker himself indicates in his contribution to this volume (see Chapter One): 'Taken individually, these elements are found in many other settings; taken together, they comprise a configuration that is distinctive to post-Soviet and other "post-multinational" settings such as East Central Europe after the collapse of the Habsburg, Ottoman, and Romanov empires'. The author does not himself fall into the trap of reification because he takes care to specify the scope of his analysis and to emphasise the danger of too limiting a use: 'it risks contributing to what I have characterised elsewhere as an "overethnicised" understanding of the social world [...]. The notion of the nationalising state is certainly not a "master concept" that can capture the "essence" of post-Soviet political, cultural, and social life. It is simply one conceptual tool among others that may help pose some analytically interesting comparative questions.' But the risks of a mistaken interpretation are thus increased tenfold.

8. Martina Avanza and Gilles Laferté (2005) are interested in the mechanisms that we locate in policy instruments, political representation operations and everyday practices. They refer to these respectively as 'identification', 'social image' and 'affiliation'.

9. Private enterprises may use records of nationality and ethnicity to assert the distinctive character of a product and build a market. Most often they use the institutional supports provided by the administration, in such a way that the process is to a great extent dependent on policy instruments (Fligstein 1996). In the event that this process became autonomous, an additional mechanism could be characterised.

operations itself focuses on the legitimisation of dividing lines and the recognition of the groups delimited (Akdeniz and Göker 2011; Bourdieu 1991; Crowley 2001).[10]

Academic inputs are provided by the activities of researchers: engaged in their own struggles, they may attempt to assert themselves by applying for institutional support. They are concerned to obtain a position of expertise by cashing in on specialised knowledge about ethnic or national demarcations. In doing this, they offer scientific authority for the categories distinguished and contribute towards 'naturalising' them in the sense of making them appear 'natural'. Although in the first instance this involves social sciences (demographics; history; geography; linguistics; electoral sociology, etc.), life sciences may also be called upon to contribute insofar as they preside over health, technological and economic choices that are justified in terms of the 'national interest' or denounced for their 'discriminatory' character (Epstein 2003; Frickel and Moore 2006; Wagner and Wittrock 1991).

External inputs are formed by all those established authorities that escape the strict control of the agents identified in the preceding mechanisms (foreign powers; foreign political foundations; foreign universities; international scientific networks; international or supranational institutions and organisations). External norms may provide new action repertoires: the emphasis placed on the protection of national or ethnic minorities encourages internal demarcations that reproduce these categories; one might also envisage an internationalisation of demands or legitimisation by reference to external models. 'Importers' assert themselves by these means and organise a transfer of the minority issue to the internal level. Sometimes they engage in a 'double game': in these cases they use their mastery of externally-accepted norms in order to claim and legitimise a position as a national expert; in circular fashion, they then use their position as a national expert to strengthen their access to external spaces and find new sources of legitimacy there (Dezalay and Garth 2011).

In the course of their *everyday practices,* individuals reach an accommodation with the categories to which they have been assigned by the preceding mechanisms. They may appropriate the identification criteria offered them, refuse them, or hybridise them and make unsanctioned uses of them. Linguistic practices may form part of this register, as well as cultural practices, the historical referents mobilised, and educational choices, etc. (Niel 2009; Verdery 1994; Wimmer 2009).

Between these five mechanisms, no hierarchy can be established that would enable a simple causality to be plotted: instead, multiple combinations should be envisioned. On the basis of the texts collected in this volume, we can locate some initial reference points.

---

10. The role played by newspapers may be included in comparison. Journalists move within a field that is to a great extent enclosed within the space of political confrontations: by the way in which they set out the problem and through the analyses that they provide, they contribute to the ethnic and national delineations made by political representation operations. Although the degree of autonomy of the field of journalism remains variable, it is unlikely that it will become sufficiently autonomous to drive a specific mechanism (Benson 1999).

(1) Some combinations between policy instruments and political representation operations are characterised here. Spokesmen and spokeswomen use the official categories delimited by government administration to give an ethnic or national dimension to their slogans, but they may also struggle to persuade the administration to adopt and universalise their own principles for perceiving and dividing up reality. In studying the Hungarian minorities in Romania, Slovakia and Serbia, Edina Szöcsik and Daniel Bochsler (see Chapter Eleven) succeed in characterising this kind of dynamic. Those political parties that present themselves as the representatives of minorities are the locus of competition between 'radicals' and 'moderates', amplified by disputes over the appropriateness or timeliness of participation in coalition governments. Internal debates focus to a great extent on the ability to have categories defined by the party hierarchy taken up by government and transformed into official categories.

(2) Combinations between policy instruments and academic inputs are observed here. Researchers have significant influence over the construction of official categories, but they also contribute towards hardening them by making use of them in their academic work and debates. In studying the Israeli position towards Palestinian/Arab populations, Sharon Weinblum (see Chapter Seven) highlights the extensive circulation patterns between institutional discourses and scholarly discourses. Some university figures keep up a lively controversy over the 'nature of Israel'. As soon as the issue is formulated in these terms, Palestinian/Arab populations find their capacity for expression restricted: the way discussions are framed leaves little scope for their demands.

(3) Policy instruments and external inputs may also be combined. Statistical constructs and educational policies are often drawn up under the influence of external monitoring or by reference to international norms; more generally, policy transfer processes can be envisioned. External resources are often used to justify an internal position by showing that it is in line with a legitimate standard. These resources may also be used to construct a posture of 'resistance', concerned to defend a national tradition. Conflicts internal to governing administrations must in any case be expected. In his contribution to this volume (see Chapter One), Rogers Brubaker sheds light on the 'counting and categorising practices of states'; he emphasises the political nature of 'choices about what to count and how to count it'. According to his analysis, 'these choices can powerfully shape prevailing representations of state and society, and these representations, in turn, help shape political debate, frame policy options, and legitimate particular stances and decisions'. In Kazakhstan, as in Ukraine, 'techniques of statistical nationalisation' may be used to serve the ends of some heavily-targeted policies, at the same time as they adopt generally-accepted international forms.

(4) Combinations between policy instruments and everyday practices should be examined with great attention. The issue is one of specifying the manner in which an individual uses officially-accepted ethnic or national categories, reproducing them, diverting them, or flexibly manipulating them, depending on the contexts. Education systems and linguistic practices provide good fields for observation. Magdalena Dembinska (see Chapter Four) demonstrates this when

studying the case of the German and Belarusian minorities in Poland between the fall of the communist regime and accession to the European Union in 2004. She concentrates on the 1991 Education Act. This text (amended on several occasions) recognises the right to be educated in a minority language; specific courses must be organised whenever parents of schoolchildren make a written request for this, without consideration for the mother tongue of the children concerned or the majority language at local level. These arrangements lend themselves to highly variable usages and provide an official basis for 'interplay' with ethnicity.

(5) Special light should be shed on combinations between representation operations and academic inputs. The resources offered by expertise in specialised knowledge are regularly involved in public confrontations. Parties make requests for researchers' expertise in order to consolidate the delimitation of the groups they claim to represent. Using the tools offered by 'critical discourse analysis', Julien Danero Iglesias (see Chapter Two) shines a light on a process of this type. He analyses the discourse of the leaders of the Party of Communists of the Republic of Moldova (in power between 2001 and 2009) and that of the coalition that succeeded it under the name of the Alliance for European Integration. He highlights uninterrupted struggles over the definition of the Moldovan nation, struggles to a great extent oriented by the context of the electoral campaign. In the course of the interactions studied, antagonistic historiographic representations were activated, with the assistance of numerous university academics: located at the frontier between academic and political spaces, the debate concerned the existence of a Moldovan history dissociated from that of Romania.

(6) Comparative research must take account of political representation operations and external inputs. The resources offered by norms for the protection of minorities are made use of in political confrontations when parties request the assistance of experts in this field. An effort to incorporate ethnicity within the definition of party orientations can then be observed: each individual ends up recognising his or her place in a party, one defined by his or her position in an ethnicised political competition. In this manner, Hanna Vasilevich (see Chapter Five) examines the representation of the Belarusian and Polish minorities in Lithuania and of the Hungarian minority in Slovakia. While relativising the role of the European Union – accession was in 2004 in both cases – she emphasises the importance of the measures put in place by the Council of Europe. In Lithuania and in Slovakia, laws protecting minorities in Slovakia and Lithuania must take account of the Framework Convention for the Protection of National Minorities, the European Charter for Regional or Minority Languages and the Charter for Local Governments.

(7) Academic inputs and external inputs may also end up combining. Inclusion in international scientific networks and funding for research projects by foreign foundations or supranational and international organisations may lead researchers to prioritise work on the protection of national minorities and contribute towards asserting the centrality of this theme internally. Legitimisation through external inputs provides support for attempts to upset the established academic hierarchy: researchers who make use of this strategy are concerned to devalue the exclusively internal resources of their academic adversaries, by presenting their knowledge as

outdated. This struggle may take the form of a split over subject areas (protection of minorities versus other research fields); but on occasion this may be organised within the actual boundaries of the minority subject area – in this case, some researchers problematise this subject area by making use of external referents (e.g. multiculturalism, combating discrimination, access to political representation) the better to disqualify the work of other academics or other academic institutions (folk definitions of minorities, philology, etc.) The construction of expertise on the 'ethnic vote' may be part of this dynamic, as is shown by the study presented here by Julian Bernauer (see Chapter Ten).[11]

(8) Some combinations are observed between political representation operations and everyday practices. In order to determine their affiliations, individuals call upon the official categories and demarcations drawn by representatives, but also actualise them in the course of their activities. Karolina Prasad (see Chapter Six) shows this in a comparative study of Chinese minorities in Malaysia and Indonesia. In Malaysia, 'ethnically-defined political parties' have been constituted. They position themselves both within the coalition and within the opposition. This double positioning takes the form of a marked degree of politicisation: the ethnic reference conveyed by the parties translates into everyday practices and enables convergence towards a critique of the regime in place. In Indonesia, the bodies representing the Chinese minority are kept away from power. One of these favours a policy of assimilation; the other agitates for integration and for the recognition of a citizenship that is blind to ethnicity. In their everyday practices – and especially in matters of educational choices – individuals accommodate to both orientations.

(9) Academic inputs are themselves combined with everyday practices. Academic works that designate national and ethnic groupings produce political effects that are all the more marked for being popularised and translated into ordinary representations. They may, however, give rise to uses that escape the control of their authors. An illustration is provided here from the Ukrainian field, studied by Doris Wydra (see Chapter Three): works of historiography feed into 'complex narrative framing processes'. Each citizen is exposed to 'Russian and Ukrainian ethnic narratives': he or she finds that he or she is offered two founding myths, two martyrologies, etc. This double register provides room for manoeuvre as regards practices and enables the existence of 'overlapping narratives'.

(10) Finally, combinations can be observed between everyday practices and external inputs. In the course of his or her activities, each individual may demand

---

11. Think tanks may form intermediate spaces between instruments of public action, academic inputs and external inputs. Their significance is redoubled when a market for expertise in 'intercultural dialogue' or 'minority rights' is constituted. Their influence can be observed at three levels. First, through their activities, models and references may be put into circulation. Secondly, various agents may then be put into contact and a hybridisation of roles may be observed to facilitate moves from one space to another during the course of a career (from Higher Education to public administration, from public administration to Higher Education, etc.). Finally, think tanks may have a powerful legitimising effect, insofar as they are presented as neutral spaces, ones guided by technical efficiency criteria (Rich 2004; Stone 2004). One may ask the question of whether the grouping they form may become autonomous (Medvetz 2009). In that case, the identification of a specific mechanism might be envisaged.

or reject a given public policy in the name of a principle trumpeted by foreign powers, or international institutions or organisations. Fulya Memisoglu (see Chapter Eight) can thus show that the 'minority policies' in application in Greece and Turkey rest on the 'reciprocity principle' laid down in the Treaty of Lausanne in 1923. Each state is authorised to intervene in the affairs of the minorities on the other side of the border (Muslims in Thrace, Greeks in Turkey). However, in the absence of a precise mechanism for its application, reciprocity is negotiated on an everyday basis, in interactions organised by public policies. Both sides monitor the position and prospects of the other minority, and formulates its demands or complaints accordingly.

The combinations thus identified may apply simultaneously. In order to simplify matters, the illustrations proposed here are limited to the relations between two mechanisms, but more complex causal constellations are formed in each case. Comparative research should consist of studying their unfolding in space and time. The prominence given to ethnicity and nationality is based on power relations whose logic and re-combinations may be conveyed without determining a hierarchy among their mechanisms or including them in a framework of linear causality.

Conclusion

If we are to attempt to understand the reasons why ethnicity and nationality constitute, within certain spaces and at certain given times, operative categories for the ordering of social reality, several approaches may be selected. The most common retains a positivist orientation and leads us to envisage comparison as a means of establishing universal causal relationships. It is possible to base one's reasoning on different lines by following principles of critical realism and by shedding light on causal mechanisms the combinations of which vary from one case to another. In this case, no attempt is made to search for a universal law. The constellations highlighted do not lead towards the framing of a causal principle valid everywhere and across the ages. Nothing prevents a demonstration that the same mechanisms lead to different effects or that different mechanisms produce the same effects. Thus, comparison takes on a new orientation.

Although often used in ways that are improper and slanted towards positivist reasoning, Rogers Brubaker's framework enables us to identify mechanisms and to base comparisons on principles of critical realism. In order to limit the risks of over-interpretation and the lures of positivism, it may be useful to reconsider these mechanisms and to widen the bounds of comparison. By simultaneously examining instruments of public action, political representation operations, academic inputs, external inputs and everyday practices, the researcher may portray multiple causal constellations. By definition, this approach cannot lead to definitive explanations: the analyses offered here must above all be considered as an invitation to pursue studies in comparative research.

References

Akdeniz, E. and Göker, E. (2011) 'The historical "stickiness" of nationalism inside Turkey's political field', *Turkish Studies*, 12(3): 309–40.

Avanza, M. and Laferté, G. (2005) 'Dépasser la "construction des identités"? Identification, image sociale, appartenance', *Genèses*, 61: 134–52.

Benson, R. (1999) 'Field theory in comparative context: a new paradigm for media studies', *Theory and Society*, 28(3): 463–98.

Bergene, A. C. (2007) 'Towards a critical realist comparative methodology: context-sensitive theoretical comparison', *Journal of Critical Realism*, 6(1): 5–27.

Bourdieu, P. (1991) 'Identity and representation: elements for a critical reflection on the idea of region', in *Language and Symbolic Power*, Cambridge: Harvard University Press, pp. 220–8.

Brubaker, R. (1994), 'Rethinking nationhood: nation as an institutionalized form, practical category, contingent event', *Contention*, 4(1): 3–14.

—— (1996) *Nationalism Reframed: Nationhood and the national question in the new Europe*, Cambridge: Cambridge University Press.

—— (2003) 'Beyond comparativism', *Theory and Research in Comparative Social Analysis*, working paper, University of California in Los Angeles, Department of Sociology.

—— (2004) *Ethnicity without Groups*, Cambridge: Harvard University Press.

Commercio, M. E. (2010) *Russian Minority Politics in Post-Soviet Latvia and Kyrgyzstan: The transformative power of informal networks*, Philadelphia: University of Pennsylvania Press.

Crowley, J. (2001) 'The political participation of ethnic minorities', *International Political Science Review*, 22(1): 99–121.

Dezalay, Y. and Garth, B. (2011) 'Hegemonic battles, professional rivalries, and the international division of labor in the market for the import and export of state-governing expertise', *International Political Sociology*, 5(3): 276–93.

Epstein, S. (2003) 'Inclusion, diversity, and biomedical knowledge making: the multiple politics of representation', in N. Oudshoorn and T. Pinch (eds) *How Users Matter: The co-construction of users and technology*, Cambridge: MIT Press, pp. 173–90.

Fligstein, N. (1996) 'Markets as politics. A political-cultural approach to market institutions', *American Sociological Review*, 61(4): 656–73.

Frickel, S. and Moore, K. (2006) 'Prospects and challenges for a new political sociology of science', in S. Frickel and K. Moore (eds) *The New Political Sociology of Science*, Madison: University of Wisconsin Press, pp. 3–31.

Goswami, M. (2002) 'Rethinking the modular nation form: towards a sociohistorical conception of nationalism', *Comparative Studies in Society and History*, 44(4): 770–99.

Horowitz, D. L. (1985) *Ethnic Groups in Conflict*, Berkeley: University of California Press.

Kauppi, N. (2005), 'Social constructivism, structural constructivism: a comparison', *epsNet*, 3(1): 43–7.

Medvetz, T. (2009) 'Les think tanks aux Etats-Unis: l'émergence d'un sous-espace de production des savoirs', *Actes de la recherche en sciences sociales*, 174: 81–91.

Niel, F. (2009) 'Désactiver les fonctions identitaires de "la langue": l'identification des pratiques linguistiques à l'ombre de l'identité linguistique nationale', in M. Surdez, M. Voegtli and B. Voutat (eds) *Identifier – s'identifier. À propos des identités politiques*, Lausanne: Antipodes, pp. 133–52.

Noiriel, G. (2006) 'L'identification des personnes', in X. Crettiez and P. Piazza (eds) *Du papier à la biométrie. Identifier les individus*, Paris: Presses de Sciences Po, pp. 29–37.

Petersen, W. (1987) 'Politics and the measurement of ethnicity', in W. Alonso and P. Starr (eds) *The Politics of Numbers*, New York: Russell Sage, pp. 187–233.

Ragin, C. C. and Hein, J. (1993) 'The comparative study of ethnicity', in J. H. Stanfield and M. D. Rutledge (eds) *Race and Ethnicity in Research Methods*, London: Sage, pp. 254–72.

Rich, A. (2004) *Think Tanks, Public Policy, and the Politics of Expertise*, Cambridge: Cambridge University Press.

Sayer, A. (2000) 'Key features of critical realism in practice: a brief outline', in *Realism and Social Science*, London: Sage, pp. 10–27.

Smith, D. (2002) 'Framing the national question in Central and Eastern Europe: a quadratic nexus?', *The Global Review of Ethnopolitics*, 2(1): 3–16.

Stanfield, J. H. (1993) 'Epistemological considerations', in J. H. Stanfield and M. Rutledge (eds), *Race and Ethnicity in Research Methods*, London: Sage, pp. 16–36.

Starr, P. (1992) 'Social categories and claims in the liberal state', *Social Research*, 52(2): 263–94.

Steinmetz, G. (2004) 'Odious comparisons: incommensurability, the case study, and small N's in sociology', *Sociological Theory*, 22(3): 371–99.

Stone, D. (2004) 'Think tanks beyond nation-states', in D. Stone and A. Denham (eds) *Think Tank Traditions: Policy research and the politics of ideas*, Manchester: Manchester University Press, pp. 34–50.

Verdery, K. (1994) 'Ethnicity, nationalism, and state-making. Ethnic groups boundaries: past and future', in H. Vermeulen and C. Govers (eds) *The Anthropology of Ethnicity: Beyond ethnic groups and boundaries*, Amsterdam: Het Spinhuis, pp. 33–58.

Wagner, P. and Wittrock, B. (1991) 'States, institutions and discourses: a comparative perspective on the structuration of the social sciences', in P. Wagner, B. Wittrock and R. Whitley (eds) *Discourses on Society: The shaping of the social science disciplines*, vol. XV, Dordrecht: Kluwer Academic Publishers, pp. 331–58.

Wimmer, A. (2009) 'Herder's heritage and the boundary-making approach: studying ethnicity in immigrant societies', *Sociological Theory*, 27(3): 244–70.

| index

Aasland, A. 28
Abhkazia 1
Abulof, U. 158
acculturation 79
Adams, J. F. 215 n.9
Agadjanian, V. 18
Ágoston, A. 248
Akar, R. 179 n.10, 180
Akdeniz, E. 262
Akgonal, S. 173, 176, 180, 181
Aktar, A. 174, 179 n.10
Akyol, M. 180
Albania 231
Alexander, G. 172
Alexandris, A. 175, 182
Alon, G. 161
Aloni, S. 161
Alonso, S. 79, 82, 83, 209, 224
Alvarez, M. R. 213 n.5, 215
Anagnostou, D. 170 n.1, 175, 182, 183, 184, 185
Andersen, E. A. 28
Anderson, B. R. O. 40, 60, 65, 137 n.14, 194
Andrews, A. 170 n.3
Arel, D. 4, 18, 19, 20, 24, 27
assimilation 21, 30 n.17, 79
Avanza, M. 261 n.8
Avital, C. 161
Ayres, R. W. 12 n.2

Badawi, A. A. 142
Bădescu, G. 215 n.8
Badie, B. 2
Bahceli, T. 174
Bakk, M. 239
Baloglu, Z. 181
Bandera, S. 63 n.4, 68, 69
Banton, M. 193

Bárdi, N. 238
Barkan, J. D. 234
Barrington, L. 64
Barry, E. 43
Barska, A. 84
Barutciski, M. 173, 174
Becker, D. 191 n.1
Beissinger, M. R. 3
Belarus 6, 70, 86, 105
    economic development in 86
    Europeanisation of 101
    Soviet policies and 106–7
Benhabib, S. 61, 66
Benson, R. 262 n.10
Berdychowska, B. 91
Bergene, A. C. 260
Berlińska, D. 87
Bernauer, J. 7, 231 n.1, 264
Bernsand, N. 21
Besters-Dilger, J. 21, 22 n.11, 25
Bhaskar, R. 258 n.3
Bieber, F. 79, 82
Bilaniuk, L. 24, 25
Birch, S. 68, 210, 216, 217, 218, 225
Birnir, J. K. 196, 199, 202, 212, 224
Biševac, S. 245, 246 n.14
Blais, A. 210, 211, 213 n.4, 215
Bloom, S. 22, 23 n.12
Blum, C. 191 n.1
Bochsler, D. 7, 231 n.1, 232, 234, 235, 243, 247, 263
Bohemia 102
Borneo 131, 132, 145
Bosnia and Herzegovina 196, 242
Botan, I. 43, 52
Boulet, C. 18, 196, 197 n.5
Bourdieu, P. 262
Bremmer, I. 210
Breuilly, J. 40–1, 51, 53

Brink, J. H. 85
British Election Studies 215 n.7
Browne, E. C. 209
Brubaker, R. 3, 4, 5, 7, 8, 11, 13, 16,
    22, 26, 31 n.18, 32, 39, 53, 60,
    65, 80, 99, 100, 101, 107, 114,
    117, 123, 125, 126, 129, 133, 144,
    151–2, 184, 192, 197, 200, 201,
    204, 209, 231, 256, 257–61, 263,
    266
  triadic nexus model 3–4, 6, 39, 99,
    107, 114, 117, 151 n.3, 169, 170,
    173, 259
  see also nationalising states
Budyta-Budzyńska, M. 83, 85, 86, 87
Bugajski, J. 210, 216, 224
Bugár, B. 241
Bulgaria 231
Bunce, V. 3
Burant, S. R. 104, 116
Burg, S. L. 81
Buzek, J. 119

Calhoun, C. 41
Canada, Bloc Québécois 82
Capoccia, G. 179
Capotorti, F. 60
Cavari, A. 151
Cazacu, M. 42 n.2
Cederman, L.-E. 195, 234
Central and Eastern Europe (CEE) 99,
    100 , 231, 248
  democratisation of 231
  EU influence and 99, 108
  majority-minority relations in
    99–100, 231, 248–9
    role of external forces 100, 108,
    231, 248
Chambers, S. 79
Chandra, K. 18, 194, 195, 196, 197
    n.5, 199, 212 n.3, 234
Charter for Local Governments 111,
    112
Chimiris, E. 65, 66
Chin, J. 139, 142

China 71, 126, 130, 135, 137
Ching, T. N. 143 n.20
Chirot, D. 123
Chmelko, W. E. 65, 66
Chmelniyckyi, B. 68, 69
Cinpoes, R. 61
citizenship 3–4, 61, 64
  as an inclusionary device 64
  national minorities and 2, 26
Claude, I. L. 175
Coakley, J. 234
Cohen, F. S. 209, 224
Cohen-Almagor, R. 153
Collier, D. 172, 179
Collier, R. B. 172, 179
Commercio, M. E. 3, 4, 28, 100, 107,
    114, 117, 256
Common Economic Space 71
Commonwealth of Independent States
    (CIS) 70
comparative political studies 8, 255,
    257, 266
  critical realism and 8, 257–61, 266
    positivist realism and 259, 266
  epistemological bases of 8, 257, 258
  ethnic minorities, study of 255, 257
    substantialist perspective 255,
    256
  positivism 8, 257, 259, 266
Comparative Study of Electoral
    Systems (CSES) 213 n. 5, 215
consociational democracy 81, 83, 195,
    196
Constant, A. 210
Coppel, C. A. 137
Coppieters, B. 4
Council of Europe 12, 100, 111, 113,
    183 n.15, 264
  Charter for Local Governments 111,
    264
  European Charter for Regional or
    Minority Languages (ECRML)
    109–10, 111, 112, 113, 264
  Framework Convention for the
    Protection of National Minorities

109–10, 111–12, 264
minority rights and 111
Cox, G. W. 211, 215
Cribari-Neto, F. 226
Crick, B. 94
Crimea, Autonomous Republic of 15,
27, 59, 63–4, 67
Black Sea fleet and 67, 72
demography and 15, 64
national identity and 64
secessionist movements (1990's) 68
critical discourse analysis (CDA) 41,
42, 52, 62, 264
Croatia 13 n.4, 196
Serb minority in 13 n.4
Crowley, J. 262
Cummings, S. 4
Customs Union 71
Cvetković, M. 244
Cyprus 180–1, 183, 186
Greece-Turkey relations and 180–1,
183
1960s conflict 183
Czechoslovakia 1, 11, 12, 101, 102
as bi-national state 102–3
dissolution of (1993) 101, 108, 118,
231
minorities in 101–4
citizenship and 103
Prague Spring 102
Slovakia, relations with 101, 232
Treaty of Trianon (1920), effect of
101–2
see also Slovakia
Czykwin, E. 85

Dahbour, O. 2
DANCEE 90
Danero Iglesias, J. 5, 264
Data Assessment for Hungarians in
Slovakia 103
Daugela, L. 117
Dave, B. 16–17, 19, 21–22, 24–27, 32
Delfi.lt 119
Dembinska, M. 6, 94, 263–4

Demetriou, O. 185
Dezalay, Y. 262
Dieckhoff, A. 2
Diener, A. 17
Đinđić, Z. 243, 245, 246, 247
Diósi, Á. 248
Duc-Fajfer, H. 94
Duch, R. M. 209
Džihić, V. 244 , 245 n.11
Dzurinda, M. 108, 115, 240, 214

Edwards, A. 131 n.8
Elfić, E. 244, 245
Eplényi, K. 239
Epstein, S. 262
Eriksonas, L. 105
Esman, M. 198
Estonia 4, 13
citizenship restrictions in 13, 26, 28
language tests, use of 22, 28
ethno-demography of 15, 16, 17
EU membership and 17 n.9, 99
language and nationalisation in
20–22, 24, 29–30
nationalising discourse in 13, 16
Russian, use of in 22
nationalising policies in 12, 14, 15,
27, 28–9, 30
Russian minority and 15, 16, 17,
29, 99
statistical nationalisation and 19
school system in 23, 24, 30
Soviet period 106
Estonian Ministry of Education and
Research 23
ethnic conflict 1, 81, 82, 94, 95, 195,
249
level of representation and 83
primordial paradigm 195
ethnic groups and ethnicity 2, 8, 16
categorisation and 194, 197, 198–9,
200–1, 202, 204, 249, 256, 259
initial reference points and 263–6
cultural cleavages and 197, 198
collective/shared interests of 191,

194, 195, 202
comparative politics and 255,
257–8, 259–61, 266–7
critical realism, use of 8, 257–61,
266
five generic mechanisms of
comparison, use of 261–2
positivist realism and 259–61
substantialist perspective and
255, 256
consociational model of democracy
and 195, 196
elites, role in creation 198, 202–3,
204
identity and 191, 192–9, 203–5, 209
n.1, 224, 256
essentialism and 7, 192, 193,
194, 196, 199, 200, 202, 203
fluidity and multi-dimensionality
of 196
historic constructionism 198–9
naturalised constructionism and
7, 193, 200–5
as relational structures 257–8
social constructionism and 7, 18,
192–3, 195, 196–9, 200, 203,
204, 256
primordialism and 194–5, 199, 200,
203, 204
race, study of and 200–1
see also identity, national; minorities
ethnic mobilisation 2, 7, 87, 192–3,
194, 195, 197, 202, 204
democratisation and 201
discursive social practice and 202,
203
regime change and 201, 202
see also minorities, mobilisation
study of
ethnic political parties 82–3, 209, 210,
231, 235–6, 248–9, 255 n.1
electoral systems and 211, 224
fissions and fusions study 237–50
fragmentation and 235–6

intra-ethnic party competition and
232, 234
radicalisation and 234, 235, 236
strategic voting, effect on 209–11,
213, 255 n.1
trailing parties and 213, 219
united parties and 235
see also under names of individual
countries
ethnic politics
intra-ethnic competition and 232,
234
government participation, effect
on 233, 249
theory of 234–5
local politics and 235
outbidding model of 194, 195–6,
203, 212
pluralism, demand for 233, 234–5
see also minorities, political
representation of; under names of
individual countries
Ethnic Power Relations (EPR) 195
Ettinger, Y. 161
Euractiv 43, 53
The Euromosaic Study (European
Commission) 110
European Commission against Racism
and Intolerance (ECRI) 175 n.6
European Convention on Human
Rights 185
European Union 12
CEE and 99, 117–20
Europeanisation of 101, 116,
118–120
national minorities, protection of 6,
116, 117–20, 181
EU accession and 118–19
EUROREG and 171 n.4
Friendship Treaty (1995) and
118–19
EUROREG 171 n.4

Faucher, L. 200 n.10, 204

Fazekas, L. 247
Fearon, J. D. 209 n.1
Feldman, W. 28
Fernandez, J. 133
Ferrari, S. L. P. 226
Fierman, W. 19, 21, 22 n.11, 23, 25, 26
Fisher, S. D. 211, 215
Fleming, M. 85, 86, 87, 89, 90
Fligstein, N. 261 n.9
Forum Minority Research Institute 231
    n.1
Fowkes, B. 114, 115
Frandsen, S. 4
Franko, I. 74
Freedom House *134*, 135, 141
Frickel, S. 262

Gagnon, A.-G. 79
Galbreath, D. J. 23
Galvin, M. E. 23
Garizan, O. 47
Garth, B. 262
Gazeta Wyborcza 88
Gellner, E. 40, 61
Ghanem, A. 3, 151, 153 n.4, 154
Gil-White, F. J. 7, 193, 194, 195,
    200–2, 204
Giuliano, E. 204
Glickman, A. 157
Göker, E. 262
Gormley-Heenan, C. 234
Gorodjanenko, V. G. 64–5, 66, 74
Goswami, M. 260
Graney, K. 14 n.6
Greece 6–7, 169
    Convention on the Exchange of
        Populations (1923) 173
    returning migrants, effect of
        173–4
    democracy in 170
    demography of 169, 185
    economy and 173
    identity and self-perception 170–1
        Greek Orthodoxy and 170
    minorities in 169, 170, 182–3,

184–5
    citizenship and 170, 174, 182–3
    education and 182, 184
    Gypsies and 184, 185
    Pomaks and 184, 185
    see also Greece, Turkish/Muslim
        Lausanne minority in
    minority rights protection and 170,
        175, 177–8, 182, 186
    EU membership and 178, 182
    reciprocity principle and 175,
        176, 177–8, 182, 266
    Thracian minority and 178
    nationalising state and 169, 173,
        184
    identity and 169
    minority nationalism and 184
    'negative reciprocity' policies and
        7, 186
    religion and culture in 169, 185
    Turkey, relations with 170, 174,
        175–6, 177–8, 182, 183
    Turkish/Muslim Lausanne minority
        in 6, 169–70, 171, 173, 175–7,
        178, 182–3, 184–5, 186, 266
    citizenship rights of 182–3
    discrimination against 182–3,
        184
    identity, spread of 184–5
Green, D. P. 195, 199
Gricius, A. 116, 117
Guboglo, M. N. 65
Gurdere, M. 176 n.7
Gurr, T. 2, 194

Haaretz 162
Habermas, J. 61
Habibie, B. J. 140, 141
Hacking, H. 19
Hale, H. E. 2, 3, 32 n.19, 192, 194
Hall, J. 2
Hall, P. A. 172, 173
Hall, S. 61, 62
Hamberger, J. 240, 241
Hanák, P. 102

Hay, C. 191, 199 n.8
Heath, A. 215 n.7
Hechter, M. 201
Hein, J. 259 n.4
Heleniak, T. 18
Hellenic Foundation of European and
    Foreign Policy (ELIAMEP) 171 n.4
Herder, J. G. 65
Hermet, G. 40, 51
Hirschfeld, L. 200, 201
    Race in the Making 200
Hirschon, R. 173, 174
historical institutionalism 7, 170, 171,
    172–3, 186
    critical junctures and 172
    Greece/Turkey minorities study and
        171–86
    institutions, role of 172, 173
    path dependency, concept of 171,
        172, 186
    state, definition of 172
Hobsbawn, E. 59
Hofnung, M. 153
Hogan-Brun, G. 20
Holm-Hansen, J. 27
Horn, G. 114
Horowitz, D. L. 79, 82, 83, 94, 194,
    209, 212, 224, 234, 255 n.1
Horváth, I. 238
Hughes, J. 12 n.9, 59
Human Rights Watch 175 n.6
Hungary 6, 101–2, 231, 232
    Fidesz Party 247
    irredentism and 232
    Treaty of Trianon (1920) 101
    Slovak relations and 101–2, 114–15,
        116, 118–19
    Friendship Treaty (1995) 114,
        115, 118
Hurriyet 176 n.7
Hutchinson, J. 2, 64

identity, national 2, 61, 191–3
    categorisation of 193, 256
    construction of 2, 5, 7, 18

use of 'the other' and 66
contestation, importance of 62
social reality, construction of 18
see also ethnic groups and ethnicity;
    minorities; nationalism
Indonesia 1, 124–45, 255
authoritarianism in 124, 133, 135,
    140, 145
Chinese minority in 6, 123, 124,
    126, 128–9, 130–1, 135, 137,
    138, 140–1, 144, 145, 255, 265
    economic position of 128–9, 131,
        140
    education and 130, 141, 265
    financial crisis (1997–8) and 140
    representation rights and 130,
        135
    Suharto and enforced assimila-
        tion 130–1
    trade ban (1959) and 128, 130
citizenship rights in 125–6, 128,
    129–30, 131, 141, 144, 265
    Consultative Body (BAPERKI)
        129–30, 135, 137
    SBKRI (Citizenship certificate)
        131 n.7, 141
as civic nation 123, 125, 126, 129,
    144
Communist Party (PKI) 130, 135,
    137, 138
Constitution (1945) 125–6
    reforms and 140, 141
democracy in 124, 133, 134, 135,
    140, 144
    Guided Democracy period 135
history of 125, 135, 137
Institute for Promotion of National
    Unity (LPKB) 130
language and language rights in
    125, 138, 141
    national language and 125, 140
minority rights in 123, 141–5
    assimilation and discrimination
        130–1, 265
    indigenous minorities 123, 141

nationalising state and 123, 126,
144
basic freedom in *134*, 135, 137,
138, 140
core nation of 123, 126, 144
discourses and 138
New Order period 137–8, 144,
145
Pancasila, concept of 125, 126,
130, 138, 141, 144
policies and 124, 135
political hegemony and 134, 135
SARA topics and 137, 138, 141
political parties and 137, 141
Golkar and 137, 138
religion and 125, 130, 138, 141
Confucianism and 141, 144
Islam and 130
'one-God' principle (*Pancasila*)
and 125, 141
Indrayana, D. 125
integration 79–80, 90, 95
ethnic representation and 79–80,
81–2, 87, 90, 94–5, 162
key dimensions of 79
of difference 81, 94
post-communist states and 80–1
see also under Poland
International Crisis Group 245 n.11,
246
International Federation for Human
Rights 17
Iran 156
Iraq 156
Ishay, M. 2
Israel 3, 149–167, 169 n.1
Basic Laws and 149, 150–1, 154,
155, 156, 157, 158
Central Elections Committee (CEC)
153, 154, 157
citizenship rights in 149 n.2, 150,
153, 160
democracy in 6, 149, 150, 151, 152,
157
'defensive', principle of 159

'ethnic-democracy' and 151, 152
minority inclusion in 159, 161–2
identity of state 149, 150–2, 154–5,
156–7, 160–1, 162, 255
definition of 150–1, 159, 160,
161
minority inclusion in design of
159, 161
secularisation and 151
threat discourse and 155, 156,
159, 160–1
Zionist project and 150
immigration laws and 150
Israeli-Arab war (1948) 153
Kach Party 154
Kadima Party 161
nationalising state and 149, 151–2,
162
alternative narratives and 161–2,
163
association law and 159
differentialist discourse of 6, 149,
150, 152, 155–7, 159, 161,
162–3, 263
Hebrew language and 158
Nakba law and 162
Palestinian/Arab minority in 6, 149,
151–63
constitutional process and 157–8
as demographic threat 159,
160–1, 162, 163
intifada and 152, 155, 156, 160
palestinisation of 153–4
political expression of 149, 150,
152, 153, 155, 157, 158, 163
rights of 154, 155, 157 n.9, 158
state, granting of to 158, 161
threat discourse and 149, 150,
152, 155, 156, 157, 160–1,
162–3
Palestinian territories, occupation of
151, 161
Gaza 153, 156
West Bank 153
Progressive List for Peace (PLP)

(1984) 154
Socialist Party, disqualification of
153
Italy 197 n.4

Jakabffy Elemér Foundation 231 n.1
Järve, P. 26
Jenkins, S. 191 n.1, 198
Jenne, E. 247
Jesse, N. G. 83
Johns, M. 4
Jomo, S. K. 129
Jovanović, Č. 246
Jubulis, M. A. 28
Jurado, E. 26 n.13

Kahane, M. 154 n.5
Kalkan, E. 176 n.7
Kamouzis, D. 179
Kántor, Z. 235, 239
Kaścian, K. 105
Kasza, J. 245
Kaufman, I. 3, 151, 155, 156 n.8
Kaufman, S. 83
Kauppi, N. 256
Kazakhstan 4, 13–14, 16–18, 70
   ethno-demography of 15, *16*,
      17–19, 28, 30
      census data and 19, 25
   linguistic divide in 19, 21, 25–6,
      28, 29
      assimilationist discourse and 21,
         28
      language tests and 22
      Law on Languages (1997) 25–6
   nationalising policies in 14, 25–27,
      28–9, 30, 32, 263
      administrative personnel and 26
      discourse and 17, 28–9
      economic 27–8
      education and 23–4
      language policy 17, 25–6, 29
      minority autonomy 27
      Russian minority in 15, 16,
         17–18, 26, 27, 29, 255

school system in 23–4
Kelemen, R. D. 179
Kelley, J. 12, 26 n.13
Kenig, O. 151
Keohane, R. 178–9
Kertzer, D. I. 19
Keyder, C. 173
Khmelnytsky, B. 63 n.5
Khoo, B. T. 138
King, C. 46 n.5
King, M. L. 143
Kirchbaum, S. 103
Klimkiewicz, B. 91
Kocoglu, Y. 180
Kolakowski, L. 61, 62
Kolossov, V. 62, 64
Kolstø, P. 19, 27, 28
Konitzer, A. 247
Kontogiorgi, E. 173, 174
Koštunica, V. 243, 244
Koutroubas, T. 185
Kraŭčanka, P. 116
Kravchuk, L. 63 n.5, 73 n.38
Kroll, H. 84, 88
Krūma, K. 26
Kubicek, P. 4
Kuchma, L. 67
Kulyk, V. 25
Kuprianowicz, G. 93–94
Kurcz, Z. 84, 89
Kurzban, R. 200 n.10
Kuscu, I. 17
Kusý, M. 102, 108
Kuzio, T. 4, 31 n.4, 80–1, 95
Kwik Kian Gie 141
Kymlicka, W. 81, 152
Kyrgyzstan 4, 100

Laferté, G. 261 n.8
Laitin, D. 2, 14, 16, 17, 21, 22, 24, 26,
   30, 194
   language and ethnicity 19, 20–6, 65
      'native language', interpretation of
         19–20
      nationalisation policies and 23–4,

114, 264
prescriptive rules and 22
see also nationalising discourses/
narratives; under individual
countries
Lanstyák, I. 102, 103
Latvia 4, 12, 13, 15, 16, 106
citizenship restrictions in 13, 26, 28
language tests, use of 22, 28
ethno-demography of 15, *16,* 30
EU membership 17 n.9
language and nationalisation in 21,
24, 30
nationalising discourse in 13, 16
nationalising policies in 12, 14
Russian minority and 15, 16, 17,
100
statistical nationalisation and 19
school system in 23, 24, 30
Latvian Ministry of Foreign Affairs 23
Lausanne, Treaty of (1923) 7, 169, 170
n.2, 171, 173, 174, 175, 177, 178,
181, 184, 185, 186, 266
Lausanne minorities 169, 174–5,
176, 179, 180
minority rights protection and 175
principle of reciprocity and 171,
175, 177
Lebanon 154
Hezbollah and 155 n.7
Leciak, B. 88
Lecours, A. 2, 172
Lee, R. 144
Lehning, P. P. 64
Leigh, M. B. 127 n.5, 132, 139 n.15
Lerner, H. 151
Lewellen, T. C. 195, 198
Liao, T. F. 216 n.9
Lieberman, A. 160
Lieven, A. 4, 16
Lijphart, A. 79–80, 82, 83, 94, 195
consociational democracy 81, 83,
195, 196
Lim, K. S. 142 n.19
Lithuania 100–1, 104–7, 110–13,

119–120
autochthonous Slavs 100, 104–7,
116–17, 120
Belarusian minority and 6, 100,
104–7, 110, 113, 116–17, 120,
255, 264
Polish minority and 100, 104–7,
110, 113, 116, 119–120, 255,
264
Belarus, relations with 101, 116–17
Agreements with 116–17
constitution of 110–11, 112
ethnic demography 101, 110
EU membership (2004) in 100, 101,
116, 264
history of 105–6
independence (1918) 105
minorities, protection of 110–13,
116–17, 119–120
EU role in 119–120, 264
homelands, role in 114–117
international conventions and
111–13, 120
nationalising state and
citizenship laws 111
historical background, use of 105
n.1, 106
language and laws 105, 106,
112–13
narratives in 100, 105–6
policies of 107, 110, 112–13
Poland, relations with 116, 119
Friendship and Co-operation
Agreement (1994) 116
USSR and communist period 101,
105, 106, 110, 119
Lithuanian nationalism and 106,
110
Ljajić, R. 242, 243, 244, 245, 246
Lodziński, S. 83, 90
Lopata, R. 111, 112, 116
Lukašenka, A. 116, 117
Lupu, M. 48, 51, 52, 53
Lytvyn, V. 68, 71, 72 n.32, 74
Macar, E. 181

McCrone, D. 2
McDowall, D. 153
Macedonia 196
  Albanian minority in 83, 232
  2001 ethnic conflict 83
Macginty, R. 234
Machery, E. 200 n.10, 204
Mackie, J. 128 n.6
Mackiewicz, J. 104–5
McVey, R. T. 137 n.14
Magyar Szó 248
Mahathir Mohammed 138, 139, 142
  n.19
Mahoney, J. 172
Malawi 197, 198
Malaysia 3, 124–145
  authoritarianism in 124, 133, 145
  Barisan Nasional (BN) 133, 136,
    138–9, 140, 142, 143–4, 145,
    255, 265
  Chinese minority in 6, 123, 124,
    127, 128, 131–2, 133, 136,
    138–9, 143–4, 145
    economic position of 128, 137,
      140, 145
    Malaysian Chinese Association
      (MCA) 136, 142
  citizenship rights in 126, 128
    Bumiputra status 128, 131, 132,
      133, 138, 143, 144, 145
  Constitution 127, 128, 129
    1971 amendment 138
  democracy in 124, 133, 134, 135,
    140, 141–2, 145
  Democratic Action Party (DAP)
    136, 140, 142, 143
  as ethnic nation 123, 129
  Gerakan Party 136, 139
  history of 126–7, 136–7
  Indian minority in 6, 127, 128, 129,
    136, 144. 145
    Malaysian Indian Congress 136
  language and religion in 127, 128,
    131, 132, 138, 145
    Islam and 127, 128, 139, 140

    religious freedom and 132–3,
      139
  minority rights and 123, 127,
    131–3, 137, 138, 140, 144
  nationalising state and 123, 133
    assimilation policies 131
    basic freedom in *134*, 135, 138
    core nation of 123, 127, 128,
      129, 133, 144
    education and 131–2, 138
    New Economic Policy (NEP)
      (1969) 138, 145
    1Malaysia campaign 142–3
    policies and 124, 127, 128, 134,
      143, 145
    political hegemony of 134
    Sedition Act (1943) use of 138
  Pakatan Rakyat (People's Pact)
    140, 143
  Pan-Malaysian Islamic Party (PAS)
    139–40
  party system in 124, 135–6
    ethnic representation in 136, 139,
      143–4
    patronage and 134
  People's Justice Party (PKR) 140,
    142
  Sarawak United People's Party
    (SUPP) 139, 143
  United Malay National Organisation
    (UMNO) 136, 139, 142 n.19
Mallon, R. 7, 193, 194, 196, 199 n.9,
  200, 204
Mandel, K. 239
Mansbridge, J. 213
MAR (Minorities at Risk) dataset 235
March, L. 42 n.3
Marples, D. R. 14 n.6
Martin, T. 13, 23
May, S. 87
Mazepa, I. 68
Means, G. P. 129
Mečiar, V. 108, 115, 240
Medvedev, D. 72
Medvetz, T. 265 n.11

Meier, P. 87
Melnyk, S. 24, 25
Memisoglu, F. 7, 171 n.5, 266
Meridor, D. 162
Michalczyk, T. 84
Milliyet 181
Milne, R. S. 132
Milošević, S. 232, 244
minorities 2, 3, 5, 39, 256
    consensus-building and 83, 94
    definition of 170, 209 n.1
        League of Nations criterion 170
        sociological definition 60
    external homelands of 3, 4, 39, 99,
        100, 120, 256
        protection role of 113–14, 117,
        120
    EU involvement in 6, 117–20
        'quadratic nexus' (Smith) and 99,
        117, 119, 120
    integration and 79, 81, 83, 87, 95, 162
    interest convergence, argument for
        79, 82, 83, 87
    international law and 109–10
    membership and identification of
        191–3, 209 n.1, 224
    political representation of 79, 81–3,
        87, 94, 169, 209–10, 212, 224,
        231, 234–7, 245
        consociational democracy and
        81, 83, 195, 196
        fragmentation and unity within
        231, 233, 234, 235, 236–7
        government participation, effect
        on 233–4, 235–7, 245
        institutional constraints on 234,
        235–7
        intra-group competition and 233,
        234, 235, 237
        one-party representation and
        235–6, 237
        plurality and 235, 245
        proportionality and 83
        strategic voting and 209–10, 212,
        213, 224
    rights of 171, 172–3, 175, 185, 231,
        233, 248
        historical institutionalism and
        172–3
        international law and 178
        policy shifts, study of 172
        reciprocity principle and 177–9,
        185
        Treaty of Lausanne (1923) and
        171, 173, 175, 179, 185
        triadic nexus model (Brubaker) and
        3–4, 6, 39, 99, 107, 114, 117, 151
        n.3, 169, 170, 173
    see also ethnic groups and ethnicity;
        identity, national; nationalising
        states
minorities, mobilisation, study of 7,
    87, 191–2, 200–5, 231
    assumptions of 191
        ethnic behaviour (EB) 191, 192,
        193, 194, 195, 197, 202, 203
        ethnic identification (EI) 191,
        192, 193, 193, 194, 197, 202,
        203, 204
    constructionist-leaning approaches
        7, 18, 191 n.1, 192–3, 196–9
        historical constructionism 198–9
    democratic politics and 195, 196
    essentialist approach to 7, 192, 194,
        196, 203
    nationalism, theories of and 194
    naturalised constructivism 7, 193,
        200–5
        ethnic categorisation and 193,
        197, 198–201, 202–4
    see also ethnic mobilisation; ethnic
        political parties; ethnic politics
Mitchell, P. 196, 234, 235
Modood, T. 87
Moldova, Republic of 5, 39–57, 255,
    256
    AIE (Alliance 2009 elections) 39,
        42, 44, 48–51, 53
        discourse analysis 44, 48–54, 264
        Democratic Party (PDM) 48, 51, 53

Liberal-Democrat Party (PLDM)
48, 49–50, 51
Liberal Party (PL) 48, 50, 51
'Our Moldova' Alliance (AMN)
48–9, 50, 51
Central Electoral Commission 42
civil war 1991–2 46 n.5
democracy, discourses and 44, 48,
49, 51, 52, 53
elections 2009, 'events' of 39–40,
42–3, 53
demonstrations and 42–3
discourse analysis of 40, 41–2,
44–54
legitimation and 42
voter turnout in 42
electoral competition in 5
ethnic identity, oppositional views
of 39
discursive construction of 40, 49,
50, 51, 52–3, 264
Moldovanism 39
as Romanians 39
EU integration and 50, 51
language use in 41 n.1
'state language' 41–2, 53
media use in 42 n.2, 43
minorities in 47, 49, 50, 51, 52–3
nationalising state and 39, 53
nationalising discourses in 5, 44,
51–4, 264
'betrayal' discourse and 44, 45, 52
use of 'nation' in 52–3
PCRM (Party of the Communist)
39–40, 42, 53, 264
2009 April elections and 42–4,
48
2009 July campaign discourse
44–7, 48
2009 July opposition discourse
49–51
Romania and 39, 45–7, 233
as 'the other' 46–47, 53
unification with 45–47, 53
Mongolia 200

Montenegro 1, 232
Moore, K. 262
Moravia 102
Moreno, L. 2
Morrison, J. 59, 63, 67
Moser, R. G. 231
Motyl, A. 3
Munck, G. L. 134 n.11
Munteanu, I. 43
Muraška, L. 117
Myerson, R. B. 211

Nadeau, R. 215 n.9
Nagler, J. 213 n.5, 215
Nagorno-Karabakh 1
Najib Razak, S. 142 n.19, 143
nation
building 4, 61, 80–1, 123, 202
civic and ethnic 52
concept of 5, 60
as imagined communities 60, 61,
74–5
state, formation of 61
nationalisation, domains of 14
economy and 14, 26, 27
ethno-political demography 14,
15–20
categorisation difficulties and 19
statistics, use of in 19–20
language repertoires/practices 14,
19, 20–6
linguistic policing and 24
prescriptive rules, use of 22
school system and 22–3
titular language and 20, 21–2, 26
polity and 14, 26–7
administration, recruitment and
promotion 26, 27
restrictive citizenship policies
26, 27
nationalising states 3–5, 11–12, 30,
31–2, 39, 80, 95, 99, 107, 123, 169,
202, 256
core nation and 11–12, 15, 26, 31,
65, 80, 133, 144, 173
discourses/narratives of 5, 11, 12,

14, 20, 26, 28, 30, 31–32, 61, 150
  motifs of (Brubaker) 11–12
  political transferral of 60, 61
ethnic differentiation and 100
forms of nationalisation used in 26
processes and projects 14–15, 25, 31, 32
use of concept 5, 11–12, 14–15, 30, 31–2, 144, 260 n.6, 261 n.7
see also language and ethnicity; minorities
nationalism 1, 40–1, 194
  classifying theories of 3
    Roger and 40
  definitions of 5, 40–1
    Breuilly and 5, 40–1, 51, 53
    discourse, importance of in 41, 51
  minority nationalism 184, 231
  post-communism forms of 12, 99, 107, 231
  as 'quasi religion' 1
NATO 12, 70, 71, 73, 101, 117, 184
Navot, S. 153, 155 n.7
Nazarbaev, N. 17
Némethová, D. 240
Népszabadság 247
Netanyahu, B. 160
Netherlands, The 135
Neuberger, B. 151
New York Times 43, 116
Niarchos, G. 175, 176, 180
Niel, F. 262
Nikolayenko, O. 63, 64
Niuńka, C. 117
Noiriel, G. 261

Obama, B. 143
O'Flynn, I. 79
Oksamitnaja, S. N. 65, 66
Öllös, L. 240
Olmert, E. 161
Ong, A. 142
Oran, B. 170, 181–182, 185

Orbán, V. 247
OSCE 43, 115, 216
Ozkirimli, U. 2
Ozolins, U. 22

Palmer, H. D. 209
Paolino, P. 226
Parks, R. 143
Pászkán, Z. 239
Pásztor, I. 247, 248
Pedahzur, A. 154 n.5
Peled, Y. 3, 153
Peleg, I. 151, 158
Peters, B. G. 172
Petersen, W. 261
Phillips, A. 82
Pierson, P. 172, 179, 186
Pirie, P. S. 61, 63
Pirozhenko, V. A. 63
Poland 16, 79–98, 231
  Act on National and Ethnic Minorities (2005) 85
  administrative territories reform (1998) 88–9
  Belarusian minority in 6, 80, 83–86, 89–90, 91, 93, 131, 255, 264
    Bialowieża National Park (BPN) and 89–90
    electoral defeat of 85, 86
    empowerment of 89
  Citizens' Committee of Solidarity 83, 84, 86–7
  communist period 80, 85
    fall of 80, 86, 231
  economic development and 86, 90
    minorities, effect on 82, 86
  Education Act (1991) 90–91, 264
  electoral law and system in 83
  EU accession, effects of (2004) 80, 264
    minority protection and 116
  German minority in 6, 80, 83–4, 85, 86–9, 91, 93, 255, 264
    convergence of interests and 88, 89

identity and 87, 88
language and cultural issues 88,
  91–2
MN electoral programme 88, 89
Territorial Reform Act (1998) 89
two cluster split of 87
Kashubian minority 84, 85, 91, 93
Lithuanian minority 85, 93
Minorities Act (2005) 90, 91, 93
minority representation in 80, 81,
  83–6, 89, 93–5
  educational policies and 91–3
  electoral engineering and 81, 86
  integration of difference and 81,
    88, 90, 91
  media policies and 91
  political mobilisation of 87, 89
nationalising state and 80, 81, 95,
  123
  dominant culture and 81
religious identity and 85–6, 91
Roma minority in 82, 93
SLD (Democratic Left Alliance) 84
Ukrainian minority in 83, 84, 85,
  91, 131
World War II and 80
ZSL 83
Polish-Lithuanian Friendship and
  Co-operation Agreement (1994) 116
Political Science Institute (Belgrade)
  231 n.1
Politika 246
Polity IV 134 n.11
Posner, D. N. 197, 198
Poulton, H. 185
Prasad, K. 6, 265
Prussia 16
Puk, A. 91
Purcell, V. 126 n.2

Rabagliati, A. 84, 85, 86, 87, 88, 89
Rabushka, A. R. 194, 212, 231, 234
Ragin, C. C. 259 n.4
Rannut, M. 24
Rapawy, S. 18, 66

Raskin, J. D. 192
rational choice theory 209, 211
  instrumental rationality and 211
  strategic voting and 211–14, 255 n.1
    definition of 211, 212
    ethnically-divided states and 212
    logic of 211–12
    measurement of 215
    SF-ratio and 215, 216–18, 222
  see also Ukraine, 1998 election
    study
Ratnam, K. J. 132
Ravid, B. 162
Razak, S. N. 142
Reháková, B. 61
Reid, A. 123
Rich, A. 265 n.11
Rivlin, R. 161–2
Rjabtschuk, M. 62
Robotin, M. 83, 235
Roeder, P. 81
Roger, A. 8, 40
Roma 82, 93, 184
Romania 1, 16, 231
  Democratic Convention of Romania
    (CDR) 238
  Democratic Party (PD) 238
  EMNT 239
  Hungarian minority in 7, 232, 233,
    234, 238–40, 242, 249, 255, 263
    autonomy, associations promot-
      ing 239
    Civic Association for Oderheiu
      (UPE) 238–9
    Democratic Alliance (UDMR)
      233, 237–40, 242, 245
    education rights and 238
    governmental inclusion and
      238–40, 249
    Hungarian Civic Party (PCM)
      233, 239, 240
    Hungarian Civic Union (UCM)
      239
    Hungarian National Council of
      Transylvania (CNMT) 239

language rights 238, 240
parties, list of *254*
party fragmentation and unity of
233, 237–40
Hungary, relations with 233
Moldova, relations with 233
National Liberal Party (PNL) 239
National Salvation Front (FSN)
nationalism in 233, 238
minority parties in 7, 83, 233, 234,
237–40
People's Action Party (PAP) 239
Romanian Social Democrats
(PSDR) 238
Rose, R. 24
Rothschild, J. 19
Rothstein, B. 173
Rouhana, N. 151, 153, 154
Rozakis, C. 178, 184, 185
Ruiz-Rufino, R. 79, 82, 83, 209, 224
Rupnik, J. 108, 114, 118
Russell, D. 79
Russia 4, 70

Sabah 127, 128, 132, 133, 136 n.13
citizenship rights in 133
Saban, I. 160
Saideman, S. 12 n.2, 209, 212, 224
Salat, L. 83, 235
Salom 180 n.11, n.12
Sanguin, A.-L. 91
Sarawak 127, 128, 132, 133, 136 n.13
Sartori, G. 235
Sasse, G. 59, 63, 64
Saudi Arabia 155
Sayer, A. 258 n.3
Schatz, E. 13, 14 n.6, 32
Schneider, G. 209, 224
Searle, J. R. 199 n.9
Sebestyén, I. 248
Seher, R. L. 195, 199
Selb, P. 209, 213, 215, 226 n.26
Serbia 1, 196, 232, 242–8
Albanian minority in 232, 242
Bosniak minority in 7, 232, 233,

234, 242–6, 249, 255
autonomy and 242, 243, 244,
247, 248
Bosniak Democratic Community
(BDZ) 244, 245, 246
Democratic Community (BDZ)
233
government inclusion and 243,
245–6, 248, 249
Muslim National Council of
Sandžak 242
parties, list of *254*
Party for Democratic Action
(SDA) 242, 245, 246
rights and tensions in 243–4,
245, 246, 248
Sandžak Democratic Party (SDP)
242, 244 n.11, 245, 246
Democratic Party (DS) 233, 243,
247, 248
Democratic Party of Serbia (DSS)
243
dissolution of Yugoslavia and 232–3
Hungarian minority in 7, 232–3,
246–8, 249, 255, 263
Alliance of Vojvodina (SVM)
246–248
autonomy and 247
Democratic Fellowship (DZVM)
246, 247, 248
Democratic Party (DSVM) 246,
247, 248
minor parties in 246, 247
parties, Coalition of (2008)
232–3, 234, 247–8
parties, list of *254*
Liberal Democratic Party (LDP)
243, 246
minority parties in 7, 232–3, 234,
242–8
fragmentation and unity of 233,
242–8, 249
National Minority Councils (2010)
243–4, 248
nationalism and 243

parties and party system 243, 247
  minority support and 243
religious rights and tension 244, 246
Roma and 242, 246
Statute of the Autonomous Province
  of Vojvodina 248
2000 democratic revolution in 247
  DOS coalition 247
2007 elections 247
2008 elections 247
Shamir, M. 156 n.8
Shepsle, K. A. 194, 212, 231, 234
Shevchenko, T. 65 n.6
Shikano, S. 211
Shulman, S. 60, 61, 66
Siiner, M. 17 n.9, 20, 21, 24
Simonides, D. 84
Simonsen, S. G. 81, 83
Singapore 127–8
  ethnic demography 128
Sipalan, J. 144
Skinner, W. 126 n.2
Skocpol, T. 172, 186
Skubiszewski, K. 116
Slezkine, Y. 13
Slota, J. 115
Slovakia 100, 101–4
  Constitution 108–9, 10
  Czechoslovakia, relations with
    101–4
  EU membership (2004) and 100,
    101, 104, 108, 114, 115, 118,
    119, 264
  Hungarian minority in 6, 7, 100,
    101–4, 107, 108, 114–15,
    118–19, 120, 232, 240–2, 249,
    255, 263, 264
  as autochthonous 101
  Beneš decrees (1945–48) 103,
    104, 115, 240, 241
  education rights 240, 241
  EU involvement in 118–19
  external homeland protection and
    114–15, 117, 118, 120
  Friendship Treaty (1995) 114,
    115, 118
  Hungarian Civic Party (MOS)
    240
  Most-Híd Party 232, 241–2
  parties, fragmentation and unity
    240–2, 249
  parties, list of *254*
  Party of the Hungarian Coalition
    (SMK) 108, 115, 232, 240,
    241, 242, 245
  political rights of 240, 241
  Slovak nationalism, effect of
    103, 104, 108, 232
  Hungary, relations with 232, 241
  minorities, demography of 101,
    108, 240
  minority parties in 7, 83, 108, 232,
    240–2
    government participation in 242
  minority protection laws and rights
    108–10, 114–15, 118, 119, 120,
    240, 241
  nationalising state and 102
    language rights and laws 109,
    115
    national narratives in 100
    policies of 107, 108–9, 110, 115
  Prague Spring, effect on 102, 103–4
  religion, role of in 102
    as mobilising factor 102
  2006 party coalition 241
    SDKÚ-DS and 241
  USSR and communist period 101,
    102, 103, 108
Smith, A. D. 1, 2, 60, 83
Smith, D. J. 4, 27 n.14, 99, 100, 107,
  117, 119, 120, 258
  quadratic nexus model 99, 117, 119,
    120, 256
Smith, G. 4, 13, 26, 27
Smith, J. E. 1
Smithson, M. 226
Smooha, S. 3, 151, 153
Sniečkus, A. 106
Snyder, T. 106

The Reconstruction of Nations 106
social mobilisation 2
Solyóm, L. 115
Soner, A. 174, 175, 179 n.9
South Ossetia 1
Soviet Union 12–13
    dissolution of 231
    multi-nationality in 12–13, 22, 32, 59
        linguistic Russification and
            12–13, 20, 32
    national homelands in 13
    nationalising discourse in 13, 14, 32
    nationalising policies in 12, 13, 14,
        30–1, 32
        'homo sovieticus' creation of 59
        Russian migration 15
    school system in 23
Spain 1
    strategic voting in 213, 226 n.26
Spiesz, A. 103
Squires, J. 87
Stalin, J. 13, 50
Stanfield, J. H. 255
Stanić, R. 244
Starr, P. 261
Stebelsky, I. 18
Steen, A. 28, 29 n.11
Stein, E. 101, 102
Steinmetz, G. 258, 259, 260
Stern, Y. 158
Stone, D. 265 n.11
Strøm, K. 235
Stroschein, S. 196
Sudan, North 1
Sudan, South 1
Suharto, General 124, 128, 130, 135,
    137, 140, 141
Sukarno, K. S. 125, 128, 130, 135
Sukarnoputri, M. 141
Sum, P. E. 215 n.8
Suny, R. G. 12
Suryadinata, L. 125, 129, 130, 140
Susser, A. 158
Syria 155
Szabómihály, G. 102, 103
Szarka, L. 240

Szász, J. 239
Szöcsik, E. 231 n.1, 263

Tadić, B. 243, 244
Tal, A. 158
Tanács, I. 247
Taylor, R. C. 172, 173
Tereskinas, A. 91
Ternovácz, I. 248
Thelen, K. 173
Tiemann, G. 210, 216
Tilly, C. 124, 134
Timor-Leste (East Timor) 1
    2006 conflict in 1
Timoshenko, J. 68
Tiso, J. 102
Tomaszewski, W. 119
Topidi, K. 108
Transnistria 1, 46 n.5
Triandafyllidou, A. 169 n.1, 182, 183,
    184, 185
Trifon, N. 42 n.2
Tsebelis, G. 196
Tsitselikis, K. 169 n.1, 171, 180, 181,
    182, 183
Turcan, V. 53
Turkey 3, 6–7, 169
    citizenship and 170, 174
    Convention on the Exchange of
        Populations (1923) 173
        returning migrants, effects of
            173, 174
    democracy in 170
    demography of 169
        minorities, classification of 169,
            170
    EU relations 178, 181
    Greece, relations with 170, 174,
        175–6, 177–8, 179–80, 181, 266
    Greek minority in 6–7, 169, 173–6,
        177, 180–1, 186
        1964 expulsion of 179, 180–1
    Lausanne minorities 169–70, 173,
        174, 179–81, 186
        Armenian community 169, 176,
            180

discrimination and 174–6
Greek-Orthodox community 169,
173–6, 177, 180
Jewish community 169, 180
political integration of 174–5
minority rights in 6–7, 170, 175 n.6,
177, 178, 181, 186
education system and 181
Human Rights Commission and
177
Istanbul Riots (1955) and 179,
180, 181
'negative reciprocity' policies
and 7, 186
reciprocity principle and 175–8,
179, 181, 186, 266
wealth tax collection (1940s)
179–80
nationalising state and 169, 179
identity, construction of 170
minority policies and 169,
177–80
Muslim/non-Muslim relations
and 174–175, 179 n.9, 180,
181
religion and culture in 169, 181
Theological School of Halki and
181
Tusk, D. 85

Udvardy, F. 239
Ugljanin, S. 242, 243, 244, 245, 246
Ukraine 3–4, 6–7, 13, 15, 59–77,
209–29
Constitution (1996) 59, 62
Constitutional Court 68
electoral system 209, 210, 216, 224,
225
ethnic parties and 209, 216
majoritarian system in 7, 210,
211, 216 n.11, 220, 224
PR and 7, 216, 225
strategic voting and 209, 210,
216, 220, 223–5, 227
trailing minority parties, effect of

219, 220–2, 223, 224, 227
ethno-demography of 15, 16, 18,
29, 59, 65
Donbas area 59, 63, 64
ethnic re-identification and 18,
29, 66
Galacia 59, 64
see also Ukraine, Russian
minority in
EU integration and attitudes 29, 67,
70, 71, 73–4
identity/ies, national 60, 61, 62, 64,
66–7, 72–5, 224
bi-ethnicity in 66, 67, 70, 72
citizenship and 64, 74
contestation of 62, 63, 75
discursive construction of 60, 62,
66–7, 69–70, 74–5
multi-layers of 61
Soviet reorientation and 64, 70–1
territory and 63–4
Ukrainian language and 66,
69–70
independence (1991) 59, 65, 224
language and 65–6, 70, 73, 74
1989 census 65
language law (1989) 22
language preference and 65, 66,
70
linguistic discrimination and 66
linguistic divide in 19, 20, 21,
25, 29, 60, 65
linguistic policing in 24
'native language' and 19–21
Russian, use of 66, 70, 72, 73, 74
school system and 23, 24, 25,
66, 73
'state' language and 65, 66,
69–70, 73
nationalising narratives in 6, 14, 18,
60, 62, 66–8, 209, 265
Constitution's role in 62
core nation and 65
identity discourses 66–8, 72
Kievan Rus and historic interpretations 62–3, 67, 68–9

political transferral of 60, 61, 68, 69, 74, 75
use of 'the other' in 67
1998 elections 7, 210
  CSES data 213 n.5, 215
  democratic consolidation context of 224
  electoral system in 210
  Russian minority strategic voting study 7, 211, 213–14, 217–27
nationalising policies in 12, 14, 29, 30, 263
  minority autonomy and 27
Orange Revolution (2004–5) 225
parties, political 68, 224
  BJuT 68, 69, 70, 72, 74
  Bloc Lytvyn 68, 71, 74
  Communist Party 68, 69, 70–1, 72, 74, 210, 211, 217–19, 224 n.24
  ethnic parties and 209
  foreign policy and 72–3
  historical narratives, use of 68–70, 74
  Our Ukraine 68, 69–70, 71, 72, 73, 74
  party identification and 68
  Party of Regions 68, 69, 70, 71, 72, 73, 74
  People's Party 68, 71, 72
  pure nation narratives 69–70
  sovereignty argument 70–74
Russia, relations with 67, 68, 69–74
  Black Sea Fleet and 69, 72, 73–4
Russian minority in 6, 7, 14, 15, 18, 27, 59, 60, 64–66, 209, 210, 255
  Communist Party, preference of 210, 211, 217–219
  minority definition and 60
  as 'others' 66
  political representation of 210, 216
  Russian language and 66, 70
  strategic voting and 210, 216–25
  as Ukraine citizens 64–5
Soviet era and 63, 69, 107

see also Crimea, Autonomous Republic of
UNESCO/IUCN 90
UNHCR 242 n.7
USSR 1, 59, 101
  see also Soviet Union
Ustundag, E. 180
Uzbekistan 17

Vajdaság MA 248
van der Linden, B. 90
Vasilevich, H. 6, 264
Verdery, K. 262
Veremis, T. 173
Verkuilen, J. 134 n.11, 226
Verschik, A. 23
Vlachová, K. 61
Vlah, I. 47
VMSZ (Alliance of Vojvodina Hungarians), VMPD (Democratic Party of Vojvodina Hungarians) and VMDK (Democratic Fellowship of Vojvodina Hungarians) 247
Vollebæk, K. 115
Voronin, V. 43, 47, 48–9, 50
Voutira, E. 174

Wagner, P. 262
Wahid, A. 141
Wanner, C. 14 n.6
Waters, T. W. 160
Watson, S. 65 n.6
Waxman, D. 151, 158
Weber, M. 209 n.1
Weber, R. J. 211
Weinblum, S. 6, 160 n.11, 263
Weinshall-Margell, K. 156 n.8
Wibisono, C. 130, 138
Wiesehomeier, N. 209, 224
Wilkinson, S. 196, 225
Williams, K. P. 83
Williams, M. S. 82
Wilson, A. 4, 13, 14 n.6, 15, 21, 64–5, 68, 210, 216–17
Wimmer, A. 204, 262

Wittbrodt, E. 84–85
Wittrock, B. 262
Wodak, R. 41, 61–63
Wolczuk, K. 67
Wong C. H. 139, 142
Wong, C. W. 131 n.8
World Conservation Union 90
World Trade Union 70
World Wildlife Fund 90
Wydra, D. 6, 209, 265

Yagcioglu, D. 177
Yanukovych, V. 68, 70–72
Yemen 156
Yiftachel, O. 151
Young, I. M. 80, 82, 83
Yugoslavia 1, 11, 12
    dissolution of 13 n.4, 231, 232
Yushchenko, V. 68, 70

Zambia 197, 198
Zaprudnik, J. 105
Zhulinskij, N. 74
Zilkić, A. 244
Zimmermann, W. 64
Zuber, C. I. 7, 196, 231 n.1, 234, 242,
    255 n.1
Zukorlić, M. 243–6

www.ingramcontent.com/pod-product-compliance
Lightning Source LLC
Chambersburg PA
CBHW072053020426
42334CB00017B/1498